Mad in Pursuit

Also by Violette Leduc:

La Bâtarde (1965)
The Woman with the Little Fox (1966)
Thérèse and Isabelle (1967)

Mad in Pursuit

**
VIOLETTE LEDUC

Translated from the French by Derek Coltman

Farrar, Straus & Giroux   New York

Originally published in France under the title La Folie en tête
Copyright © 1970 by Editions Gallimard
This translation © 1971 Rupert Hart-Davis Ltd and
Farrar, Straus & Giroux, Inc.
All rights reserved
First American printing, 1971
Library of Congress catalog card number: 78–148709
SBN 374.1.9508.0
Printed in the United States of America

Bankruptcy. To be made bankrupt. At fifteen I used to read the
bankruptcy announcements. That was my reading: hunting down
life's failures. All my life I have combed provincial newspapers in
this way.

1944. Was I bankrupt? Was I about to become bankrupt? The
railway stations had exploded into fragments, the roads were
ploughed fields, my money lay asleep in my suitcase, a great city
would soon pull itself together again and throw me out. I was in a
cleft stick: my bankruptcy was ineluctable. The bullets whistled
over the roofs. Having fled into a flat on the quai Malaquais, I sat
huddled in an empty bathtub. The guns fell silent, I stood up in
the bathtub and craned my neck. I stepped over the edge, I pushed
the window ajar and looked out into the rue Bonaparte. I leaned
out. I was spying. If I leaned out too far, I would be killed. No, I
wasn't spying. I looked down at helmets and sandbags, I looked for
Paris beyond the barricades, along the banks of its river. Paris was

empty, Paris was disdainful. A tree bowed in submission, a tree staring at us with all its leaves: summer. A crack. It was death: just a puddle. I closed the window, climbed back into the bathtub, sat down, pressed my forehead against my knees. Not a man, not a woman to call friend while the guns worked off their evil temper outside. I was afraid, and my tears dripped into the bathtub. Abruptly, silence. I emerged from the tub, trotted over to the window, opened it slightly, leaned out, then leaned out farther. Two stretcher-bearers were carrying away a corpse on a litter. The hand had slipped out, still warm, still soft. The boots gaped open, a muddy blanket covered the body and face. A dead man. The first I'd seen. The stretcher-bearers were matter-of-fact, apparently preoccupied with other thoughts. I heard a whistling sound. A pistol: a lone man somewhere keeping the fight alive. The dead man was lugged farther off. I closed the window and crouched down in the tub again, such a long way from my suitcase, such a long way from my cash.

The guns fell silent, we emerged into the streets, I took possession of my old quarters once more.

The noise of the trash bins being dragged across the yard at nine every morning, that was all I had now to fill the void, the void left by the happy birds since I had gone from my Normandy village, since I had been forced to do my waking up once more in the black den on the rue Paul-Bert. I must get used to it all again, and I couldn't get used to it again. I moaned, I wailed with my head on the towel I was using as a pillow slip. Paris, while my eyes were still unopened, had sunk its claws in me. I went back to sleep, and Paris shook me with less consideration than if I had been a prisoner due for execution. I turned towards the wall, I listened, and more trash bins assailed me. I threw back the covers, I offered a leg, an arm to the slaughter between sleep and waking. I wanted to stagnate, to muse, to ponder, to browse among the old rubbish in my head. Impossible. There were women draped out of the courtyard windows shaking their dusters; their brazen voices clashed like swords. I pulled the covers over my head. To escape, to bury myself. With moans of laziness I rejected the rain, I rejected the sun they were discussing from their windows. If I opened my eyes a little, if I lit a Camel, I was faced with millions of people all wanting nothing to do with me. If I opened my eyes, I couldn't avoid comparisons. In the village, in one of M. Motté's rooms, the light took me by surprise. White pepper with no blinding power. In the village I began my day with the simplicity of a bird's swift peck. In Paris, in my black den, I had merely the peelings of the day, the peelings of the night, the remnants that the flats in the sun discarded. The sickly hints and layers of my own marasma.

If someone crossed the yard, if someone tore himself free of his dwelling, then the clatter of his steps would always reveal it to me, and my den would begin to flame, the dead stove glowed red, the lid flew open and Gabriel stood there, flames flickering from his shoulders. He was escaping, he would always be escaping, Gabriel, my ex-husband. The stranger's steps faded along the passage, and someone got back into bed beside me. It wasn't Gabriel's ghost. I don't believe in ghosts. It was Gabriel, the Gabriel who didn't want to go. And that was Gabriel too, rushing so joyfully out into the street. Already my past and present locked in a war of attrition. My tears no longer wet my handkerchief: I battered at the pillow, I smashed the skeletons of the two lovers into tiny fragments, I sat motionless there on my bed. Change, sweet sadness, growing old: turf, a lawn on the mantel where your wineglass stood ... Our lawn, Gabriel, a grey lawn, the colour of our silence, our endless silence lying there, our dust. I hurtled out of bed, I polished away at the stove till it was a funeral monument glittering as bright as your shoes ever did. Gabriel had never got around to mending the lamp and the shade. I found the pieces all over the room. Our walls had hummed and murmured night and day. They skinned us alive, those walls of ours. And now I shave my eyebrows and my legs with your Gillette blades, I said to myself, now I bleed at the moment when you bled.

Now I am discouraged before my story has even begun. Spring in Paris is crucifying me. Every shoot emerging from the earth tells me I am withering. A Sunday in spring, and Paris wooing her passersby. Our sun, a smelter's white arm along a bench. The merry-go-round will start at two o'clock, pretty sun inside its painted frame, pretty waxed moustaches of the young lover on a postcard, that rose, that nightingale will tell you of my love, sulky sun in front of the métro gates, in front of the knots, the ropes, the crickets, the toads in my insides: they are my dead, they are your dead, and they don't want to come out today. Winter the giant will come again, winter the giant will put his cheek against mine again. I am old, I cry out for winter to return. If January covers me over with its snow, with its ice, with its hoar frost, then my hair will turn white less quickly. First day of spring. How not to worship it? Hey, a little restraint there, spring, you're melting my butter. Jonquils, leafy branches brought back by car late in the evening, I loathe you all, I despise you. A prisoner is daring to find fault with you from behind the bars she has forged for herself... Leaves, flowers, buds, you have let yourselves be duped. I don't know your dead, you city dwellers, you lily-of-the-valley raiders, I only know mine. They were so simple when we met, when they glanced so briefly into my eyes. They were all the men, and the women, and the children there on the corner of the rue de Montreuil, there in front of the Cave des Pyrénées where they often have the cheap port advertised. They disappeared around the corner, and then full stop. They were the dead and they were the living. That rosé celebration wine, that timidity in the spring sky up there, shall I be able to drink it down, like all the others, in deep refreshing draughts? It will be difficult. They are persecuting me, I am being persecuted. The dribble, the slime, the poison on the rosebud that is bursting with the millions of children my womb refused... The velvet of my pubis on the velvet of a pussy-willow branch: the correspondences are held chords in my imagination. Birds of the evening and the morning, I am deaf; come and die on my back. Yes, they passed by me on a street corner. It wasn't a trial, it wasn't a judgment. Just a meeting. I gave them my blind woman's eyes, they gave me theirs. Where are they? Futile question. I walk beside them all. Beside every one of them. Men, women, children I have met in the street all the length of my existence, you will be my unfinished prayer for always.

February 1945. The most extraordinary month of my existence. It did not follow January; it did not precede March, April, May. It was wholly separate from other months. It was twenty years old, a bay leaf torn out of time. I laughed at the word marvellous until February 1945. It was a gaudy fair balloon, a guttersnipe, a spare part, a penny banger for people who want to work up their enthusiasm. That February was marvellous. I wept for thirty years, I embroidered that February. I can't find what date it was that particular day. It was snowing: the trash bins and their lids were sliding over cotton in silence. I rushed to the window. It wasn't snowing. The trash bins stood in an orderly line under the lean-to beneath my window. I leaned on the sill, I mused in the miserly silence of a courtyard between two tenement buildings. There was a knock. Mme Faury was wild with joy, she informed me, because her scrubbing brush wasn't lost at all. She apologized, she would clean the toilet at the end of the passage tomorrow or the day after, who knows, perhaps in a moment, the main thing was the scrubbing brush there in her hand, being brandished for me to see. You look and look ... and then in the end you find it just when you've given up looking. We exchanged a few conventional courtesies, drawn together by a scrubbing brush. I was totally bewildered. It was absolutely the first I had heard about the lost brush. I made my decision: the manuscript must have a new folder.

Clothed in my reeking rabbit coat, shod in a man's boots, my legs armoured with stockings hand-knitted of natural wool, I set out at a gallop for Mme Aubijoux's book-cum-stationery-cum-delicacies store.

'I'd like a folder,' I said to her.

Mme Aubijoux was counting back numbers of magazines. She raised her eyes. 'You want a folder for that?'

She patted her pile of magazines into shape.

'Yes, for this,' I said, with a detachment I would not have believed myself capable of a quarter of an hour before.

My pages slid out from their grubby folder and I gathered them all together again on the transparent sarcophagus where shiny brown fish were dozing in rows beside chocolate drops.

'You'll be losing the lot!' she commented rather crossly. She walked to and fro across her store, picking up other magazines here and there, clutching them against her bosom.

'I haven't lost any up till now,' I said.

A customer put down the money for a newspaper and vanished.

'Thank you,' Mme Aubijoux remarked to her store.

The pile of unsold magazines was taking up all her attention. She had forgotten me. I coughed.

'Do you want a folder with strings or just a plain one?' she asked, without glancing at me.

'A folder with strings...'

Another customer put down the money for another newspaper and disappeared.

'Thank you,' she said to the two revolvers on the cover of a Western.

At last she served me. She brought out three folders with strings onto the sarcophagus.

'They're files,' she said.

I rejected the royal-blue file and the emerald-green file in favour of the orange file. It cost four francs. It was a pre-war file, she informed

me. A third customer made his exit at the same time as I did. I heard
a third thank you.

*

I lit the two lamps that were still working and crammed the stove
with fuel. Another knock. Butter. A curse upon me, a parcel of
butter. To whom could I sell it?

February 1945. With a little charcoal, a little gasoline, with two
bicycle tyres, the French were setting out to find supplies for themselves. The number of black-market dealers was declining. They
were still feeding the old, the sedentary; but the others were out
combing the countryside for themselves and doing very well at it.

I kicked the parcel along the floor towards the hole that served me
as a kitchen. The writing filled me with distaste: a seducer's letter
written to myself. I could have stamped and stamped on it, that
butter, even though it could procure me the gold I had refused to
buy. I no longer looked at my money: it was a big zero. But I did
pace to and fro in my black den with a piece of paté on a slice of
bread. I wanted to be like the woman of action I had once been: that
woman who had never had time for lunch. How alive and inviting it
was, the orange file on the table. I opened it, executed several glis-
sandos with the little strings, I counted the punched-out stars. My
pages were held in place. Pulled tight. Imprisoned. Birds of a
feather flock together, I thought to myself, glowing with satisfaction. There was still no title. My thumb, too small just like my
mother's, gummed a strip of white where the title would be. The
name of my street at the top right-hand corner was very neat. Perfect, perfect. I wrapped up the file. I always hide things, always
transport them concealed in grey paper wrappings.

Ten past one. The reporters were feeding their news into our
wireless sets. I took a long time over washing myself beside the old
cast-iron stove. That day, the lather from my soap in my armpits, in
my groin, had the nuptial freshness of mock-orange blossom. I put
the shoe on one foot while the other soaked. Sitting on the chair
Hermine had left behind, one foot tightly clasped in its mahogany
suède, the other lying in a beatitude of warm water, I stretched out
my arm, I took up my book again, and to the sound of the *musique
concrète* played by the tenant overhead on the ceiling with her
furniture, her carpet beater, her pad of steel shavings, I went on
reading *Philosophical Fragments*. I didn't understand a word. I
forced myself to go on. If I stopped, then the dirty clothes to be

washed, the windowpanes to be cleaned, the mantel to be dusted, the
rug to be brushed, all cried out: Hey there, we're dirty, you know;
time you gave us a wipe ... I was ashamed at battling on for nothing.
The brass doorknob, for instance: I was neglecting it simply so
that I could die of boredom reading books too difficult for me. I was
letting it tarnish for the sake of words, sentences, paragraphs that
were more obscure to me than Hebrew or Sanskrit. I had wept over
Spinoza, and now I was making a fool of myself over Kierkegaard.
I threw the book away: my problems began to melt and vanish like
candles. But how to kill all that time until seven in the evening?
That was one problem I couldn't evade. Should I brush a little dark-
blue eye shadow on my lashes? No. Let my eyes stay as they are:
sad, and small, and sly.

*

Come on, old thing, do try to reek a little less, I said to my rabbit
coat as I pulled it on. But I didn't nag. I went over to my other
friend, my iron stove. I packaged up the orange folder in its grey
paper wrapping. The fortune-teller arranges, disarranges, rearranges
our future on a tabletop. She makes crosses or enchanted circles and
semicircles with her cards. I was arranging, disarranging, rearranging a future I had no faith in whenever I opened and closed my
exercise book in front of a wood fire at night in Normandy. I say
it again: I grew in some way at those times. I was awake, everyone
else was at rest, half past one in the morning chimed, the clock's
pendulum swung garlands of brass flowers and coral nests to and
fro. Time was at work, the village melted in my hand, and it was
the hand of a child just dropping off to sleep. I raised my eyes from
my exercise book, the shutters gazed back at me through the glass
panes, the world lay all in a doze. I straightened my back, the wood
fire was taking an eternity to die, and I took myself for a spark on
an ocean of shadows. I was alone, I was courageous. I was wholly
absorbed by my word-covered pages. I did not puff out my chest.
All that mattered was Maurice Sachs's advice: 'Write down your
childhood memories.' That phrase 'childhood memories' is a booby
trap. We can't rediscover our first impressions, our first sensations at
the age of one, or two, or three. Ah, how whorish adults become,
attempting to exploit the little children they once were. I am sixty, I
look at a white cloud just as I looked at it when I was four: with
tenderness. I can't recall that child, she hasn't grown old. I coughed
beside my wood fire, warning the silence of my presence, an ir-

rational courtesy. Then, over the slate roofs at half past one in the morning, the glittering music began again. If I dragged my gaze away from the closed shutters, from that space between window and shutters like a cool cellar on the hottest day of the year, then I felt my gorge rise. Too much meat, too many sausages to be dispatched.

I tucked the orange folder under my arm, I said goodbye to the silence of my night-time vigils in a village. I carried, hawked, proffered, lent my pages to Bernadette, to Marcel Arland, to Clara Malraux. Bernadette explained that I was to be the new colt in her 'stable'. I laughed without gaiety. My pen is not a thoroughbred, it cannot sail over the hurdles of words. I shall always be a short-winded beetle. I have often wished for a last resting place for my pages, a definitive drawer that would become the fodder pit of my solitary evenings. I would open it and drink from my private spring.

On that February day in 1945 I was to meet Bernadette, on their behalf, at seven in the evening. We were to proceed to a café where I was to place them in other hands. I left my black den with a presentiment. The day to come would be unique, different from my yesterday and my day after tomorrow. Though presentiments disturb me, they also ravish me. We enter and emerge, at the same instant, from an indefinable event. It is almost an orgasm.

*

February 1945. Paris had been liberated, but I hadn't been liberated from my lust for profit, from my pinchpenny tenacity, from my aspirations to trafficking, my inclinations towards the illicit, my desire to start from nothing and surpass myself. The money, gained by my stevedore efforts, lay asleep, and I did not dare awaken it. My mother said the wisest thing would be to put it in a strongbox at the Crédit Lyonnais. No, I thought, I'm not using the money but I still possess it; putting it in a bank would mean I had abandoned it. It would be putting it into boarding school, the way I'd been put into boarding school. My mother said she wasn't going to leave it at that. Her advice terrified me, her advice was torture to me. The bank: a trap waiting for my nest egg. The bank: an abstraction. The abstract fills me with despair: I can't grasp it. 'We'll go down into the vault, it'll be safe there.' I don't want my money to be under bombardment. Picture books, fairy stories, they never meant much to me. But when I unfolded my wads of money, then it was the pages of those neglected books I was turning. My money was the innocence, the carefree childhood I had been cheated of. The man who looked out at me from every note was the witness of my doggedness along the paths, across the plains, through the woods, along the hedges, in the rain, in the snow, in the wind, in the frost. He was the end of the road. And twenty years later I still haven't changed. I am suspicious, I am on my guard. In June 1965 I am sleeping with a cheque, some shares, a considerable sum of money under my pillow. I switch on the light if I wake up, I lift the pillow, and my ticking pouch looks very much like my towelling pouch of twenty years ago: as white as a dove's down. My love of money purifies the container.

*

February 1945. Paris had been liberated, and I was torn between a village in Normandy that no longer wanted anything to do with me and a city in which I had no wish to rot. Stop, have pity, my heart had often pleaded with me on the way uphill. I didn't listen to it. The most stupid of challenges to the most essential of motors. If I were to cease trafficking and prospering, I would drop. The wood-cutters, all the woodcutters, with a single axe stroke, would fell me to the ground. I thought I could escape my fate by amassing money, by emerging from my leaden diving suit of laziness. I hadn't escaped my fate. My ideal? That of a beast of burden. To keep going beneath my load, weary beyond endurance; not to moan among the loving couples in the Place de la Contrescarpe at eleven in the evening. To collapse after having encircled a cathedral of hawthorns in my arms, soaked up the rain from the apple trees in flower. Paris, you made me afraid.

*

February 1945. Paris had been liberated, but I could not liberate myself from the farmers. I had denounced them. One winter morning I was walking along with head held high, shoulders back, honest gaze, squeaking shoes, indifferent eyes, light suitcase, aerial gait— why, I was riding on the wind. Without looking, I could see the twitching curtains of the curious, hear the whispering of hidden mouths. The little town nearly two miles from the village was a place we had avoided during the war because of the inspectors patrolling there, and we would have liked to go on avoiding it after the Liberation. Impossible. The lorries we must clamber on to with our wares all stopped there. We sat with our teeth clattering from cold and nerves. Despite glass after glass of Calvados, we sank, there in the café where Maurice Sachs had drunk before he went away, that morning of mist and pouring rain. I never thought about him now. For time must elapse before it starts to sap and torture us. The same policemen who had turned their backs during the war now prowled around the trucks: they had their eyes on us.

Last in line, I was just taking the hand of another black-marketeer in the lorry, just about to jump up, when I heard a smooth voice: 'Come with me, please...'

The lorry left without me, carrying off the kind black-marketeer. He was gesturing to me still, asking why I hadn't climbed in. Why not? Because a finger had been placed on my shoulder. I turned and saw a sausage with a bitten nail on its end.

'You are under arrest,' the policeman said.

The lorries gone, the town lapsed back into lethargy. On that winter morning a cat, dying of hunger, lay languishing in the steam from a solitary boiling laundry copper.

The policeman was not without delicacy. We walked down the main street as though we had nothing to do with each other. Things changed as soon as we turned off it.

'Let's get a move on there,' he said. 'I've got other things to do today, you know.'

He was young, slim.

I walked on in front of him, along a side road where the roses go on flowering into November. The sight of those flowers, and the thought of the lucky black-marketeers now on their way in the lorry, filled me with despair. I felt sick at my own obstinacy in going on with the petty profiteering game.

'Naturally I'm wondering what it is I've done,' I said to the policeman.

From a passageway two purple hands hurled a bucket of water at our legs.

'...What you've done, eh? You'll know soon enough. With those sacks...'

'What sacks?'

'Your sacks.'

I began to understand it all: the sailor's little boy had told them everything. I had often caught him hanging round M. Motté's house. He used to follow me till I turned off the path.

The doors of the police station opened easily enough, so it couldn't be very terrible.

There was a second policeman in the characterless entryway. The place looked less and less threatening. Except that my expert's eye told me the tiled floor got a thorough washing every day. The second policeman was short and thickset. He wore his cap over one eye, a little more roguishly than the first man.

'We've been expecting you,' he said.

'She's all yours,' the one who'd brought me said. Then he disappeared into the back of the building.

'Come in, Paris-Beurre, come in ... Make yourself at home.'

I was acquainted with the phraseology and the witticisms of the policeman with the tilted cap. I remembered drinking with him at the poacher's house. We used to clink our cider glasses, our glasses of rot-gut. He never called me Paris-Beurre then, though.

A third policeman was typing in the wretched office.

'Take off your coat. We're going to play Paris-Beurre now,' the second policeman said.

I had written fashion articles during the war for *Paris-Soir*. That was the allusion, I realized. But how had he found that out?

'I call you monsieur, so call me madame,' I said, almost choking with self-control. 'I don't joke at your expense, so please don't joke at mine...'

The thickset policeman's tone changed in a flash. 'That's enough chatter, Paris-Beurre! Now take it off. Come on, off with it. No messing about!'

He advanced towards me. A bull in police uniform. Why such hatred, I wondered.

'What must I take off, monsieur?' I asked with a pitiable smile.

Hatred? It was too grand an emotion for so mean a room.

'Your coat, my dear, your cache-butter,' he said, with a leer that revealed all his quite attractive teeth.

At that point the policeman who had arrested me tiptoed back, positioned himself with his back to the door, and folded his arms.

The short, thickset one finished lighting an army-issue cigarette. He blew the first puff in my eyes. 'Not made up your mind yet, then? Not going to take it off? Come over here, Paris-Beurre!'

I went to him. He sat down on a stool.

He felt me all over. His cigarette smoke was getting in his eye.

'Little Miss Paris-Beurre has it all over her,' he informed his colleagues.

The policeman at the typewriter nodded in confirmation.

'Be so good as to remove your coat, Madame Paris-Beurre,' the policeman on the stool said.

Tears welled up in my eyes. I took off my coat.

'Just look at that!' he exclaimed to the others.

I had twelve kilograms of butter around my waist. Here is how I carried it: I knotted several handkerchiefs together to form a belt. Then from this belt I hung four burlap bags, pinned on, each bag containing three kilograms of butter, and spaced around my waist so that I wouldn't sit on any of them. It was a heavy and uncomfortable load. If the handkerchiefs came loose, then my knees banged against the blocks of butter as I walked.

'Just take a look at that!' he repeated.

I handed over the twelve kilograms. Where would all that butter go? In what saucepans would it melt? Would they sell it and make money out of it themselves?

'Sit down, Paris-Beurre, since now it's possible for you to sit down again...'

I put my coat back on. 'What about the case? Don't you want to look in that?'

He brushed at one leg of his trousers. There was ash on his thigh.

'...Here, my attaché case. Go on, open it!'

'Legs of lamb we're not interested in,' he said.

He lowered himself nonchalantly onto a corner of his desk. My attaché case wasn't transparent, but it certainly contained a leg of lamb, plus some chops.

'...But the name of the farm that sells you all this butter, Paris-Beurre—now, that does interest us. I'm waiting.'

He swung his feet. First one, then the other.

'Can I go now?' I asked, having done up my coat.

He brought his fist down on one of the sacks.

'God in heaven, it's hard!' he exclaimed.

The others smiled.

He slid off the desk, then walked towards me and planted himself in front of me. 'Come now, Paris-Beurre, did I arrest you simply to let you walk off scot-free?'

'You arrested me?' I said, bewildered. 'Is that what being arrested is?'

'Cigarette?'

I took the army issue the short, thickset policeman offered me. Then regretted it immediately: he was buying me. I refused his light.

'Aren't you eating? It's lunchtime,' I said.

I began to cry.

The secretary-policeman stopped typing. 'We could all go and eat if you told us who sells you all that ... We could go then ... It's your fault.'

My tears ceased.

'There are some questions I could ask you, too,' I said sweetly. 'The leg of lamb in the case, for example. Who told you about that?'

'We'll tell you that later,' the secretary-policeman said.

'Later, Paris-Beurre, that's right, we'll tell you that later,' the short, thickset policeman said meaningfully.

'You're getting on my nerves with all this Paris-Beurre,' I said stamping my foot. 'Why can't you stop it?'

All three burst into laughter.

'And you, why can't you stop this bungling black-marketeering, eh?' the short, thickset one asked me, his voice abruptly hard.

*

The questioning began. The woman known as Paris-Beurre was required to give the name of the farm from which she obtained her supplies; otherwise, she would be thrown into a cell. Yes, with the mice. Yes, with the rats. Yes, with the spiders. Yes, on the hard earth floor. Yes, with the potholes in it. Yes, with lumps on it. Yes, locked in with her own deranged imagination. Yes, against the slimy wall. Yes, cut off from the rest of the world. Vileness isn't the policeman, it isn't Violette filled with panic and begging on her knees. No, vileness is the name of the farm, should it escape from my lips. The hours go by, night falls, I am a little girl afraid of a dark dungeon. I am dying of fatigue, I am afraid, afraid. I am afraid of myself. Am I going to dirty myself, am I going to soil myself in that elegant cranny of my being where I am sometimes so pleased with myself? All those years spent paying what I owed in the farms, all those years of remaining silent because silence was necessary, what are they? So much dust in the wind if I betray just one name. Have I worn myself out for castles in the air? I'm so tiny, monsieur, how can you expect such mountains of filth to come out of me? I must be parted from what I bought with my own money, and now, in addition, I must be a traitor. The hours pass, night has fallen, the rats are waiting, the mice expect me. The secretary-policeman continued to type, to smoke cigarette after cigarette; the sentinel-policeman remained at the door with folded arms. Frogs croaked 'Paris-Beurre', crows cawed 'Paris-Beurre' ... I took hold of myself again, I struggled, I found my last shreds of strength in the clasped hands of the black-marketeers sitting in their lorries. A crystal bell tinkled among the swarming bells of Notre-Dame on the evening of the Liberation. Don't speak, be strong, it was telling me. Whereupon the short, thickset policeman held up the threat of his cell for that evening, for that night, for tomorrow, for later. I believed everything he told me. My panic, my terror whenever they came to the village... And now I was in their hands.

I gave up the ghost at about seven in the evening: I told them the name of the farmers who sold me most of my butter. The short, thickset policeman was radiant. He said 'Good night, madame,' without even glancing up at me: he was already at work on the name in front of him. The sentinel-policeman accompanied me out into the street, then vanished into thin air. I was shaking: you are a traitor, and now they can have their dinner.

*

I was running along the road, running back to the village. No houses to left or right. Why should there be? There never have been. And anyway I've just denounced them all, so there can be nothing left now to hang on to. A road between fields, between banks, between ditches. And what good would houses do me, I ask? I run, I run ... with thousands of eyes in my head... Evil eyes. I felt such affection for the houses' eyes down in the hollow of the village. The fallen tree was no barrier to me. A name on my lips, and now the houses' eyes will be veiled, like the eyes of birds that have died of cold. I must go down and warn them: the police will be coming to your house, you must destroy the evidence.

I ran with my mind elsewhere for a mile and a half, with the clean and prickling cold against my cheekbones.

Violette... Yes, you there in front of me. You mustn't run towards me like that, Violette. You musn't throw yourself on me as if you were just leaving the village, because I'm on my way there. Don't get in my way, Violette, don't keep me from going. Why are you spreading your arms out like that as you run towards me? Let me stretch out my arms towards the farmers' houses, I want to let them know what's happening. Traitress, don't start all that again, weeping blood, clotted blood and salt regrets with your face against mine, no, what's done is done. If I had a double locked inside me, that double would be my enemy. We would say yes together when what we ought to say is no. So I ran. I ran on and on.

Stop, have pity, my heart pleaded.

I turned into a field, I stumbled over the clumps of earth. I fell and stifled a cry. I was sitting by a can someone had thrown on the field. There could be no doubt: it was my kerosene can. The one I used to carry around from house to house, in 1916, before we had our carbide lamps. I touched it. How strange, I thought to myself, it is less cold than my hand. No, it wasn't my kerosene can with its swinging handle. A piece of uselessness, kicked every day by a passing idiot. I laid my hands on it. Its battered shape consoled me for the wrongs the police and I had done to me. The air was ice. I was being sawn through at the knees. I stood up.

'See you again,' I said to it very quietly, without being able to see it, without having seen it.

I crossed the furrowed field. The cold laid steel posies against my temples.

*

Village, my village, I am going to warn them how I have betrayed them; but first, first a last embrace. Tomorrow I shall leave you at dawn, or else they will point at me in the street. Cemetery, always open to the night, I must tell you how guilty I am. I have come to make love to you, village. They are all warming themselves indoors, so they won't see me. Remember, remember how you were swaying with haughty hollyhocks the day of my arrival. I remember the sound of your flocks next day. Village, you were a voyage of discovery. The grass cooling the edges of the watering place, tresses streaming out into the water, held prisoner between the mossy stones. Village, this is our last evening. I can't give you back all that you've given me; I'm not breaking it off. Village, village. The rain ceased falling, you were playing barcaroles for me, and I suddenly glimpsed the little calf, trembling on its new legs. I was resplendent with fresh straw. There is going to be frost. Your roofs are being skinned alive. Why can't I quiet the poplars? I have become an undesirable, a motionless wanderer. I love you, you tear my heart out. I am going, I am taking you with me, tomorrow I shall leave you.

February 1945. Paris has been liberated and I am imprisoning myself. In what? In the search for a smell. I go into Guerlain.

'You haven't something spicier . . . ?'

'. . .'

'You haven't something a little less sweet . . . ?'

'. . .'

'You haven't something a little less spicy?'

'. . .'

'You haven't something sweeter?'

'. . .'

The saleslady applies the scent to the back of my hand, she
sprinkles me with her disdain, and I buy nothing. The sleeve of my
rabbit coat wreaks havoc on their counter, my boots are intruders
on their carpeting. I apologize as I leave, but I persist in my quest. I
ask at the cosmetics counters of Printemps, of the Galeries-Lafay-
ette.

'You haven't by any chance a scent like an apple tart? A caramel apple tart...?'

Two salesgirls choke back explosions of laughter, a supervisor looks me severely in the eyes. I leave.

That smell of apples cooking in an oven, that wandering presence in the meadows, in the paddocks and the orchard, by turns shy and boldly tantalizing, it was my witness the day I was betrothed to the Orne and its byways. In the depths of a wood, out on a plain, between two hills, beside a railway track, or by a harrow, my grandmother Fidéline, so long dead, everywhere invisible and everywhere resurrected, was keeping an eye on her apple turnover. I was seeking that smell in Paris while so many scents fearlessly invaded my village. Fidéline, a word in your ear: I am carrying my childhood tears in an orange folder. Writing was a secret; but now I am a peddler, and the orange folder contains wares to be sold on the open market. That laugh along the quays from the Châtelet to the display windows of La Belle Jardinière, that laugh just by my arm as it presses the pages tight against me, it's Maurice Sachs's laugh. I stop in front of a cage. Two birds in captivity. They aren't birds, though. With their ashy-blue feathers they are soft exhalations from my very soul.

Maurice, without any intent to hurt, exclaims: 'And why, my dear, should you not go peddling a few pages that you have written?'

I feel my feet slipping, and the whole city quakes: that little house he promised me in Poitou has vanished forever into the abyss.

I pull myself together. The birds on their perch, remote from the crowd and the noise, are looking me over. My defects glitter back at me from their eyes as I am jostled on the sidewalk. What a trajectory of moss roses and crowns-of-thorns between the being that is imprisoned and the being that is free. And the bars are a trellis of love. My tears lend the sky an added beauty. I am seized by a temptation to hurl my orange folder down into the Seine, to buy those two smoke-blue creatures, to shut myself away inside their cage with them. That calm of theirs on their perch is going to my head. Paris has been liberated, Paris is being reborn, and I am wandering along its quays searching for the wilting and the weak, for whatever is dying of thirst or withering away. A pitiable tuft of wall-flower, its petals the colour of port wine, still smells good, nevertheless. A beam of sunlight falls upon it and I breathe in its scent: a timid gate-crasher beside the reek of gasoline. Often I remake things,

things that have been made without my approval, and so I remake
them to my own taste. So I turn back, I create a wallflower of an
even darker colour. Oh heavens, the snapdragons! How beautiful
you are, how resplendent in your seed packet! The future cannot
evade us: all we need is a watering can and the salesman in his
grey coat.

*

It's not difficult: you go into a café on the Place du Châtelet and
you ask for chocolate. You take little sips, you replace the cup in its
saucer, you pick it up again, you sip again, you stir the spoon round
and round the cup, you blow on the steaming liquid it contains, you
look exactly like all the other chocolate drinkers at four in the afternoon. In Paris I wear myself to a shadow attempting to merge into
the background, to be anonymous. I hide the orange folder on my
lap, I cover it with my rabbit coat, I drink my chocolate. Gérard,
the thirteen-year-old boy I once read my paragraphs to ... Gérard
has been deported, Gérard is dead. The paragraphs are in my
orange folder. Paris, I put up with you, so just leave my dressings
undisturbed. I have my dead I have to bring out and put back
again. Gérard complimented me with his eyes. I didn't raise a
finger to help him. I didn't raise a finger against him. I was neutral:
that is my sign of the cross. To die is to be wise, since to die is to
stop. But I don't want to stop my black-marketeering, I don't want
to be infected with my father's idle ways, I don't want to hear my
mother nagging at me because I'm like my father. The solution:
to work if I want to give birth to myself.

*

I ring, then listen to the uneven clumping of her high heels: Bernadette is heavy on her feet. The door of her apartment, tucked away
in a corner of the old building, swings open.
   'Hello, darling ... How well you look today!'
   Untrue. I don't look well today. My baggy eyes are a disfigure-
ment. Every day Paris adds another pair of unlovely smudges beneath my eyes.
   She continues: '... I absolutely must find you a young fellow!'
   I have complained to her about my solitude, but I haven't asked
her for a young fellow. I don't believe her anyway. I know she
won't find me one. Words, conventional phrases, Parisian cant: 'I
absolutely must find you a young fellow.' If I complained that she

is hopelessly inefficient as a procuress, what would she say to that?
She would laugh. Sometimes her mixture of upper-class manners
and mock plebeian heartiness gets on my nerves. A young fellow.

Some Apollo of the boxing ring or the cycling world perhaps?
A young fellow. Sparkling teeth? A member rubbed shiny with tooth-
paste? The impulses of a champion even in his sperm? The phrase
'young fellow' doesn't suit Bernadette. But politely I observe and
record. I produce the requisite smiles, expressions, silences. I don't
believe in it all but I do believe in Bernadette's compassion. And so
you should, ungrateful creature. Only the other day she was lending you her bed, her telephone, her bedside table when you were
nearly dead with panic. She is one of the world's resurrectors. She
has resurrected dozens of neuros (neurotics) as she calls them. But
once you have gone, once the door is closed behind you, then she
has to unload it all; otherwise, she would be crushed by the sheer
weight of all our confessions and lamentations.

'How are the packages going?' she asks.

'Badly, very badly! What will become of me if I can't earn my
living any more?'

I would gladly collapse on the spot. But it would be disgusting.
To be a slug on her floor would be obscene. Order holds sway inside
that head of hers. If I were to collapse, I would be spattering her
little book of maxims.

She examines herself in the mirror over the hall table, this 'good
sort'; she tames a lash or a brow with one finger and a little spit...
It's for your sake she is putting on her pillbox hat, for your sake she
is getting ready to go out.

'... What will become of me if I haven't got a job any more?'

'We'll find something else,' is her reply.

Her Italian madonna fingers insert themselves into the black kid
fingers. The telephone rings.

'Hello, my darling... How sweet of you to call...'

If she were my mother I'd strangle her. Scattering her endear-
ments right and left like that. My frivolity is greater than Bernadette's, you see: I am taken in by her façade.

'Shall we go?' Bernadette asks. 'Gégé has arranged it all.'

'...'

She closes her door, then notices the great sad birds flapping past
in front of my eyes.

'Trust me,' she says. 'It's a dead cert.'

We set out for the Café de Flore.

Since enter the furnace we must, in we go. Furnace? A beehive gone mad. Every bee a queen, all drunk on royal words. Seven in the evening. Tobacco smoke like smoke from locomotives. Insane to think we shall find a place. Café de Flore, garden of gossip, horticultural show for the latest crop of scandals, and then the dried teasles that were this morning's freshest tittle-tattle ... Giacometti is over there, scribbling on his copy of *France-Soir*. Pascal, the waiter whose evenness of temper is variously attributed to indifference and self-control, finds seats for us. A free table, a miracle. The owner, eyes on the floor, walks among the customers following some mysterious trail. Effeminate homosexuals sip fizzy drinks; the metal chains they are wearing fizz and sparkle too, like the wild hopes they have come out in tonight, glittering into life every time the door of the café swings open. Has he decided to come, the friend, the one they long for? They are on fire as they wait for him. I sit down facing Bernadette and look at them, wait with them. Other homosexuals, intent on ignoring the effeminate ones, walk up and down the aisles, looking for something that isn't there, then leave again as quickly as they came. They are here in force this evening, the homosexuals, erecting a wall between the ordinary world and theirs. Present, Bernadette. Present, old soldier, old pensioner. Ghosts? Where are there ghosts? Over by the cashier's booth. Maurice ... Maurice with his tall hat. Maurice shaking hands with everyone. Hunted, charming, pulling a sob out of his pocket. Maurice, a Charvet handkerchief wound around his fist, Maurice laughing in order not to cry, Maurice departing with that dragging step of his towards the back of the café, preparing to ply already heavily laden vessels with his charms, because Maurice always gave without counting to those who needed nothing. Why is yesterday imitating today like this, why am I struggling in the meshes of the past? I can't hear what Bernadette is telling me; I can't hear what I am saying in reply.

I wait, I fix my eyes on the door. I hope, I pray, I am estranged from her without ever having met her.

I used to sit near the door of the Flore, to the left; a great cloak fell gently over my shoulders as I entered. Paralysed, dazzled, smitten with astonishment, I looked, I drank from the very spring of life: her presence. I wrapped myself in my cloak, I journeyed over a face. I emigrated, I landed on two eyes, a nose, a mouth. I became a butterfly with no more than a single hour to live. I fluttered over her forehead, a cool beach.

She will come in soon. I can't picture it. Twenty past seven. She's not coming.

'Twenty past seven, Bernadette...'

'She promised Gégé! Now come on, sweetie ... there's no need to be so on edge!'

Bernadette doesn't like doubters.

'Do you think she's working up on the first floor?'

The heat had brought a flush to Bernadette's face. 'Of course she is! All this noise is unbearable,' she added.

I go on waiting: I am between the teeth of a great grinder. I go on waiting: the grinder is about to start. Will it be dramatic if I don't meet her? No, it won't be dramatic. And yet my hands. Ice around the orange folder. I am ashamed: Bernadette will have to hand her my pages.

'Twenty-five past seven! She's not coming...'

'Don't be ridiculous,' Bernadette said. 'Why shouldn't she come, for heaven's sake?'

I looked at her so long before I spoke to her. Does she know about them, all my stations on the way up to her?

We bear the names we deserve. Mine is a blow from a stick. Simone de Beauvoir's is a carriage and pair. I shall never be able to separate her first name from her family name. How could I? How could I separate the azure from the sky ... I say her first name and her family name aloud, I am walking in a formal French garden, I am haughty and preoccupied, I move onward through the statues, carrying my lace handkerchief, and I do not raise my voice. Her first name and her family name in my mouth: the chaste almond inside its skin.

Towers and their arrow slits: so many little girls with whom I dally I like their sexes split with that neat line. I'm not a sex maniac. I see what it is permissible to see. At the age of eight I stroked a baby's crack with a sprig of chervil. Its eyes, above the chervil, were enigmas making fun of me. One Thursday I went up into a tower. My sprig of chervil had been long since thrown away. One always believes these things. But the slits in the tower disturbed me. Upright in the worn staircase, I made two strokes, a savage journey there and back, inside my own lips. I folded my arms. What was going to happen? The arrow slits above and below were questioning. Furious, belligerent, I put my eye to one of them. The baby in the alley was showing me its sex. I went closer, I gazed at a narrow landscape in the slit of a tiny child's sex. I went down the stairs, I avoided the arrow slits' eyes: enigmas making fun of me. The chervil has withered, the baby has been thrown into the dungeons and forgotten. Those games have never been pursued farther.

My eyes, my two doves in silken harness: her first and second names.

*

I have already told how I first read Simone de Beauvoir's name and the title of her novel *L'Invitée* in a scholar's office. He placed the book in my hands. To say that I was stirred would be inadequate. I read and reread that name, that title: a woman was writing on behalf of millions of other women, as though all women were capable of writing. I read and reread Simone de Beauvoir's name, I remembered the solitary sea at one in the afternoon, the sun, and the crests of the waves. Printed on that cover, the two names were both near and distant, just like the sea at one in the afternoon while the natives are eating their lunch of shellfish. I often search for the scent of incense. It is funereal, it is complete in itself. I read those two names on the cover of that book, and I was breathing the scent of incense.

*

During the war, always friendly and considerate, Blaise used to bring us the Paris papers in our Normandy village. I remember a paragraph informing me that the 'poet-thief' Jean Genet had been released from prison, and that Jean Cocteau had helped to secure that release. Jean Cocteau glimmered only faintly in the paragraph, with the modesty of a lamp about to run out of oil. Who was he, this Jean Genet none of whose work I had read, none of whose work had been published? The word 'thief' coupled with the word 'poet' displeased me. The label strangled the poetry. And thus labelled I saw Genet wearing Aristide Bruant's big floppy bow. I also read that Simone de Beauvoir spent her mornings writing in the Café de Flore. The information upset me. I had made phone calls every day to the Café de Flore asking for Pierre or Jacques Prévert, for Jean Grémillon, or Marcel Carné, Jean Aurenche or René Clair, in the days when I was a switchboard operator and errand girl. Now I asked myself: is writing just like making films, mere play-acting? Blaise explained that it wasn't like that at all. It was just that in a café authors could find the warmth and the hot drinks that just couldn't be had in their homes. No, Sartre and Beauvoir weren't making a spectacle of themselves. I made myself a promise, I took a solemn vow: I would see her writing in the Café de Flore before the war was over.

*

The post offices began refusing packages, so I took my goods in to Paris myself. My wares once transformed into cash, I rushed off to spend Saturday afternoon at the hairdresser's. On Sunday morning, standing on the worn carpet of my room in the Hôtel du Cénacle, I dressed myself in a Bruyère dress, I made myself up for my wedding, my wedding with Saint-Germain-des-Prés. My painted nails, my ten witnesses. A last glance at my expensive snood, at the fringe of hair arranged in a fan over my forehead, and off I set—to begin leading my other life. Self-sufficiency incarnate, walking on my Cazals cork-soled shoes. At half past ten in the morning I entered the Flore. I sat myself down on the banquette to the left inside, and I was attending high mass. Do you like going back to the same church for the sake of a stranger's name carved on a prie-dieu? I do, I do. I edged over towards the left-hand door till I was only a yard or two away from the steam-beclouded manageress. I ordered a brandy.

*

And so, my wares disposed of, a cloak falls about my shoulders. I am warmly ensconced in my box. The café is silent, customers few and far between. The silence of an orchestra in the second before the concert begins.

I live and look. What gives me life? A sudden shimmer. At what do I look? At the sun dancing in a dust storm.

I call the waiter over. 'Is that Simone de Beauvoir?'

'Yes, that's her,' he answers.

Her hair, a feat of engineering and a diadem. Drawn back from her face, then sweeping forward again in a curve towards the middle of her head. Without her knowledge, it was paying tribute to her great forehead. Her forehead. Yes, a beach. I fluttered over it, bustling and busy, a butterfly with only an hour to live. Yes, I said it before, and now I am saying it again.

I hid my hands beneath the table. I was seeing a woman writer more and more clearly.

I ordered a second brandy: a routine was being established.

Simone de Beauvoir was writing a book. Where? In the very oxygen I was breathing. There were only ten yards or so between her hand holding a fountain pen and mine holding a cigarette. A woman, dressed like anybody else, was writing her books in public, yet without so much as a glance around her. Her industry was making her invisible. No, it wasn't play-acting.

'A little beyond, on the same seat, that's Jean-Paul Sartre,' the waiter told me.

He straightened up. Why shouldn't he have been proud of those intellects he tended to, why shouldn't his customers have taken comfort from the nearness of those authors creating their works before our eyes, without show and without false modesty?

I had read *La Nausée*. I had been overwhelmed by the passage about the root, by the part about a jazz tune coming into being. The pages were rough with fresh filings. His talent: medically a counter-irritant. So that was who had just come in, his torso armoured in a sheepskin-lined lumber jacket, his pipe screwed between his teeth. If I see them close to, if I see them from a distance, even when I see them again in a photograph, I want them to burst, I want them to explode, Sartre's lips. They are flowers and they are healthy abscesses. They are the coming-to-a-head of the prodigious gift he has of understanding everything. Sitting in the Café de Flore, Sartre covered page after page without pausing, without removing his pipe from his mouth. His concentration and his facility seemed to me supernatural. I looked at them both, both sitting on the same banquette, writing as though they couldn't stop... What am I as I look back? A sentinel at the gates of literature.

*

I returned to the same table the following Sunday and ordered my brandy as before. Simone de Beauvoir was writing at the same table at the back of the main room, dressed in the same short fur coat.

The waiter brought me my brandy, I lit a cigarette. A whippet under a table raised its eyes to me: it was an indefinable promise.

I hurried out of the café back to my room in the Hôtel du Cénacle.

'What a little face she has,' I whispered to the wardrobe mirror.

I could look at myself without loathing because I was also seeing the face of the woman who wrote in a café.

'Why "little"?' I asked out loud. 'She has a face, just a face.'

That 'little' signified my need for tenderness as I recalled a serious, a remarkably modest face. I would have liked to protect her without ever going any nearer. It gave me a soft and tingly feeling to think of myself as a useful little beetle. I went back to the café. They had both gone. The man whose bare feet were blue with the cold had gone too.

Sunday after Sunday I went back. I was terrified by my increasing boldness. I slid round to the left as soon as I was inside the door. If my place was taken, then I waited outside. I walked to and fro along the terrace, I simulated detachment and amused interest. Would my place be free soon, Pascal? I swung my handbag: I must throw people off the trail. My place was free. Quick now. I took it avidly; I shredded and devoured her forehead, her cheek, with my eyes.

Then I left the café at the same time as the man whose bare feet were blue with cold, the man with the thin and ravaged face. It was Arthur Adamov. He too wrote without blotting a line.

On Monday morning I shut my snood away in my wardrobe in the Hôtel du Cénacle, I got back into my black-marketeer's harness, I walked to the Gare Montparnasse, and, sitting in a third-class compartment, I stared at the train window, at my box of matches, at the window strap, at the brown patch on the back of my hand, at the corner of my nail, at the lace holes in my boots ... I could see her little nose again, so unsentimental, so ungrotesque. The train picked up speed. Heavens, it's raining. A salutary rain lashed the window as Simone de Beauvoir sat writing in a café.

Long months passed before I went back to gaze at her from a distance in the Café de Flore.

'Half past seven! I tell you she's not coming...'

'And I tell you she is!'

I wanted to believe Bernadette. It was impossible.

Bernadette was chatting to the film writer Jean Aurenche at another table.

Thirty-two minutes past seven.

Utterly resplendent, wholly sure of myself, I turned my head towards the sun: dressed in her short fur coat, she was coming down the stairs of the Flore without seeing anyone. She was in a hurry.

Bernadette signalled to her.

'How do you do?...'

The conversation was brief. No, she wouldn't sit down. She took the orange folder from Bernadette's hands. 'I shall read it. Good-bye,' she said to us.

She had scarcely stopped before she was off again, still in a hurry.

Other customers recognized her, whispered, gave admiring glances.

Now, twenty years afterwards, I am walking in a wood. A muted rain is falling, and I walk on through a damp autumn.

'How do you do? ...'

A leaf ought to fall, but it doesn't. I walk on against the current through a torrent of dead leaves.

'How do you do? ...'

The voice is husky. A leaf ought to fall from an almost stripped bush, yet still it doesn't fall. My boots in the dead leaves: along with the shimmer and the satin rustle, the sound of the sea churning off a shore. The voice had a plashy note.

'How do you do? ...'

I go home: first relic of the autumn, the box is pink. I go home as I went home twenty years ago, after she had said that how do you do to me: alone, my head full of tears. A young girl in a white dress opens the shutters. Did it rain for long? A dream, all a dream.

*

'Hello,' I said in a dead voice.

I counted on my fingers. Nineteen hours had gone by since our visit to the Café de Flore.

'Hello,' I said in a rusty voice, the voice of a wakened sleepwalker.

I waited, preparing to reply: no, I'm not going out this evening. I'm too sad, I have no profession.

'Hello,' Bernadette said again. 'Is that Violette?'

'Speaking.'

A pause.

'Hello, Violette? Simone de Beauvoir read your pieces last night. She wants to see you. Call her now at the Flore.'

'I should call her?' I repeated without grasping what it meant.

I hung up. The floor of the telephone box opened, I fell down a mine shaft. I was picking stars, or rather they were alighting on my hands. The blue gleam of the anthracite pile brought me back to earth, or rather to the floor.

I called the café. They went looking for her. Would it be better to live or vanish?

'I like your reminiscences,' she told me, 'and I'd like to talk to you about them. Would four tomorrow afternoon suit you? Upstairs at the Flore?'

'Yes,' I answered, dumfounded.

I hung up the receiver violently: nothing was in its place any more. I was trembling.

I said yes, yes, and then again yes, to the silent telephone.

My life till then: a trajectory leading up to that yes, a long impulse towards that yes.

I emerged from the telephone box. A humble creature, a widow who has married off her daughter, who is going out to buy milk and bread at dusk, at that hour when the wick is drowning in its tallow in the church. If you do not lack humility, then you know how to accept what is given you. To make love. It was enough to breathe in the ozone of an electric event, it was enough to smile at my lowered eyelids. I paid for my call, and I was a murmuring hive.

I bolted the door of my dark den, I improvised dance steps. I concentrated on not even touching this extraordinary news. I had to live my thousands of years of happiness before four o'clock to-morrow came, and yet I had to be so thrifty with them too.

My hair washed for her, blooming with rollers, I emerge to run my errands: I am Hercules, I am secret, I have a secret. My street? An iron bar, and I bend it. My joy? A windowpane. What is that rustling against the walls, sweeping the sulphur along the inner edge of the pavements? My giant wings. I say thank you to the crate in the gutter, to the war on the boozer's nose, to the runny nose of a weeping child.

Simone de Beauvoir had said to me over the telephone: 'Would four o'clock tomorrow suit you, upstairs at the Flore?'

I was early. I waited under the clock, in the entrance to the Saint-Germain-des-Prés métro. I am always early. I waste my time with an excess of punctuality. That dusty shred of cobweb fluttering crazily against a grille, that silk stocking dancing up and down on a string outside its window half an hour ago ... they were me before my time. I am early, I wait, I am nonexistent. It's not boring, I nibble at myself. I imagine other minutes between the minutes, other seconds between the seconds. I double the money of the time that is rotting me minute by minute, second by second. An insect advances slowly across my grave: the needle of the clock. I am early, I spin time out, I have time to sell. The seconds climb, the seconds descend; I see defeats and victories interlayered. I see time sweeping everything up before it. In a quarter of an hour I shall meet Simone de Beauvoir. At four o'clock I shall be the privileged person in Paris to whom she is speaking, I shall be the sole person to whom she is giving her time. The seconds will climb, the seconds will descend, but I shall have forgotten you, clock.

The doors of the métro bang, fevered travellers pass in, pass out, and I assume them all to be idle, thoughtless creatures. To appear before the appointed time would be impolite. And I ask the clock to hurry, and the travellers go in, and the travellers go out, and the travellers bump against a milestone begging a clock for more speed. Some raise their heads. Four o'clock to them is just like four o'clock yesterday, just like four o'clock tomorrow, and how I wish I could be one of their herd again. Three minutes to four. To get back to my black den, to vanish at the moment when it happens at last. Below, the clangour of the trains sounds like the iron-lattice gate of a lift as it opens and closes in a hospital, but I'm not ill, I'm not injured. I am a swinging door.

I walked into the Café de Flore two minutes late. I had let two minutes escape me somehow.

She was waiting for me upstairs, by a window. Her grey jumper, her ornamental earrings, her wide, barbaric necklace moved towards me. I was happy and I was crushed.

'Good afternoon ... I thought we'd be quieter up here ...'

Your greeting is too vast, your kindness too perfect. I ask only to crumble away, to be dispersed by the four winds, shattered in tiny fragments.

'Good afternoon ...'

I remember her voice the first time and the second time I met her, and it begins all over again.

She says how do you do to me. I count the blue patches in a winter sky.

She says good afternoon to me. The trees quiver beneath their violet veiling.

Yes, there is a slight veil over the voice. It is a painful parting behind a screen, it is a melancholy felt at one remove.

*

She asked me to come and sit next to her, on her right.

Yes, I took tea. Yes, my childhood memories gave her pleasure. Yes, I would fix the end. Yes, it would be best to use the passages about Sachs for something else. Yes, the first number of *Les Temps Modernes* was ready. Yes, they were starting a review. Yes, they would pick a passage for the second issue. Yes, Albert Camus was

editing a new series of books. Yes, she would give him my manuscript. Yes, I must change the end. Yes, Sartre would read it. Why
should I not have answered yes to the paradise she was bestowing
on me? Sitting beside her, after having gazed at her so long from a
distance without any hope of ever getting any nearer, how could I
have argued? Now she had fallen silent, and while she drank her
tea I made ready to say yes yet again. She asked me how I had first
thought of writing. I told her how Maurice Sachs had pushed a
penholder into my hand. The apple tree and the basket amused her.
She said it was a rich notion he'd had. Where was he? Was he coming back? She talked to me about *Le Sabbat* too. Sachs, I could
sense, would have amused her without ever touching her. The
authenticity in Maurice Sachs was too deeply hidden. She was going
back to her hotel, would I like to walk part of the way with her?
Her kindness ... it was a happiness that felt like an agony. She
refused to let me pay for the tea. She pulled on her short fur coat,
she went on talking to me about my childhood, about my mother.
Would she be able to read all these things I was telling her? What
did I do when I wasn't writing? I was in the black market. I see,
the black market. I was walking beside her, we were passing the
outside table of the Deux-Magots, then the Rhumerie Martiniquaise ... She didn't want to interfere in my affairs, but it was
rather remarkable. I was involved in it less and less these days, the
black market. Ah, Le Havre, Cherbourg... Could I write something on that perhaps? I don't know, I don't think so, I wouldn't
dare... She left me on the corner of the Boulevard Saint-Germain
and the rue de Buci. But of course we would see each other again, she
would send me a note, no, no! Why not telephone her in ten days
or so, in the morning, at the Flore...

'Goodbye.'

'Goodbye...'

She turned on her heels. I ran to Bernadette's and told her everything.

'Bravo, my dear, you've made it,' she said.

Bernadette seemed to be satisfied with her new colt. Some colt—
short-winded as soon as it's written a single line.

*

That same day, at eight in the evening, I was at table, I was sculpt-
ing Petit Pâtre soft cheese onto my bread. Hermine and Isabelle
came into the back den, they unrolled a carpet of graveyard flowers

under their feet, they stationed themselves at opposite ends of the room. Hermine near the door, ever ready to escape; Isabelle between the double curtains, ever ready to rush in. I moulded another piece of cheese with my thumb. I listened to the sound of my own chewing, and from time to time I ventured a glance towards Hermine, towards Isabelle. They were patient as statues are patient, they gazed as blind women gaze, they were silent as the dogs of figures on tombs are silent. I bit into a russet apple, I got up from the table.

I walked to and fro, I pretended not to notice them. Bunches of lilac in our boarding schools, lilac bushes into which we dived together. The scent of our lilacs caught my nerves on the raw.

'What have you come to see?' I asked Isabelle. 'There's nothing' to see. That's how it is.'

Isabelle was wearing one of my long fancy nightdresses. I recognized, without quite recognizing it, the shroud of a corpse that has just been exhumed. A remnant that revealed nothing: Isabelle's body was nonexistent.

'What do you want to know?' I insisted. 'I have nothing to say to you. That's how it is!'

I waited for her to lower her eyelids. Those active, those wild eyes with which Isabelle once pierced the darkness, in our dormitory, were condemned to withdraw into themselves. I placed my finger against her temple. Isabelle wasn't made of marble, but neither did she have that apricot warmth I remembered. Is she dead? Is she alive? Worse: she has changed. Married? Children? Her long hair had grown even longer, it was sweeping the carpet of funeral wreaths. A torrent of tears, her tresses. I worked out Isabelle's age. You don't crumble away into dust at forty. I tried to lift the yellowed hair, to see the swell of her hips again, reassure myself that it was really her. I wasn't able to: her hair was as heavy as the lid of a tomb.

'Don't torture me with that questioning smile,' I told her. 'You were always jealous I remember...'

Isabelle's profile did not alter. There was the same bubble of innocence rounding out her cheek.

'All right, I'll explain,' I said.

I told her all that had happened to me: it was more heart-warming, it was more overwhelming than friendship; it was more agonizing than new love, it was more demanding than morality, it was stronger than incest, it was a greater subjugation than religion and yet dependent solely upon myself; it was stricter than the duty to be faithful; it was, on my side, a magical stubbornness; it was a renunciation that outstripped my imagination and for which I had that moment been born; it was nothing at all, it was passion. I didn't mention my pages to Isabelle; she hadn't changed, she wouldn't have given a damn about them. I told her: you, Isabelle, you will die with me, and yet I have turned the page. I told her . . . I know my future because I shall renounce . . . Renounce what? I have no idea. I told her . . . I shall see her again, the woman who writes in a café; what will I become? Isabelle was snickering at me: a toothless idol.

I didn't even speak to Hermine. I had no interest in finding out what had become of her.

*

Oh God, am I free then? Don't say yes, don't say no. You don't know of my existence, you wander up there in your heavens. I am free: Hermine and Isabelle have gone, and I shall see the woman who writes in a café again. My body? My sex? A rubbed-out pastel. Am I really free? Too free: Simone de Beauvoir wants nothing from you. Your reality? Your pages. And don't forget it, never forget it. She telephoned you only because of them. We are a long way from sixteen-year-olds twining their arms round each other's waists in doorways. They belong to the same world. She is sweet and kind, she asked me if I would like some tea . . . She is kind but she is close. Careful! Reefs ahead. Don't go looking for faults. I know nothing about her. But I do know how she closes her file when she has finished writing. How does she close it? The way we close the door of a house we are leaving forever, determined never to go back. But that's stupid; tomorrow she will be writing again, tomorrow she will have to go back. Maybe, but I'm not wrong: after she's finished writing, she shuts herself up too. I don't know where she goes, who it is she goes to meet. Maurice has set me on the road; now she was advising me. Vocation: a gaping void. I read over what she had read: a woman of great talent followed me across my pages. Knowing that she had read those words went to my head. My gestures, my tics, my impulses, my moments of dismay, my cries, my crises, my astonishments, my treasures, my ordures, my falls, my leaps, my waverings, my returns to stability, my ecstasies, my agonies, my collapses, my recoveries, my abasements, my errors, my humiliations, my crashes, my flights . . . words that from that moment on would belong to her. If I don't succeed in expressing

myself, what will become of me? I took out the pages about Maurice
Sachs. She was quite right there: it didn't hang together. I raised
my eyes. Crass creature at a table, fists pushing up my cheeks, I
stared sightlessly at a face battered by grief, the Madonna in a
reproduction.

No, I wasn't the grovelling slave of what I wrote. No, I don't go
into a trance before I write, or after I write. Polishing a piece of
furniture has equal value. My style is breathless. My style! What a
way of putting it. I might as well say my Louis XVI bidet? Anyway.
If you need to boast of something, that means you haven't got it.
As for application, yes, when I try to write I certainly have application. A bee on a flower. Yes, I gather all my forces together then.
My ideal? The honesty of the cobbler. I grit my teeth, I circle a
television aerial, a cowled chimney in my sights; those are my
depths. I set free a sensation, a comparison. It is daylight, that's
my darkness. I have a cross, I do not try to avoid it on my quest for
the exact word. My hope of attaining my goal is also my precipice.
If I found it, that word, I should not be exact, I should be exactness
itself. There are only definitive words. No others exist. I have my own
gold fever when I'm on the trail of that word: a factory girl's
diamond. If I can't find it, then I go out and wander past the
closed bistros at eleven in the evening. The chairs piled up on one
another are eloquent and I am dumb. What are you turning into,
would-be writer in the street? A sheet of trampled newspaper teased
by the wind out on a freezing sidewalk. And then, and then ...

I've finished writing, I hurl myself on the washing to be done,
the linoleum to be scrubbed, a jazz programme on the radio, a
Bach cantata. How kindly he is, the friend that places the boiling
hand of the everyday in mine when I leave my worktable. I don't
skimp, but I don't work overtime either. I would like them, I long
for them, the tempests of creation ... I'm just not in that league. The
hiccups? I abandon my paper. Cold feet? I close my notebook. If
my pulse slows down, then I run as fast and as far as I can from
all those words that can sometimes transport you with ecstasy, sometimes bore you stiff. And yet, and yet, if I warm my feet, if I cure
my hiccups, it is so that I can go on writing. Sometimes I dream of
aphrodisiacs I could soak my pen in, so that the words would be in
love with me. I love my adjectives, yes love them, but one must not
overdo things, and I don't abuse them. To qualify is to take an
absent being in one's arms. Everything that we write must be absent.
Were I to describe a stone for a hundred years, my words would not

have the hardness, the disdain, the cold exclusion of the stone. I give myself to adjectives body and soul, I die with pleasure for them. What a ball thwack in the middle of my racquet when an adjective sometimes appears from nowhere. I write, I follow the scent. My pen, my pack are ready to leap. But there are the lullabies. And the *gymnopédies*. Tender variations across the sky in early March, over towards the Place de la Nation ... Come back in December, my innocents; come back in January, my silky ones: let me capture you, I'm going to qualify you, I'm going to exploit you, I'm going to destroy you because I'm going to betray you, tender variations in the sky, towards the Place de la Nation ...

I was listening to Couperin at three in the afternoon, my breast heaved with emotion at such stateliness. I was seeing tender variations in the sky with Couperin in my head even at six that evening ... How am I to fuse a formal drapery of music with the pink wake of an angel? By opening a matrimonial agency. Then I could marry adjectives to sounds and colours and scents from morn till night. I had eaten and drunk God when I read that Vincent Van Gogh once qualified the smell of turpentine as *mystic*. That adjective has stayed in my bloodstream. But my struggle to be sincere is making me pedantic. I must not wallow in such satisfactions; it comes too close to repudiating them.

*

A week ago I was sitting beside her, on her right hand, upstairs at the Café de Flore. I cast furtive glances at the comb in her hair, and it was the first time for us. Her tortoiseshell comb is unremarkable enough: chestnut-coloured, inserted in her black hair at the back, between the diadem of hair above and the skin of her neck below. I have had her comb in front of my eyes for a week. It is her, and it is not her. It is her in her absence and it is a presence that makes me thirsty; her comb obsesses me. I look for it everywhere. The teeth of her comb claw at my throat. Why her comb? Could it be because of this:

'I want to sit down, I'm tired ... Can I sit down?' I asked Fidéline.

Fidéline squeezed my hand harder. She was sending me a message: Sit down? You know that would be silly. Night is falling, the grass is wet.

Our knives slid from our fingers. I enclosed her thin legs and her long, shiny dress in my encircling arms.

'I want to sit down,' I said, buried in her skirt.

Fidéline let our basket of dandelions fall. 'It's very silly, at this time of day ... It's damp. Oh, all right ...'

We sat ourselves down on the sparse clover. The plain was drowning in the mist; but we knew that plain by heart.

'It's as though we were at the sea,' I said to Fidéline. I gave her my arm, I tapped on the back of her hand, I wanted her to look at me when I was speaking to her and when I wasn't speaking to her. I wanted her to look at me always.

'Why do you say that?' Fidéline asked me. 'You've never been there.'

I didn't dare explain it to her: the sheet of dew on which we were sitting, the sea ... The immense dusk, the sea ... The sound of the bugle lost on the plain, the sea ...

'Look,' I said to Fidéline, 'look!'

I stood up. I could see it better.

'If it's a dandelion, don't pick it! Our basket's full already,' Fidéline said.

'It's a piece of a comb,' I cried.

I was cleaning it with the hem of my pinafore.

'Do you want to see it?'

'It's dirty. Throw it away ...'

'It's not dirty. Don't you want to see it?'

'No, I don't want to see it. Throw it away!'

I put it back where I'd found it. I burst into tears.

*

I look and look for her. The time, waiter, it's important. Ten to four, you say? Must I suffer from my own punctuality for another ten minutes? Ten to four, are you quite sure? Who can be sure of the time? You over there, customer! Why do you smile as you look at me? Is it possible you have guessed who I am waiting for? Yes, go on cutting the pages of your book. A writer is crying out to you from every page, O cutter of paper. I sensed it, she is coming in now, at this moment, and everything is transformed. The Café de Flore? Swept with bright beams, a sun, my sun, brazen flash of trumpets. You can look at me now, customer, I am transformed, I am opening my window, I can hear the sighs of love from all my subjects. She is climbing the stairs, I am certain of her arrival, I am a majesty and a simple mortal. I'm going to see her again, I'm going to receive her; order in my palaces, I say; yes, she is climbing the stairs, she is

about to walk through my gardens of clipped hedges where nothing
has been left to chance. My palaces ... the unoccupied tables in a
café. My clipped hedges ... the slices of fruitcake.

She holds out her hand to me, she has taken the jump into
friendship. I remain on the edge, I love her so much. She dares to
apologize for being five minutes late, she dares to. Don't address
me as though I were your equal, you offend me when you do that:
you demean me in demeaning yourself. She is friendly, she is
attentive; I wonder which rung I shall fall from; the picture is
never big enough to take in everything on her face.

'Have you been working?'

'Yes, I've been working.'

And yet I felt dissatisfaction at the confession. It would be too
easy, too insipid if we were both to be so satisfied with ourselves.

Simone de Beauvoir opened the orange folder.

She read, I stagnated. I didn't dare look around me. Too flighty.
I didn't dare look down at one of my pages: it belonged to her.
Where was I to hide myself while she read the changes I had made,
on her advice?

'I shall take it with me,' she said. 'Sartre can pick a passage for
our review, then you can correct the proofs.'

Someone else was listening, someone else was swallowing like
that. Joy strikes, and we are somewhere else.

She opened the orange folder again, flicked once more through
what she had read.

'You know, I really do like this,' she said in her husky voice.

She closed the manuscript up again.

I lowered my eyes at her compliment. My crown of bay: my
lowered eyelids.

Later, she said: 'I'm reading a book by Genet. I'll lend it to
you ...'

A book by Genet ... She was giving me a piece of tremendous
news, yet not telling me what it was. She would lend me the book
she was reading at that moment: I would be nestling warmly in
the pocket of her little fur coat.

*

Sartre selected three passages for which I found a collective title in
the texts themselves: *A mother, an umbrella, a pair of gloves.* I
really thought I was the cat's whiskers. Sartre has selected three
passages, I have found a title for them in the texts themselves ...

Just listen to her. She is mad with vanity. You will burn your wings, my tattered little moth; writing will no longer be a secret. You are exposing yourself now. I am telling my life, writing has become my life. Believe me, I don't take myself seriously when I scribble on those sheets of paper. Should I go on telling it? Should I stop? But if I stop, then I am doing away with Simone de Beauvoir. It was she who helped me write my books. I went on writing for her sake.

*

Her name was Paule Allard. She was one of their friends. She received me in the editorial office of their review, she showed me the first issue of *Les Temps Modernes*. I held it without holding it. With excessive respect. It wasn't published yet, but it was doing very nicely already, their review. Quivering with life even through its thick cover, all that freshly picked, weighed, screened, red-hot new material.

'I have your proofs.'

She was looking for them. My proofs. A double meaning. My heart beat faster, my hand trembled on account of my childhood griefs printed out in black and white.

Paule Allard was patting them into a neat pile, the proofs I was to correct. But how can I ever make them come out differently now, I asked myself, my mother's steel-blue gaze or Fidéline's hemorrhage. I was losing my own identity as Paule Allard laid my mother's fits of fury, Fidéline's celestial gentleness, into my outstretched hands.

She took them back again. She enclosed them in an envelope, my proofs.

The linotypist's lucidity made my heart sink. I wondered what he'd thought of it. A judge, among the monstrous rotating presses, passing sentence on my work without parting his tight lips. Verbs and adjectives will have been weakened, others will have been strengthened in the printing house. My book? Replayed on a checkerboard. My style? The gasping of an asthma victim.

*

I went off to daub my face with pink, with red, with black, in the basement of the Deux-Magots; a man left his sheets of paper, stood up, shook my hand across the table, talked to me for five minutes. It was Sartre. I love Sartre's face. They say he's ugly. He can't be ugly: his intelligence irradiates all his features. Hidden ugliness is the most repugnant. Sartre's face has the honesty of an erupting

volcano. When he walks into the Dôme, into La Coupole, he is a
bull collecting his strength, he is a meteor. He is a spray of icy water,
impetuosity itself. There are some faces that will deny you even a
flicker of the eyelids. They are imprisoned in their own starch. I love
his bottom lip, like a white Negro's, his squint, his wandering eye.
His shipwrecked eye, a surge of light, Sartre himself when he plunges
into our muddy waters. His eye in the Cartier-Bresson photograph
... the quiver of a light-filled brush. Vincent Van Gogh painted a
young man with the stem of a cornflower between his teeth. I know
of no face nearer to Sartre's than that. It is the generosity of a newly
ploughed field, Sartre's face.

That day he said: 'You ought to work up the section about the
epileptic in the park.' I would have liked to, but it was beyond me.

His voice transfigures him. When I listen to him, I understand
just how far the timbre of our voices betrays and informs against us.
Sartre speaks, and first and foremost his voice is irrefutable. Sartre
speaks, and it is so dense yet so airy between the words. It's more
than melodious: it is percussive. In twenty-two years, Sartre has
talked to me for a maximum of ten minutes. The second time, after
having laid his paper down in the same way on his table in the
Deux-Magots, he said to me: '... The titles of Hegel's chapters are
more tiring than the text ...' I have never got over that.

*

I think more and more about Simone de Beauvoir. She keeps vigil
in my black den during my sleepless nights. No comb, no broad
brow, no diadem of hair. She is a rock in the darkness of the den.
Yes, you're not mistaken, that rock is her, says the unhappy wind
clamouring for refuge at my window. I stare at the rock; the darkness is cold against my eyelids, between my lashes, and I remember
the dampness of a freshly watered garden. How can I give her the
treasure of a garden when it smiles in happiness after a summer
shower? How can I become for her the harmony of a river meadow
after a gentle fall of rain? A river meadow would win her heart,
whereas my big nose, my mouth ... I stand tall: I am going to see
her again. And having seen her, I shall become tiny once more.
Afterwards: the indifference of geography maps on every face, and
my own threadbare handkerchiefs my only tenderness. A shiver, a
swell, the breeze, a quivering. I move with the springy, plimsolled
step of a gymnast, I dream of my next meeting-to-be with her, and
I fall, feet together, from the horizontal bar. The shiver, the swell,

the breeze, the quivering ... less the agitation of the acacia leaves
than my clairvoyance....

*

She has said she will introduce me to two of her women friends. I
am intrigued, I am intrigued.

*

They were all three discussing William Faulkner and his book *The
Sound and the Fury*, when I arrived at the Café de Flore. Simone de
Beauvoir was unable to contain her enthusiasm for this tale told as
an idiot's stream of consciousness. Colette Audry added pertinent
observations to support this view, while Nathalie Sarraute, the third,
more recent, more distant, less decisive, remained silent, or else
gave us to understand that after all, upon reflection, yes, when you
thought about it, when you looked rather more closely, then Faulkner, well it was clear, Faulkner was not so great as people claimed.
I felt she was splitting hairs. But I was instantly fascinated by the
weight, the lassitude in her intonations, the undercurrents one became aware of when she stopped speaking, when she halted moment-
arily, when she set off again. Even if she was mistaken, she wasn't
just saying whatever came into her head. The time had come for me
to take the plunge, so I took it. Enthusiastically, I explained to them
the role I thought heat, the fatality of the heat, played in *Sanctuary*.
I said it was a Greek tragedy, that Popeye was like the fate of the
Atridae. I wasn't trying to show off. My excitement and my enthusiasm made up for my lack of intelligence, for all the objections.
Or so I hoped, so I prayed. Abruptly I fell silent. What if she,
Simone de Beauvoir, took me to be more intelligent than I was?
What would happen then?
    Colette Audry and Nathalie Sarraute also talked, without self-
satisfaction, about the books that each had written. Extracts were
appearing in *Les Temps Modernes* and both were to be published by
Gallimard. I felt sorry for Nathalie Sarraute, though without letting
it show. Writing tortured her, writing made her ill. Time fought
its way onward, I was being crushed by that weight, by that flag-
stone, by that monument she carried every day on her shoulders once
her fountain pen had been unscrewed. And yet the ardour in her
eyes left me a hope. Two firebirds. She expressed her tragedy and
her passion for literature by means of distant insinuations, enig-
matic waverings, probing silences, questioning looks, and pauses

that were pools of promise. She laboured to explain, she laboured before venturing to explain herself, she laboured to get each detail
right, she laboured as she questioned everything she had just said,
she advanced step by hard-won step across ruins and crumbling foot-
holds, over black ice, over worm-eaten scaffoldings, over the
shakiest of constructions, over condemned catwalks, over treacherous repairs, so that there was always the risk she might fall and never
recover; she explained again that she didn't like Faulkner all that
much, she was sorry, it was a pity, that's how it was, after all the
last word has never been spoken, but really, she exploded, she didn't
like him one bit. She inspired me with curiosity, so that I longed to
read her inner life like a book. The idiot's tale in *The Sound and the
Fury* appeared twice as difficult in my eyes because she read it in the
original language. Without dominating the conversation, she went
back over the point she had been making, she went on musing,
among her books, in the sheltered hollows of her reading; she continued to concentrate on the idea that we liked Faulkner and that
she didn't. She lowered her eyes, she looked like a pious churchgoer
searching for the truth in prayer. She stared at the red tip of her
cigarette: she continued, for her own satisfaction, to weigh the pros
and cons.

It stared one in the face: literature was her reason for living. I
imagined a scientist in love with love, a scientist doing research on
love, making experiments on love in a laboratory full of complicated
apparatus. Nathalie Sarraute was like that. She did her research, she
made her experiments on and with literature, which was what she
loved most in the world. She smoked Gauloise after Gauloise after
Gauloise. I remember her cigarette packet poised on the edge of the
café table, about to fall. The blue of that packet was more real than
nature, and she smoked with total conviction.

Colette Audry and Nathalie Sarraute left. Sitting on her right
hand, on the banquette, I told Simone de Beauvoir the truth: that
I preferred Nathalie Sarraute's sadness, torments, agonies, collapses,
undercurrents, waverings, bewilderments to the physical and moral
robustness, the intellectual lucidity, the constructive approach of
Colette Audry.

Yes, she would lend me the Genet book.

*

A thoughtful being, a publisher. He puts a couch in his waiting
room; he considers his authors' comfort. But the authors already in

print rarely sit on it. They go upstairs without waiting; they are familiar visitors. The others, the hopeful, the candidates, those who have been summoned, can moulder away on it at their ease. It is perfectly kept, this waiting room. And yet, and yet there is a faint, a very faint mist over everything all the same, a mist of microbes, of miasmas draining our hearts and souls of all their strength: our apprehensions. The pulse weakens, you don't dare to sigh, you don't dare to swing your foot. True anxiety prefers to hide. Two hopefuls sit side by side ignoring, avoiding each other. The project they share is a barrier between them: to be published. If one of them is asked to go up the stairs, if M. X. is ready to receive him, if a third hopeful walks down those stairs only too evidently at ease, then conflicting scents fill the waiting room: triumphant incense and chrysanthemums rotting on a grave. Will he live by his writing, or will it drown him one day, the aspirant who has been called in, the aspirant about to be received in one of the offices of a publishing house?

Some of the visitors cause a great stir. They inform the receptionist, whom they have known a very long while, that they are expected. They have made it, they are the big names who do not need to give their names. The hopefuls gaze at them expressionlessly. It is too good to be true. And there isn't the time to admire them now, these great names; you are about to go over the top, about to die in the attempt like as not, while they are already walking in triumph. Some of them are very old, gossipy, affable, playful, frisky writers: they are living proof to the hopefuls that writing, writing on and on, is a preservative. Possibly; but the hopefuls would rather finish their lives like Nerval, or running arms perhaps, rather than climb those stairs in a warm topcoat, with a comfortable hat and a shiny bald head.

Lastly, there are angels in the waiting room. They are the people who don't write, those who haven't sent in any manuscript, those who aren't tearing themselves to pieces inside. They are the people who work with the printers, who are from outside the publishing house proper. They are neither rivals nor brothers to be held at a distance. They are anonymous. They will help you if your manuscript is accepted. They are what is termed production.

The lobby or waiting room of the house of Gallimard was not then, in 1945, what it has become since: elegant, beautifully decorated, every detail in place. It was less well looked after, more intimate, more human. A kindly air of free-and-easiness has persisted.

You see it in the heavy, green-painted front door, almost always ajar. You walk past it; you are a dressmaker or a tripe butcher. You say to yourself, 'Why not me? All I've got to do is give it a push . . .' A generous door, a tempting door, a permanent invitation to the world. Push it, slip inside even though you know no one there, hand over your newborn manuscript to the nun on duty, and you'll see . . .

Here I am then, in the lobby. I am a privileged hopeful. Someone has read my pages, someone wants to talk to me about them, and I can therefore hope for a contract. Here I am, alone, at fault, wavering because I am obliged to disturb the receptionist at her switchboard. It crackles and she soliloquizes. She says: 'M. Queneau isn't in yet. I'll get back to you.'

A plug is withdrawn, a hole breathes.

'I'm putting you through to M. Mascolo. Hold on . . .'

If, in her melodious voice, she were to say: I am trying to locate M. Sophocles, he is in this morning; I am trying to find M. Aeschylus, he isn't in his office—if she were to add that M. Euripides won't be in this morning—I should not be astonished in the least. This is the world of literature, and everything is possible on the telephone. Her hair sometimes falls across her eyes; she is putting her heart and soul into the job. She is struggling with names, with presences, with absences, with messages; she is a little untidy, she has beautiful breasts. Who can tell me what I am doing there, standing in front of her, with my half-dozen childhood memories to publish? She is doing something useful, I am floating.

My heart was softened towards her by her collection. She was arranging, then rearranging her little fairytale animals on the ledge beside her: the voices had found one another now.

She took up the cigarette that was burning itself away in a saucer. She was about to ask me what I wanted.

'Hello,' she said. 'M. Gallimard is engaged . . . Call back in a little while.'

Was he talking to an André Breton, to a Michaux, to an Apollinaire of twenty?

'I have an appointment with M. Albert Camus,' I said during a brief calm.

'Who should I say is here?'

I should have expected it. She had no idea of my name. I wasn't expecting it. If I had been asked to bend my head, to show her my bald spot, I should have been less embarrassed. But I told her my name.

'Hello ... M. Camus's secretary?'

She was going to the trouble of finding out if I was expected. All I wanted was to take to my heels, to order a plate of sauerkraut somewhere near the Strasbourg-Saint-Denis station, to consult *La Semaine à Paris*, to melt away into a cinema audience. The froth of a Kronenbourg in a goblet, the froth sliced off with the waiter's wooden skimmer ... Life, yes, life without sheets of paper to be scribbled on, was a masterpiece.

'M. Camus's secretary asks whether you'd mind waiting a moment ...'

Nothing is simple, and I wasn't expecting that either.

I mouldered on the couch. I deliquesced. A man, not a very tall man. The appetizing complexion of a pink prawn. He was coming down the stairs. A small, ornately wrinkled face, made up of odds and ends, yet somehow not ugly. One of those faces that nature made while her eyes weren't on her work. The eyes sang immensities. A joyous shadow in a loose worsted topcoat. He approached the switchboard. His presence was a balm. He put a finishing touch or two to the arrangement of the fairytale animals; he spoke in a low voice to the receptionist, taking care at the same time not to disturb her work. At last a little human intimacy, at last a ray of reality. M. Queneau, M. Mascolo, M. Sophocles, M. Aeschylus, M. Gallimard, M. Euripides, they were all before me at last, all in one, clear-skinned, bright-eyed, and in excellent humour.

'You can go up now,' the receptionist told me.

I walked into Albert Camus's office. The grey carpet, the putty-coloured mackintosh over the armchair took me by surprise. Silence once more, absence once more. I waited for him briefly.

How did he get in? There he is. Standing there. Unruffled. Serious. Grave. Indolent. Modern. Romantic. Solitary. There he is, looking just like his photographs. Everything is measured, everything is aloof: his body, the suppleness of his body, his bearing. His youth is behind a mist; the beauty of his face has been misted over. He has the deep look of someone who is attached to nothing. To speak in his presence would be clearing one's throat, merely clearing one's throat and no more. I realize it that first instant: I shall not meet him, he will not meet me. Definitive? No, ephemeral. Impalpable, his presence, the silhouette of a distinguished explorer. My presence, too, has become impalpable since he entered. Because I cannot reach him, I feel a desire to hurl myself upon him physically. He murmurs distinctly; the result is harmonious and monotonous. I listen, he speaks: an abstract politeness on both our parts. He was sitting, now he stands. Green coolness, green mist, green froth of green plants making a patio in an office. A room-filling unobtrusiveness: the beautiful raincoat over the armchair is doubling for a man who is tired. Why this curtain of melancholy between us? The attraction of a being constantly in flight. Silken face, magnetic face; nowhere for a caress to cling, nowhere for a hand to rest ... I should have taken him for the hero of *Armance* even if he'd been a floorwalker in the Bon Marché.

He moved sparingly from one point to another. I examined him from top to toe. Silent tread of an exile, discretion of a forbidden alien, sobriety of a young diplomat. I no longer knew where I was, I no longer knew what I was there to do, I no longer knew what this contract in front of me meant.

I lifted my pen to sign at the foot of the last page.

'You're not going to read it?' Camus murmured.

'No, I'm not going to read it.'

I signed for a book to be published in the Espoir series, after *Le Dernier des Métiers* by Jacques-Laurent Bost, after *On joue perdant* by Colette Audry: a combination of titles that was scarcely encouraging.

As he showed me out, Albert Camus murmured that he would try to find a title. The telephone was ringing in his office, I didn't dare tell him how much I had liked the simplicity, the austerity of his first book, *Noces*, and he would have been wasting his time listening to me. There was no doubt, no possible doubt: we had not met.

I mustn't forget it, and I haven't forgotten it: I was met out on the landing, not by Camus's secretary, but by Jacques Lemarchand, moving in his shyness, lost, gangling in a black suit. I took him at first for a student from the provinces doing a part-time job between lectures. Stirred—yes, I was stirred by his tact, his finesse, his delicacy. Saddened—yes, I was saddened too, and how, because he was suffering, at that time, from acne of the face.

I descended the stairs in triumph: I was the holder of a contract.

I walked over to the switchboard as the man in the light worsted topcoat had done earlier.

'Mademoiselle,' I said with self-assurance, 'could you tell me the name of the writer to whom you were talking a little while ago?'

'But, madame,' she replied, still conjuring with her plugs, 'we get so many of them here, writers ...' She thought a moment, 'Ah, you mean Louis Guilloux,' she said.

'The one who moved your little animals ...'

'That's him,' she said. 'Hello, I'm putting you through to M. Brice Parain. Hold on, please ... Yes, that was Louis Guilloux!'

'Thank you very much.'

I had read and reread *Le Sang Noir*. Now I almost knew the author.

I emerged through the green door. They were repairing the road. God, among the navvies, was re-creating the world for me with a shovel and concrete.

I met Nathalie Sarraute and Colette Audry again at the Royal Saint-Germain. The counter of the Royal Saint-Germain was at that time one of the most frequented havens in all Paris. The workmen at midday, then at seven in the evening, were nomads, gypsies, exotics. They stole in among the intellectuals, the strollers, the idlers, the artists. A plumber's canvas bag, a carpenter's toolbox would set us dreaming between the gold of a Suze and the emerald of a Vittel-menthe.

Kafka was the fuel of our blaze that evening. I felt myself coming closer and closer to the cockroach and its bowl of milk in *Metamorphosis* every time Colette Audry called Nathalie Sarraute Natasha. Natasha ... An adult Russian was becoming a child. Was she Russian? I was alone between the two of them, a cockroach in my brain, a cockroach in my heart. Colette Audry is chivalrous. She rushes to champion the people and the ideas she loves. That evening she wanted to convince her friend, to convert her to a belief in Kafka's genius. Nathalie Sarraute was still more depressed than she had been at our first meeting; she explained how much Kafka demoralized her. I smiled: she was really going too far with her inexhaustible reservations. I smiled, but I understood her intellectual discomfort: she doubted others because she doubted herself. Her gaze drove me to panic. The two firebirds had kept our appointment too. I would have preferred her to be a little fonder of alcohol. Mineral water exclusively. We are unpredictable to ourselves, thank goodness; else, where would be the spice in life. I found Nathalie Sarraute's sobriety exciting me; I found that in order to attract her attention I was beginning to drink, to drink, to drink. I am shocking her, appalling her, and I am in my seventh heaven. It is Colette Audry's turn to be alone between the two of us. I am playing the *enfant terrible* in order to attract Sarraute, in order to shock Audry. But she's seen it all before, Colette Audry. Her fiery eyes, her glances shooting off in all directions tell me that she is upset on

Natasha's account, she would like to make me behave so as not to upset a sensible woman.

We were together all evening. I said: 'I've read Virginia Woolf.' It was a barefaced lie. I said: 'I don't like Virginia Woolf's books,' simply because Nathalie Sarraute seemed to idolize her. I let fly my arrows, I wanted to transfix an admiring heart beating in a brain. In all, I had read exactly ten pages of *Orlando*, and those ten pages had gone right over my head. Now they were helping me to wound a fanatic, to pierce an Early Christian of Letters. I wasn't jealous of her intelligence and personality. I was jealous of her ardour and her conscientiousness. I was like a bandit observing the comings and goings in a villa from his hiding place in the shadows. I lurked near her shrubbery, near the books she took down from her shelves, the books she read and reread, then put back again. I lurked beside her while she weighed, while she compared, while she reflected, while she argued with herself. I lurked beside her while she came to blows with herself over a truth, while she analysed, while she vivisected, while she rejected or magnified according to the results of her experiments and her reflections. 'Colette Audry calls me Natasha because I'm Russian,' a bewildered child suddenly informed me. I learned that she had lived in France all her life. A Russian, with the finely drawn lips of a woman consumed by unease, a woman burned up by an intellectual fever. Nathalie Sarraute was using her own being as fuel: her eyes revealed the fire inside. She was always on her guard: she was mistrustful of others when she was talking; she was mistrustful of herself when she was silent. She gave me a sense, with her sober air, her inner discomfort, of a shower that must burst and fall, that doesn't burst, and yet the sky is so black. Colette Audry questioned her about her work. She replied with such lassitude, such reticence, such absent-mindedness, such exhaustion that I could see her work hidden away inside a labyrinth, a maze into which she was obliged to make her way every day in order to write, to suffer, to sacrifice herself. The 'Ah's' that came so often from her mouth were not exclamations but unavoidable facts that crushed her. I didn't like Virginia Woolf's books: 'Ah.'

Nathalie Sarraute was smitten to the heart while leaving you free, so free that you began to wonder whether you were in fact free at all. Nathalie Sarraute said 'Ah' like that—in a dying and penetrating voice, expressing such good will towards you when you had disappointed her so—in order to make you love what she loved or not love what she did not love.

I went back to my black den and thirsted for her there. She will always leave me thirsty for her. I remembered how she leaned over the cigarette she was taking from her packet. She was a lady and a student. Was it the lady or was it the student who thought of me as feckless, throwing money away right, left, and centre, even though back in my room, now, I was counting every coin I had spent?

*

I should never have written Simone de Beauvoir a schoolgirl letter if my childhood reminiscences hadn't taken her fancy, if Camus had refused to publish them, if Sartre hadn't opened the door of *Les Temps Modernes* to me. All that, I said to myself, all that is her. She gives me what she promises me. She inspires me with the strength to write even when I don't. And when she asks me 'Have you been working?' if I answer 'I have been working' then I am the highest hollyhock flower on the stem. I have worked, I have written *Train noir* for *Les Temps Modernes*; you asked me for it, I will show it to you. The contract signed in duplicate, the twenty-thousand-franc advance on sales, they are you. Do I have ulterior motives? Am I trying to create a situation by using the hidden byways of sentimentality? The unconscious, my eye. Remember Sachs. He used to tell you about the unconscious. According to him, it is a titan. It is strong, it is cunning, it knows how to get its way, the unconscious. It has burrowed out, it is still burrowing out deep chambers inside you where Isabelle, and Hermine, and Gabriel are begging. I can't think what they'd be begging for ... You. You just as you were, in the days of Isabelle, of Gabriel, of Hermine. They're wasting their time. If I were told I must never see Simone de Beauvoir again, I would not lift one eyelid to plead with her. I know that better than my life, better than my own breathing. What she gives she gives, once and for all. What she does not give, she will never give. I have understood that. There is nothing sentimental in my tenderness for her, the tenderness that I shall have to restrain until the end. Spring, I thought you were young. I have met her and you are old. I set off along country paths, the blue of the sky reproves my mourning, I have nothing to learn about good and evil, I have learned it all, I stammer incoherent feelings, and it is for her. What is my feeling for her? My lowered head. I am thirty-eight, I have just been born, I am awakening. Spring, no cymbal clashes of cornflowers and poppies. At the very most, the gentle music of pale primroses. I am awakening to face a problem: an emotion to be contained, to be hidden, to be openly confessed to myself, then dammed up when I see her again.

Let us run with the wind till she has read my letter, till she replies to it. Will she reply? Her beauty would be no different if she weren't a writer. No, that's not true. The limpidness of her face is also the limpidness of her time spent writing. She wrote in a café, I watched her on one volet of a triptych, it was as though I was praying. I will make myself invisible, she will forget my stupidity. I shall be gay. Sartre and she are devourers of realities; your half-opened daisies won't even catch their eye. I fled the other day so as not to pass them in the street. But I saw them all the same. She had put her hand on Sartre's shoulder. I ached with happiness. He walked along the rue Bonapartre, and she trotted. I remembered the beginning of an Apollinaire poem. A man riding along on horseback, a woman trotting beside him.

*

Simone de Beauvoir has replied to my letter. She can give me friend-ship, and she will. My future repaired and guaranteed. One word made me weep: the word 'mirage'. It wounds me. She didn't in-tend to wound me. She has explained that the feeling I have for her is a mirage. I don't agree. I don't like that word 'mirage'. It's a cheap word, a pinchbeck word. In the desert, it signifies vast crazed visions for the sake of a glass of beer. I don't take it seriously. I can see where I am going when I attach myself to her: along a road on which I shall have to warm myself up again every time I say good-bye to her. Come now, she never asked you for anything. She could have rejected you totally, and you were afraid she would. Her life is elsewhere. She wrote that herself. 'My life lies elsewhere.' Honesty. Cruelty? 'My life lies elsewhere.' Shot like a bullet. Sartre is inside that word 'elsewhere', and that consoles me, that will continue to console me. I shall meet them again in the street, I shall make my-self invisible, and afterwards I shall sing. Her answer to my letter is definitive, a judge's summing up. I could never have imagined so much frankness in reply to my unbridled sentimentality.

*

We are having dinner together this evening, for the first time. The nativity of an evening. I close my eyes, I open my hands, I flatten myself against the door of my black den like an inlay; my evening with her glows through my hands like a candle. I leave myself, I lose myself. My hope, an orchard. My sky, a scent of flowers. When I was fifteen, when I was sixteen, this evening, yesterday, now, my setting suns, I raced with tigers the colour of fire, the tall irises were funereal in the schoolyard. Wind, fine weather, light, sea, ocean, all alone, happy, content, and the sand in the hourglass caressing time as it passes; sssh, rose, sea, and ocean, and falling asleep, I am the tree of silence, we are having dinner together this evening.

*

There has never been a bar of soap that has not consoled me, as I unwrapped it, for the child that cried and would not sleep. The uglier its colour is, the more consolation I draw from it. I am a devotee of soaps the colour of pink icing. Sleep, my baby, go on sleeping, I say to the new bar of soap, and as I rock it I am rocking myself. I sit down beside my bowl of water, I clasp my hands around the soap's mica box, and it is as though I were devoting my existence to the repose of a being eternally asleep and yet not dead.

Make me light with your lather, wonderful pink Camay, and this evening I will give her the weight of the bird when it plays with the branches, I will give her the gaze of the wood's undergrowth, the smile and the coyness of the unfolding leaf, I will bring her the frothing chestnut tree. I will give her the gleam at the end of the path through a wood. Above all, keep your voice down when you talk this evening, you Northerner. I paint my fingernails, I paint my toenails, I will be new, I shall arrive with my splashes of blood. My arms, my legs, my veins, my arteries, my bones, my blood, my breast, my building, all the buildings, my country, many countries, cold, warm, hail, ice, the equator are all netted, all contained in one and the same word. The word hope. She will walk into the café in less than ninety minutes.

Panic at seven in the evening: the minutes are meteors; the meteors are bringing me too close to her. I emerge from my black den.

*

At seven-thirty I entered the Deux-Magots. A customer paid his check and offered me the place I coveted without even seeing me. Everything is going my way tonight, I said to myself. I sat down at the table facing the door and imagined to myself, for the sake of a little harmless sadism, that she was looking for me at all the other tables. I hid my bunch of flowers on my knees. Why have I been

for twenty years, why am I still, a young man who brings flowers?
I am just not comfortable if I see her again without having brought
a plant or some flowers : I have lost an ally. I pulled my skirt down, I
folded my arms, I worked on my expression until I had made my
whole face empty, natural, available. It was the opposite of play-
acting. A friend is about to appear, the gardens will be more beautiful
than a king's supper in his palace. With one click of a nail I remove
all the customers. War, peace, life, death, health, sickness ... the
fixed point around which the revolving door is turning. Waiting is a
revenge on the future. When she arrives, then I shall wring the
future's neck. The others will recognize her, but she won't be the
spring waters from the mountains for them. Less noise, please; I'm
waiting for her. That camellia-face, the face of a child who is waiting
too ... No time, too late. A tragic roaring in my bowels. Faces,
things in the café turning blue, blowing up a storm for me. Two minutes to eight, time plays no tricks, time marches on, eight o'clock is
a thunderous blue, the storm prowls around us, still in the distance,
making up its mind. Burst now, storm, she is about to come. Time
passes, I am suffocating, it is unbreathable. Wild gestures from the
trees, the necessary wind before the storm; oh, let her come in now,
let there be an end to it.

She comes in. A glinting bubble. All that happiness in waiting
for her without a drop of comfort is swept away. She is beautiful,
she is modest. She looks for me, I make no sign. The movement of
her head as she looks for me: that of a bird. Her arrival, a legend
whose hand I will have to shake. There are so many ways of making
love. I can make love to what I see: a being walking towards me.
I have her at my mercy, she is here. She was there, she was giving
me back the beauty that had made me tremble. I came to attention
again. I handed over my bunch of flowers. She parted the paper
slightly; the noise was unseemly in the extreme ... She said, 'How
pretty ... how pretty they are ...' and her kindness annihilated me.
She handed the flowers back; how was the shiny paper envelope
to be closed again? Even with my hands cut off, I would have
brought her flowers from then on between my stumps.

She informed me that I would soon be receiving the proofs of my
book. The prospect of signing copies of my book at Gallimard's
went to my head for an instant. She was so simple, and when she
announced that my first book was about to appear, then that was
so simple too ... Everything became possible. I would have sworn
that I read Marx, Hega, Heidegger with the greatest ease. Her

radiation, that is the secret of my self-confidence. She talks to me.
Outwardly, I present a show of discipline, industry, obedience,
docility, humility. Inwardly, I am so happy, so free ... And the tone
in which I say 'Oh yes?' in answer to her! Those 'ah, yeses' signify:
I am an eagle, I am hovering over this café, I am about to carry you
off. She strips all unnecessary mystery, all unnecessary sanctity from
things. That is why I take myself for her. Her clumsiness when she
is using a lighter, when she wants to knock the ash off her cigarette ...? Those are my pinholes, the chinks I fill with my tenderness for her. I say to myself: she is vulnerable. I didn't want her
to carry the flowers in the street. It would look ridiculous. I would
be ridiculous instead. Perched up on my stiletto heels, it was all I
could do to keep up with her between the Deux-Magots and the
Golfe-Juan, where we were to eat.

I told her about my evening at the Royal Saint-Germain, but dishonestly omitting the attraction Nathalie Sarraute exerted on me. I
was afraid of offending her. Offending her? She asks nothing, her
life is elsewhere. Her emotional life, her literary life, her philo-
sophic life; in short, her life as a woman and as a writer. Her life
with all the wonders of its day-to-day events. I behaved as though
she were the most jealous woman on earth. I passed over Nathalie
Sarraute in silence, over my excitement as I listened to a summing
up of Valéry's importance emerging from those abstract lips. What
titillation there is inside my head when Nathalie Sarraute, nobly
drugged with literature, is there beside me!

Why was I unable to be honest every time I talked to Simone de
Beauvoir about Nathalie Sarraute? I was afraid—as I always shall
be—of losing her. There was only one solution: remove everyone
else. Yet I talked about Simone de Beauvoir to Nathalie Sarraute
without the slightest restraint, about all that she represented for me.
And Nathalie Sarraute talked to me with restraint about Sartre,
about all he represented for her.

*

It's fixed: she will leave the Genet book for me with the cashier of
the Deux-Magots tomorrow.

*

Simone de Beauvoir explains everything without long speeches. If
I say 'I'm not an intellectual,' she looks annoyed. 'You are an intellectual, because you write,' she replies. She proves it to me: to rebel

means to prove one's honesty. She showers me with proofs and explanations at an unbelievable rate. And while it's going on, I renounce my dozing daisies. But I go back to them afterwards. 'Have you been working?'—'Yes, I've been working.' That's the essential thing. Judges and moralists go and get yourselves stuffed, because I have answered her question, and the tree can drink the sky's blue the easier for it. Her life is elsewhere. I understand that and shall never understand it. She told me yesterday: 'My life is elsewhere.' Yesterday: twenty years ago.

What is she? What will she always be? A girl. Simone de Beauvoir will always be the girl that climbed out of our taxi first, when we stopped in front of where she lived. She was giving me what she promised me: I was saved. No, I wasn't saved from the black streets, from the wan intersections, from the lonely exchanges between the red and green lights, from the gathering speed and determination of my taxi along by the walls of the Garde Républicaine. Now we were swinging around the Spirit of the Bastille, and I recognized my own neighbourhood. That bowed back in front of me, that kindly determination to get us across the desert of Paris ... I warmed my heart against a man without a neck. Alone in the taxi, alone in the sleeping city, I felt pity for myself. Throw me the trapeze so that I can go through my dreary tricks, come on, throw it.

'It's been a fine day today ...'

The driver: '...'

'It can't go on being this cold.'

The driver: '...'

'The forecast says it's going to get warmer.'

The driver: 'You believe in them, do you, those forecasts? Well, no forecast's going to stop me going fishing tomorrow!'

'I think you're quite right.'

There is nothing I wouldn't stoop to, just so I can tell him I think he's quite right.

'Good night, monsieur.'

'Good night, little lady.'

I opened the door of my building, I was a harmess old man's little lady. I would never see him again.

*

My big nose. I wasn't forgetting it. I would thrust its company on Simone de Beauvoir for five or six hours together. I made myself up: I saw it magnified. I sat next to her: my nose disappeared. Happiness, a feather duster that can dispose of anything. Then I would leave her, and think of myself as a repulsive man who has been paying court to a very beautiful woman. If I called attention to it, then she talked about my baroque face; but no, I wasn't ugly ... I am nearing my sixtieth year now ... the pine planks, the worms, the earth, the dust will soon be of more moment than the flesh and bone of a big nose. Still, I don't forget what she was obliged, what she is still obliged to put up with every time she looks at me. When I leave her at five in the afternoon, when I find myself back on the métro platform, I watch with inner dread the behaviour of the old men towards the young girls just out of school. And yet I am not one of those old men; she is not one of those girls. A lie. You were, you are a foul old man who comes ringing at her door with a pitter-pattering heart. Do you know what you're doing with all this self-indulgence about that big nose of yours? You're pulling her down to the level of people who look no further than a pretty face. I don't think that's true. No, the discouraging thought for me is this: if we aren't intelligent, then the spectacle we make of ourselves with our unpleasing features is a hundred times more tedious. My nose has been shortened, I confided to her once. 'What it must have been like!' she exclaimed before she could stop herself. That Golgotha is in the past now, and I do not hold it against her. Conclusion: my fear of being her is worse than my panic at imposing my nose on her.

*

One Sunday afternoon I went into the Flore with Blaise. We chatted, we watched, we made comments, we laughed about everything and nothing, and I threw surreptitious glances at the place where I used to sit while watching Simone de Beauvoir write. My eyes encountered Gabriel's. His eyes had a nasty look in them. Yes, I hadn't made a mistake; there he was, sitting in my place, in the place from which I used to watch her, from afar, from nearby, working on hour after hour. He wasn't alone. A woman with a disagreeable face was leaning towards him, attracted by him, by the look of it. I was at the zoo: a forty-year-old beaked and ancient monkey, I was staring at my double, a forty-year-old beaked and ancient monkey wearing a turban. She looked quite ill-tempered.

Gabriel stood up, came over, ignored Blaise. He had aged, he was already a sprightly old man. It didn't make me sad, it just repelled me. He was someone I didn't know.

'Can I have a word with you?' he threw at me.

I made my apologies to Blaise and followed Gabriel to a table where I had once gossiped with Bernadette and Jean Aurenche. Memories everywhere.

'Do you still want a divorce?' he began. 'I want to make another life for myself.'

'Of course I want a divorce ... It was you that wouldn't agree.'

He didn't speak. He was angry. He mustn't be thwarted.

I told him that we would get a divorce and that I would take care of it all.

Gabriel hadn't changed. He was satisfied and at the same time he was hurt.

I had been his 'chap,' his 'little chap.' Ripe strawberries hanging from snow-covered pines would be more real than that memory. There are some beings that die more than others.

'You're writing ... Things must be going okay for you,' he said after a long silence.

'How do you know I'm writing?'

He brushed at himself with one hand. He will always brush at himself like that. A speck of dust is the brink of despair to him.

'I just know,' he said. 'You have things in *Les Temps Modernes.*'

I hadn't the heart to ask him what he was doing, whether he was happy or not.

He had given me calluses, Gabriel. My sufferings, my passion and my raving for him, where were they? Was suffering merely dreaming that we suffer?

'You mustn't keep her waiting.'

I was enchanted with the detachment I felt as I said it.

He didn't answer. I had disarmed him.

Then suddenly I was moved to the brink of tears, I was floored by a great wave of feeling. Gabriel had put his hands on the table. He was so proud of the bottle-green gloves she had knitted him, and he was showing them to me wordlessly. A whole season of memories leaped out at me: I remembered a scarf knitted for Maurice Sachs while Gabriel looked on, Gabriel dressed only in a towel, a towelling loincloth ... I must make him happy now, now that everything is over.

'She knitted them for you?'

'Yes,' he said.

We shook hands: we would get a divorce.

*

I got the divorce, all in my favour. I met him later on in a grocery in the neighbourhood. He turned his back on me. I was no more than an old shrew who didn't come up to his ankle. I hear he is married again, this time to a schoolteacher (the turban? the disagreeable face?), that he has moved to the country. Future assured, fresh air, quiet life, hands cosy and warm in knitted gloves. Gabriel has made it in life. Sometimes he feels nostalgia for a certain dark den, for a certain crazy creature; of that I am certain. But it passes with the breeze and the clouds. He is safe from life's storms forever now.

'Would you prefer an ordinary pen or a fountain pen?' Jacqueline Bour asked me.

What should I reply? Her musical tones masked my answer. She questioned me, expressed astonishment, made all the necessary inquiries, was infinitely conscientious. And it was all pure music.

'Would you like to come with me? It's all ready for you,' she also said.

I followed her; I listened to a contralto in cool undergrowth. You walk into her office on a hot summer day, you refresh yourself among the flowers on her printed dress. She looks at you: there you are all cool and calm again.

I walked behind her into the room lined with glazed bookcases. She was making the same gestures she had made yesterday, the same gestures she would make tomorrow: presenting the paper knife, setting out the cards with the critics' names on them. She moved hither and thither, simplifying the publication of a book with her

courtesy. And yet all those books, those authors, year after year ...
She must be bored with it all ...

'What shall I write?' I asked in anguish.

I fanned out a bunch of cards. I read the names of André Billy of
Alexandre Arnoux. I didn't know either André Billy or Alexandre
Arnoux, except through their articles.

'One writes "With the author's respects," ' Jacqueline Bour said
from the doorway.

I was grateful for her 'one.' If she had answered: 'Our authors
write this or that at the top of the page, above the title,' then I
would have walked out. I would have shouted: 'I'm not one of them
because I'm not an author.' 'With the author's respects.' The formula chilled me. I made ready to dip my pen in the ice compartment
of a refrigerator every time. 'My respects, madame.' People had said
that to me once or twice, when they'd mistaken me for someone else,
and I'd always taken it to be an expression of scorn.

'With the author's respects.' I wasn't prepared for that pompous
formula. I had forgotten it since my five years working for Plon.
But, after all, I wasn't there to reform publishers' publicity depart-
ments.

'I'll be back in a moment,' she said.

'I'll be back in a moment': banality of banalities. That day, in
that building, in that room, at that desk, holding that pen, it was
unforgettable. It was Fidéline's 'Softening Balm' when I had an
earache. She would be back in a moment—and I would have handed
out an incalculable number of respects.

'I'll be back in a moment.' She had said it the day before, the day
before that, the year before, the year before that, she would say it
tomorrow, the day after tomorrow, in a year, in two years, in
exactly the same tone, to a beginner, to another beginner.

She left the room. The atmosphere changed.

I hadn't dared to look my book in the eyes before. I had thrown
it surreptitious glances, first from one side, then from another, not
daring to attack the front cover, the title, directly. Left to myself,
I did dare. How thin it was! A pamphlet. How gloomy it was with
that maroon frame! How dismal with its mortar-coloured background. Why hadn't they given me the proper white Gallimard
cover with the red title, the young blood of literature, the pulse of the
very newest trends? Did it mean I hadn't deserved it? I had adored
that cover in the windows of so many bookstores all over Northern
France, and now I had been cheated of it. I belonged to the Espoir

series. I felt my book was appearing in some provincial branch in a sullen country town somewhere. Threaten me, torture me, if you wish—I shall never manage to open it. Had I done so, then I should have been reading the words of a Violette Leduc who died as she wrote them. To write, I said to myself with the slim volume in my hand at last, is to destroy by destroying oneself.

Each word had already begun to die when I read my book in typescript; each word had died a final death when I corrected the printer's proofs. I had expressed myself as well as I could. I had believed in the promises, in the conquests, in the caresses, in the embraces, in the love battles of my pen with the paper. And it had all been no more than the struggle of a dead woman with the dead. My follies when I was eight ... crushing flowers in my hot, moist hand; smelling my hand; discovering insinuations of nostalgia one day during a heat wave—no, I don't want to see my follies transformed into printed letters on a page. Go away, book, leave me here, leave me with my flowers safe in the paddock of my memory: they are flowers scented with love and sweat, they aren't commas. Let me go, book, and I will go to the mass for the poor tomorrow at six in the morning.

Silently, solitarily, I took up the paper knife belonging to the house of Gallimard. Since the pages must be cut, let us cut them. I didn't believe in myself or in them; I had no recollection of Simone de Beauvoir's encouragements, of the sincerity of her judgments. My mother, to whom I had never dared give my pages to read, my mother was hovering on extravagant wings in that room where the press copies are signed. I listened to her wings rustling, I forgot the proper names I must copy out. She flew out of the office, she left me the scent of her Caron face powder: 'Love no Other.' The piled-up copies of my book on the table, the bundles of cards began to sap my strength once again: I was growing, I was multiplying myself only to make myself the more null and void. The scent of the powder vanished too.

I slid the card into the signed book. I was bored. I got up, I moved away from the table's unconcern. I approached the bookcases against the wall with the precautions of a cat burglar. I read some of the titles, some of the names, I read the greatest names the house had to offer. The one that stuck in my mind, that day, was Saint-John Perse ... A name like that, it wasn't going to crumble away easily. I returned to my seat carrying a portable steel safe. What was in it? A sun hat, a deck chair, a garden in Touraine—in short, everything

Strand Book Store

828 Broadway
New York, New York 10003
212.473.1452
strandbooks.com
strand@strandbooks.com

Sale: 4613825

Date: 04-01-2016
Time: 06:29 PM

Mad In Pursuit
0374195080   Item Price: $7.50 $7.50

1 Items

Subtotal: $7.50
Sales Tax (8.875 %): $0.67
Total: $8.17

Credit (Visa) Payment: $8.17
Card Number ************6323 XX/XX
WILLIAMS/KYLE F
Approval # 402481378

Amount Tendered: $8.17
Change Due: $0.00

Printed by: kara   Register: BASE3-Shift1

April 1, 2016 06:29 PM

Hardcovers/Merchandise are returnable
within 3 days for a full refund.

All other books, excluding
clearance items, may be exchanged
or returned for store credit
within two weeks of purchase.

Receipts must accompany all returns and exchanges.

Follow @strandbookstore
Show us your #STRANDHAUL
Happy Reading!

needed for reading Saint-John Perse amid a carnival of birds surrounded by cats snapping up lizards ... Proust, Breton, Apollinaire,
at that table, on that chair. My hand? Their hand. With the paper
knife with the sawing noise of the pages being cut. I cherished them
with my sixteen-year-old self, with my twenty-year-old self. I have
never felt as close or as far from them as on that day.

Jacqueline Bour came in balancing another pile of books that
reached up to her chin. I was stricken at the thought of her. All
that work for nothing, I said to myself. I knew I wasn't laying the
ghost of the person who had written *L'Asphyxie* during those nights
in Normandy. I shall never be rid of her, that brave heart sitting so
straight near the flames of her wood fire. This first book about to be
offered for sale made my heart sink like the thought of a promise
given that can never be withdrawn. I wrote, I wrote ... 'With the
author's respects.' I fidgeted with my arms, my legs, my hands, my
fingers: why should all these critics in Paris and all over the country
read *L'Asphyxie*? I wasn't any awaited messiah. Why shouldn't
they read *L'Asphyxie*, since I'd been told that ten new books
appeared every day and they skimmed through them all? But as my
courage returned, so my presence of mind waned. So many names
and first names copied out mechanically ended by confusing all my
thoughts. The piles of books with their white flags sticking out gave
me a boost; I was impressed by my production figures.

'Have you finished?' Jacqueline Bour asked. 'Very good.'

This remark finished me off. I interpreted it as follows: 'Have
you at last stopped writing for good and all? Have you understood
what it means to write while Mallarmé, on our shelves, has been
watching you wasting your time? You have given up the idea? Then
that is very good.'

She would send me my author's copies. But she handed me five
or six there and then, done up in a little package. The package dis-
patcher in me noted and approved the careful wrapping, the beautifully tied knot. The paper knife and the unused cards were left
ready for the next author. Tomorrow morning the table would be
neat and tidy again with the same names to copy out. I had a dizzy
vision of myself in a great factory where the machines never stopped
turning, night and day. Where is Gaston Gallimard's office, I
wondered. Where was this 'Gaston' that Maurice Sachs talked about
so often? That office, that Gaston ... safe from the intrusions of
beginners.

'Come back and see us again,' Jacqueline Bour said in a friendly tone.

I would rather eat my own liver raw than go back there soon.

I stepped onto a bus, I took heart again. I displayed the package of books very obviously on my lap, just as I had displayed the number of *Pour Elle* with my first story in it on the métro that day. The girl sitting opposite me was taken up with her wristwatch. We have been brought together, you shall not escape me. The woman next to her and the man next to me got off at the next stop. The ground had been cleared, now I could speak. I fixed the girl with my eyes, and fairly quietly I said: There is a book in my package, and I wrote that book. What would happen? Nothing happened. The girl went on looking at me and then, after a short while, without even a glance down at my package, she shrugged her shoulders and fled out onto the platform. I took her seat and kept an eye on her. I was hoping she would say to the conductor: There's a madwoman on your bus. She asked him the time, they checked their watches, and at the next stop she jumped down into the street. Why could that moment when Simone de Beauvoir told me over the telephone that she'd read my pages not be prolonged? I can say it again: that was my only moment of wonderland. The farther I travelled from the Gallimard building, the more my hopes of recognition rose. One glass of port at a bar and I was off. What if I turned out to be the thunderclap and the earthquake of modern literature ... I could see them, all those critics ... they devoured my book overnight, they were telephoning one another, sending telegrams to one another, fighting to be the first to get an article out on *L'Asphyxie*. After the second glass of port, my ears were buzzing: I could hear the frenzied din of the Bulls and Bears in the Stock Exchange as the critics wrote their articles on the blackboards, and my price was going up and up. I made the rest of that day into a trophy to present to Bernadette: I was still the new colt in her 'stable' and I hated to disappoint her.

*

Weeks and weeks went by during which I was a constant prey to inner imagination. Were they reading *L'Asphyxie*, those hundred or so critics to whom my book had been sent? Every day I waited for my name to be pronounced over the radio; I didn't miss a single literary programme. I also kept watch for my name in the headlines of the newspapers, and I gobbled every piece of literary gossip. Nothing. Silence. Absolute silence. I didn't give up hope. It was the silence before the cymbal clash. I was to be the cymbal clash of the new young writing. One Sunday afternoon I bought a copy of the newspaper *Libération* a hundred yards down the street from the Poccardi Restaurant where I had eaten lunch with Gabriel the day we were married. I went back to my place in line for the next show-ing of *Citizen Kane*. I opened the paper, and my eyes fell upon some literary reviews on page 2. The critic, a woman, after having praised Jacques-Laurent Bost's *Le Dernier des Métiers* and Colette Audry's *On joue perdant*, went on to call my book 'thin' and dismiss it in five or six lines. I went into the cinema with death in my heart. I didn't hold it against the woman critic. She had just been teaching me my lesson, meting out my punishment.

More punishment followed: a three-line thrashing in *Nouvelles Littéraires*; Robert Kemp condoling with me, convinced that the meagre results before him had necessitated a back-breaking labour on my part; André Rousseaux in his column for *Figaro Littéraire* making fun of my 'gobbledygook,' and quoting a passage in gobbledygook. His sadism consoled me somewhat, but I cried all the same.

My cheeks still wet with tears, I ran into the antique dealer Hagnauer, who was only too delighted to give me the news that Cocteau had read my book and was telling everyone else to read it. Encouraged, I walked round for hours and hours. I had developed a method: that of the bird's-nester. I slowed down when I was twenty yards away from the bookstore, then I stole up on it very gently so as to surprise my book in the window and receive a shock from it. But all the nests were empty. Except once. Where? The dispiriting window of the Polish bookstore on the Boulevard Saint-Germain. How old and worn it looked in the very back row! If I buy it from them, then they'll take it out of the window; if I buy it from them, I shall be nothing but a dusty rectangle after I have gone. I looked at it for a long time. One afternoon I was preparing an assortment of vegetables to make my soup, a wild hope seized me, the knife fell onto my one sad leek. I threw on my clothes. The journey to the Bac station was interminable. I arrived in front of the Gallimard bookstore on the Boulevard Raspail, in front of its eclectic windows, completely out of breath. But it must be in them. It wasn't. The large-format books, the rare editions of Valéry, of Gide, of Apollinaire, disdainful and withdrawn, rejected me utterly. The bastions of modern literature cannot be overthrown just to make way for your little pile of turds. Oh God, how I begged outside those windows ... If I had only been sure of what I was writing, I should have been saved ... Baudelaire and Rimbaud, were they sure of themselves? But I wasn't Baudelaire, I wasn't Rimbaud. Ten new books published every day. How can you expect them to display such a flood? An hour, even if it were just for an hour, each of us in turn ... Where has it gone since I did all that signing? Where has is gone to earth? Have the bookstores received it? I should die of shame if I had to ask them. Writing must be a sin, or why should I prefer to conceal it? My guilt was coming back. Window displays and bookstores whispered to me in the night: 'You'll never amount to anything, you'll never amount to anything at all,' just as my mother had once dinned those words into me in the past. I shall hand in my cards. Hand in your cards to whom? To the bookstores, to their windows, to the publisher.

I was unable to control myself when I saw Simone de Beauvoir next. I gave her a full account of my situation as a misunderstood writer. I didn't restrain my tears, I lost my temper with myself out loud. I belittled myself, I annihilated myself in order to soften her heart. I dug over all my grounds for rancour, for bitterness, for lamentation. I had explosions of lucidity when I was with her too ... boring her would serve no purpose. Better to keep quiet and suffer alone in my den. Then I was back in the grip again: I must conquer her with my tears. I raised my voice: I ought to just stop writing. I was appalled, between the floods of tears, by my own arrogance, my own coarseness, my familiarity with myself in her presence. The more I complained, the more I believed I was achieving a success in the emotional field. Complaining implies a desire to attract. Simone de Beauvoir didn't grow impatient with me, but that brought me no joy: I was convinced that without being detached she was nevertheless indifferent. In fact, she was simply waiting, moved and sympathetic, for me to finish unburdening myself of my griefs. Why was I alone, why did I want more and more to be alone while I was there beside her? She had nothing to give me, I had nothing to ask of her. But between the beginning and the end of every sentence, what impossible love I was bringing her! I shall never know what the word 'love' signifies where she and I are concerned. I don't love her like a mother, I don't love her like a sister, I don't love her like a friend, I don't love her like an enemy, I don't love her like someone who is absent, I don't love her like someone who is always near to me. I have never had, never will have a second's familiarity with her. If I didn't know I was going to see her every two weeks, the darkness would swallow me. She is my reason for living, even though I am not part of her life.

So I railed before her. I didn't want to write any more, what was to become of me? I had no profession ... I omitted to mention my notion of managing a Maggi or Hauser dairy branch... Simone de Beauvoir didn't interrupt me in the way I often interrupt her. She told me that I must go on writing, that I must be patient, that she would think about it, that everything would turn out well in the end. She told me all that without any hesitation. I listened to her inside a grotto. Outside: two bunches of wisteria flowers with their melting blue. Her eyes. She comforted me and reassured me without my having deserved it. I left with the certainty that I was being looked after.

*

The lady at the desk of the Deux-Magots handed me the copy of *Miracle de la Rose* Simone de Beauvoir had left there for me. It's heavy, I commented. Yes, it's heavy, the lady at the desk replied. The book was bundled up in a piece of torn paper. I am always moved by Simone de Beauvoir's awkwardness. She is hopeless with her hands. I ought to have brought my shopping bag: a work weighing at least two kilograms... It was tiring, it was cumbersome. How was I to carry it except pressed to my heart? A book to read; a cruise; we set sail.

That evening: *Miracle de la Rose* weighing down my bed. The book is inside a chest, between two covers that fit together. I have brought a de luxe edition home with me: it's a first. I am not turning pages, I am lifting engravings. Each page has the serenity of a sheet of thick blotting paper. My fingers touch the homespun of a monk's habit, my eyes finger the texture of the prose on the page. The title, at the top of every page, is light and airy: the letters are restful like empty hospital rooms. I read and reread the name Barbezat. I read and reread the term 'hand press.' I see the publisher Barbezat before me, even though I don't know him. He is bustling about surrounded by a teeming crowd of little medieval people; he is labouring on Genet's behalf with his hand press. The size and weight are almost those of a Bible at the foot of a pulpit; they require a lectern, special arrangements. I lean my elbow on the pillow, we tilt, the book and I together, towards the wall, and we

begin to give ourselves to one another. I am falling into my reading
of *Miracle de la Rose* as one falls in love.

*

Nineteen years have gone by since that evening. I am about to reread *Miracle de la Rose* in the ordinary edition. I take it out with me
every day, along with my beggar's scrip and my feed of oats. Scrip?
No, my bag has no hole in the middle, but it is an old word I have
a certain weakness for. And oats? Like a horse, I feed up my hocks
to run through the woods. I take the book out of my scrip. I settle
myself down on the moss and pine needles. It is closed and yet it
pours out light. A fly skims the title, an ant crawls over the cover,
a grasshopper hops onto the name of Gallimard, a gust of wind
blows them all away. The day the postman brought it me, this
book, I cut two pages of it at random with my knife that cuts the
goat cheese and the pure pork sausage, and I read those pages
again with the same fervour, the same enthusiasm.

'We know of no executed victim whose execution alone has haloed
him as we perceive the saints of the Church and secular heroes of
past ages haloed, and yet we know that the purest of those men who
received such a death felt in themselves, and on their disjoined
heads, the touch of that astounding and private crown whose jewels
are all ripped from the darkness of the heart. Each one knew that in
the instant when his head fell into that basket with its sawdust, to
be picked up by the ears, handled by an assistant whose part in this
seems to me strange indeed, his heart would be gathered up by
chaste, gloved hands and then transported into the breast of an
adolescent boy bedecked as for the festival of spring.'

I stopped reading at that paragraph and looked at my hands:
the swollen veins in them terrified me. Quite exceptional, the
atmosphere and the temperature as I copied out those lines of Genet.
Not hot, not cold. All around me, all—all—all is gripped, is held in
velvet pincers. A spasm, a fit of immobility as far as the eye can see.
The certainty of an imaginary memory joined with an event that will
not take place. I am in a wood, and at the same time I am in Paris
with the same calm, I am going to the cinema, I am meeting someone who loves me, and I love him. Everything is alive, everything is
breathing in the wood, and yet everything seems to be dead without
being stiff: is this then a supernatural atmosphere? Is it this im-
placable immobility that is working in my favour? I step out of the
taxi, my lover is waiting in the entrance to the cinema. An eccentric

fires three revolver shots in the heart of the wood, at which the bells
of a sheep flock cover the hillside in blossom. I close Genet's book.

I walk, I look for trees with bark twisted into strange shapes;
clouds stretch themselves in the sky: sensual delights. They keep me
company, they are all I have. I have an appearance of happiness, I
have an illusion of foreboding when they stay a little longer than
usual over me. I am less abandoned than I thought before. I wait for
them, I observe them, I compare them, I interpret them. I say to
them: 'You're late,' 'How you've made me wait for you,' 'Ah, so
there you are?' 'I'd quite given you up,' 'You're too big,' 'You're
too little,' 'Goodbye, is it goodbye already?' 'Very well, goodbye.' I
am from the country of great heavy clouds: they are my flocks
moving to fresh pastures. I say to the white clouds, I say to them:
Profits: zero. Love: zero. Pleasure given, pleasure received: zero.
Affection given, affection received: zero. Kiss given in the morning,
kiss received in the morning: zero. Kiss given in the evening, kiss
received in the evening: zero. Explosions of surprise: zero. Delirious
happiness after reading a letter: zero. Unexpected visit: zero.
Moment of meeting: zero. Return to life after a declaration of love:
zero. Tears of joy: zero. Tears of happiness: zero. I should lose my
reason if I didn't have you, little white clouds. I should go home
dull-eyed, leaden-footed, bent-backed. Old women, so unfortunate,
still have aspirations. Is she cold? Is she e'sso co'd? my mother would
say to me when I was little, as she pulled on a sixth woolly. What
made me warmest of all? That excision of the letter *l* from the word
'cold.' Is she co'd, is she e'soo co'd, I repeat along the roads while no
one in the world looks out for me.

*

I sit and read *Miracle de la Rose* again. Fever, palpitations, shivers,
just the way it was when I read it first, nineteen years ago. I was
an adolescent of thirty-eight, I was discovering the happiness of
adoration, the joy of admiration. Now I am an adolescent of fifty-
seven, I am discovering the happiness of adoration, the joy of admiration. For whom had I caught that fever? For whom was I in a
swoon? For Harcamone, the convict condemned to death. I reread
Genet and my heart beat faster. In twenty years' time it will beat
faster for the Colonie de Mettray entwined with, superimposed on
the prison of Fontevrault. Jean Genet trembled so much in prison as
he read *Jeunes Filles en Fleurs* that he couldn't go on. There on
the other side of the photographic plate is Proust, Proust with his

Time Lost and his Time Regained. I am the prisoner of both. I
read and I drown: their periods engulf me. The paper of the
ordinary edition makes no more noise than prison slippers as I turn
the pages at ten in the evening. Ten in the evening, the prison
thrums, tattooed men smile at the arrow-pierced hearts on their
arms, then leave to make love on a bed exactly like their own. And
I grow beautiful with the soft down of their whisperings. He is
called Divers. He is called Bulkaen. Genet writes: 'I am dead.'
That too is a marriage to oneself amid great pomp. He tells me
about himself in his books. I see him so sad and fragile. I can open
Genet anywhere. The griefs and agonies in Genet are my litanies. I
am raised up like Harcamone; see how I hover over his majestic
misfortunes, his sumptuous experiences, his rituals, his carnivals, his
metempsychoses, and Genet's ultimate alchemy when he transforms
imprisoning chains to flowering bracelets. I close the book; a harvest
of blue in the sky takes over from it. Why the obscenities, I used to
say at one time. Now I say: why disguise the word 'cock,' since the
word melts away in Genet's myrrh and frankincense. Every book
he writes is a commemoration of transfigured sufferings. At his
high mass I hurry to be early, to get a seat in the front row.

*

I began to write L'Affamée in my den, at the table where Gabriel
used to turn up his nose at my Rivoire et Carret noodles. Sitting
down to write at a table, in the artificial silence of a tenement courtyard, in the unhealthy chiaroscuro of an all-but-windowless room,
required more ritual preparation than in the country. I had perforce
to re-create as best I could those bracing nights of mine and their
black, untroubled oceans. I did my hair with great care: the noises
of the city died in the silken movement of the brush; the silence
of the fields, the woods, the gardens came back to me between the
teeth of the comb. Everything had been silence; everything was
becoming silent now. I powdered my face, I spread roses on my
cheeks and on my lips. And to make myself worthy for the grave
ceremonial of writing, I put on a blue-and-white checked smock.
Enclosing my wrists in the cuffs of the smock was like an ascesis.
My bound wrists lay before me. I presented them to the hair-cracked
ceiling. Removal men in your Northern province, you stole a little
girl's heart with your leather bracelets. And when I was sixteen,
seeing photos of Cocteau in the papers, I observed that he wore
the cuffs of his shirts extremely tight. I snipped off the buttons from

my smock cuffs, I sewed them back on again, I thought of him, I felt myself nearer to those swift and darting hands. I threw back my shoulders, I approached my table as I would have approached an exam. To write, as I have said, is to gather oneself together, to be a savage bee. We lead the way so that we may be led. Finding the exact word means concentrating oneself into a single point, but it also means wandering through the labyrinths of impotence.

Motionless at our tables, we are divers scouring the sea bed for an infinitesimal gradation. Sometimes I made a show of nonchalance of having all the time in the world; I hovered over the subject to be explored; or else I sang the opening of Liszt's E flat concerto at the top of my voice, then bent over my exercise book, then stopped singing: there was no way of conjuring fate. I was terrified by what was going to happen. I turned my eyes away from my book, much as we turn our eyes away from someone we love. Love vanishes if we insist too much. I coughed without needing to cough. I sat down at my table, I opened my ink bottle, I listened. Someone outside! Someone coming to see me. But not coming in. Someone will come, though; someone will come in. Who? I don't know. Finesse. I dipped my Blanzy-Poure pen in the ink, I wrote, I told about Simone de Beauvoir without mentioning her name. I told of my torments, my wretchedness, my anguish, my distress, without ever addressing her; but she was the character with whom I was occupied on every page. Every word was dedicated to her without my ever telling myself that she would read it. I referred to her simply as 'Her'. I should have been showing off if I had named her. She was everything, I was nothing.

Now I call her by her name; yet I still insist: she is everything, I am nothing. I have undertaken to write my autobiography; therefore, I must say 'Simone de Beauvoir'; but it wasn't easy. I was attached to her in my exercise book just as I am in life: with too much discretion, too much submission, too much punctuality, too much self-renunciation. To become an encumbrance to her would be to lose her. My tact is inspired directly by her. Her strength, her modesty, her severity add up to form my invisibility. The word 'love' is a word without meaning when I am talking about her. It's as though I were to say 'spring water' instead of 'ground glass.' It is so much stronger, so much more real than infatuation. It is an emotion that dares not make a move. My feeling for her reaches a paroxysm of well-being if I can sacrifice myself for her work, for her harmony with Sartre. I told all this indirectly in *L'Affamée*.

To write is to liberate oneself. Untrue. To write is to change nothing. As soon as my exercise book was shut again, I once more threw my arms around that impregnable keep I could never embrace. I ask myself, I shall always ask myself why I wound myself, why I suffer on her account when I want nothing from her more than the hours she has decided to give me, the hours that she does give me; more than her beautiful face that I want to see again, that I do see again; more than her slightly husky voice that I would like to hear, that I do hear; more than her exceptional intelligence that I am able to appreciate when I listen to her; more than the affection she shows me by shaking my hand when I arrive, by shaking my hand when I leave. Who can explain to me why I am a bull losing its blood when someone tells me she has given a little of herself elsewhere? To repeat such things is to murder me. I don't want to be jealous. I want to be silent. The more she keeps me at a distance, the more she protects me from an inner deterioration. Right at the start of our relationship, she eliminated all idea of intimacy between us forever. I keep on my toes, I watch myself to see that I appear to her in the best possible light. She said to me recently, 'I know you.' She said it without animosity. Arms broken, legs shattered, blind, I left pushing one foot in front of the other. She is a psychologist. Not a nook or a cranny escapes her. If I don't bother her, if I don't force myself on her, then I won't lose her, that's how I've worked it out.

I don't desire so much as a hair of her head, so much as one of her nail parings. What do I desire from her? Nothing, 'oh nothing. I don't want to lose her. Her journeys, her departures, the pale fawn leather of her suitcase against her carpet ... Twenty years during which I have been glimpsing her between two trains: the time of my arrival, the time of her departure. Five minutes before she leaves me—for it is always she who leaves me, even if I have gone to visit her—I think I shall die of a dizzy terror at our relentless punctuality. I may laugh and sing, stupefy myself and intoxicate myself, I may amuse myself, study, read, or sink into the depths, I may love another being but she lives inside me and will live inside me always. Would I kill myself if she abandoned me? It would be worse than that: I should wither away. I should search everywhere, and in vain, for my labour of writing if I didn't see her every two weeks. Our misfortune, our great misfortune is this: we want to sate ourselves. She rations me without intending any coquetry. The past in the present, the present in the past, that is my book *L'Affamée*.

I wrote in the black den, I searched and searched for an image, for an adjective. My pen suddenly snapped up the image as a dog snaps up a fly. I would be writing, then suddenly nothing. Forty days of drought could be upon me in a second in that desert. My vocabulary shrank to nothing. What was I to do? How was I to define blue, my favourite colour; how was I to define the eyes of a Siamese cat? Elbow on the table, I closed my eyes, I gritted my teeth, I puffed out my lips, I creased up my eyelids, I made myself hollow so that I would receive a visitation. I prowled, I wandered, I made sudden raids, I snatched up all sorts of blues: the blue of the blue bag in the cool water waiting for the washing to be rinsed, the blue of the sky when it opens into a celestial wound between two clouds, the blue of a storm between the branches just before it rains. I rejected all those blues. The blue in the eyes of a Siamese cat was more elusive, more milky, more sensitive to cold. The blue of long wanderings, a shivering of the soul. It was an endless pilgrimage into the blue. A slow progress floating in a blue boat, on a blue river, between blue-tinged lianas, with thousands of Siamese up in the trees. At last, without being able to capture it, I had thrown my net round the adjective that would sum all that up. I was breathing it, it was in the air, yet I couldn't find it, that adjective more indispensable to me than oxygen. I made myself hollower still. Make up your mind, don't run away. The liquid blue in the eye of a Siamese cat? No, no ... that's no good. The real writers have gathered in their harvest, what is there left for me to glean? I must give up. No, I refuse to give up. The adjective does not respond to my prayer, I must lay my penholder down on my table ... I come to myself with closed eyes, creased eyelids, arms outstretched— have mercy! I need an adjective.

Writing. Love after love is over. I was bent, I straighten myself: my desire to write better. If you knew how irresponsible I am when I am applying myself, when I am concentrating myself into that one point. I am juggling with glittering ideas. Once my exercise book is closed again, I accuse myself of living. To die writing. Style. The impenetrability of a style. The clarity of a style. The bounties of a style. Style: risking my neck for it. I write, I have no future, I abandon it on the page of my exercise book. An absorbing labour. The roadsweeper's broom is truer and more real. I close my exercise book, I put my Blanzy-Poure pen away in the drawer.

*

Two or three times a week, at about nine in the evening, I waited for Nathalie Sarraute in a bar on a quiet street off the Champs-Elysées. The pianist fluttered over his keyboard. I drank two or three neat brandies, I smoked cigarette after cigarette, dressed in my moulting rabbit coat, my hair in somewhat frizzy bangs. The pianist improvised, finishing off with gentle runs through the high notes; he played snatches of popular tunes, *Tea for Two*, *Cheek to Cheek*, *The Man I Love*, and then, once again, his fingers were fluttering in another improvisation. The barmen officiated behind their bar, underneath the bottles and the flags; glasses glittered into a second life reflected in the shakers, the lampshades soothed the light, the alcohol warmed you without burning you. The pianist made me feel seasick with his swaying torso. His instrument, churning out its barley-sugar jazz, charmed the adulterous couples. Customers came in, but it wasn't Nathalie, again it wasn't Nathalie, still it wasn't Nathalie. Eighteen minutes late, what does she think she's up to? Coming here is a drag for her. Don't be unjust, don't be so mistrusting, she has a husband, children, she has duties and responsibilities. Nineteen minutes late; she can't think much of me or she'd be here on time. It's deliberate. More customers came in; it was Nathalie, last of all, the one who slipped in without anyone noticing. A spear-thrust in the belly. She was coming towards me with her tired air, her feverish eyes, superb in her reticence, clothed as always on these occasions in her long Tuscan lamb coat. Her billfold clutched like a missal ... I insisted, I insisted ... she gave way; I paid for what we drank most of the time. I would have given her even what I didn't have. She never carried a purse.

Once Nathalie Sarraute had shaken off her inner life, she was like a little girl stepping out of a sledge. I played my role of inveigler, the role I had played in the furnished room in Vincennes, with my Basque beret tilted to one side. If I drank brandy neat, it was partly to put on a show of being an alcoholic, to be noticed, to be admired. Not to be 'sensible' seemed to me to be fabulous. Ah, with what enthusiasm I played the *enfant terrible* during those evenings! I wanted to frighten Nathalie Sarraute the way others want to comfort people. She encouraged me, she thought I was sincere. 'You're unbelievable, you're fantastic,' she said. Fantastic. I ordered a sixth brandy in order to be even more unbelievable, in order to be even more fantastic. I was deceitful with her. I allowed myself to tell her that she ought not to torment herself so about her work—she would arrive half dead, devoured with torments—and yet at that very moment her lassitude, her torments fascinated me, ravished me. We talked about Camus, about Gide, about Kafka; she weighed their talent or their absence of talent with a thousand-kilogram weight which she lifted in slow motion; the barman brought me a seventh brandy. I threw in: 'His talent is just staggering!' I tapped a cigarette on the table even though I was still smoking one. 'Do you think so? Are you sure? Ah...' She was doubtful and she wanted to believe me.

Nathalie Sarraute was forever on her guard in the Ascot's leather armchair; she often delivered herself of those 'Ah's' in a drained voice. She grieved me, she infuriated me. And yet, my girl, just look at her, think, listen. She is an angel and a martyr as she says 'Ah' like that. I lost heart. Her armour of 'Ah's' was unassailable. And then, in order to compensate, I uttered monstrosities. Nathalie Sarraute was profound; therefore, my surfaces had to glitter. I wanted to interest her, to subjugate her, even though I knew my labour was lost in advance. I was no longer the fervent adolescent in love with literary refinements that she had remained. I listened to her with a great deal of inner calm but I listened with a sexual mechanism ticking inside my head. I wasn't a friend: my attention wandered as soon as she began telling me about her difficulties at her writing table. A strange kind of egotism, a strange kind of vanity that attempted to dazzle another with glasses of brandy. It wasn't that I didn't care. I prefer people to conceal their torments as writers. I was too demanding. I was deaf and blind during a test of trust. Nathalie Sarraute's reserve and economy, her bearing, her speech, her caution, as of some great carnivore at nightfall, all enchanted me. I would have liked her to be equally economical when she told me about her writing; I would have liked to see her falling at my knees in the bar of the Ascot, begging me to decide whether she should go on writing or not.

I am telling the whole truth, and if I just make myself look foolish, then so much the worse for me. I would have liked her to yield, and she was inflexible. She is bringing them on herself, these torments of hers, I said to myself, I can't stop her: to write and torment herself about it, that is her cross, that is her life. She grieved me, and I told her so without evasions. I can still see her telling me about Dostoevsky, describing him on his knees at the feet of a great lady. He was begging for compliments. He was forgiven, he was always forgiven everything. Nathalie Sarraute's thin lips would swell up if I asked her, the following week, to tell me that story again. The weaknesses, breakdowns, contradictions, bad habits, lies, eccentricities, betrayals, pettinesses, deceits of a genius are his fruits; are ripening while he is disconcerting us. Maurice Sachs telling me about Max Jacob... Nathalie Sarraute conversing with passion about Shakespeare in a bar off the Champs-Elysées... They exhausted me, those beings in love with literature. What a calamity, to have ovaries in one's ears. I would leave her, and I would be thirsty. I could have begun my evening with her all over again.

I don't remember when I began to complain about Sartre and de Beauvoir, those two innocents who had fished us out of the void. I said to Sarraute: 'We meet them, oh yes we meet them all right, they give us a moment, of course they give us a moment, they give up their time to us, of course they give up their time to us, not too much, a little, they pay attention to us, of course they pay attention to us, anyone can see they do, but they never talk about themselves, so what are we to them? Are we guinea pigs for their psychology? Why don't they talk about themselves? Are we zeroes? The less they talk, the more we confide in them—that's inevitable. It's unjust, it's horrible. We leave them, we are disgusted, we vomit out what we have just told them. They aren't misers ... they ought to open up to us since we open up to them.'

I had been within talking distance of Sartre on two occasions totalling about five minutes. Now, sitting beside Nathalie Sarraute, I was waxing angry, criticizing, running down. As if I talked to Sartre every day, as if Sartre and de Beauvoir owed me confidences, conversations, hours of their presence. If I pass a streetsweeper sweeping a Paris street, I leave him to the exercise of his profession, I don't disturb him. Why should I want to disturb Sartre, or Beauvoir? Nathalie Sarraute took to complaining in the same way that I complained. But she dared to complain to their faces. I didn't dare. I camouflaged my feelings. To reproach Simone de Beauvoir for her discretion meant running a risk of losing her. I sentenced myself to a life of duplicity. I supported Nathalie Sarraute in her rebellions and thereby won her favours. I kept both of them.

Entirely submerged by my joy at seeing Simone de Beauvoir again, I forgot my complaints, my grievances, my criticisms, my intention of begging for at least a semblance of confiding in me, for a less inexorable use of our time. When I am with her, how is my cellar flooded with sunlight to complain of too much light... It is quite true that I was lacking in honesty, in probity, between the moment when I left Nathalie Sarraute outside the Ascot and the moment when I shook Simone de Beauvoir's hand as she walked into the Deux-Magots. I don't regret it. I should have lost what I could never have replaced, had it been otherwise. Where my role becomes despicable is when I complained about Nathalie Sarraute to Simone de Beauvoir, about Nathalie Sarraute complaining about her difficulties, her problems, her torments, her sufferings as a writer. I was unable to sense the inner gestation. I wouldn't write this if Nathalie Sarraute hadn't become a success. If I telephoned her, if I told her how much I should like to see her that very moment, then she hurried to my side. I went back home to my den more thirsty for her presence than before, and I became afraid: I must stop playing with fire. Three days later I was clamouring for her from a suburban telephone kiosk, I was hurtling across Paris to reach the Ascot. Her lucid ravings, her unshakable enthusiasms, her rejections, her reticences, her indulgences, her severities, her pad-locks, her bolts, her microscopes ... all stimulants for the sexual mechanism up there in my head. When I walked away from her, it was on a tightrope.

*

Suddenly a series of small happinesses, small satisfactions, small traps, small pretexts for vanity. Hagnauer tells me again that Cocteau is giving people my book to read ... Robert and André Payen see me through the window of their bookstore and call me in: Louise de Vilmorin has been in; she likes my reminiscences. Madeleine Castaing has been in too, and she has read it; what's more she told them she's given it to Elise and Marcel Jouhandeau ... Romi was so happy to see me happy ... at which, on impulse, I made him a present of the manuscript of *L'Asphyxie*. It is good to be given warmth like that. I listen to them all, turn and turn about, and I feel tenderly towards myself, towards them. In their eyes I can see all those windows where I'd looked in vain for my book. I go home, I wash out my blue-and-white check smock so that I shall be able to write better. If it were true, if writing were on occasions a con-solation ... But I have to live, and I have no profession. The fly on my neck as I wash out my smock refuses to move. It's unpleasant, but I mustn't flick it off; it's a friend, it needs me. How alone must you be to want to keep, to protect a friend inside a fly?

That evening we were eating at the Golfe-Juan. Simone de Beauvoir asked me if I wanted to go on and end the evening at the Pont-Royal bar with Arthur Koestler and his wife. I said yes. By taking me into the presence of a writer who was her friend, Simone de Beauvoir was heaping on me a humiliation as great as the joy: I was being given too much.

The bar is in the basement. It has thick carpets, deep armchairs; people talk in low voices there, and every time I go in I'm reminded of the strange atmosphere of the Russian church on the rue Daru. It is somehow stifling without being too hot, and the bottles of gin and Scotch are the icons. The stairs down to it have a nonchalant twist to them, and every customer emerges from the wings, walks onto a stage as he enters. A pause on the last step is an unnecessary precaution: it's too late, there you are already, between the friendly barman and all his cultured customers. It is one of the places in Paris where people shout least. It is just a series of chapels: priests

discussing manuscripts, publications, new books. The conversations
are like church services being intoned in vast and comfortable armchairs.

I followed Simone de Beauvoir to the far end of the bar. A cor-
pulent man, average height, greeted her with open arms. He called
her Simone. I was shocked. His spoilt child's face, his thick Mongol
lips reminded me of my cousin's. Simone de Beauvoir introduced
me. He shook my hand without interest. Koestler and Beauvoir
plunged into an argument. Sitting there beside her, dumb, I was
her dictaphone. I existed in the shadow of her glory as I smoked my
cigarettes.

Ten o'clock. I turned my head, I recognized him without knowing him. He was hesitating on the bottom step.

'Genet!' I exclaimed.

'You know him?' she said.

I had intrigued her.

'I don't know him, but I tell you it's Genet!'

Someone had pointed him out to me several months before among
the Flore's outside tables. Where? There, wearing a white pullover.
'There' was a long way off. He was just leaving, he was surrounded
by people and had his back to me. How could I have recognized
him in the Pont-Royal bar?

I replied to Simone de Beauvoir, but I didn't take my eyes off
Genet. He was opening a path for himself; now I had a better
view of the belt of his raincoat carefully buckled around his waist.
Genet was insinuating himself between the armchairs.

There he was in front of us.

'Genet...' she said, pleasantly astonished to see him that evening.

I was still lingering over Jean Genet's raincoat buckle. I was keeping his face till later.

'Hello, Beaver,' he said.

A supernatural simplicity.

She introduced me to Jean Genet.

'I've read your work,' I put in too quickly.

I didn't know whether I'd ever see him again, and I wanted him
to know that I had. He smiled at me. One hand stuck in his raincoat pocket, he looked like a passer-by who has walked into the
wrong place. His smile, which he kept on his face, meant: You
went a bit far there, but I shan't hold it against you. Genet's pale
eyes bereft me of the power of speech. They entered into me, his
cold eyes.

He sat down in the last remaining chair, opposite mine. A kind of stiff-mannered explorer dropping in on a visit, lowering himself to our level, crossing his legs, placing a hand in a grey kid glove on one thigh.

'So, you like what I write, then?' he said after a long while.

Unthinkable to speak anything but seriously to him.

'You are the greatest of all!' I said at one gasp.

A shadow passed over his face. I lacked delicacy.

I looked at him, I looked at him ... My impulsiveness seemed to have saddened him. Did he believe me?

'Simone de Beauvoir lent me *Miracle de la Rose*,' I told him.

He looked at me without seeing me.

Then he gazed with the kind of sadness that blanches all expression at the young man who was bringing him a brandy.

I had been breathing in a scent of ceremony, the effluvia of death and pain in all their ritual pomp—incense, in a word—ever since Genet came in. Genet's mouth: an unbelievable surprise. It had remained that of a generous and happy child.

He sipped a mouthful of cognac. He did not disappoint me. That sip was truly the ceremonial and the simplicity I expected of him. He brushed the glass with his lips, he condescended to take a pinch of reality from this world of ours that was not his.

Without removing his glove, he took a packet of Gitanes from his raincoat pocket, then lit one. Not a single useless gesture, an ascesis in the economy of his flick to put out the match. This man, I said to myself, is a ceremony.

'If you knew how I loved *Miracle de la Rose* ...'

I had leaped into the fire. I had lost my head, I began dancing in the flames: ... Harcamone, when you set him free, when he flies away ... Harcamone, a sort of great mythological petal above the prisons ... I didn't dare say it all; my clasped hands expressed it.

He tapped his cigarette on the edge of the saucer; he was conscientious with his ash: it mustn't fall outside.

'No kidding? You like my books, then?'

No kidding. Genet is charming when he is unsure of himself. No kidding. I was seeing a Genet as sensitive as an aspen leaf.

He looked over at Koestler, entered for a moment into their discussion, then emerged from it again: 'I read your *Asphyxie*.'

In anyone else the omission of the article would have struck me to the quick. On his lips my flayed title enchanted me.

The discussion between Beauvoir and Koestler was becoming

increasingly animated. I wasn't alone: Jean Genet, without saying anything to me, was keeping me company.

I love hearing a transistor radio slightly off-station; it sends out gusts of music at you as though music were a wild, untamed element. And Jean Genet, preparing to leave us, thinking of other things, was sending out gusts of affection at me in just that way.

He stood up. He was going. Without having taken off his gloves.

'Shall I see you again?'

'Let's have lunch together,' he answered, 'I live in the Hotel Fleur de Lys.'

He left without shaking hands.

I followed him with my eyes. His astounding presence. A lord, a boxer you would have said.

I said good night to Simone de Beauvoir five minutes later.

    *

Three days later I walked down into the métro at Faidherbe-Chaligny; I returned to the surface at Richlieu-Drouot. In what state? In the state of a dunce staring at a wall: he has forgotten what little he ever learned. But now Genet had come, Genet was walking the earth to avenge me. He kept his foster parents' flock ... he didn't go to school ... but he knew ... with his crook and his cape ... secrets of beauty.

I searched for his street, I searched for his hotel, I didn't know whether I was coming or going. I will not conceal it: Simone de Beauvoir no longer existed. I was impelled by the exaltation and the faith of a cripple hoping for a cure. I did not realize that a great book, a great writer carries no weight in the great cauldron of Paris, at the Drouot intersection, at a quarter to noon. I searched at a quarter to noon, at the Drouot intersection, amid the irritation and hardness of the passers-by, near all the great department stores, I searched for the Hotel Fleur de Lys as I had once searched at seven in the evening, along the rue du Ranelagh, in the mist and langour of the green plants at the windows, for the house where I was to see Maurice Sachs. I made my way towards Genet with more good sense. No new dress, no new hairdo. I knew what to expect: Genet was wholesome, I respected him. He cast a spell over me. I often reread the passage in which a nun drowns herself and leaves us with the memory of her big behind. It revived my horror of having a bottom that was too low and too fat. And yet, as I searched for his street, for his hotel, as Maurice Sachs disappeared farther and farther into Germany without my noticing or caring, I was making my way towards Genet with the delicate nuances of a new beginning shimmering inside me. A homosexual and a genius: what unheard-of sacrifices, what sweet self-immolations awaited! Where was my sex at the moment when I was on my way to see Genet. No sex. I was an angel. That's what people say. That's what they believe. A man-eating angel, so watch out. Oh, shut up! How could I have a sex, I am all fervour, all admiration. Exactly. We know what they've led to in the past. Shut up. I'm just warning you, since your memory seems to have deserted you. Shut up, shut up, I am newness itself, freshness itself.

I ran, I halted, I set off again, I brushed against the wall of the Bibliothèque Nationale with a certain arrogance: Genet was expecting me for lunch! Poor girl. There's still time: go into the Nationale, check to see if Genet's books are on the shelves, read him, then read him again, don't go to see him, it will be terrible. Believe us, Genet is not in your league. What is my league? The cinema on Thursday afternoons with the old women and the children, among the candy-munchers and the orange-peelers. It's horrible, the spoilsports lurking inside me. Doesn't the silence of a great library tempt you? You could lavish your adulation on him in his paragraphs ... I'm forty years old; I'm not afraid of living yet.

I walked around the Square Louvois and found myself irritated by the great still trees. This Jean Genet was at least worth a day of storms. The sun was being miserly, it seemed to me; nothing was glittering. It's because he's asleep, I told myself, he has so much sleep to catch up on ...

My fever rose higher and higher. I opened my purse, I read, I re-read 'Hotel de la Fleur de Lys,' written in my handwriting on a scrap of paper, I didn't dare ask where it was for fear that someone should reply: it doesn't exist.

I tripped over the stick of a rich idler; I was forced to ask, after all. What more could he tell me? I was there. Had I no eyes to see with? Yes. I apologized. Sweet Jesus, a miniature hotel, a miniature porch, a miniature façade, right in the middle of Paris.

I went in his room. I found myself at the bottom of a basket: the chaos in Genet's room. What an absence of literature and calculation his room represented. The writer was disclosing himself more than he had done in *Miracle de la Rose*, in *Notre-Dame des Fleurs*; he was letting me see his daily life from the very outset. Chaos of cigarettes, ashes, manuscripts, underwear; I averted my gaze, I was already carrying relics away with me. Disorder is surrender: we want to set things free. Genet was surrendering to me all the things to which he surrendered himself. I was not prepared to light upon his unmade bed. I forced myself to breathe again, I searched for the nonexistent odour of sperm on the sheet; I wanted to find a sperm stain, but there wasn't one. I refused to give up. Pious and exalted priestess of homosexuality in Genet's books, I took it upon me to breathe in the immaterial odour of sperm from the half-open packet of Gitanes, from the damp cigarette end in the ashtray, from the collar of the shirt lying on the floor. Humble, infatuated, wily-eyed as an old priest during the collection, I was hunting for the celestial dispersion of a penis, that of Genet's characters. No traces of cock here, I said to myself. I wanted to emancipate myself so as to come closer to him. Come back, my past: snow on my shoulders. My past, unctuous in the tube of Elizabeth Arden cream that I use, that Genet used: he was just finishing shaving as I entered.

'It's good, that Elizabeth Arden,' I said to Genet as he looked at himself in the mirror above his basin, as he smoothed his cheeks with his at-last-ungloved hands, as he tended his skin, his complexion, his features.

'Do you use it?' he asked with interest.

He apologized for being late. I would have liked to apologize for being on time.

Then Genet coming and going, Genet with the great V of his open shirt, my sly glances at Genet's armour, at the entanglements of silvered hair, and other glances at his gaping shirt. His armour, his silvered entanglements ... I adored them with the cheek of friendship. Beware: Genet is strict, Genet is vigilant, Genet is in a state of alert.

Genet pulled on his jacket, we were about to leave for lunch. There was a knock, someone walked in. Genet introduced him to me.

'Lucien, my son.'

Instant jealousy. I am often jealous without admitting it, without showing it. I am not jealous of other people's belongings. I am jealous of whatever suddenly deprives me of a presence, of attention. Then my cheeks flame, my heart burns and is eaten away in glowing embers, and in my head—what is more, in all my body—a grotesque wind instrument, a sort of tuba, thrums so loud that I have difficulty in subduing it, in preventing everyone else from hearing it.

I admired Genet; therefore, I controlled my jealousy of Lucien. Twenty-two. Laughing eyes. Tanned skin. Short, well-muscled. Steely, but juicy. He gave my hand a straightforward shake. Good-looking, small features, but no, not insipid. I was aware of invisible biceps. Why was Genet playing Daddies?

'You got it?' he asked Lucien.

'Course I've got it!' Lucien answered.

His accent had the Mediterranean in it: the acme of naturalness, of gaiety, of simplicity. Living with Genet, for Lucien, was whistling a happy tune. I could have writhed on the floor at his feet.

'They didn't make any trouble about giving it to you?'

'They gave it to me without my asking.'

I didn't try to find out what it was.

Genet sitting between us in the taxi gave me the feeling of a victory won after a hard fight. I was crossing Paris with the uncon-cern and the gravity of a hero at last taking his rest. Genet on my right was a street, store windows, a Rolls, an apprentice, a water-colour above a roof.

'You're going the wrong way,' he told the driver. 'We're not going to the Madeleine, we're going to the rue Saint-Benoît ...'

I listened, but I couldn't catch even the timbre of that amazing voice. We were passing the bar Le Trou dans le Mur; we had left the Opéra behind us.

'... I'll cross the Place de la Concorde, then go along by the river,' the driver said.

'The Cour du Louvre would have been better,' Genet said. 'But still ...'

That 'but still ...' completed the process, and I was cut off from them entirely.

Will you come back, Maurice? Le Trou dans le Mur, a bar where you waited for me. I looked for it, that very bar, with it right under my nose. Yesterday you were there. With you absent, it is a chapel for laying out the dead. It's so small I thought the whole thing was a joke, but there you were, down in the basement cutting the pages of a book, your gaze, as always, drowned in sadness, harassed, it seemed to me, by your sleepless nights, by alcohol, by your spinning-top days of a man torn apart, by your manufactured bustle and energy. Come on, have a Manhattan ... The words rose from the dramatic blue haze of your ill-shaven cheeks. Will you come back? I long for it as I long to die when I am in pain: without believing it will happen. Ah, how near we always are to confusion and resentment ... For two straws I could begin to loathe this Jean Genet who towers above you, who is so sure of himself. You were all meanders, he has not a fluctuation in his being. You were all unction, he is an astringent. You floated, you were infinitely accommodating, credulous. He is tough. You burned your wings. He keeps himself at a distance. Your sufferings, your longings, your regrets ... and now? Is your heart still set on it, conquering Paris? But taking his genius, Maurice, and giving it to you, even that would do no good. He has something that can't be transmitted.

And Lucien? Lucien here in the taxi? Genet is separating me from Lucien, and so much the better. I want him to be alone, Genet, quite quite alone, like the strip of silver paper swaying in the heat, up on the fruit-tree top. I want him naked, I want him wholly alone and wholly naked, lying straight in the burning sand, with an aluminium rattle decorating his sex. I would be a wall, or barbed-wire entanglements, or a chip of wood, and I would look at him. That is my version of Genet's glory, my version of Genet's genius.

He smoked his Gitane, silent, humorous, wise and sensible. His hand was so white it looked like the dimpled hand of a Benedictine. The driver was taking us along the Seine; the plane trees were quivering, the pomp and the calm of every kind of grey was clothing both sides of the river; the buildings, temperately, were singing to us. I thought I was wasting my time looking out of the window, so I returned my gaze for an instant to Genet's generous mouth: no change. The perspectives opening from one bridge to the next ... so many perfections. And I thought: sitting beside him like this, in this autumn elegance and warmth, do I deserve it?

'I love the "Beaver," I really do,' he said as he opened the restaurant door. 'She is so alive ...'

He gave me another gilded autumn by evoking Simone de Beauvoir's vitality suddenly like that. Five minutes before, she hadn't existed; now she was streaming through my whole being.

Duplicated menus with small, blurred blue writing always depress me. I have to shout for help before I can eat. Too much to choose from. I held it out for Genet to look.

'I shall have a lapin chasseur,' he said.

He was smiling out of the corner of his eye.

A rabbit huntsman. Without him I should never have noticed what an odd expression 'lapin chasseur' is. I began looking forward to further revelations from Genet's prose.

We all three had lapin chasseur.

Intimidated, petrified, dumfounded, I did nothing to liven up the
desultory conversation. I had piled too many Pantheons on the
restaurant table, thickened the air with too much silent homage.
And I can't write down what Genet said because he didn't say anything.

Had I been preceded by my reputation as a boring and stupid
woman? I hoped so, ardently.

Fired with admiration, with fervour, with religion, I nevertheless had ulterior motives in visiting him. I had written a piece on the
hands of labourers, when they are going home on the métro and
rest them on their knees. And I had brought my pages with me.
Simone de Beauvoir wanted to publish them in *Les Temps
Modernes* and I needed a title. I opened my purse as Genet was
finishing his dessert and I handed him my piece to read. He read it
through, without comment, then he gave me a title for it immediately: *Les Mains sales*. I was staggered by his logic and quickness
of mind.

Genet, taking Lucien with him, left me sooner than I would have
wished. I went back to my den, I walked with my back less bowed,
I had acquired reserves of oxygen to breathe in the métro. He was
there, sitting opposite me, his piercing gaze, unspeaking, yes, his
severity of a little while ago exactly, but now. A child that has
suffered. More than me. More than us. And a child that had
neither sold nor lost its chastity. I put on my blue-and-white checked
smock, I continued to write with the industry and tranquillity of a
hired clerk. I stopped, I looked up at Simone de Beauvoir's eyes
on the wall of the den. Writing about her on every page, without
naming her, meant throwing myself in front of her eyes as I might
have thrown myself in front of car headlights in the night.

*

Simone de Beauvoir is interested in everything. She never forgets
anything. She remembered my projected lunch with Genet and
interrogated me about it as soon as we met next time at the Deux-
Magots. I concealed nothing. Suddenly a silence. Oh, irresistible,
unforeseeable. Suddenly a silence from Simone de Beauvoir. It signified sympathy, attention for what I was telling her. And yet,
during that silence of hers, I had a presentiment that I was admiring
Genet too much, that I was raving. Simone de Beauvoir's discretion
is remarkable. She never interferes in anything that is not her
business—though that didn't prevent her from sensing the dramas

I was heading towards. Her silence, that day, was like the quivering silence before a storm. I went on telling, telling... She agreed, she uttered Genet's name with warmth. I got everything mixed up together. I began telling myself: I count for her just as she counts for me; her life isn't elsewhere because there she is beside me and she is full of warmth. I also told myself that she didn't waste herself on every comer. Suddenly another silence from Simone de Beauvoir; suddenly I was ashamed of displaying my madness, my fever for Genet to her. I was stealing the emotion she awakened in me, to apply it to someone else; I was provoking her with what I was taking from her, I was challenging her without taking into account the fact that she counted more than anything in the world. She had lent me *Miracle de la Rose*, she shared what she loved. I was uncomfortable by the time I neared the end of my story; I was telling too much. I stopped talking about Genet altogether. How did I come back to her? By lighting her cigarette. Every time I lit her cigarette, she said thank you in her husky voice, a thank you behind a veil. I lit my own; I gazed at her forehead with wide-open, with huge eyes: it was there, exactly there, her kindness and her willingness to understand me, to understand us, to understand everything. Her forehead was all that.

*

I left her, I fumbled for my keyhole with a blind woman's fingers. No light outside, no flashlight. I walked back into my den, I switched on the light. With my purse still on my arm, with nicotine staining my fingertips, I wrote a letter full of raving and convoluted sentimentality to Simone de Beauvoir. I tore up one, two, three, four envelopes after having written her address on each one of them with ever-increasing care. Next morning I posted my letter express: I was proud to be giving the people in the post office such a famous name. What was I hoping for? To live with her? Derangement, presumption. I would never have dared. To travel with her? Aberration. I wouldn't have dared to do that either. She will always be Simone de Beauvoir. She will never be Simone. Oh, admirable aloofness I wish I could melt away in my own tears. These twenty-two years, have they been twenty-two years of unreality? Here I am in front of the building where Sartre lives. Before she vanishes, she says to me: 'In two weeks' time ... let me hear from you.' She wants her mind set at rest about me, so all is not lost. And she also says: 'Goodbye, work hard...'

Goodbye. Work hard... Good solid advice, her advice to me. It's true, her fountain pen is burning her fingers, she moves off with tiny steps towards the elevator. She vanishes, I leave, my heart contracts, I am excluded, I am the wanderer outside, now, and in two weeks' time. I leave, I am an ice block of despair. I am all emptiness and uselessness; everything is a matter of indifference to me, I walk down the steps of the Vavin métro station. She has left me, only three minutes ago, but she has already forgotten me. Sartre has so much to say to her. I hand my ticket over to be punched; it's enough to make you blow your brains out. Vanished in smoke already, her goodbye, her wave of the hand as she walked up the gangplank to go on with her writing. And I am left in Paris with only my skin to inhabit, and here I am wasting my time till midnight with comic energy. If I were to go to the film she told me to see, yes, I am her little pet seeing what she has seen and liked. The chaos in my room created as I dressed this morning ... a catastrophe has taken place, and all those involved have fled. The open scissors bear witness to the bunch of flowers arranged for her. The scissors are closed, so who is lying? The cut flowers or the scissors? A frail smile for my painted nails, my flowers in her room are faded and obsolete, the gardens are Peggy Sage on my finger ends. They must be wiped out with acetone and cotton.

*

In the night I weep: my book is not being bought. My book is missing from the bookstore windows. My book is never mentioned. One moment printed, the next gone forever. A shipwreck that no one noticed. The more I try to understand, the less I understand. I settle myself down at my table, I go on, I do not see beyond my exercise book. Just as well; otherwise, I should be bitter, otherwise, I should say to myself that it was already all over the moment I began to write. Then I plunge into the publishers' advertisements in the weeklies, in the magazines. I am never there. I don't ask for publicity; whom would I dare to ask it from? Camus is so distant, so distant it would feel as though I were asking him for the moon itself if I had the audacity... Why am I not among the new books being published, along with the other writers who have written a first book? It is a mystery, a mystery undermining me. The publisher is ashamed. The publisher's readers ... they are ashamed, too. I have been whisked out of sight, I am a rabbit who has vanished into a top hat. It's not the publisher's fault, it's literature's fault.

Literature laid a trap for me. I let myself be caught in it, I am preparing to be caught in it again. Where am I going to end up? What am I going to become? A husk if I don't write. To write is to preserve. To write is no more than that.

It was three in the afternoon in autumn. I was writing the last pages of *L'Affamée* while Mme Faury was cleaning the landing outside. From time to time her broom banged against my door; I would stop writing, cock my ear, listen to the silence around my table. She went back to her own room. What calm. Or is it the city holding its breath? I stretched out my legs, I took my ease in my retreat. I closed my eyes. I was the silence, I had no face.

I finished my sentence. The sky was a weight on our building. It was three in the afternoon in autumn. I wrote, I wrote.

There was a knock at the door of my den.

Strange, I wasn't expecting anyone. It must be Mme Faury. She'll have lost her brush again. No, she went back to her own flat. It can't be her.

The knocking was insistent.

I stood up, I stretched in the half darkness, in the smell of the bleach exhaled by the floor I had scrubbed that morning. I thanked myself for having polished the armchair and the dining chairs, for having washed through and ironed my blue-and-white check smock.

I wouldn't be at peace with myself like this if it were a visit. It can't be a visit because I'm not expecting anyone. What a good idea it was to wash my hair yesterday evening. Still, I'd better open it, who can it be?

'Genet...'

With someone else. With someone in the shadow.

They came in.

Genet in my den ... am I dreaming? No, I'm not dreaming.

He kissed me, I kissed him on the cheeks.

'Is it cold out?' I asked him. 'Your cheeks are so cool...'

I didn't hear what his answer was. They were cheeks blazing with festivity on Christmas Eve. They had come, the turkey was in the oven, it would be tender.

It was so simple, it was so generous, this unexpected visit of his, that my generosity, transmitted to me by Genet, fell in its turn upon the stranger.

'Take the armchair ... sit in the armchair,' I said to the stranger.

He did so without any fuss.

He gave his glasses a little push, but without lifting them. His hands were well-kept.

'We've been eating lunch at the Véfour, so we came round,' Genet said.

Yes, it was all as simple as ABC.

I forgot the stranger, I forgot his well-kept hands, his precise gestures rectifying the position of his glasses. I bent my head, I cooed like a sucking dove for Jean Genet.

'I've brought you someone who's read *L'Asphyxie*,' he said.

A reader... A real one... There with me. Now I bent my head for a Jean Genet who had brought me a reader. A reader with glasses, glasses I can touch; a reader with manicured nails, nails I can brush with my own fingertips. 'I have brought you someone who has read *L'Asphyxie*.' Easy to live through, easy to hear. A flesh-and-blood reader.

The stranger turned his head towards my notebook.

'You're working. We don't want to disturb you,' he said in a slightly cutting voice.

I listened in Genet's eyes to what the stranger was telling me. I was embarrassed at being taken too seriously, but pleased at being treated so considerately by a man whose existence had been unknown to me five minutes before. Genet looked at me with a kindly smile. He was preparing to leave. I took fright.

I closed the notebook of *L'Affamée*.

'There, that's that,' I said, numb and stupid by this time, but aglow with pride.

I suggested they stay for some cognac.

'We haven't come here to disturb you,' the stranger insisted.

Genet said nothing. He was beginning to find the whole thing a drag.

'I'll be back in five minutes,' I cried from the door.

I flew out still in my smock, I knew our Paris-Médoc branch didn't close in the afternoons.

The manager took his time coming up from the cellar while I boiled with impatience. At last he appeared. A bottle? No, a whole bottle was too expensive. A 'flash' as they say in the groceries? Yes, that's more my mark. I wanted to be hospitable but not spendthrift. I flew back once more, carrying my 'flash' in its wrapping of tissue paper.

I ran up the stairs two at a time, I looked down at the shine the Kiwi polish had produced on my shoes. I opened the door with the savagery of a warrior queen.

They were talking quietly together. They stopped talking. The stranger stood up, was apologetic. I was going to too much trouble. He was taller than Genet and impeccably dressed. Too much trouble, I was going to too much trouble. It was heart-rending to feel myself becoming important.

'Give me that,' he said.

I handed over the 'flash'. He uncorked it.

I fetched three glasses, my head empty. Where was Genet? Where is Genet, I wondered. Where can he be, Genet? I can't see him anywhere, I'm just a machine mechanically pouring cognac ...

'Just a little ...'

'Only a drop ...'

I took a first mouthful, and my eyes lingered on the stranger's cuff-links: golden chestnuts in their prickly cases. I learned by heart his springy mattress of close-cut black hair.

Genet merely wetted his lips. He blamed his liver, and I thought of all that prison food. The stranger was silent. His lips brushed his cognac; he seemed to be doing his best. What constraint was it that suddenly left me? Why was I suddenly able to fill my glass up again without embarrassment? We scarcely spoke. Genet smoked his Gitanes without offering them round. His boorishness didn't shock me: he had so many years to make up for, so many years during which he hadn't been able to smoke as much as he wanted. Genet is alone; he doesn't bother with our idiocies.

The stranger offered me his cigarette case. I chose a Gitane with its number showing; I selected it with care, without hurrying, from among all the other carefully arranged cigarettes. My hand trembled.

We smoked, we talked off the top of our heads; the stranger pushed back his glasses again, keeping his myopia in the centre of its frame. My book *L'Asphyxie* was brought back into the discussion. I believed what the stranger told me about it, but he said it all with too much warmth, too much conviction. He really made me seem too important. I would have liked to hide myself under his compliments. He was mistaken. My Blanzy-Poure pen and my squared paper did not merit such eulogies. I was heartbroken at having my heart warmed so. I sat there opposite him; everything was in its right place: my shoes were properly polished, my smock freshly washed, its cuffs tightly buttoned around my wrists, the spike of my belt accurately inserted in the last hole. I was suddenly pierced by one of those meteor-notions that flash abruptly in and out of one's mind: I had been sitting opposite him like that always.

He rose from the armchair.

'Come and have dinner with me at home with Jean ...'

'Accept,' Genet said to me.

I accepted.

I kissed Genet goodbye.

'I shall kiss you, too,' I said to the stranger.

He seemed pleased.

*

Two days after their visit, in the rue Chanzy, I met our landlady. I can move up to the sixth floor, into a front flat, I can move into my two-room at last. Move ... What have I to move? Nothing. A new contract has been drawn up, I must take what I have asked for. I pretended to be delighted; I was crushed. Yes, Madame Virgoniazzi, goodbye; yes, I will sign your contract. I fled, I rushed away to cajole the den I must now abandon through my own fault. I ran back to it without even buying food for my meal.

You were waiting for me, my darling. You are always waiting for me, my adored one, with your disfigurements, your blisters, your mouldy stains, your blotches. Wait, wait, we're going to be closer to each other than ever ...

I turned the key twice in the lock, I fastened the peep hole shut.

Den, dark den, my heart is beating like this for you. I am going
to leave you. In your corner I was pregnant, over by your window I
considered an abortion. No tears in my eyes, yet I should like to
weep. Thick-growing griefs everywhere; yes, I will be silent now.
It is a terrible thing: I accept leaving you, yet you have done me
no harm. I am going away without you. Your walls were damp,
but to me you seemed a place for meditation. I walked through
your cloisters, you were so dark. I am packing up and leaving; what
a slap in the eye for you! You, so regular, so humble with your lack
of sun. I shrieked, I tore myself apart, I lived off you. I am terrified
at the idea of moving. Den, let us thrash this out: I can't go, I can't
just turn my back on you. To live and die in the same burrow. Already I am remembering you. You are secret, you are discreet, you
kept our clamourings, our vociferations to yourself; our circus was
a closed circle. Gabriel didn't come, I spat fire and brimstone, the
stove hurled out its glowing ashes, you were silent. Would he
come? I waited, and he came.

*

It was a professional mourner who walked into the concierge's lodge.
My humility was no hypocrisy. My life was a long wall of misfortunes and I was hugging it as I walked. The more I shrank against
it, the more my hair fell over my wretchedness. Whose widow was I
then? My own.

'I'd like the key,' I told Mme Moutiers.

She was making sauerkraut, unsurprisingly, for she was from
Alsace.

'Ah, you want the key, do you?' she said as she scattered peppercorns over the mountain of blond tresses. 'You want to go up and
look at your new flat, I expect. Have you made up your mind?'

What a plate of sauerkraut, what abundance. The good fortune of
others is never well-stocked enough: it is our kind feelings towards
them.

She wiped her hands and handed me the key. 'How it will suit you
up there!'

'Do you think so? Do you really think so?'

'Do I think so! You'll have the air, the sun ...'

I looked down at the key, doubtful of the whole world.

'Quickly, up you go,' Mme Moutiers said.

Why am I not a trash bin? I could be emptied, I could be filled, I
could be carried from here to there, I could change places without

having to become aware of my new surroundings.

I climbed the six flights of stairs. Up you go, my girl, otherwise you'll be dead of nostalgia before you've even left your dark den downstairs. I consoled myself with the memory, the intention, the future of my personal pleasure when my finger is between my lips. Its advance will be even more cloudy from groin down to toes, I can tell you that, first floor. I was on the discard pile, I was just a foil for others, now I have found a blind partner: my finger. I was poverty-stricken, now I am receiving gifts; my love for myself, the phantasms that fill an absence, I can assure you of that, second floor and third floor, just like it. The cloud, the famous cloud, the invader, the cloud of pleasure in the belly, in the legs, the underwater flora in my entrails, and I am dissolving, the grace of a few drops of water wetting the sand; yes, a labour of love. I end in the calm and the putrescence of dead leaves; that is how I can describe it to you, fourth floor, fifth floor; it is a reflection, this pleasure for which I exhaust myself. All my postures, dear den, I gave them to you in a looking glass. My door with its spy hole is lamenting. It is my soul, it is looking for me down there. My history in that den is a long one. Shall I ever have done recounting it? Gabriel is buried there, he must be carried elsewhere. I oughtn't to have come here. Four doors on each landing: they will eat me alive, the ears inside them will ingest me. I have come up here to intrude; they will resent me. Oh, that ladder in the stairwell, I'd never have imagined that ... but of course it's the fire escape ... How beautiful it is!

I turned the key and walked in.

Two light rooms. An airy kitchen with a hood over the stove and a window. A box room, private water-closets, marble mantel. So it's taken me forty years to achieve this: a flat just like the flats of all those modest persons who emerge every day so well-pressed, so well-brushed ... That air of false innocence will do you no good, little flat; all empty places have that, you're not going to conquer me. Who will protect me, who will prevent me from moving in here?

'Mule, stupid stubborn mule, can't you see that your den is doing you harm? You'll ruin your eyesight working all day by artificial light ... It's undermining your health, you stubborn fool. Oh really, you obstinate idiot! Be reasonable, for heaven's sake! How are we to get you out of there?'

My mother, will she help me carry up my clothes, my table, my divan?

I signed the new contract, then wondered if I would really move

1947. An autumn evening. Seven in the evening and autumn in
Paris. I was light, I was dawdling over the city's roofs, I was tipsy
without having had a drink, I hugged the chimneypots in my arms.
1947. Autumn, autumn. The darkness at seven o'clock in the evening
in autumn is young and sprightly ... I powdered the sky with my
face powder, I veiled the lights with my voile handkerchief, I was
happy, I was carefree, I was looking for his street, what had got into
me? Nothing, I was just living. The bus made its way along the rue
de Courcelles, the flower-seller dipped into her basket on the avenue
de Villiers, I remained silent, I was expansive, I kept my eyes fixed
on the ineffably pink sky over towards Levallois-Perret, and everywhere there were nests, nests. The air was warm ... the breath of
our bistros on my lips. I hopped along the lonely benches, along
the ledges of the roofs. What if I didn't go to visit this man after all
... what if I were to shut myself away in a cinema? So odd, the
way I had washed my smock and my hair before his visit, yes odd,

very odd indeed. Goodness, here I am. That's me, the young lady staggering with the weight of her future as she climbs into a taxi. Where is she going? To see this man. No, it's too close to take a taxi. I could see *Les Rapaces* in the Latin Quarter. Shall I? Or shall I go to his dinner? Advise me, big garage across the street, so neat and tidy, I have to choose and I am afraid of the choice. Kisses, kisses, kisses while I wait, kisses blown to the great fragile masses of the autumn trees in the Parc Monceau. I am afraid, and I must make up my mind. What is there to be afraid of? The autumn is caressing, the city is warm and padded, what could possibly happen to me? Salutations, cocked snooks, then finally respect and consideration for the park gates. It is shy, the park, in between the big pillars. Does he live on this street, this man? A window opens. Oh la la la, the kitchen is down in the basement. Really posh stuff. What if I went to see the film instead? Panic? Dismay? No, self-possession. The city tonight is a success; the last leaf refuses to fall. Just now I was flying ... Hop over the gates, surprise the lawns and the chairs still posed as they were left; avoid walking on the children's sandcastles, share the mystery of the thickets with the solitary statue—and not ring his bell. I should displease the lord, the boxer would be angry. I ring the bell. So much the worse, I'm ringing his bell. I am not where I ought to be. Who says so? My blood, my arteries. Still, those old-fashioned stained-glass panels in the staircase window are reassuring. I would never have expected him to live on a ground floor. He isn't coming to the door. A good sign, I can escape now, I shall get there in the middle of the film.

The door opened, I walked in.

      *

I'm going to slip, I'm going to fall down on the black-and-white marble flags. They are too big, they are too black, they are too white, they chill my heart; just one sign from you, God above, and I will vanish.

'Through here,' the servant said.

I believe, I always shall believe that all servants despise me totally. They are blaming me for having brought my mother into the world, for having made her a housemaid. They accuse me as they wait on me: why aren't you below-stairs?

I followed him; he led me away from the celestial fluidity of a face, a sculpture poised on a pedestal. I had scarcely arrived, and already I was aware of a tangible past existing within an uncertain present. Mirrors, too many mirrors, limpid mirrors from ceiling to floor. I was afraid. I was going to fall on the polished flags, and I would witness it, the dissolution of my image in a mirror ... Ivy streamed out of urns in every mirror. A red felt portière swagged to one side kept me warm; what more unexpected than a current of warm air at the bottom of the sea?

The servant was waiting for me. He indicated a tiny room in which there was space for one at most. On the instant he took my worn rabbit to hang it up on one of the hangers in the dear little closet, Genet ... His raincoat. The apartment into which I had not yet entered swelled inside the tiny cloakroom. I tidied my hair. Whose were they, the leash, the forest-coloured gloves reflected in the mirror of that minute room? Fingers snipped out of moss spoke to me of country walks, of comings and goings round a country house. Escape now, there's still time, you'll be free in a forest, the gloves were telling me.

Out of my depth, bereft of voice, of saliva, of the power to breathe, I powdered my nose. Its mattness reassures me; I can persuade myself it has been removed from the foreground.

I followed the servant again. We walked back round the sculptured face; the lines and curves slid round me with the abandon of shooting stars. I followed him through into another hall, walking on tiptoe because of the anguish the black-and-white flags inspired in me.

Open french windows, a gust of autumn; I could breathe better. Two of the park trees were sleeping outside, black on black. Who was lighting the pictures suspended on their wires? Who was scattering that dusting of private light over each of the portraits, the landscapes, the figures? Every painting was lit like that: they all had the self-confidence of paintings in a museum. I would have liked to run there and then. It was raining this morning, I thought, and I was out buying fresh cod, it was raining quite humbly and my lips wove silk in the air. Throw me out into the street, butler, slam your door on me. The air is soft this evening, the air is coaxing the padlocks and the bars, I have come to make myself a prisoner. Infinity; a moment ago I touched the fringes of infinity; I don't dare breathe.

The servant opened two white doors trellised with gold; I lost myself in contemplation of a red sofa, of bracken fronds quivering with health. I plunged forward into his drawing rooms, into his world.

The doors closed behind me. The servant had abandoned me.

Genet, sitting at the far end of the second room, began to rise without eagerness. The stranger leaped forward, taking over from Genet.

'How kind of you to come ...'

'...'

I found his politeness somehow disappointing.

'You didn't have too much trouble getting here?'

'Not too much,' I answered, scarcely moving my lips.

I no longer belonged to myself: he was depriving me of all I had received in coming to see him. He was taking away everything except my eyes to recognize him with. For what being other than myself was my heart beating? Did to live mean to vanish, then? To vanish and to remain rooted there in front of him staring through two portholes. I stared at him, at him and his abstract glasses: I was learning his face as I had once learned mountains and rivers.

'You're late,' Genet said reproachfully.

'I'm not late!'

Genet had come too close. He was coming between us.

'Come now, Jean ...' the master of the house said. 'You mustn't be so strict ... What a terrible man he is,' he added laughingly.

He turned towards me.

This man who was leading me over to a fabulously comfortable armchair, who was giving me Genet's place, was being my protector again without even knowing me. Here I am in society, and I think it's never happened to anyone else. One of my slates has worked loose, I don't know whether I'm coming or going. Protector; have you thought what that means. This man has power, but he isn't hiding you under his wing exactly. It doesn't matter, I'm burning with curiosity.

I refused the armchair. I didn't dare take a place that belonged to Genet.

The servant brought in a tray with drinks on it.

I preferred the sofa; I sank back too far into its cushions. My skirt rucked up, my knees were almost knocking against my chin. I wished I could cut my legs off, I was encumbered by my femininity.

Genet sat beside me and the master of the house took Genet's place. Yes, I would like a Cinzano bianco. I didn't know there was such a thing as Cinzano bianco ... Jean Genet, despite those eyes turned inward to scrutinize his inner secrets, was observing all the same. He was reflecting among the Louis XIV furniture, among the museum paintings. I knew nothing at that time of his moods, his angers, his outbursts, his scenes, his games; and yet I would have wagered then that he was deliberately controlling himself. He was gazing with an absent air at the wood fire that had been laid in the fireplace. I lost my self-assurance: Genet was refusing to speak.

He had come and he was blaming me for having come. He was blaming me for it without turning his head, without attempting to help me understand why. He smoked his Gitanes; he was alone, unbending. Withdrawn inside his own boundaries. Withdrawn inside his lucidity, his perspicacity, his severity, his integrity, obedient to his own rituals, his own laws.

The master of the house served our drinks, centred his myopia, pushed at the bridge of his new glasses. The same gestures he had made in my den: memories so soon. A shy man reassuring himself with the touch of a personal object worn every day. Our memories, in the beginning, when we are building up an edifice of love, our first memories are innocent children. I forgot Genet. He talked, but I didn't listen to what he said: a genius was wearying me, some great construction work about to be undertaken.

The cut-glass goblet was too heavy, it weighed the weight of the butler, the weight of a white marble flag, the weight of a black marble flag. I threw sly glances at the painting that covered one entire panel nearby; but I didn't dare linger on it, I didn't dare gaze at the silver of another, I didn't dare put my glass down on the low table, I didn't dare do anything except say thank you before, then after, he took out his black leather cigarette case, before, then after he offered me a Gitane.

'Thank you, monsieur ... Yes, I'd love one, monsieur ... Thank you, you're so kind, monsieur ...'

I was polite twice, three times, in order to see his melancholy-tinted eyes twice, three times again. Today they are cornflowers in my hayloft.

'A little more Cinzano?'

He was trying to put me at my ease.

'Yes, monsieur ... Thank you, monsieur ...'

'Call him Jacques!' Genet cried, unable to stand any more.

'Yes, why not,' the master of the house agreed.

He had wanted to laugh, then stopped himself. He puffed out his cheeks, he put his fist up in front of his mouth, he let out a sound between a sob and a chuckle. Because he was moved, he was standing the situation on its head. It was the emotion of a shy little boy and a modest man. This sad man with his austere appearance was capable of amusing and being amused. His playfulness went straight to my heart.

They talked to one another; Genet asked him if he really liked Louis XIV furniture ... Hurt, the master of the house struck back. They went on talking, I continued to settle in. I no longer listened to them overmuch; I sank back further into the cushions and enjoyed the increasing confidence my Cinzano was bestowing on me. I wandered among the paintings without making it too obvious, I smoked my Gitane beside a heady young lady stretched out on the grass to my left, I drank my Cinzano beside a humble peasant girl bathing on my right, I watched her dipping her feet in the water of a stippled blue stream. I remembered my own feelings of well-being when bathing my feet.

The servant announced that dinner was served.

Genet rose listlessly to his feet. It was my fault: he had to put up with us. I was distressed on behalf of Jacques, who had invited him. If only I could light that fire, then sit Genet in the fire so that he would warm up, so that he would soften, relax ...

I found myself back in the hall. The bracken fronds frothed; Jacques asked me if I was working on anything, and he seemed to come to life. He put the whole of himself into what he was saying. I was overwhelmed with pleasure, as though he were my favourite child. He made precious gestures as he spoke. A flower opened in the place of a hand. One gesture, the hand thrown out in front of him, the middle and index fingers separated from the thumb, displaying the cuff of his shirt—the finest of lawns, of voiles, his shirt —that one gesture made me uneasy because I kept wondering if it was studied or not, because I kept wondering if my father made gestures like that or not.

He made that same gesture again as we passed the ivy streaming down from the urns. We were just entering his dining room. His golden chestnuts in their spiky cases ... he was wearing the same cuff-links he had worn the other day ... the other day when he was sitting in my tattered armchair ... the other day when he was drinking my cognac out of a glass that began life as a mustard container ... I was hypnotized by the sight of my den held up for comparison with his sumptuous apartment.

During the meal, that gesture of his proved the leitmotiv of his caustic wit, the accompaniment to his cruelty, the *nota battuta* of his harshness, the overture to a successful sally, to the perfection of one of his oral portraits, sketched as he ripped meat from bone with eager teeth.

Either he would extinguish the environment in which he lived with those sad eyes of his, or else, if the conversation was languishing, he would bring it to life again by pulverizing a film, a book, a political figure. Once again his hand and wrist would be thrown out in front of him as if to give concrete expression to a criticism, a judgment, a condemnation, and then he would end with an extremely courteous 'Don't you think?' I didn't think anything; I just stockpiled. I was dumb. And I should add perhaps that this talker served himself last, as is only proper, I should add that this ethereal creature ate with the appetite of an ogre while seeming scarcely to touch a morsel.

*

During the meal I began to look back from a distance, tenderly, at my two Spontex sponges. They were soaking in a saucepan that I no longer used for cooking, my two sponges. Though the memory of them didn't prevent me from appreciating the smoothness of the cordon-bleu cooking in front of me. Dishwater, my soups at home. No ... thank you very much, I said to the butler when he offered me the tureen again. I returned, in thought, to my two darlings in their bleach and water, to my spongy wheat waiting for the harvest. My Spontexes were purifying themselves while I dined in town, so I wasn't wasting my time. I said to them: goodbye for now, clean yourselves properly now, I'll see you again later. My mood darkened. Why was Genet talking to Jacques about Italian poplars for Lucien. What a fuss he was making, sitting there opposite me ... I existed. Had he forgotten it? I turned to the thought of my mother, of Simone de Beauvoir ... No, there was no one for whom I existed. Did I exist for myself? Too difficult that, too deep. Genet was like my mother. They will neither of them forgive others for their childhoods. The constancy of their sufferings. No, I'm sorry, Genet, I'm sorry, I won't do it again. He was describing to Jacques exactly how the poplars must be placed, he was making a sketch. I realized, I sensed, that I was not on the same wavelength as Genet. I lacked gaiety, lightness of touch, spontaneity. I was nothing, whenever he appeared, but a lumpish cobblestone. I admire him, I idolize him to the point of stupefaction. Genet needs the cheek of a Paris urchin, the effrontery of a little gipsy boy. I am not witty, I am not intelligent. What do I feel for him? An incomparable love for his books, a love that overflows onto their author, a love for which he gives not the tiniest damn, and I know that. He can neither tolerate nor forgive me my heaviness.

I consoled myself with Jacques's lined curtains. Who could ever reach you and hurt you behind lined curtains as thick as that? Genet was describing to Jacques the house that Lucien was building with his own hands ... My abandoned woman's eyes settled on the dead rabbit, warm inside its fur, a wild rabbit hanging from a hook; supple, docile, that death ... a relaxation, a siesta after a banquet of wild thyme. The canvas was suspended with a piece of ordinary string. No frame. Gone all the gilding now. The colours seemed the more naked for it, like a landscape that is concentrating itself, stripping itself down before a storm. Genet was still talking about the Italian poplars around Lucien's house ... The huge chandelier hanging down over the table intimidated me. Their conversation ceased.

'Who painted that picture?'

Jacques leaned over towards me. 'Do you like it? It's a Soutine.'

'Do you like it?' A social formula. He likes it, that's the important thing. I didn't say anything in reply: that was my way of acquiring the picture, my way of giving bunches of luminous dandelions to the dead and transfigured rabbit.

The butler brought us spinach covered in a white sauce. As I savoured it, I offered more luminous bunches of greenstuff to the rabbit. I had been a child, yes, I had had all my wishes granted every time I surprised a wild rabbit, his chaste white bottom, his charming little tail, in a path, in a wood, crossing a plain. Something ephemeral, something instantaneous: the snapshot pause of a presence. Then an innocent in flight like a criminal. Soutine had fixed my brief moments of ravishment on canvas.

*

Now the meat.

What a drama! Suddenly I realize the piece of meat I had put in my mouth was too big for it. Extrude it onto your fork, then return it to your plate. Do that? Do that here? While Jacques makes his polished gestures over there, while he eats away yet somehow remains completely detached from what he is eating? Better to leave the table and escape forever. Even if I were to push it from left to right, from right to left for days, for weeks on end, that piece of beef, I should still be no better off. I had to get rid of it. How? Yes, a drama, my cheeks alternately swelling as it travelled from one to the other ... they were bound to notice eventually. Oh, what a pickle I'm in now. If only I'd gone to see *Les Rapaces*... My ice cream on its stick would have melted away in my mouth. And what if they ask me what I think about the Italian poplars. Italian poplars? Never heard of them. You've never seen an Italian poplar? I've got a swelling, can't you see? My cheek gets swollen when I become depressed; no, it's not tobacco I'm chewing, it is the fruit, the ripe round fruit of my great grief.

I managed to reply to them, to enter into their conversation despite my alternating gum boils. I begged my incisors: a last effort, a quick slice, one good bite. But they were worn out, poor things, and there was no help from them. The butler changed our plates. Not the slightest progress. Where was I to throw my fibrous lump? Horrible situation. Chewed meat, slippery with saliva, cannot be laid upon moquette, or spat into crystal. I had to conjure it away, the mass in my mouth. But how? I walked round and round the problem inside my head ... At that moment Jacques opened his cigarette case with one hand and offered it to me. An idea. I coughed, I coughed ... I coughed fit to burst. I waved the case away: no, really, I couldn't smoke ... Genet raised his eyes and stared at me. I buried my face in my napkin, I rid myself of the lump of meat. The transfer accomplished, I helped myself gluttonously to gâteau and cream. Genet asked for a Gitane. It was the moment for my lump of meat's second transfer: from my napkin to my left hand. I smoked and ate more comfortably. We rose from the table at half past eight.

As we passed the urns and the streaming ivy, Jacques put his arm around my waist for a moment in a gesture of affection. With the wine's help I was now accustomed to the two drawing rooms, to the bookcases, to the golden trelliswork. One quick conjuring trick and the saliva-soaked meat was safely disposed of in my purse while the master of the house was busying himself with the liqueurs. Free at last. You can invite that woman to your house any time ... she's not amusing, of course ... she's not witty ... she's not even well-read, but she does know how to behave. And yet with the kind of life she leads at home ... she ought to jump at your throat like a wild beast ... in fact, she's lonelier even than a wild animal ... always in curlers ... no sunlight ... no light at all ... with a garden of trash bins outside her window ... Not only is she ugly but she's lifeless, too ... Who was saying all that? I was. To myself.

I was often married when I was nine. The cigar smokers used to give me their paper bands. I used to wear them on my wedding-ring finger, tied on tightly with white thread, and then I would exhibit them in the local stores. I was as puffed up with pride as our pigeon-fanciers' pigeons.

Jacques opened a box made of some pale wood. I used to open my pencil box in the same way, just for the pleasure of opening it. He offered the box to Genet and Genet pierced and drilled his cigar with a match. They sank back into the cushions. Genet continued to rake out his Havana with his match. I watched him, and it seemed to me that he himself was glowing with satisfaction when the cigar drew better. Jacques smoked with the serenity of those who can let their eyes rest upon their acquisitions: furniture, pictures, friends. Genet busied himself with his dimpled, waxen hand; Jacques abandoned his, the one holding the cigar, and let it hang outside the armchair; his hand was more masculine than Genet's. I smoked my Gitane, I drank my Cointreau, but I didn't put their paper rings on my finger. That's what growing old is. Not daring any more.

We didn't talk much; Genet's presence muzzled us. Yet Jacques laughed wholeheartedly, and exclaimed: 'What a terrible man! Isn't he terrible?'

I didn't answer.

Towards the end of the evening he asked me if I would like *L'Affamée* published in a de luxe edition, at his expense. It wouldn't appear till after the ordinary edition. Genet decided that Pauvert should be given the job. I drank Jacques's words, though the project itself held little interest for me. Jacques was thinking of me, that was what counted first and foremost. I was in love with the grateful Violette inside me: a misunderstanding was being born.

I asked him who had painted the picture that covered an entire panel on his wall, the one of the young woman lying in the grass.

'Do you like her?' he asked me, as though he was quite prepared to give me his Courbet on the spot.

The world was at my feet. The misunderstanding was growing fast.

He escorted us out as far as the dainty cloakroom. The french windows had been closed.

The care with which Jacques handled my rabbit coat irritated me. I could have wished the evening was beginning all over again at the moment of our parting.

'Does he live alone?'

'Why should he live alone?' Genet answered in the taxi. 'Ah, I'm going to Pigalle now...'

A smart guy, very offhand.

In a hurry to change atmospheres, in a hurry to leave me, Genet got out of the taxi without having offered me even the illusion of an illusion that might have warmed my heart, without having accepted even the illusion of an illusion that would have irritated him. A vaguely athletic figure, a vaguely English figure, moving off into the warmth of a Pigalle autumn inside his raglan-sleeved raincoat, wearing his boxer's nose.

'Take me back to the Place Clichy,' I told the driver.

I got out of the taxi; the fare would be less now. Was that the real reason? Yes and no. I had to have my métro, my dear dear métro... I had to have its faces and its trooping herds, I had to have its smell of distress, I had to get close to them all down there, try to lose myself in them.

'Telephone me!' the master of the house had said in glacial tones.

His handshake, next to the melting lines of a Modigliani sculpture of a face, was a cold medallion clutched in my clammy hand.

*

What do you say we follow that great flayed creature, that tall solitary dame along the corridor of the Dauphine-Nation station? Look how covered she is in wounds, in hacks, in cuts, in every kind of hurt that causes pain but doesn't kill... Let's stay close to her. Is she never going to finish counting and recounting her sixteen stations? Oh well, if it eases the pain for her... She's off again, like a sleepwalker that can't walk straight. How bowed her back is, she's bending under the weight of something. No, she's weaving about in all directions. We're going to have to pick her up. Poor old bag, get on with you now, take your eyes off that Lysis brassières poster. Hey, now she's talking to the girl in the advertisement, she's a maniac. Let's get closer, come on, let's get closer so we can hear. What can she be muttering, poor old dear, has she lost her wits? Lucky for her, the corridor is empty now. What's she saying?

Hey, watch out, Mme Orator, someone's coming. Nothing to be afraid of, though. A couple of beggars or something. Now come on, what is it she's saying, old bowback there? Yes, she's got her strength back, she's yelling that she doesn't like men with glasses, that she loathes men with a mania for pushing at the bridge of their glasses. She's a crackpot, there's no doubt about that, now she's wiping the brassière girl's eyes with her tongue ... not men with glasses, not men with glasses, she's gasping, and she's practically pushing a hole through that poster, she's stark staring mad. One moment she turns her back on you, the next she's full-front. Ah, madame is doing her little act, her imitation of a saint with closed eyes that stare straight at you; madame is possessed, she is reciting, her head is about to fall into the basket ... And still the men with glasses, she can't leave that alone. They are idiots, they are easily scared, they are evasive, they are weak, they are double-dealers, you have to go a long way to find their eyes. She's smiling. Who's she smiling at, then? At her own eyes full of tears? It's impossible with her. How she's aged! And yet she was pretty old to start with. Madame is doing another act. Madame is casting her pearls and her hiccups before us, what is she saying? ... Their faces are more naked, more abandoned, more vulnerable when they are wiping their glasses. She is telling her beads, following her idea round and round. Their drawn faces, their faces unseemly with sadness, their immeasurable countenance. Oh, belt up, you old bag, otherwise you'll finish the night in the police station.

*

She loathed men with glasses; she said: I loathe men. She sat down on a bench at Porte Dauphine-Nation, she said I'm going to sit down on that bench. She had no strength, she said: I have no strength. She felt her legs giving way; she said: I can feel my legs giving way. She had a funny feeling of faintness; she said: I have a funny feeling of faintness. She wasn't sure of anything; she said: I'm not sure of anything. She was hostile to men with glasses, she was tired, she was drained of everything, she was suffering from an attack from she wasn't sure what. She said to the rails in front of her: I don't want anything to do with men in glasses, I'm tired, I'm drained of everything, I'm suffering from an attack of I'm not sure what. Everything was rushing away from her: the rails, the chocolate machines. She said: everything is rushing away from me —the rails, the chocolate machines. She didn't really feel sick; it was as though she were discovering she was pregnant without actually discovering it altogether. She loathed men with, with ... Not enough strength to finish. It was a discovery of everything inside everything, this vague nausea. It was a total earthquake inside her body. What was it she loathed, what was it she couldn't bear to look at, what was it she wanted to vomit up since she wasn't pregnant? It had to be spoken in the end, but her body was falling away from her, so was the kiosk on the métro platform. No legs, no strength left to articulate. Beaten. She said: I loathe men, I loathe, I. She said: let me fall asleep rather than start all that again. She would have liked to live by proxy, she would have liked to die; then all this wouldn't keep on and on in this way. Who was crushing her? Why this change, this new and weakening alteration throughout her body making her say she's pregnant, she's not pregnant, she is pregnant ... If she could only throw up.

Now she's on her feet. Cracking, contracted. Broken by the effort, she sits down again. She addresses her purse: yes, they look around like spaniels when they hunt for their glasses on all fours. Here comes the train. Now it's leaving again. Better to weep, to forget wherever one is, to see it through one's tears, to speak it through those tears as though it were a great injustice. They have haggard eyes when they wipe their lenses, they are at bay, it is their melancholy, and their eyes are like irises past their best. Nothing has happened to me, so why am I a child being thrown out of a window. I am sure of nothing except the hole in my métro ticket, and that hole knows, it knows that everything is beginning all over again. You know, don't you? You know that everything is going to begin all over again.

Let us sing it at breakneck speed, the news inside me is spreading now, I feel better, I am reborn, the news inside me is panting faster than my breath itself. I shall take the next train.

She took the next train.

Avron, reject among stations, that is where I shall rest ... I'm so little, Mama, I'm only a little girl, hide me under your skirt, won't you? Who will hide me under her petticoats? I'm a little girl who does all her homework ever so well, who learns all her lessons and twiddles her thumbs, so you mustn't disturb me. I don't know anything, I'm a very tiny little girl who lives a long way away from everything. I am learning to unlearn everything, I am concentrating very hard on not knowing things. I shall take the last train. I love. Iluviluviluv. How quickly I said that! What do I love? I love the choirmen and the workers who wear leather aprons. I drank Cinzano bianco, I was a little girl who drank Cinzano bianco. I've missed the last train, so now I shall walk.

One, two. One, two ... quite a good pace, so I was drinking Cinzano bianco, I wasn't looking where I was going, and suddenly I was caught. The laundry being done in my ears, the waves wash it towards me, the waves wash it away, the waves are saying it, then saying it again and again, the rock has shifted, it is going to be terrible, it has been shifted and shaken to its foundations.

Go to sleep. Go to sleep.

Was it the speed of her frenzied heart, was it happiness, was it the shame of having entered a world where she could be no more than the merest passing insect, was it the triumph of a beggar who has gate-crashed a banquet—she couldn't get to sleep.

She did not find sleep until she had remembered her two Spontexes, her darlings soaking in their bleach only two steps away from her bed.

*

I didn't talk about my first dinner at Jacques's house much to Simone de Beauvoir. I hid that event from her. I wasn't deceiving Simone de Beauvoir, I was cheating her. I didn't say: he runs the tips of his fingers over his thick, yet indescribably light thatch of hair. I didn't say: I was proud of him during dinner, he didn't flatter Genet. I didn't say: I wandered away into regions where I had been unhappy to the point of death and suffocation while he amused us. I didn't say: sometimes the little boy inside him didn't burst out laughing when I expected it. Simone de Beauvoir doesn't ask questions. She makes no demands, yet she controls me utterly. I fear her. But she would no longer have been the one and only if I had told her all about that evening. So I didn't pause to describe anything; I was running a hundred-metre race, I talked as quickly as I could, I deliberately hurried my account along till it was out of breath. The wind blew into my mouth and chopped off my sentences. I spoke colourless nothings: 'He's rather nice, he's a friend of Genet's, it was Genet who introduced me, he came to see me once, Genet brought him.' — 'I remember,' she said. I was hoodwinking her, I was concealing my emotions from her. Yet Simone de Beauvoir heard me out with her usual kindliness.

'If it means you'll be less on your own, then it's all to the good,' she commented.

How not to love her? No, she doesn't take the poetry out of things. She simply puts them in their right place, sensibly, straightforwardly Though the deeper meaning of my evening on the rue M. escaped her, because of my own concealments, she had nevertheless still managed to simplify relations with the furniture, the garden, the receptions I still associated with my father and his parents. I had been thrown out into the gutter with my mother, now I was being asked to sit at their table. I felt myself less free to be alone, to be sad, after I had taken Simone de Beauvoir back to her front door in my taxi. There was another being living in the depths of me. I said goodbye to her relieved and yet burdened by what I had not said to her. She was delighted at the prospect of seeing *L'Affamée* brought out in a de luxe edition. She was irreproachable. But there was another thing I hadn't dared confess to her : the project I had conceived of dedicating my book to Jacques, the book whose every page, every line, every word had been written for her.

Jean Genet is making great strides. Louis Jouvet is putting on *Les Bonnes* at the Théâtre de l'Athénée. Mixed feelings: I am not absolutely delighted by the rapidity of his fame. Is Genet pleased with the production? With the rehearsals he is going to? I've no idea. The two actresses playing the maids are said to be admirable. We discuss it with Simone de Beauvoir; she tells me the life story of the Papin sisters, she tells me about their crime. I'd never even heard of them before. I listen ... the stairwell, the iron from the ironing board, the eyes torn out of their sockets, nothing needed changing, nothing needed to be added. Genet is taken up with his rehearsals. Even if I were to meet him, I wouldn't dare question him. Patience.

The first preview was announced, and I was invited to it. In turn, I invited Marie-Louise Villiers and her husband, the doctor Raoul Carasso who wrote under the name Raoul Carson. We had the best box of all. I was not a little proud of Genet's solicitude. I was as moved as if Jean Genet had built the box with his own hands before having the tickets sent round to me. A glittering house, packed with the curious, the blasé; in short, all those people who are bored wherever they are but can't bear to miss anything. How was I dressed? I'm trying to think. Ah yes? My grey jersey skirt, then my knitted top with the wide green and purple stripes. Both bought at Jacques Fath two years before. What shoes was I wearing? My shoes from Cazals, by now looking far from new. I was a friend of the author's, I puffed out my chest. I gazed at the iron curtain: it was guarding Genet's privacy. It was raised, then lowered again. If they could only see Genet, all these bored people, all these busybodies; if they could only see Genet spreading his Elizabeth Arden cold cream on his cheeks after he's shaved! Genet all alone in a café in Pigalle, in Clichy ... Every now and then I leaned out of my box: I looked Parisian high society up and down.

I am concealing the all-important thing. I was caught. The sprouting seed in my head, the sprouting seed in my breast. The seed of my absent one. Yes, he is smoking at this hour, far from the theatres and the noise, smoking his Havana with its mulatto's skin; his hand lies in surrender on the velvet of his armchair, detached from everything, witness to the long hard day of a man of action. I am very glad at heart: he has not come to the preview. I can construct a temple for his solitude among the clatter and chatter of the audience down in the stalls.

A box, during the performance, is less full of rustles than a brushwood shelter concealing hunters on the watch for game. Inside a box everyone can live the life that he will never dare to have. He can deceive, he can be free in thought, he can dare to be himself. I was pregnant, that evening, in a box in the Théâtre de l'Athénée. The sables, the minks, the scents, the sequinned dresses reminded me of my condition. Nestling beside every spectator there, I was a warm fruit. The signal for the curtain to rise. Yes, my little one, yes, we're both lovely and warm here; you inside, me outside. Disturbing harmony, moment of discovery: not a gesture, not a movement. Heart's modesty, mind's modesty, my whole being's modesty: fruitful relaxation. Don't raise your eyes; above all, don't raise your eyes. Be prepared, receive, protect; one false movement and you lose your child. I ripen, I am warm with blessedness, I store up riches inside myself, my heart is suckling a fruit, my head as well. When is it I'm waiting for? For now. I give birth to a being elsewhere.

The curtain rose. The production was a disappointment to me. Where were the Papin sisters? The Parisian commercial stage had drained all the blood out of them. Couturiers and perfume houses had infected those two provincial tigresses with banality. Jean Genet's ceremonial writing, his periods, were used as embellishments for the white fur bedspread. The word 'madame,' which he uses so often in the play, echoed in Meaux, in the church where Bossuet delivered his orations. The maids were too eager to leave their attic for 'madame's' room. The play took place in Paris, and monsters who once lived in the darkness had become mere parlour-maids in the light of day. The Parisian atmosphere threw the characters off balance. A slick aesthetic transplant. Too slick. Perplexed, dumb, I spent the intermission clutching the hand of Philippe Erlanger, a friend of Marie-Louise Villiers and Raoul Carasso. Several days went by, and I refused to read the reviews. I went my own way, loose-tongued and pretentious, a mine of self-importance; in short, among a small circle of idiots I did not refrain from tearing Genet's play to pieces. And what is more, I was being dishonest, because I didn't really believe what I was saying, because I didn't honestly give a damn. For me, Jean Genet's genius is in *Notre-Dame des Fleurs*, *Miracle de la Rose*, *Pompes Funèbres*, *Journal du Voleur*. His place in my world was so high that to write that play was, for him, a fall from grace. I preferred not to linger over the idea that I would be seeing him again.

*

'Telephone me! Come and have dinner again!' Jacques had said.

I telephoned from the coal merchant's little bar.

Simone de Beauvoir and Jacques are both ignorant of the fact, but they have inflicted martyrdom on me over the telephone. They are pale and wan at the other end of the wire; they won't come out, as the photographer says of the underexposed plate he is trying to develop. I call them, and all I hear are feeble negatives. Simone de Beauvoir is more lively, she goes straight to the point; but I have to be in the deepest depths for that point to spur me into life. She has spoken to me, I am about to hang up, I feel remorse at having awakened so many dead people who have nothing to do with her, who have nothing to do with me. The telephone is silent, the dead have gone back to sleep. Can it be the power of the desert lying between us? It's possible.

'I'll be seeing you,' she says with warmth, just as she says it in the street, as if she were thrusting a tube of energy into my hand, a two weeks' supply. Then I walk out of the café I have been telephoning from. I am free. I can do whatever I want.

'Who shall I say is calling?' the woman at the switchboard at Jacques's factory asked.

If I could talk to you in a universe where nothing is surprising, I thought, then I should reply: Say it's the nonexistent calling. As soon as the idea of going to his house again took shape inside me, I had ceased to exist.

'Hello,' he said. 'How are things?'

His voice was sharp. I was mincemeat. His voice distressed me. Why should he throw a polite formula in my face? I hadn't deserved his bad temper. What had I done to him since the other day? Ask him how things were with him? In my turn? No, I hadn't the courage. I mustered all my strength, I answered: 'Things are fine thanks, monsieur...'

Neutrality. I felt sick. Putting oneself through a grater just so that nothing will show, so as not to be importunate, how demeaning. How vile it is, on occasion, self-control. What a tyrant, shyness. Yes, the receiver would have fallen from my fingers if I had been compelled to ask him how he was. I wiped my nose with one finger: it was shiny, I didn't want him to see it over the telephone. Ought I to hang up now, or is he going to speak to me again?

'Would you like to come over for dinner next Friday?'

'Yes, that would be fine...'

Now I was reduced to the state of an animal half beaten to death. I would die of cold and starvation under a porch rather than thank him for his invitation.

I'm sixteen, monsieur, I used to be more than sixteen, but now I'm not any more. You're so attractive, that's a heavy weight to bear. The rivers are slow; the barges are moving along them, taking dictionaries out to dump them in the sea; the letter *r* for the word reason is going to sink forever.

'Till Friday, then!'

'Till Friday, monsieur.'

Call him Jacques!

Later on. Being his valet gives me consolation.

He horsewhipped you with that 'Till Friday, then.' He shook you off over the telephone. He slapped your face. He kicked you after inviting you, he brushed off what he had said to you. A caesura. But worse than any final break. I have just one piece of advice for you: fly away forever in the smoke from his cigar. 'Till Friday, then!' Good riddance to bad rubbish, that's what he was saying to you, just when he'd asked you to visit him. Yes, I thought, you came to see me, monsieur, I didn't go out looking for you. Is this a rejection or is it a game? Already doubts and tiffs and callings to account.

I emerged in ruins from the telephone box. My imagination was unable to encompass the coldness he had shown.

The coalman was behind his bar.

'I'd like a Cinzano bianco,' I said.

'We haven't got that.'

'I'd like a Cointreau...'

'That you shall have.'

The coalman with his smeary coal-dust makeup, the coalman with his empty sack on his head. The coalman looking like a nervous monk. The coalman with his dark-brown hood dusted all over with coal dust, with his dark-brown bag on his head like a mock penitent. The coalman's bone-china white eyes: he's just been out delivering his nuggets. To bite into his dazzling teeth, to nibble his pink lips. My eyes had watched the coalman pour himself a glass of wine just as the savage beast had clawed me over the telephone. Pooh, it's not deep, it's only a beginning, there's still plenty of time to get the hell out of it. But my baby, what's going to become of him? That, a baby? An idiocy, a shrivelled hazelnut in my heart, in my head ... A little sun and it will ripen. We'll go on Friday, my little one. We'll go, I promise you.

Next Friday, what did I go back to?

*

My tiny cloakroom. My hanger. My urns. My ivy. My swagged portière. I was acquiring the habit: I took, I helped myself. Throat constricted. Hands too cold to powder my face. Someone else's hands. Curving cheek of the sculpted face. Open the brackets, close the brackets of love. My satin. My sofa. My bracken. Frothing. Shameless but dear to me. French windows closed. Was it no longer autumn this evening? Later, later, portraits, landscapes, figures, hoods of light above you all; later, I can't take in everything at once. Less zeal, butler. I walk over to him, but it isn't two minutes' pause I need, it's a century. Bracken, you chatter too much. Where is my baby? On my forehead, in my heart, in my head.

The butler opened the doors.

A wood fire, I cried to myself. Thoughtfulness. His thoughtfulness. It is the autumn itself, triumphant in his fireplace. I was being offered a wonder: a reconciliation when nothing irreparable had occurred: I was reconciled to Jacques before I had even set eyes on him again.

Where is Jacques? I can't see him. Be cautious, advance with measured tread, be brave, be careful to hide what you know: that you love him.

Where is he? Where can he be? Take care, relax your grip on yourself for a moment and you'll be shouting 'I love him' in his drawing room, you will be struck down by lightning before you've even seen him again. Where is he?

Two boxers ran at me. I felt a moment's panic.

'Bahia! Blitz! Here, I say!'

It wasn't Jacques's voice.

He got up from the daybed by the fireplace. 'Jacques has told me such a lot about you...'

'Ah. Jacques isn't here?'

'Jacques is away.'

I had been too bold. His face changed.

The two boxers threw themselves on me with all their weight.

'Don't be afraid...'

I was afraid for my silk stockings.

'They want to play with you,' he said.

'Yes, I know.'

'...Jacques is away on business.'

'Yes...'

He was holding the boxers by their scruffs. He turned his head up towards me. 'I am Jacques's friend.'

I looked at a flame in the fireplace. I didn't fall, the flame was still upright.

I was pale, did I feel unwell, he asked it with a genuine, kind smile. Me, unwell? Me, pale? Oh no, it was something else entirely: the lights of cottages in the dusk, all through my life, after heady and ecstatic walks, those lighted windows in the distance, going out one after the other. Jacques wasn't there.

He had gone back to the daybed, he was reclining on it.

Jacques had chosen him, what was there for me to add?

Then the boxers jumped up in slow motion after him, settling themselves down beside him. The man who was away on business was showing me how he lived when he was not entertaining.

'They love you,' I said, picking my way.

The eyes of Jacques's friend lit up. His smile transfigured him. 'They never leave me!'

There were pink rubber dolls' heads, white rubber cutlet bones lying around on the drawing-room floor.

'Bring some Cinzano bianco,' he said to the servant.

Jacques had told him everything.

'Jacques doesn't like me to drink,' he said, obviously rather pleased with himself.

He added a great deal of water to a very little Pernod.

I said: Thank you, monsieur, when he gave me a light. I was to call him Denis.

Blitz lay asleep, his black lips pushed back, a little pink bud, the tip of his tongue, protruding. Presumably he was Jacques's favourite. I was drinking my apéritif in the bosom of a family; as I looked up at Denis's profile, I thought of Manolete.

> *

I took a second helping of fish, I took a second helping of everything in order to please him. He had taken Jacques's place. Yes, the urchins; yes, the belone oysters; yes, the Morbihan oysters; yes, the oyster beds near Arcachon...

I had composed my sentence well in advance. 'So Jacques will be back quite soon...'

He was surprised. He stared at me for a moment, then failed to reply.

We were the same age and we had affinities: we were both to be numbered among those who had known want. His appetite staggered me.

The dead rabbit in the painting, the peasant girl dipping her feet in the water of a stippled blue stream, the closed bookcases... Jacques had disappeared so that we could be left in sole possession of it all.

The servant opened the dining-room doors at the end of the meal and we returned to the drawing room.

Denis had slid down onto the rug, in front of the wood fire, and I let myself down too. He was playing with a twig. Blitz was asleep on the sofa, Bahia on the daybed. The room, with its windows closed, its thick, lined curtains drawn, had withdrawn to leave only the fiesta in the fireplace.

'I love Jacques,' I said as I stared at the flames.

Without answering me, Denis got up and stretched out on the daybed. He lit a cigarette and told me that he would have to leave me soon. Would I like a liqueur? No, there was nothing I wanted.

*

One two, one two. I hobbled along on the heels of my André shoes. One two, one two. Alone in the deserted streets. Alone at eleven in the evening in this neighbourhood where there is not the shadow of a shadow to be seen. One two, one two. I kept going, brave little girl. One two, whatever did I say that to him for? One two. It's a defeat. it's a disaster. An irreparable gaffe. One two, one two. If I didn't have the noise of my heels ... Why did I jump in head-first like that? One two, one two. I could have hidden it, no one was making me tell. Last time I got into a taxi with Genet ... He's in Clichy, in Pigalle ... not a hope of help from that quarter. The métro. The métro is all I have left ... once again.

It was Sunday. It was three in the afternoon. I was reading an instalment of Richard Wright's *Black Boy* in *Les Temps Modernes*. There was a knock. Someone had got the wrong door: on Sundays I'm alone in the world. Better open it, though. Genet. He came in without a word. Grey kid gloves. Pale suède shoes. Fancy Italian shoes. I preferred him in his crepe-soled ones. Freshly shaved, but we won't mention the Elizabeth Arden cream; new raincoat, raglan sleeves, tiny pink-and-beige check. I kissed him, but he obviously couldn't care less. Like my mother. They neither of them have time for kisses. He sat down in the armchair, where Jacques had sat that first day. His gloved hands along the chair arms: two still lifes. Their tints of moss and fog gave me all the details of Genet's long walks through Paris. Once I saw him through a bus window, I remember, alone, a flaming torch. In those days his severity was his beauty. Genet, the treasure trove of morality. Is he ever indulgent? If he is, then his indulgence is silent. It makes us think we are murdering that poor child he once was. Genet has no weaknesses other than those he is prepared to grant us.

'Have you seen *Les Bonnes*?'

'Yes, I have seen *Les Bonnes*. You gave me tickets.'

What had got into me? I usually vanished when he appeared. But that day I was still there, uneclipsed, still me. I was daring to lie down again on my divan, where I was before he came in.

Genet was staring at me, scrutinizing me, probing behind my eyes. What was going to happen?

'Do you like *Les Bonnes*?'

'I'd rather not answer that.'

I could see the steel in him, I could see the glittering reflections from the steel structure inside. Genet was staring at me, scrutinizing me, probing behind my eyes. The question had been asked. It was terrible. He was giving my opinion too much importance. Let's forget about *Les Bonnes*, I felt, let's not talk about it any more, I prefer the indirect approach.

'Do you like *Les Bonnes*? Answer.'

The voice had not risen. Genet was quite calm still. He knew what he wanted. His gloved hands had not budged on the arms of the chair.

'Don't force me to answer ... Genet. I prefer not to answer.'

'I want to talk about *Les Bonnes*.'

Genet was staring at me, scrutinizing me, probing behind my eyes. Genet crossed his legs. I detest him, I thought, the air is getting thinner in here, I hate him, what have I done?

I pushed myself up, I swung round till I was sitting on the edge of the divan. I had been wrong. My strength was ebbing, I was tensing up.

'Very well. Since you wish it, we'll talk about *Les Bonnes*. No, I don't like *Les Bonnes*, I don't like the production ...'

'I don't want to hear about the production. Tell me what you think of *Les Bonnes*.'

I threw myself savagely back onto the divan.

Savagely I told him: 'I prefer your books.'

I waited.

'Go on,' Genet said.

He waited too.

I threw discretion to the winds. 'Does one expect Racine to write poems by Rimbaud? Does one expect Rimbaud to write Racine plays?'

Genet didn't answer. He got up from the armchair and I got up at the same time.

'Are you going?' I cried in a panic.

His face was unrecognizable. I saw an earthworm, it was writhing in my dark den. He was right, he rolls up when he is not understood.

'Are you going?'

He advanced upon me, he threw me down with all his strength on my divan. He opened the door of my den. He slammed the outside door. I heard him cross the yard.

I wept for a long time, with increasing pleasure. A child forgetting why she is crying. I submitted, I accepted that it was all beyond me. After two hours of grief I turned my head: the armchair stood out from all the rest, I was seeing it through opera glasses. Opera glasses bring you closer to the people on the stage but they also cut you off from them. You close in on what is happening in the distance but without participating in it. My lips trembled; they swelled with grief; my pain was no longer mechanical. Genet rose from the armchair once again, then again, ten times, a hundred times, intent on escaping and hurling me out of his path. Genet all alone on a stage was escaping, then beginning his escape again and again, down there, down there where I could never reach him again. I had no recollection now of *Les Bonnes*. I could think only of Genet, see only Genet. A page of my relationship with Genet had been turned once and for all when I stopped weeping.

*

My mother rushed in from the country, eager to help me move. Next day she was forced to take to her bed. Influenza. She subsided into laments over her wretched existence, over the detested country life that was being forced upon her. She let herself go. I didn't weep when she told me how she was learning to milk: I bled. To start on a new trade is a weary business when you are of retirement age. You must wear boots or clogs to work in a cowshed, but my mother had not been able to. The weight was too much for her city dweller's legs. I told her she must persevere, that clogs are warmer in winter. I feigned chilly indifference while I was yearning to exact revenge for the wretched childhood she had been forced to undergo.

She sniffled, she blew her nose, she shivered with fever, she coughed, she told me they hadn't enough money to buy a herd. I told her to sniff up some eau de Cologne; but she wouldn't. Two cows, and two fields, which Michel was attempting to cultivate without having had any experience. No, she wouldn't touch my grog; the smell made her feel sick. Flu is something you have to warm up, like children's feet. My mother sat up in bed, she found her voice again to explain how she raised her chicks near the boiler in the kitchen. I was unappreciative. She still had a little girl of seven beside her, a little girl who wanted her to be elegant in front of a mirror. I am obsessed with how she dresses. The quality of the eggs she took to the poulterer's amazed the farmers' wives ... Her mother's instinct was never idle.

The concierge found someone to help us from up the street. I took my pots and pans, my books, my clothes up to the sixth floor. My mother accused herself, apologized for being ill, promised me an outing to Saint-Germain-des-Prés as soon as she was better. That ball of black hair on my pillow ... my chick taking advantage of the warmth from a kitchen boiler, my brown egg, I will never sell it.

'How awful I feel!' she said every time I prepared to make another trip.

They carried up the divan. I stood in the centre of that white rectangle and lived through a death agony, there in the void left by my divan. My mother climbed the six flights of stairs wrapped in a whitish, yellowish burnous. I had wrapped her up in the colours of anaemia. Death in my heart, I handed the key of my den to the concierge. The three doors on the new landing terrified me more and more.

*

'Are you listening?' I said one morning, after we'd finished breakfast.

Ten o'clock. The sounds of the street outside. My grinding teeth. Oh, for the sleep, the cotton sleep of my yard in winter.

'It's a busy street out there,' my mother thought aloud.

'It's a street!'

'How difficult you are. Think how lucky you are to be living in Paris.'

'Without a penny, without a future.'

'It was your choice.'

I would wake up, I would get out of bed aching, without even the strength to pick a reproach. A couple of fine figures we make, I said to myself. Money or no money, we certainly need prettying up a bit even when we are just staying in; we scorn the cheap robes

in the big stores so that we can make scarecrows of ourselves with
our short skirts that don't cover our long nightdresses. And as for
our lumpy old woollen jackets—rags and patches would be more
honest. Bah, she would have answered me, that bottom lip thrust
out in rehearsal for her old age.

'Are you listening?' I asked again.

'I'm always listening,' my mother said. 'You smoke too much.
You oughtn't to smoke in the morning. What is it you want me to
listen to?'

'...When I'm out, the pavement gives way under me.'

She stretched her head up very tall. 'What do you mean?
Explain?'

'...When I'm out, the ground suddenly flies out from under me.'

My mother sighed.

'...I'm walking along, and I have to find a wall, a store front to
support me.'

My mother gave an even deeper sigh. 'You don't get enough to
eat. It's the same for everyone these days.'

I cut a cigarette in two and smoked half. I was obeying and dis-
obeying. I went on.

'I can feel life draining away; the earth is going to open up; there's
nothing to rely on any more ... I keep going, holding on to the
walls; people think I'm drunk; and my body is empty, absolutely
empty. Is it serious? Do you think it's serious?'

My mother took a deep breath, like a physical-training instructor
giving a demonstration. 'No, of course it's not serious! I see what it
is now.'

'What?'

'Stupid, you ought to be pleased.'

'Why?'

'It's your change of life.'

She was smiling at me: I had the innocuous sex of a little girl
again, I was worthy of her trust. I was her peace of mind.

'My change of life? That's impossible.'

A threat of storm in her face. 'And why "impossible"?' she said
in a different voice.

'I'm too young.'

My mother shrugged her shoulders. ' "Too young"! You poor
goose...'

'Why "poor goose"?'

'Poor child, you've certainly earned it,' she went on. 'Now you can reap the benefit...'

'What benefit?' I asked.

'You can take someone.'

'...If you want to "take" someone, then you must be made a little different from me.'

'What's wrong with you?'

'Oh, nothing: I'm ugly.'

'Be a woman,' she cried, 'and you'll find someone. Be a woman, for heaven's sake!'

Being a woman meant being deceitful. I didn't want her to say it.

'These unpleasant spells, can they go on a long while?'

'They can go on for ten years.'

'Ten years?'

'Oh, yes. And consider yourself lucky. There are some women who go quite crazy.'

'Perhaps I'll go crazy!'

'Ah, if I only had all you have now, you'd see,' my mother said.

She sat dreaming. I wondered whether what I had would enable me to take men the way a restaurant owner takes the trout out of his tank.

*

I can't describe my mother. She was ageing now. She was a master-piece cut adrift and floating with the stream. Time, if I let my gaze rest truly on her features, time had deprived me of her jabots, her big-brimmed hats. Why remember when everything must vanish anyway? I clung on to her nose: that didn't change. Sometimes, when my heartbreak was unbearable, I took it out on my mother's eyes because I couldn't find the old steel in them any more. I cast a veil over them, the inner eyelid of a bird, and time ceased swindling me with its drawn-out degradations. Sometimes I was nothing but regrets; I had still not sufficiently exhausted those hours, those minutes, those seconds during which my mother had been sure of her elegance; at those times I pulled down her mouth, I hollowed her chin, I emptied her eyes. That hardness in her face, where had it gone? What do you think of a blanquette de veau for lunch, she asked. Answer me, where are you wandering again? I am hiding in your voiles, in your boas, I am wandering among your laces and your alpacas, I am standing to attention inside your starched fronts, I am holding back my tears behind your little veils, I am offering you your hatpins on their tray; open the pages of *L'Asphyxie*, pierce, prick, torment my heart, at seven years old, at five, it is all yours. Ah, the dizzying flights of time. Listen Mama, listen to me now: I was a painter in my childhood, I gazed at you, you gazed at yourself in the looking glass; believe me, my portraits of us both were works of art; I painted them with my passion, with my fresh eyes, though you can't see them because I carry them mingled one in with the other here inside me. Don't destroy my work with crackling varnish, don't crumble away.

We ate the blanquette. Our champagne? Our laments: her dismal life; her hard labour. I sat, an impotent recording machine: there was nothing I could do to extricate her.

I complained in turn about my book's not selling.

'But literature is your life, all the same,' she said.

She had me by the short hairs: she was talking about the past while referring to the present. Those days when I was discovering Proust and Dostoevsky at night, by the light of a single candle, an adolescent allowing herself to live at last. The great writers were my sustenance, in those days when I drew a little sustenance too from the fleur-de-lis on my paper knife.

I explained to my mother that though literature was perhaps my life, it was not exactly a job. I was living on the profits of my black-marketeering still, and tomorrow heaven knew what was going to happen.

'If it isn't a job, what is it?' she asked.

'Wait, I have to think about that ... Yes, what is it?'

*

Literature is this: taking the imitation-leather shopping bag down from its nail, setting out on my errands, feeling the presence of my battered billfold through my woollen glove, crossing the street, looking to see if the owners of La Mandoline café are behind their counter, pushing on as far as the Pingouin wool shop, lassoing all the bundles nestling in their pigeonholes with a single glance, retracing my steps, crossing the main street, seeing the hoar frost of heavy seas on the flank of a cod, choosing the freshest mackerel, caressing, though without buying, the skin of the mushrooms, smelling my fingers, because I love the earth.

I go into the butcher's. I'd like a nice juicy piece of meat ... He slices a piece for me: a promise of strength ... The steaks shimmer on the white marble.

I retrace my steps. Prime quality the oranges, the bananas, the grapefruit sold in the open market, beside the Hôpital Saint-Antoine.

I pay for my pound of oranges, I turned my head ... Could it be the weight of an anemone on my shoulder? Is it the light finger of a season, spring come early in the fragile winter, pointing out a rift in the clouds, there above the hospital? The birth of a colour in the sky, hope all-powerful. I go back into the fish dealer's. I shall eat alone, I shall begin with moules marinières. I have the ten francs, here, you can give me fifty.

What tender emotions above those skew-whiff aerials! It is March, it is April, hovering there over the hospital, so shy still, just beginning to open. No white wine for my mussels, I'll use vinegar instead. I have my parsley, my bay, my onions, my thyme. Write? How could I? I am blind. I have the film of a dead bird's eye swimming in front of mine. One is pale pink, the other is pink with a hint of orange. The shading of a rift in the sky, the refinement, the simplicity of sweet peas. I halt, the watches in four windows are all keeping time, I have the sky's cheek against mine. On again. Two pounds of ordinary potatoes, please. Big ones, for french fries.

And I dawdle past the bears in the Nouvelles Galeries. They are wearing bibs, they are sitting in baby carriages. A packet of Lux, a packet of Omo; and while I'm here a saucepan scourer. As long as the shading and the rift ... Gone, all that grey has resumed possession of the sky, everything is softening, everything is imperceptibly stirring, the city has been aired since that fragile colour appeared. Let me have an endive, it's got more taste; lettuce is so insipid at this time of year. Can I eat it tomorrow, this plum? Can't you see it's wrapped in special paper? I was dreaming of a hound in the sky, following the scent of those tender rifts ... I'd like a Karcher beer. Is it fizzy? First fruits in the sky, that's what they were, and I have gathered them. Blue Gauloises, please, three packets, and a box of matches ... No, I haven't any change. Now let us sit down between the merry-go-round and the métro. One can never be too careful, we must lower the basket as gently as possible onto the seat. What long hair she has for ten, is she ten? What gravity; the merry-go-round's only customer. I've had enough of always recognizing myself all over the place. I shall rearrange my things in their basket. The leaves are fresh, they are raspberry leaves.

Here I am, melting on a seat, with my errands perfectly run,

useless, indispensable to whom? A troglodyte, and in a way not unhappy to be so. Sitting just by the merry-go-round, I dream of a
merry-go-round. Its refrain runs through my life, love far from
love, another love for love, my basket beside me, the lid neatly
closed, the raspberry leaves? The tender shading in the sky a while
ago now, my lips not moving, my lips bursting with words and sobs
that do not emerge—is that writing, is that not writing? I can tell
myself a story; the mussels will be cooked in next to no time. I
could be a ploughman, I would begin my day at four in the morning, I would have a team of percherons because I'm of the old
school, I prefer the swing of their great hindquarters to the fits and
starts of tractors. I would chew my tobacco, I would take my snuff,
the day would disentangle itself from the night, the timid, mouse-
grey daylight would drop its scarves around my neck. Quiet, quiet,
day is breaking, and from a simple petal Chartres explodes. If it
meant not speaking, writing, since it is love . . .

*

I shall leave this flat, I shall leave it as soon as I can, I promised myself. I hated the noises from the street, and the noises didn't like me
either.

'Eat,' my mother said. 'Eat, eat . . . Why don't you eat?'

She was putting me back into boarding school at the age of forty.
Who else was there to cure of her childhood griefs? Jacques? He
has no time for my ministrations. Too bad. One man on earth is
my little boy, and it's he. Jacques, my little boarder in his college.
Why not a festival of sentimentality? I shall come and see you
twenty times a day in the visitors' room, I promise. I'm different
from all the other mothers: we're going to work together on your
escape. In the night, my child, I shall steal you from under the head-
master's nose. I shall run off with you across the roofs, and right
away the future will smile at us. Don't be afraid, I shall carry you
on my back. You will have to hug my neck, you will have to hang
on to me, I shall hold your calves, my sonnikins, you will see the
stars, I shall run, you won't be scared, you will jounce against my
back, I shall be a father, a papa.

*

'What do you think of her?' I asked after we had returned to our
table on the terrace of the Flore.

My mother pondered. 'I think she's sly.'

'Sly! What do you mean, sly?' I said in astonishment.

My mother seemed unshakable. 'What do you want me to say? I thought she was sly...'

I understood less and less. I stammered out 'She's beautiful... don't you think she's beautiful?'

My cheeks were aflame with my determination to convince her. 'Yes, she's beautiful,' my mother agreed.

'How nice she was, how kind she is...'

'Yes, very nice. She said two words.'

It was true. She had said just two words.

'But can you tell me what you mean by "sly"?'

When my mother is exasperated she puffs up her cheeks, she lets out a long pooooooooh that is also a fart, she breathes her self-conceit at you before she replies.

'What a bore you can be! Give me a Camel.'

I offered the packet.

I had dragged my mother upstairs as soon as we set foot in the Flore. It was four in the afternoon. Perhaps Simone de Beauvoir was working up there. I was right. Alone, among the empty tables, she sat writing in the silence and half darkness.

'Good afternoon,' I said.

'Good afternoon,' she replied.

'I'd like you to meet my mother...'

'How do you do, madame,' she said to my mother.

My mother hadn't dared to reply.

'Goodbye,' I said.

'Goodbye. Telephone,' Simone de Beauvoir said.

Then we went back downstairs. We had found places out on the terrace. Boulevard Saint-Germain today, Porte Champerret yesterday. It's called amusing yourself. You're thirty, twenty-five, and then? The room upstairs at the Flore was filled with a vast *tableau vivant*. The chairs, the tables, the ashtrays, the carafes... the walk-ons, the extras. She was writing in the centre of the *tableau*, cut off from them all, at one with the world she was transposing. Permission to look at her for five minutes, good afternoon, goodbye. Then a child follows her mother down the stairs.

'What are you thinking?' my mother asked.

'Nothing. And you?'

'Nothing,' my mother said also.

She was writing at four in the afternoon, withdrawn, modest. I watched her on the awnings of the cafés, I flung open my arms: I enfolded the immense *tableau* in my arms, the sand mingled with the water, the water with the sky, the sky was a prisoner in the tableau. Everyone talking; upstairs her silence; a fringe, the fringe of my hair, between her silence and the noise of the conversation.

I wonder where the present moment is. The past devours the present, they both slide into the sheath of the future. How can I preserve my mother from age and time? By hesitating—was she fifty-nine or was she sixty that day? Was I thirty-nine or was I forty? A year snatched from under the executioner's axe. Miracle and frivolity, she had opened her purse, she was looking at herself in her mirror as she had when she was twenty-five. My mother doesn't like seeing herself too close: she keeps mirrors at a distance. She is haughty with her own image. I admired her movements, her performance; I missed no detail of the act. It was not an impulse, it was a resolution. Her face, as she observed herself, as she recognized herself, was the face of a dedicated scientist. As the silence of trees saps her energy, so the buzz of idlers chattering on a café terrace injects her with vitality. She was born in a Northern village, but she is a real Miss from Ménilmontant. Rotten sods the both of you, I said to myself, thinking of Michel and my stepfather. She always wants me to tell her how old she looks: it sends shivers up and down my spine. She was making signs of the cross with her mirror: up and down, right and left ... Let her see herself young and elegant before she goes back to their smallholding. I want her radiant, I want her without memories. She was still making her signs of the cross, superbly apart from the English, Swedish, German, American men at the other tables.

'They all are,' I said out loud.

She went on with her manoeuvres.

'They all are!' I said louder still.

'What are all what?' she said impatiently.

'They're all men like Maurice Sachs, men who don't pay any attention to women.'

Satisfied with her inspection, she shut her purse.

'Aren't you ever going to get tired of men like that!'

We became pensive, we withdrew into ourselves.

'Whatever happened to him, I wonder, that poor man?' she murmured.

She eyed a slender young man who looked like Lord Alfred Douglas. His mouth was like a sabre slash.

'Why "that poor man"?'

My mother left Lord Alfred to his beauty.

'Why? Because he was a good man,' she said quietly. My mother ruminated. What was she predicting for us with the twitching of her lips?

'Am I getting old, Violette? Am I finished? Answer your mother ...'

Anything, but not that.

I said: 'Shall we both have a Pernod?'

'Answer me. Am I old?'

Anything, but not that.

She petrified me. Quick, a red herring. I said: 'Where shall we eat this evening? Have you any ideas? Oh, but I was forgetting the Payens ... we have to meet them.'

'Answer your mother!'

Anything in the world, but not that. Your mouth, your elegance, your slenderness, they are my jewelry, the glitter of my memories.

'Answer your mother, I tell you. Am I an old horror?'

'You know perfectly well you're not an old horror!'

'How unfeeling you can be with your mother sometimes.'

'Why tell you what you already know? You don't look your age.'

'You've always been unfeeling towards your mother.'

'That's not true. It's utterly untrue!'

How could I ever dare pass judgment on your youth, how could I ever dare pass judgment on your age? Ask for the Big Dipper, the Little Dipper, Cassiopeia, and I will hand them to you while you re-create beauty for yourself.

'I don't want to be an old bag.'

'You're not an old bag, you're not an old horror.'

Real concern rejuvenates.

Ageing is a problem. Every problem brings us a renewal. Once she was a city dweller, a businesswoman, a fashionable woman; now she is a chicken breeder in the country, in a desert wilderness ... What am I to do? I love her: I shall lie without lying absolutely.

I proved to her that she was up-to-date, broadminded, it seemed to me. It wasn't every mother who would go out drinking Pernods at five in the afternoon just to boost her daughter's morale.

'What wouldn't I do to see you happy!' she said fervently.

Time had spared her little black lashes. Her blue eyes became calm again too quickly.

'Look,' I cried. 'There she is, she's leaving.'

Simone de Beauvoir, with quick short steps, was leaving the café.
I never thought about her age. She was first and foremost a writer.

'How horrible you made me in your book,' my mother sighed
after a long silence.

'I was transposing,' I said evasively. 'That's what literature is all
about. It's fiction.'

I was being dishonest. What I had written in *L'Asphyxie* was
the truth.

'It is fiction then, really?' she said with supplication in her voice.

She was pretty enough to eat, she was putting herself in my hands.
I will become God, if she wishes it. My ambition, if I had to look
after her, would be unbounded.

The bells began ringing in the church of Saint-Germain-des-Prés,
at seven in the evening. No steeple will ever be as lonely. I listened,
I was set free; my throat: a bird; the sky: a plume of spray. Joyous
migrations as the bells ring. The presbytery there in our furnace,
standing back, masked with leaves, one window lighted; the bus
taking its time, reminiscence, reminiscence.

The sound of the bells, odd in Paris somehow. I dreamed on the
terrace of the Flore: they are burying a little girl of five named
Violette and her mother, aged twenty-five, named Berthe. The
priests are saying the mass in front of mirrors; the two corpses are
turned to face one another. The little girl is in her shroud of
broderie Anglaise, she is wearing white gloves, she is entreating;
her gloves are still moist. The mother is wearing her big velvet hat,
she is in her petticoat, with high button boots. The notes of the
organ unwind around them. That evening the bells are ringing in
Saint-Germain-des-Prés.

'If you see him, you must point him out to me,' my mother said.

'He's annoyed because I don't like his play,' I said with profound
sadness.

'Annoyed? A man like that, annoyed?'

'Yes, annoyed.'

It was moving, her astonishment mingled with admiration.

It was simple to be sad because of her in the indifference and
the animation of a café terrace.

'That man can't be annoyed, he has suffered too much,' she said.
'I'd like to see him, you've talked about him so much...'

'I'm keeping my eyes open for him,' I said. 'I'm told he comes
here.'

I was looking for him in every passer-by. If only I could invent him, create him for her just at the moment when she felt the desire to see him.

We left the café. Two young women in black trousers threw themselves on our table.

The rustling of the falling dusk against the rustling of neon advertisements; a tender, tender astonishment, a rose reflected there above us—the sky.

We walked along the boulevard. She staggered; her high heels were too tiring for her, I scolded her, I told her Cuban heels were ideal, she gave me her arm, she didn't answer me, I gave her my approval, I straightened my back, I supported her, I let her go for a second, I returned to her side, she took my arm again, for her sake I stole the murmur, the fragility, the nocturne being played in the distance, towards the Place Médicis, I brought her a posy of darkness gathered from the lawns of the Jardin du Luxembourg.

Old women sitting on benches allowed me to glimpse an old age without losses or commotions.

'Is it far?' she asked.

'We're there.'

Reassured she suddenly became ecstatic: 'Why don't we eat at the Reine Pédauque? Do you remember, my naughty little girl, do you remember how we liked it there ... Do you think it's very expensive? It would be a mad extravagance...'

'It's impossible. The Payens are expecting us.'

'That's just a bore as far as I'm concerned,' my mother said.

We arrived in front of the Rhumerie. They were watching for us. I presented my mother to Andrée and Robert Payen and to Romi.

'If the ladies would just come up,' Romi said.

The ladies stepped up on the dais. It is a little theatre where the customers are actors who sit and watch the spectators pass by. I drank several white-rum punches. Romi explained to my mother that he liked my little book, my gaffes, my greeds, my moods, my shiny raincoat, my beret, my long greasy hair, my short hair frizzled like a nylon scourer; he egged me on to drink another punch, he was proving his friendship, his sympathy. My mother was silent. Was she sulking? Was she being tragic? She was countering the others' polish with her disdain. Ah well, she had always been difficult to please.

'Oh, God!' I cried.

I stood up.

'What's the matter with her?' my mother said.

A glass toppled over.

'It's him! It's him, now!'

Genet was walking past the dais of the Rhumerie. A beggar began playing his tin whistle.

Now he was moving away, freed from me without having even felt my weight. He was walking in the direction of the Danton cinema.

'I tell you it's Jean Genet!'

My mother was getting annoyed: I wasn't controlling myself.

I stood up, I sat down again.

'Behave!' my mother shot at me.

'Your daughter is crazy about the stuff that gentleman writes,' Romi put in, as imperturbable as ever.

'I'm in a state,' I confessed.

Genet was striding along.

'... If I don't run now, I'll never see him again.'

I made up my mind.

I pushed my way through the customers, but I was brought to a stop near the café Mabillon: impossible to cross. Where is he? I can't see him. Paris, you wouldn't dare do that to me. Paris, give him back to me.

A yard away from the newspaper kiosk, at the corner of the Boulevard Saint-Germain and the rue de l'Ancienne-Comédie, it was him; half a yard from the newspaper kiosk, it was him still. Along Berteil's display window, it was him still. I could make out the names of the papers in various typefaces: German newspapers, English newspapers, American newspapers, they were all giving me back Jean Genet. Genet is back!

I began to shout: 'Genet ... Genet...'

He didn't turn round.

I kept shouting: 'Genet ... Genet...'

He was striding along with his companions.

'Genet ... Genet...'

At last he turned round to look. He had recognized me.

'Genet!'

He didn't slacken his pace. Now he was shouting at me: 'Fuck off!'

His companions didn't turn their heads.

I could see him. He crossed between the silver studs, he passed in front of a terrace where students eat their french fries and sausages out of cardboard containers.

My mother greeted me on my return with a stormy frown. 'Well?'
Her thoughts were wholly for Genet.

'He doesn't want to see me any more.' I sobbed.

'You mustn't upset yourself,' Romi said.

'Leave her be,' my mother said to Romi. 'She's drunk.'

'Me? Drunk? How can you say such a thing? Can't you see how
unhappy I am?'

Genet was avenged.

He'll be here within a quarter of an hour. The chestnut gâteau is a
success; the cold tap is running gently over the bottle of Champagne.
My mother insisted on inviting him. He'll be here any moment now.
He is coming, I am full of dread. He will come, there's no doubt
about it, and yet the knowledge is also a presentiment.

'Be calm,' she said.

'I am calm.'

She was stretching up on tiptoe, exploring the street. 'I'd like to
see him.'

'You will see him!'

'I'd like to see him from a distance first.'

My mother opened the window. False alarm. She closed the
window.

I went over. The roofs, monotonous. The chimneys, homely.
The sky, absent. Two particular chimneys, higher than the others,
two chimneys feeling the cold, were stealing Jacques away from

me. Would he come?

'Come here,' she said. 'You can point him out to me.'

I went over.

'My hands are burning hot,' my mother said.

I could sense it: she was expecting my father. My father? Can I say that? I leaned forward, I could see nothing.

The street looked only half alive.

'He's late,' she said in a sad voice.

'Don't get upset. Late? No, he isn't.'

A blonde woman, tired by the look of her, was watering geraniums on a balcony. Four minutes late. I looked for him down in the street. Jacques was just closing his car door in front of the Maggi warehouse.

'This time it's him!'

My mother leaned out too far. 'Where? Quickly, show me, show me!'

I didn't understand her impatience, her fever. My father: a few bone fragments in a vault.

'The tall man over there, the tall man in navy blue, on the far pavement, that's him,' I said.

My mother looked at him. Suddenly she pulled back into the room. 'Close the window!'

I closed the window. It wasn't my father.

We stood there staring at one another. He was taking a long time.

'You made a mistake,' she said. 'He'd have been here by now.'

Why wasn't he knocking at my door?

As I pulled the door open, Jacques appeared.

*

'Where is your mother?' he asked eagerly.

'Straight ahead of you.'

He is so eager to meet my mother. Did I invite him? Has he come? A castle of cards crumbling between my hands.

'Will you permit me to kiss you?' he asked.

I should be overjoyed, I am crushed. He is kissing her just as he kissed me when I visited his home. I am defeated, why did he come? What are they saying? Their words are indistinct, they can hardly reach me, are there just the two of them, there seem to be so many of them. I feel weak, I need the support of my wallpaper, of this bright bird, of its branch. I love him, he is taking my life from me. I erase, I blot out, there is nothing I want, nothing I can recall beyond this happiness so far in excess of my deserts: him here.

'Why are you still standing in the hall?' my mother asked.

Why? I love, I am about to set sail, I am an obsolete liner, I am doing an emigration waltz round and round him. Now that he has walked through my door, I am too overwhelmed to move.

I walk over to them, I talked to them about this and about that. I was struggling for my life; I didn't want to be captured again by this handsome man in his impeccable clothes.

They talked, they talked. I observed him, I analysed him detail by detail; I was the prey of a navy-blue suit, of a white shirt, of black shoes. I thought I was learning him by heart; I tensed to my task. Impeccable. A little neglect would have made him less anonymous. Jacques. Who was he? A character out of a book by Senancour, by Fromentin, by Benjamin Constant ... a being impalpable, chaste, withdrawn—just what it takes to stir up, to release unreason and madness inside your head. Who was Jacques that day? The sky through the window; the bare windowpane; the handle of the window; the tremors of two green plants. He absorbed everything into himself and left me nothing: it was a magic spell. I was forced to prop myself against the fireplace.

Courteous, considerate—even his perfect manners could not protect him from his melancholics, from his moments of nostalgia, and he would be absent himself from us for a while, even though he remained standing beside us. He parched me with thirst. His eyes, blue with the wan worn blue of myopia, gave me vertigo: too much empty space. He seemed to be weary of the moored boats and the trees that receded into the mist every time he took off his glasses ... I was no longer my own possession, I offered him everything, I gave him everything, and at the same time I was making predictions to myself: I would have to hide from him for always what I felt for him, I would have to cut off my hands so as not to comfort him or offer him their warmth.

'Violette has told me so much about you,' he was saying to my mother.

How calm, how measured, how level headed ... It's too good to be true. He is as much in control of himself as he is of me; already I am shouldering my cross. I recognized those quivering nerves at the corners of his mouth. Sometimes I found him pale and wan, tense with gloom. This man who was so successful at everything he undertook, perhaps he was really unhappy underneath, weak, adrift in life ... I set up traps, I spread nets, one day he would call for me ... I didn't see that I was myself the prey I was catching in my traps and my nets. What sadness emanated from him when he looked outside. In vain you control yourself, watch your own moves, prosper; suddenly the black tears are sliding down your cheeks, you are no more than the tiniest chip of gravel under the smoking tar.

Jacques was looking at his mother in my mother's eyes. I understood that. Too much tittle-tattle between our registers of births and deaths. I will not dwell on the point. Jacques adored his mother; Denis had told me that. Was he about to start discussing my book? The model was there in front of him, how would the model behave, how would it react? I shivered. Little boy, my desire to protect you would be less wild and overwhelming if you were less strong. Talk to my mother about *L'Asphyxie* ... No need to be afraid, he is discretion itself.

Will she talk about Genet, that day at the Rhumerie Martiniquaise? I pray: let him know nothing of Genet's severity towards me, of my ungovernable admiration. It's true, I do hide what I feel for each of them from the other. I hide Jacques from Simone de Beauvoir, but I don't hide Simone de Beauvoir from Jacques. If my heart were a mask, I would slap it on my face. Then they would forget my unpleasant features, my sins. It's true, I do conceal my attachments. The person I am on my way to takes over, I abandon myself to that particular one, but without forgetting the days ahead reserved for the others. Where is the harm? Everything can be forgiven me: no one loves me, no one will love me. Am I being unfaithful to them now, as I copy out my work on August 15, 1967, at eleven thirty-seven, as I give them

the silken rustle of the olive trees in the tall grass, the silken rustle of the leaves, the green light, the elegant light of the cypress, the inconstant blue, the icy blue, the frozen sheen of the sky's indifferent perfection.

the panting breath of the breeze, its shyness, its caprices, the distant hills drowning in their blue-tinged tears?

No, I am not being unfaithful to them. I am seeing, I am looking, for them.

My mother didn't talk about Jean Genet to Jacques, but she did tell him the trouble I had gone to over the meal. She was revealing my heart. I gave a little cough; she changed the subject. Jacques told her how much he liked what I wrote. My mother said nothing.

They ate with ogrish appetites. I wasn't hungry. The weight of knife and fork was too much for me. Seduced by Jacques's affability, my mother was waiting on him, giving him the best piece of meat, tilting the dish to spoon him out more juice from the sirloin. A lot of things happen in a year, my mother often said. A lot of things were happening in less than a year. Sitting in my skin, my kingdom of white clouds, sitting in my armchair of doves' down, I gazed down at them, listened to them. Yes, Jacques agreed, I would have more air, more light, more sun up here. Does a loving soul need air, light, sun? She has her glowing prison bars, her glittering bowl, her heavenly body for a jail. My mother and Jacques agreed on every subject under the sun. Where was I to fit in now, there wasn't the smallest gap between them, what was I doing there with them anyway? Just existing. Violette? A figure cut out of a picture book, hung over them by a thread tacked to the ceiling. She didn't want to leave that place downstairs, monsieur, you don't know how stubborn she is, you just don't know how pigheaded she can be, she was ruining her eyes, I told her so. I hope you insisted, madame. And our 'flash' of cognac, Jacques, forgotten already? She lived in pitch darkness, monsieur, I don't even call that a room. Quite honestly, I must tell you, it was like an animal's den. You rub your hands together, you help me to disown it. Quite honestly, you have no idea what I have disowned in the person of my beloved den : those who have gone. Except that they will still go with me into the grave, naturally, we can jettison nothing.

Jacques was speaking to me about the best position, the best arrangement for my worktable. I have a table? That's news to me. I write? A second piece of news. He knows everything, I know nothing. He has come between me and myself. When I am with him, I am a lump of love. I am a poor hunted hare: every time I find a place to lay my head, I am hounded out of it. I am numb, my fingers are asleep, my legs weigh me down, I can't lift my arms, I have been sleeping under thirty-six blankets: a long sleep of love before I was awakened by my love for him. She'll be so much better off with two rooms; yes, so much better off. *Auf Wiedersehen*, my friends, goodbye, I'm off back to my cell now. It's dark, my heart lies on my lap, I am weaving a garland for him ... Fidéline, we are trimming our sails ... we are leaving with Jacques. Oh yes, you are welcome, welcome, we shall all be fiancés together, all three of us together.

It was terrifying how far I had gone by the end of the meal. As Jacques talked to my mother, so he also whispered confidences to me : I decided, this morning, that you should have my spiky chestnuts to look at—yes, my cuff-links—and I've kept my promise; I want you to know that I'm wearing them for you today, just for you. I am trying to please you with what I know pleased you before, with what I hope will please you in the future. I was washing my teeth, I left the brush sticking out of my mouth, I was in a hurry, I wanted to find the blue suit I was wearing the very first time you came to see me. I finished brushing my teeth, happy at the thought of appearing before you at once similar and different after knocking on your door. I want you to be anxious, otherwise I wouldn't set such store by you. You often avoid my face; I understand that; let me offer it to you in other ways: on the frame of my glasses, on my cigarette case, on the poplin of my shirt, on my linen handkerchief, on the curve of my vest. My gestures, my expressions of a strong man who is playing at being playful or ingenuous, I give you those too. And let me make it clear: I was actually hearing his voice.

*

Old squash, you're forty, give up all this starry-eyed nonsense. Leave it to the fifteen-year-olds, and your shame with it. I have no shame. I'd be ashamed to be ashamed. Shame would be too late anyway; I've bought my ticket: destination fascination. If his intelligence weren't as carefully groomed as his appearance, then it would be different. The other day he was talking about Baudelaire with such ardour ... We run after what we have lost, poor child. He is rich; Hermine was poor. She obeyed; he gives orders. You broke her; he will break you. Hermine was a woman; Jacques is a man. His cuffs ... what about his cuffs? They have the grace of a rose at a young girl's neck: secret bonds. But never forget it, poor child, this love-at-first-sight of yours is not reciprocated.

How are they getting on with their lunch? They have had second helpings of sirloin, of juice from the meat, of salad; they are just polishing off their cheese. I eat Jacques as I play at nibbling what is on my plate. It is raining. Will he make up his mind to love me? It is raining so discreetly. Ah, how well-mannered the sky is, it won't interfere in this affair of ours. It's raining; no, thank you, no, I won't take cheese. It's raining. The pride, the tremor at the corner of your mouth, that's where the little boy can't be consoled, the little boy who had to eat up the lentils that made him feel sick. Men get over their childhood. All right, then he isn't a man. I don't give a damn, not a damn in the world. He is what he is: a sad heart. An irresistible being, a distant being.

Come quickly my little boy half past four and school is out jump

into your mommy's arms she got here first she got here before the
other mommies before the bell rang and she saw your scarf and
your topcoat in the corridor she saw you running ahead of the others
she felt you bang ten times against her chest before you came running
up to her with your arms wide open the radiator didn't keep my little
jewel warm the stove was out my heart let's lose no time sit down
on the edge of the sidewalk just do as I say give me your tootsies yes
I'm kneeling down don't be afraid I'm not going to cry or pray
I'm just going to warm you up if your friends make fun of us then
I'll kill them there what luck I'm wearing my waistcoat that's easy
to open put your tootsies between my breasts press my poppet press
press yes you do like it you wanted a turtledove in a cage my love
where do you think I can find you a turtledove in a cage mommy
hasn't got an automobile mommy can't go and find you one in the
woods mommy hasn't any money for the man who sells the seed
down by the river but that doesn't stop her heart beating under your
tootsies while she warms them up for you so you have it after all
your turtledove in a cage tomorrow I'll buy you some new laces I
don't want your bows to come undone hang on to your mommy's
arm my little Jesus unless you want to fight them I'll wait a bit further on and pretend not to notice you can roll in the dust and hit
them with your fists mommy is always telling you you must do
what you want except crying mommy dies when she hears you
sobbing mommy will explain why when we get home very well if
you prefer to hang on to my arm then hang on to it give me your
satchel to hold you'd like a bar of chocolate a cake the others have
them they are going into the baker's mommy heard you mommy
has no answer her purse is very naughty it plays tricks on her when
she looks for her money it hides it from her it doesn't want to let
her have it the naughty rascal look it makes you think it's empty
but it isn't tomorrow the purse won't tease us so it will say I was
hiding your money just be patient my darling boy I'll make you some
toast why should we go to the baker's we have some bread I'll grate
you some chocolate you can put that on your toast if you like mommy
has seen some threadbare patches on your topcoat she will darn
them while you eat your tea don't you think we're happy come on
quickly let's get home walk a little faster if you can yes my precious
later on you shall buy a turtledove.

They were eating their dessert, they were taking second helpings of
crème Chantilly and chestnut purée just as they had taken second
helpings of the sirloin, the meat juices; a compliment to my mother.

Jacques was determined: he would publish *L'Affamée* in a de luxe edition. He would take over the book's publication entirely, and in addition he was going to give me 100,000 francs in royalties before the book appeared. Quite a sum. For a moment I thought of it as a measurement of love. He was giving me 100,000 caresses and 100,000 proofs of tenderness. I didn't tell him but I had decided to give him the manuscript of *L'Affamée*.

My Blanzy-Poure pen was worth 100,000 francs, my exercise book was worth 100,000 francs, my short sentences that filled me with despair were worth 100,000. I was cheating Simone de Beauvoir, I was depriving her of a dedication that was her due, I was misappropriating my manuscript; I was worth 100,000 despite my misappropriations. Failing to sell five hundred copies of *L'Asphyxie* still left you with 100,000 francs. Not seeing a single one of those volumes in a bookstore window still enabled you to earn 100,000 francs. The sadism and the ironies of certain critics were bringing me 100,000 francs. Receiving 100,000 francs. That was something that had never happened to the ant living with Maurice Sachs. My mother served coffee, I forgot the 100,000 francs, I forgot the writer he was looking for in me. Maurice Sachs, Jean Genet, Simone de Beauvoir, Berthe—my mother, all forgotten too. I had just been born. I had come into the world a convalescent. Jacques: my first walk outside.

*

Three days later I said: 'The hundred thousand francs ...'

'What hundred thousand francs?'

My mother was tying up some parsley and thyme for her beef stew.

'The hundred thousand francs he promised me. I'm going to collect them this afternoon ...'

'You wouldn't do such a thing!' my mother said in a shocked voice. She inspected her stew. 'Don't do it, Violette ... You know I'm right, don't do it.'

'What are you afraid of? He promised them to me.'

She threw the onion skins into the garbage. 'You know I'm right. Just don't do it.'

I took the towel out of her hands. 'Don't work, I don't want you to work. Sit down. Rest.'

'I was just wiping my hands. How sharp you are with your mother!'

'No, I'm not ... Oh, you don't understand!'

She wasn't a housemaid any longer; I wanted her to dictate, to give orders. I wanted her to sit resting and fanning herself while I got ready to go out and ask my father for money.

'Are you going?'

'Yes.'

'It's a mistake. You're making a mistake.'

The journey from my street to his factory in the suburbs was long and complicated.

I stepped off the bus; the film posters on the wall of a block of flats forced themselves on my attention. I seized my opportunity. I disengaged myself from the avenue and its hellish traffic; I began reading the poems, the sonnets, the love letters written on the names of the actors, on the titles of the films. Taking the full force of the wind, two steps away from a disused railway track. Half drugged, I began clutching the bars at the top of the embankment. The sleepy tracks passed their calm on to me; the grass on the slopes of the embankments was not stunted. My anguish, my emotion, my reasoned despair, lying there below. Rails to London, rails to Amsterdam. What good would London and Amsterdam do me with him? The grass was conciliatory; but the rails, running forever side by side, told me I should always be apart from him. I walked along underneath his wall; I had come to visit a prisoner in his tower. I saw his car with its top down standing in front of the main entrance. It was running, escaping on the spot, his car. There were poplars lending grandeur to the factory's garden ... He loves trees and will never love me.

I started up the narrow staircase: what if at the top step I found a grille, an undernourished face, a little sad mouth through one diamond of the trellised grille, packages expected of you, letters longed for from you, what if I found a strong man who had become weaker than I ...

His secretary told him I had arrived. I waited a long time.

Typewriters were machine-gunning ground-glass partitions behind which shadows rose and sat down again. Why was I having to wait so long?

He caught me unawares when he came out of his office.

Radiant, he was that. Strapping, he was that. At ease inside his skin, he was that. At ease in his fawn suit, that too. Vitamin C for my brain, his black, brush-cut hair. Money, for some people, what a springboard, what a guarantee of a safe landing! I was seeing him again; yet since that visit to my flat I had never left him. You eat, and you forget your hunger. No, he had never left me. I shan't ever sleep with you, yet you will have lived inside me all the same, I thought. A block in front of me. The block has eyes, a nose; I have just arrived in the world, it feeds me, it brings time to a halt, it is the first moment of my existence. I possess everything and I no longer have anything at all. My hands, which will never be able to say to him come to the Jardin du Luxembourg, come to the Louvre, come to the cinema, come to Sète, come to Narbonne, my hands are porcelain figures. Break them, oh, break them. Not allowed to live, not allowed to die. Will you have me as your dog? I'll run through the woods for you, I'll come back towards you; dumbly I will question you, you will be my rest after the woods and the forests. You were a dam in my path. Earthworks were under way. Surprise, overflow, cascades of astonishment. You are there, I spread all around, I am the earth, I am advancing towards you through the sea. I am not moving, I am not looking for you, and yet I am on my way towards you. Suddenly I look at you. I am serious, I look cruel; that is because I am absorbing your surroundings as well, the space to your right, to your left, the space where you are not.

'Good afternoon! How are you?'

I can't answer. You speak and I become a little stick balanced on the tip of your fingers. I should be presumptuous if I dared to answer: 'And you, how are you?' I was a great mass, I was immense, you were there with your unsubstantial glasses, I asked for nothing more. Now you speak to me, you trample my garden down. Why are you so curt? Who are you fighting? I arrive and you draw blood at once. Why this barbed wire?

We went through into his office. The horrible panther-skin rug did nothing to comfort me. I didn't say to myself: L'Affamée is certainly worth 100,000 francs. I was there to beg the money he had offered me. Nor did I say: Jacques is not a publisher; therefore, this de luxe edition represents his friendship for me. I didn't want his friendship, I didn't want to be a woman who wrote when I was with him. I wanted to be a woman swooning with love.

His dog, which had been asleep under his desk, ran towards us.

He called it Blitzou. He said: 'Here, Blitz! Now, Blitzou, watch it.' He wanted to be stern and affectionate at the same time.

'He recognizes you,' he said to me.

He was talking about me in order to talk about his boxer; it was a pretence of intimacy.

The boxer stared at me, paws spread. Then it turned round: I was supposed to stroke its back. Its little docked tail quivered. I asked the boxer for strength and courage when I could no longer look at Jacques, when I became afraid that he would see what I was concealing from him.

You gave your paw, you earn his love. I have often wept without tears to be in Blitz's place.

'Here, Blitzou! Don't bother Violette.'

The dog wasn't bothering me. It went back towards its master.

'You great ... dimwit!' Jacques said in a gruff, kindly voice.

The gruff, kindly voice inspired you with confidence. A whole programme of privileges and protections for Blitz. I picked up the crumbs.

'How is Denis?'

The secretary came in.

'You can bring me those letters to sign. I shall be leaving early.'

Where was he going? A business appointment? Pleasures? Fine books to choose? Silks to feel? Paintings to take another look at? A whole city of art from which I was inexorably locked out.

The secretary went out.

'Denis is very well, thank you, Violette.'

An impeccable answer.

'I've come for the hundred thousand francs,' I said without preamble.

A shadow passed across Jacques's face. Only for a moment, then he was in command of himself again.

'Of course,' he said. 'Would you rather have a cheque or cash?'

'Cash.'

The secretary came back in.

Her out-of-date, provincial air enchanted me.

'Would you bring me a hundred thousand francs, please,' he said to her. 'Small denominations?' he asked me.

'Yes, small denominations.'

Was my mother well? Yes, my mother was well; yes, she would soon be going back to Charente. I fumed with impatience at all this formality.

He described the grey cover for the de luxe edition of L'Affamée; I told myself I was sponging off him. I had stopped saying: I am taking what he has offered me.

The secretary returned to the office.

He took the bundles of new notes from her and laid them on the edge of his desk. It seemed to me that the act of giving them to me was painful for him.

'Do you want to count them?'

That hurt. No, I didn't want to.

I bundled the notes into my purse.

'When shall I see you again?' I asked anxiously.

'Telephone me,' he said coldly.

He loved money; I was depriving him of the 100,000 francs he had offered me. I understood him; I continued loving him while also continuing to love money. I was begging for a dinner so that I could be near him, but he refused to be more specific. I left; I had obtained nothing. In ruins. Unhappy. Laid waste. That is the nearest I can get to what it was like every time I said goodbye to Jacques. 'Come to dinner on Friday ...' I would have been free and happy with 100,000 francs in my pocket if he had said that.

He walked out with me to the entrance. Kiss on the right cheek, kiss on the left cheek; money, friendship, I have given you everything, what more can you want, now I am going back quickly into my office. I shall be safe there, on the other side of my padded door, with my dog lying asleep untroubled by beggars.

I dawdled outside, I had obtained what I came for. I traced the names of the actors on the poster with one finger, then the red title of their film, standing beneath the windows of the block of flats while the automobiles flashed past at breakneck speed. I retraced my steps to be with the railway track again. It was Jácques at peace, it was Jacques disappointed by my visit. The grass was breathing with Blitz's lungs. Everything waiting patiently, everything simply living or sinking into silence. I followed the rails of the disused railway track until my eyelids hurt.

Why, I asked myself, why must one die of hunger in the presence of someone who overwhelms your heart? Why should one love without eating, without drinking, without getting dressed, without paying for a roof over one's head, without smoking a good cigarette, without seeing a good film, without collecting the radio from the repair shop? As love is necessary, so money is indispensable. To love is a considerable labour. We cannot be sure it won't cost us our necks. Love must be fed, love must be given to drink, love must be kept amused, love must be provided with shelter and warmth. What is there degrading in the fact that the being you love and who does not love you is kind and generous towards you? The older I grow, the less I think of myself as guilty for having loved people who didn't love me.

*

My mother handed me my stepfather's letter to read. A cow was about to calve. They hoped she would be back soon. We sent them a telegram: she was coming home.

Our last apéritif, our last dinner out, our last good night in bed. Her cardboard suitcase ... Slip me inside her fur-lined slipper before she goes.

Next morning I went with her to the Gare d'Austerlitz. I went into the train with her, I found her a seat next to a window, over-looking the platform. I put her case in the rack, I handed her her newspapers, I kissed her knowing she would not kiss me. Other passengers lifted their eyes from their magazines: they sensed my fever, my anguish.

'You must take care of yourself, think of your health,' she said to me out in the corridor.

She went back into her compartment. I pushed my way out past the passengers in the corridor; my lips were moving. I halted outside the toilet; I was praying.

I looked up and saw her sitting in her seat, with her case above her head, her newspapers in her string bag, her hands on her knees. I jumped up as high as I could, to see better. I talked to her as though the window were lowered: 'Eat properly, read, don't get bored, they're sure to be there to meet you, don't worry.'

My mother looked out at me without any reaction. Was it indif-ference? Was she concealing her grief? I couldn't tell, I shall never know. My mother is often a stranger to whom I don't dare put direct questions.

I sent her a last wave: I left before the train pulled out. I was choking. I blew her a few kisses. Her face remained expressionless.

I ran along the train towards the exit. I was talking, talking. I was talking out loud about her poor cardboard suitcase, about her frizzy permanent they'd let get too hot, about the scuffs on her high-heeled shoes; I said: it's too painful, it's not right for it to be so painful. It was she who was going back to boarding school, it was I who was leaving her behind in the visitors' room on October 1. I quietened down at last after three hours of tears, laments, moans, sobs, and stammering in my room.

I cannot recall, I will not recall where and how Genet and I were
reconciled. A chance, a merciful stroke of fate. Reconcile ... I shall
never be weary of that verb. I say it slowly, my eyes are beaded with
happiness. Reconcile, reconciled ...

Genet took me to visit Paul Morihen's bookshop. It was Paul
Morihen who was to arrange for the sale of *L'Affamée* in its de
luxe edition. We arrived in a taxi, which to me was a disappointment. I prefer walking through the gardens of the Palais-Royal. I go
back there on pilgrimage sometimes: the kiosk that sells the toys
and candies is my basilica. I listen, I look, I am astonished. Children's games are immutable, mysterious. The rules of bouncing the
ball against the wall have not changed by a single handclap or a
single twirl of the wrists; the hopscotch frame has exactly the same
number of squares; 'salt, mustard, vinegar, pepper' is still the mass
being sung for a whistling rope—they are all religions that children
respect. They amuse themselves, yes, but they punish anyone who

makes a mistake. Those tiny, noisy, inoffensive hordes stir up a
yearning in me for silent countrysides, for out-of-the-way villages
where the poor man can be an object of adulation. Moreover, I
should like to have seen how the windows of Colette, Colette the
writer, were getting on.

I walked through the bookshop door and recognized him. Leaning over one of the tables, surrounded by all those costly and luxurious books, Cocteau was drawing naked young men with broad
strokes of his pen on big sheets of paper. Their sexes saddened me.
They were too conspicuous.

'Good afternoon ... Have the books I ordered arrived?' a customer asked.

'Just a moment, I'll go and see,' the assistant said.

Genet, having presumably already met Cocteau that day, had
abandoned me. He was talking to another assistant, one dripping
age and distinction. Grey hair? No, little silver chains.

Genet was turning the pages of a huge book. He was making
comments.

'...I'm frightfully sorry, they haven't come in yet,' the first
assistant said to the customer.

The old assistant was eating Genet with his eyes. Genet was
enjoying himself, he was saying 'No kidding?' He was at ease, he
felt cossetted.

'What a bore!' the customer said. 'I was counting on having
them. You promised me they would be here...'

Cocteau was opening vast parentheses, closing supple parentheses
to make the bodies of his boys.

'...I was counting on them too. I was sure I'd have them for
you today. Would you like me to telephone you as soon as they come
in?'

'I wanted them this evening. I wanted them to give to a friend.'

I was straining to hear things that weren't my business. I was
excited and I was intrigued. I was enjoying myself and I was a
hypocrite: I couldn't decide whether I was on the side of the impatient customer or of the friend whose education was being fur-
thered. Those whiffs of Platonic perfume in a bookshop ... so old-
fashioned.

'Give him a Vauvenargues. We have him in a really magnificent
edition. Shall I show it to you?'

'A Vauvenargues?'

Cocteau's hand skimmed across the paper.

'...I wanted to introduce him to Proust...'

Jacques and Denis had pursued me even here. They were putting their tongues out at me from among the rare books. Genet had forgotten me, Cocteau hadn't noticed me there beside him.

'Shall I show you the Vauvenargues?'

'No...'

On a fresh sheet, Cocteau began stretching a slim S through that firmament of adolescent naked bodies. Another sheet, another stretching curve. Why should they not be discharges of pleasure... His pen held vertically like that ... a water-diviner's rod, penetrating the beautiful sheet of paper.

'... The Vauvenargues you mentioned, is it bound?'

'Of course, monsieur.'

'Show it to me quickly. I'm in a hurry.'

Ah, yes: 'You can bring me those letters to sign. I shall be leaving early.' He was Jacques and he was not Jacques, the customer. What bookshop does he go to—Jacques. Genet is chatting away over there, Cocteau is absorbed in his drawings, Jacques is here without being here, Denis is being given all of Proust and a bound Vauvenargues ... Why did I come here with Genet at all?

'It's magnificent, your Vauvenargues!'

'Shall I wrap it for you?'

'Oh, yes. It's a gift...'

Jean Cocteau.

Cocteau the diviner, Cocteau the source of inspiration in others, Cocteau the coach, the trainer. Photographs of Cocteau in *Comoedia*, sketches of Serge Diaghilev, of Nijinsky, of Stravinsky by Cocteau, glittering plumes from the fakir Cocteau's turban, his supercharged gems reaching me even in my provincial town. Cocteau's reckless phrases, Cocteau's *Opium*, Cocteau's sharp profile, Cocteau's ascetic nose, Cocteau's *Enfants Terribles*, Cocteau's *Parents Terribles*, Cocteau's electricity, Cocteau's dynamite, Cocteau's magnetism, Cocteau's long fingers and long eloquent hands, Cocteau and Radiguet on the beach at Mimizan...

'Georges!'

'Yes.'

'Can you deliver this package for me out to Passy?'

'Why not?'

'I can't see your bike anywhere.'

'It's parked on the rue de Beaujolais. Shall I go now or have my break first?'

'Have your break. You can go after that.'

Another impatient customer? Another friend?

There was one aspect of Cocteau's appearance that I had been following closely, with untiring fidelity, for more than twenty years: those slender wrists so tightly clasped in the supple cuffs of his shirts. If a picture of Cocteau appeared in a newspaper, I threw myself at those wrists immediately. The comfort, the rectitude of a wrist tightly clasped in its band of cloth. Did he pull the material tight with infinite care, as though he had slit open his veins? Or was it merely a detail in a dandy's dress?

Cocteau's nose astonished me in all his photos. It was someone else's nose, because it was the nose of a hermit, of someone profoundly silent, of a moralizer. His nose freed me from the tyranny of my own; it laid down a rule of life for me; it helped me to understand the frivolity of my messy and disordered laments about the ugliness of my face. I looked at it a long while in every photo, that long nose. Always held up to the wind, always sniffing for the scent of a new talent, his nose. His profile brought me such comfort, the comfort you get from knowing you have a well-sharpened pencil at the beginning of an ethics lecture, the comfort you get from whittling down maxims in a pencil sharpener ...

How was I to say good afternoon to him? Good afternoon, Jean Cocteau ... Too familiar. Good afternoon, monsieur ... Too ceremonious.

'Good afternoon,' I said under my breath.

He lifted his head without abandoning the trajectory of his line.

'Darling, have you just been standing there? You should've said. How do you like my drawings?'

I wondered whether the laxity of his speech was studied or not. I preferred his ceremonious nose. But his instant familiarity warmed my heart.

I didn't answer his question. Cocteau didn't care one way or the other. He was absorbed in his work again.

'You know who I came with?' I said.

'Did you tell her how much I liked *L'Asphyxie*?' he called across the shop to Genet.

His voice was vibrant, metallic.

No, it wasn't dry, his voice, it was generous. It was like his 'You should've said.'

Genet didn't hear what Cocteau called out to him. I was in seventh heaven. Their presence was more to me than compliments, and Genet would rather joke with old shop-assistants. I didn't want Jean Genet to talk to Cocteau about my book. That would demean Genet and his genius. I understood that from the very first: a woman that writes is for him an intolerable zero. It was his duty to forget her; it was my duty to help him forget her.

Cocteau was drawing at breakneck speed, he was racing across the paper. A foot, a calf, the pen shot upwards, a slender youth. Gone his watchtower nose while the buttocks ballooned, while the sexes yawned. His cheap doodles displeased me without grieving me. I had seen some of Cocteau's beautiful, incisive portraits. That day he was simply trying to charm his paper, to titillate decrepit Barons de Charlus. His pen cascaded between their legs, dawdled at the tops of their thighs; I wouldn't, I mustn't see their bodies naked. That would be too simple. The more clothed they are, the more they disturb me. I give my soul to damnation, I thirst, I hunger in the V of their open shirts, along the broken line of their undershirt. I caress the texture of their underclothes with my eyes and morality; men, women all cease to exist. There is only delicate linen, the satisfaction of a fetishist. Their sexes, when they invite me into their homes, where are they? Sometimes beneath snow, sometimes on a branch of pussy willow. The skin of their whole bodies is a sex. These slender young figures without personality, with the cheeky faces of any Paris street-urchin, created solely for the sake of their much-publicized members, their scattering of hairs climbing upwards towards the conquest of a navel, no, they were tedious in my eyes. I prefer those masterpieces of rapidity, Cocteau's sketches of faces.

'Tell me, do you like it . . .'

'It's pretty . . .'

He didn't care what my answer was: he didn't look up to see what my eyes were saying. He had surrendered to his own speed and was no longer master of his gifts; he allowed his pen not the slightest moment's pause except when it dipped in the bottle of China ink. Squandering of a talent, heartrending proof of an artist's extravagance.

All the same, his drawing didn't stop him talking to me. He asked if I was writing, if I was happy. A strange association: writing and being happy . . .

Not that I didn't take the opportunity to complain. I complained all right. I poured out as much as I could in the way of laments while at the same time following the embroidery of a pen round the orifice of a cock, over the macarooned surface of a ball. My book wasn't selling, I hadn't a job; I had no money to live on, a little, it would soon be gone; I was alone, too alone ... Genet, at the back of the bookshop, laughed that laugh of his that is too perfect to be truly gay.

'Write a play, that will bring you some money,' Cocteau told me, without pausing as he sketched in the face of a youth with a full erection.

What a shame if Simone de Beauvoir had walked in at that moment, not concealing that she had overheard everything I'd said. I wasn't alone: she gave me a whole evening of her presence, five or six hours of her time twice a month. I was a privileged being. I wasn't dying of hunger yet, and above all I was incapable of writing a play. I didn't want to offend Cocteau. Offend Cocteau? What presumption, what ambition. He won't give me another thought once I've walked out of here. Does Jacques think about me as I'm trotting between his home and the Courcelles métro station at half past eleven in the evening? Does Jacques hear the rhythm of my soles and heels in the silence of the streets, along by the iron railings of the Parc Monceau? No. He is entering his private world of slippers, of toilet waters, of bathrobes. And also the world of Saint-Simon, of Proust, of Cervantes. No, he doesn't think about me. Twenty minutes to midnight. The park is a chaos of dark shadows, his dressing room glitters with light ... One two, one two, one two ... I have the heels on my shoes, and they are all I have. He isn't thinking about me? One two, one two, they are all I have on earth. Why should he think about me? He has taken his mind off things, now he will go to sleep.

Cocteau stopped drawing at last. 'Good afternoon, my darling,' he said to me, as though I had just walked into the shop.

Being a sorcerer, he had sensed that I like kissing people on the cheek. He stretched his neck, I kissed him.

'Why shouldn't she come and stay in my house at Milly?' he called over to Genet.

'A good idea,' Genet said without turning his head.

'Will you come?' Cocteau asked.

'Yes, I'll come,' I said, embarrassed.

*

Jean Genet was to come and have dinner in my room the day after next.

Genet is coming to dinner with Lucien, with Gérard Magestry. I advance across the floor on my knees with my dustpan and brush; it's wonderful winkling all this dust out from the cracks between my floorboards. Steel-wool pad beneath my foot, I scrape and scour, a painful labour. The Negro boy on my bottle of Miror laughs at my cleanliness as I polish the marble fireplace and count my wrinkles in the looking glass. You will have the eye, yes the sheen of a night-walking cat when he arrives, marble. And darkness will have come, with its thousands and thousands of tiny black children's heads; the darkness will look at Genet, the eye of the marble will fade. We must work, we must sweat, we must pant, we must wash down the baseboards, we must crawl across the floor for him on our knees.

*

Not the next day but the next, I opened a safety pin and used it as a compass to check the distances between my four piles of salami. Genet is a stickler for such things; he likes everything to be just so. I also checked the distances between the salami and the pieces of gherkin. If a thing is worth doing it's worth doing properly, I told myself as I hummed *Tiger Rag*. The world was my oyster. Except for my worry over the piece of sirloin. Was it marbled enough? What exactly did 'marbled' mean, applied to meat? There was always the dictionary, of course ... No, not enough time now. He'll be here soon. I pushed my finger into the piece of meat. No reaction. Its fuchsia-pink texture sank under the pressure, then slowly rose again. I dotted it with butter, I rewarded it with a sprinkling of thyme and bay.

I had only the one tablecloth. I ironed it a second time. Genet must have clean linen to rest his elbows on. The knife now, on his right? As if Genet cares. The knife on his left, then? As if he gives a damn. But I do care, I do give a damn when I am entertaining him. Not that I'd ruined myself buying the flowers: a bunch of anemones I'd found reduced. I sat down at the table, head empty, heart empty. A tired housemaid, passing through just before her employers came in to dinner, had been overcome by the whiteness of the napkins.

Limp, slimy, I dragged myself across Jacques's table to reach the silver jardinière in its centre with my bunch of anemones and their admixture of harsh leaves. Denis, I felt sure, bought the flowers for their table himself, then arranged them himself between two candle-sticks. Any paucity in the flowers themselves was made up for by the furniture and the pictures. Why didn't we collapse under the weight of roses when I went with Genet to eat at Jacques's house? Surely Genet was worth a greenhouseful of lily-of-the-valley in mid-winter. The carefulness of a wealthy man filled me with sudden anger. I forgot that if the rich were to give you all they have, they wouldn't be rich.

I was half dead with fatigue after my long cleaning session; my weariness was making me bitter: a sandwich on a greasy table would have satisfied him.

A ring at the door. Him.

It was Gérard Magestry, Madeleine Castaing's brother.

'Is he here?' he asked.

The door across the passage had just closed. Someone had been looking to see who was calling on me. I was being spied on.

'Have you seen Jacques recently?' Gérard Magestry asked.

He is an old schoolfriend of Jacques. He made his way over to the table laid ready in the room.

He sat down on the divan and accepted my offer of vermouth.

'How is it he's not here yet?' he asked again.

Gérard Magestry had met Genet at a dinner given by Jacques.

After so much preparation I couldn't find the glasses, then I had to disappear in search of a corkscrew. I found Gérard Magestry on my return looking through *Ruysbroeck l'Admirable,* which he had picked up off my coffee table.

'Are you reading *Ruysbroeck?'* he asked in very reverent tones.

'On and off,' I said in embarrassment.

I gave a sigh of relief when he put the book down again. Genet might arrive at any moment and the book would have irritated him. He would have taken us for blue-stockings. I handed Gérard Magestry the corkscrew.

He opened the bottle of vermouth, then smiled at the ordered symmetry of my salami slices.

I ran out into the kitchen. I had been preparing this meal since the evening before and the cress for my soup still wasn't pounded. I wondered what I could have been thinking of.

The blow of a fist on the door.

And the soup still not ready, I said to the biggest lump of butter on the sirloin.

I opened for Jean Genet.

'How are things?' he said.

His air of health. His ease of manner. His self-possession. His nonchalance. His peremptory tone. His presence, as perfect as a perfectly tied knot. Yes, a definitive presence. A storm shower sweeping away all your mists. Genet pumped oxygen into the city, into the apartment, into my existence. Lucien came in after him.

'It's not bad, this place of yours,' Genet said.

'Do you think so?' I answered.

He stood there, grey suède gloves on his hands, beige suède shoes on his feet, English-looking topcoat with raglan sleeves and tiny check on his back.

'I invited Gérard Magestry . . .'

'Ah, you invited Gérard Magestry too?' he mimicked mockingly, intrigued and won over.

They all sat talking together in my room while I got on with the meal. Lucien came and asked if he could help. What a treasure of discretion, a sudden, silent apparition there beside me. A sprig of thyme to season your heart, that Lucien. A precise presence, a tousled presence. He could inquire without asking questions; he just used those mischievous eyes. The grace and gay whirl of a Fourteenth of July. His one wish in life was to build houses. Genet was enchanted by that ambition and was helping him. Genet loathes literary people. He prefers people who work with their hands. He has his feet on the ground. Other than my mother, I can think of no one who is less a dreamer than he.

The oven had been hot a long while and the walls were covered with condensation. Lucien put the sirloin in the oven. I moved into action. I beat, I banged, I thumped the cress in the mortar with my pestle. That green pulp of pulps came to my rescue. The finer the pulp I could reduce it to, the less Genet would reduce me to zero. Lucien suggested opening the window, both because of the din I was making and because of the heat from the oven. They were quarrelling, bellowing their heads off in the kitchen opposite. Lucien closed the window again.

'Is he in a good mood?' I asked Lucien under my breath.

'Oh, in a very good mood,' Lucien said loudly.

'How nice you can be!' I said to Lucien in a whisper.

Someone was tiptoeing towards us. Genet? That would be too much. He's going to catch us. But what are we doing wrong? I didn't dare look to see who was coming.

'Your tom-tom, my children, it's becoming a bit wearisome . . .'

Gérard Magestry . . . and not only that, but the singsong tones of Maurice Sachs. Ah, what a glow of friendship I began to feel for this

man who was talking out there in my room, who was keeping
Genet company, who had allowed me to stun myself with a pestle
and a pile of cress.

'I've finished,' I told him proudly.

Gérard Magestry disappeared again. After the waltz of the skim-
ming ladle, the waltz of the fresh cream in the cress soup. Four
odd soup plates in Lucien's hands, the ladle and the saucepan in
mine.

'You go first,' I told Lucien.

He set off with a nonchalant tread; I took cover behind him.

'I hope you've been helping Violette,' Genet said to him.

Genet's affection and kindness tilted towards Lucien.

'I think you'll like it,' I said to Genet.

I displayed my cream of watercress.

'Jean doesn't like soup,' Lucien whispered in my ear.

'Is it good?' Genet asked.

I sank like a stone: he was turning the pages of *Ruysbroeck
l'Admirable*.

'I dunno ... Haven't read it ...'

I was speaking badly on purpose. So as to melt, so as to vanish.

Gérard Magestry looked me in the eyes: he sensed my embarrassment. Lucien went into the kitchen to have a look at the sirloin;
Gérard Magestry's eyes followed Lucien's departure with a hint of
yearning that made me sad.

Genet laid the book back on the coffee table and smiled an ironic
smile. Pages turned by a woman's fingers; that meant pages sullied,
pages infected with stupidity. *Ruysbroeck*? So much cock if I'd had
the presumption to read it. I didn't say to myself: Genet never
comes outside himself; therefore, Genet is unable to interest himself in what I read. I said to myself: I am a woman; therefore, I am
a piece of grit scratching his eye. Supposing I were to cut my
throat, supposing my head were to roll at his feet without splashing
his suède shoes ... I should nevertheless still be a woman, a mould
for pressing out children. Genet takes Lucien in his arms, to hell
with repopulation.

I asked him if he would like to sit down at the table.

He sat opposite me. I was between Lucien and Gérard Magestry,
sitting on the edge of the divan.

'I'll help you to the soup, Genet. Shall I?'

He didn't reply.

I served him with my cream of watercress with devotion. I served him first. I understand it now. I was ladling non-earthly sustenance into his plate: the space between his sentences with the white eyes of the salami; the blood of his poems in his glass of wine; and on the sliced gherkin his own excrement when, as a little boy, he sat educating himself as he shat and gazed at Nijinsky's face before wiping his bottom. I gave the leftovers to Gérard Magestry, Lucien, and myself. I watched him eat. He is a rebel, he has no time to savour his food. How would I know what he talked about? I had the joy of having him sitting there in my home. I couldn't work out why the dimpled hands, the short fingers of this Genet so prestigious in his grief and his pain were like those of Maurice Sachs. Sachs devoured, Sachs engulfed. Genet is never out of his depth, Genet is a judge.

'I can't change the plates because these are all I have,' I told them, delighted at being able to confess it.

'Why should you want to change them?' Genet said wearily.

He eyed my bedside lamp. 'Who gave you that?'

'Madeleine Castaing. Do you like it?'

'It's not bad,' Genet said.

'How did you guess someone gave it me?'

'He guessed, that's all,' Gérard Magestry put in.

I looked at Gérard Magestry. He was smoothing things over.

Lucien followed me out into the kitchen and plonked a kiss on my cheek. He could sense how uncomfortable I was feeling and how hard I was trying, this twenty-year-old little boy. But what was all that chattering and twittering? It was coming from the sirloin on its dish in the oven. Gaily chattering, mindlessly twittering, the rich sauce was wholly ignorant of Jean Genet. Lucien opened the door of the oven. His eyes shone: he was young, he was hungry. He closed the oven again.

'Jean is very fond of you,' he told me.

He gave me another kiss.

'Jean'; a miraculous draught, a bulging net when Lucien, rubbed with garlic and basil, with sage and rosemary, pronounced Genet's first name.

We cut into the meat. Cooked to perfection. I regained confidence somewhat.

'You carry it in,' I told Lucien.

'No, you,' said Lucien, wanting to boost my self-importance.

Gérard Magestry, having crept over without a sound, was watching us.

'Don't leave him alone in there,' I said in terror.

I placed the salad bowl in Magestry's arms, the dish of creamed potatoes in Lucien's. We set off in high procession.

Jean Genet sat all alone at the table deep in thought. I halted with the sirloin held out in front of me in the doorway. I was brimming over with gratitude. Genet was using my chair I had polished for him, my floor scoured with steel wool for him, my ashtray ... Genet was smoking a Gitane with the patience and amiable resignation of a husband, a lover. Genet in my room, in the chiaroscuro of my bedside table, took up so little space ...

He stubbed out his Gitane.

'Light the candles,' I told Lucien.

We laid down our dishes in turn. I sat down opposite a man who was changing. He seemed in a bad temper despite his silence.

Gérard Magestry carved the sirloin; Lucien was talking and joking, Genet riposted without zest. I like the way his forehead is losing its covering, the way his hair is greying so early. The little stiff hairs on the neck of a man going bald—a veil. My transparent veil on the first page of *Miracle de la Rose*.

'You first,' Gérard Magestry said to me.

'Are you mad? I shall serve Genet first ...'

'As you wish.'

Jean Genet raised his head and communicated with Lucien. He was exasperated but he controlled himself.

I seized his plate, I placed it on mine. All eyes were on me except Genet's. He had lowered his gaze, his complexion was becoming muddy: I was embarrassing with my unguents and my vaselines. Before long, I would be buttering his penis for him to improve his appetite. I picked out the best piece of meat.

'Take the flowers out of our way,' I said to Lucien.

He removed the anemones.

A hole, Genet, shall I make you a hole? A hole for the sauce in your creamed potatoes. I am fortifying your prose with all this cooking of mine, I am your nurse bringing you juicy meat, I am nursing your ceremonies, your solemnities. Compost, fertilizer, manure for the rosebush, you could never number its flowers; they are the words in the books of Jean Genet. They bloom by day, by night, today, tomorrow, in the future. Every day, every night a reader opens a Genet book, discovers Jean Genet. The reader is a rosebush too; his flowers open to receive Genet's words. That is what I felt as I served Genet.

'Why are you paying attention to no one but me? I'm not the only one here,' he said in a fury.

I heard the words from a distance, from a great distance; from my galley already far out at sea.

Gérard Magestry poured wine for us all. We set to and ate with good appetite, without taking any notice of Genet's silence. The atmosphere was growing heavy.

I kept my ears pricked while I washed the plates in the kitchen. Was he talking, was he brightening up? Genet wasn't talking.

'Carry in the gâteau,' I told Lucien.

Lucien came out with me each time and supported me. He didn't say so, but he was trying to keep me from becoming depressed and collapsing.

'You're the one who ought to carry it,' he said.

I carried in the gâteau. It was called 'Autumn Leaves.' Coiling, uncoiling, convex, concave flakes of chocolate hid a treasure in their heart. Just as dead leaves hide little pools of flowers in February.

'I won't serve you,' I said to Genet, 'since you prefer to help yourself . . .'

I said it without rancour, with perfidy, without animosity. I who will never succeed in being simple with him—at that moment I was. My logic filled me with a sense of well-being. I was doing what he wanted.

I served Lucien and Gérard Magestry. Then Genet took his share of gâteau last.

I remember, we were just setting out on our conquest of 'Autumn Leaves,' with forks poised. I raised my eyes. I wanted to see if Genet was enjoying the gâteau I'd bought. Jean Genet was fixing me with a stare so hard that his face was shrinking, creasing. I looked for his generous mouth and nose, his ever-fresh eyes. He presented me with the crumpled sketch of a fetus, the skimped face of a pygmy. That instant lasted an eternity.

He rose from the table, pulling the tablecloth towards him.

'Come on, Lucien, we're fucking off.'

They left the flat at a run, amid the muffled noise of bottles rolling on the floor, amid the crackling noise of breaking plates, amid the frivolous noise of shattering glass.

We were sitting one next the other on the edge of the divan, we were sitting at a naked table. Wine was running from the two overturned bottles, being absorbed by the polished floorboards. Eagerly, the wine was running over towards the window, the rivulets meeting, forming lakes, stains, threads of blackish blood. Ah! that reek of boozy women in my room.

I began to tremble.

I turned my head towards Gérard Magestry. He hasn't particularly astonishing eyes. He has eyes. In which, at that instant, I saw an impulse, an intensity of effort to love and rescue his neighbour. It was a supplication: I mustn't suffer.

'Get dressed,' he said. 'We'll take a taxi, we'll go to his hotel.'

They seemed quite useless to me—his plan, his decision; but the sheer speed of his reaction saved me from collapse.

I got up from the table. Red wine cascaded off my smock, the same blue-and-white checked smock I had been wearing the day Genet brought Jacques to see me. I could see how it had happened: Genet had tilted the table towards me as he got up, before pulling the tablecloth with him as he went. I skirted a kind of bizarre rockery: porridge with rubble sticking out of it...

'Gérard Magestry!' I wanted to shout to shake off the nightmare. No voice came.

He was waiting for me at the door.

Where to hold on, what to hold on to? My building, with the same abruptness Genet had shown, my whole building tilted forwards till it met the building on the other side of the street. Walls, doors, windows were joining against me, because I had been punished without having done anything to deserve it. It was the greatest affront of my life. I didn't stumble, I didn't lose my balance, I was too sad, I was too old, I looked down at my feet. Coiling, uncoiling, convex, concave flakes of chocolate made me think of cockroaches in a pool of blood; drops of wine still slithered down my smock, falling on the red blotches below.

The two buildings parted as abruptly as they had met; a refinement of cruelty. I was too lucid to lose my balance. A sound of squealing brakes in the street, the street that Genet had fled into; it was a taxi howling in pain. I still couldn't get out Gérard Magestry's name.

I wanted him to come for me, to take me away from those spoons lying unharmed on the floor.

At last I left the room, I abandoned the wine soaked tablecloth on the floor. I followed Gérard into the still-unfurnished other room, I held out my wrists in the tight clasp of my smock cuffs. Gérard Magestry took off my smock, a reddened rag. He looked for my coat while I made signs to show him where. He couldn't find the door of the closet.

I was howling without Gérard's being able to hear. The smock sodden with spilt wine ... I didn't want to part from my smock, from my six o'clock in the evening: me all alone, me all nice and clean, cleaning the watercress on my lap. What a success my dinner was then!

Gérard Magestry found my coat. I left everything to him, humble in my weariness. I offered him my arms, I offered him my back, I offered him the buttons of my coat even, so that he could help me. He went out first.

'Where is the switch for the stairs light?' he asked.

'There isn't one. Don't fall, whatever you do...'

'Come on,' Gérard Magestry said, 'come on ... Don't let's waste time!'

'I'm coming, I'm coming, Gérard Magestry...'

'We can pick up a taxi at the intersection,' I said. 'At the Faidherbe-Chaligny intersection.'

I switched on the light in the passageway. I was afraid he would have to wade through garbage. The passageway stank because of the refuse the tenants scattered around the trash bins.

We came out into the street. From the black sky completely relinquished to the darkness there fell such great, such heavy drops ... A cat fled. No, it wasn't raining, Gérard Magestry wasn't wet. A louring sky, a wicked sky refreshing my memory: he had run out of my room, he couldn't stand me, he had fucked off. Gérard Magestry kept up a steady pace, and I jogged to keep up with him. We were going to try to see him again. Doors, garages, wood partitions, windowsills, advertisements painted on a grocer's iron partition ... My street. Rue Paul-Bert. I trotted on with my eyes fixed on Gérard Magestry, on his long nose, on the sharp outline of his long nose. It glowed with a gentle ardour, with a gentle eagerness. Gérard Magestry's long nose, that night—the hope of flight into happiness. My pain, my grief ... a meditation in the chiaroscuro of the rue Paul-Bert. An omen if our faces are birds.

We found a taxi at the Faidherbe-Chaligny intersection.

'Where does he live?' Gérard Magestry asked.

'The Hôtel de la Fleur de Lis, near the Bibliothèque Nationale.'

We didn't exchange a single word during the journey.

Gérard Magestry took my arm to help me over the threshold of the hotel. Was I going into hospital?

The night porter checked to see if the keys were there. 'He's in his room. I don't know whether I can disturb him...'

'Why not?' Gérard Magestry said, looking me in the eye.

The porter telephoned up.

'He doesn't answer,' he said.

Gérard Magestry took my arm again. 'Keep ringing, and say we're down here waiting...'

His face swelled with generosity. There are so many ways of weeping without shedding tears. Gérard Magestry was weeping by giving me his arm.

'You can go up,' the porter said.

The situation was changing; Gérard Magestry released my arm. He smiled so broadly, his mouth nearly reached his ears. Two small children flew over to a hotel staircase.

'Knock,' Gérard Magestry said when we were outside his door.

'I don't dare.'

He knocked for me and we went in.

Genet, on his back, was lying with his eyes open, with his shirt generously gaping. I shall not be ashamed of what I am going to write. He who gives does not go mad. I fell on my knees beside the divan, close to the silver wires tangling in the V of his shirt. I worshipped him, before looking at him, before speaking to him. My worship went beyond Jean Genet. I lifted my head at last for my sun. Chin pressed against his chest, Genet was lying resting, looking straight ahead of him. Then, without restraint, still on my knees, I took him in my arms. I covered his neck, his cheeks with kisses. Genet inspired me with extraordinary forbearance. Kneeling beside his bed, I asked his forgiveness for what he had done to me.

'Is it over now?' I asked him.

'...'

'Is it over? Is it really all over?'

'...'

I covered his neck, his face with more kisses.

'Yes, it's all over,' Genet said.

More kisses, more more, you are dead, love, more kisses, more more, kisses right into the depths of your eyes; they are often pale grey. It is agonizing for me; we are reconciled, yet there is a void behind your eyes. Love, quivering mirror, your eyes, love, I sway, you are alone, there is no help for it, it is you who are intimidating the desert, and yet you do have your bed to go to sleep on all the same.

'May I telephone you?'

'Yes. Telephone.'

I was exploiting him from my knees, I was extorting another reconciliation for the future.

Genet, without expression, chin on chest, meditating behind drooping eyelids, bore with me.

Gérard Magestry helped me to my feet.

I said good night to Jean Genet and he stroked my hair. Was he dreaming he was tender?

*

The flat reeked of wine. My doors, my walls, my windowpanes, my window frames: gusts of stale wine. The abominable smell was a lie: Genet isn't a drinker. I let myself fall veeeery gently, I pulled my gloves on veeeeery slowly; the building opposite stared at me with its cold eyes. Poor wretch, you keep on and on, you do your duty; it just hasn't got through to you, has it, that time is nothing, that it's the fragility of the night that counts. He had come into the bar of the Pont-Royal with his gloved hands, the ivy streamed from the urns the first time. I went to see Jacques. Hurt. Hurt ever so. Still hurt? Yes, still hurt. I am limp and pull myself together into a heap. What have I done to them? They obsess me, they occupy my thoughts all the time. I love and I ought to be silent. Is there going to be an end to this business with Genet? Genet can't stand me, that is the end of the business. For them my lakes of sadness beneath my eyelids, for them my cool wells of love. For them. Take off your gloves. Love? Always always love? To throw our death off the scent? The hollow beneath my tongue is a pit of misfortune. Long nights, long days, November rains, December rains, I love Jacques and will never have done with loving him. *Miserere, miserere.* You stretch yourself out through the centuries, you recline on them, my sadness. As though spattered, as though vaguely spattered with a desire for myself. Don't seduce me, don't tempt me, Violette. Not here, not now, not on the marble and the floorboards. You can take refuge in that at any hour of the day or the night; therefore, you have not been utterly abandoned. Yes, I have myself, nothing but myself. I am stirred by that idea, and that stirring deep inside me is a harbinger. I yield to its suggestion. Thickets quiver; they are my uncertainty, they are my certainty before I begin. I can dream of nothing but that, I can look forward to nothing but that tonight, and in the nights to come.

I open.

I open, stretched out on marble, on floorboards. My darkness vanishes. A light is in my limbs, I shall see my fever and its quivering.

My arms stretched, my feet in my shoes, a clawing of metal against my flesh: my suspender-belt clips. My knees too tightly held in my stockings, my condition.

My stockings, my suspender belt, my shoes, a refuge, several refuges, my old age, my old ages, you forced yourselves on me, now I am going to forget you. I pull off my gloves.

My dark shadows are not fluttering in shreds, they have left me. Sometimes I want to see in a mirror with the electricity turned on.

Fully dressed. Bundled up. On marble and deal boards. Free and yet driven, keeping fierce watch. I set out, I am a sentinel. I listen to the murmurs in my belly. That weight of pleasure, before the pleasure, will expand into a cloud. Too many shooting stars, ah, too many.

I check my gloves in my pockets, just like that, for no reason, for the sheer pleasure of an unnecessary precaution.

My hand. There she is, sweet little thing on the floorboards, my ignorant darling. They can cut it off if they like. I should still find myself with my meat.

I think about it. I close my eyes, I wonder whether the comet will agree. I invite it, we will whirl in the heavens together. My finger. My rubber of stars. The comet will come down. Down even to my ankles.

The sleeve of my coat is brushing against the back of my hand. It's not the first time. My elbow is not free enough.

Humidity, scraped flower. My secret language is beneath my eyelid. I shall be broken, I shall be blessed. I shall be a couple torn apart.

I hesitate. My head swims with the suspense.

Conspiracy. I contain a continent of clouds. A conspiracy in my entrails. I shall be powdered. In my legs and in my feet. A raving madness down there where nothing speaks. I shall be a dawn and I shall be minced chitterlings.

Fully clothed, fully shod. I burgle my sex. I plunder my caresses. I steal what belongs to me.

I was walking in the meadows, a book in my hand. I was far away from everything, I looked at everything, I looked around everywhere. The weight was trying to fall between my legs. I desire, am only able to desire, myself. Sparrow, you fly away, but do not blame me. I stretched out in the grass, I held the open book near my face, a handkerchief was hiding my hand, and I watched the material as it moved.

The brain is in a vice, a narrow narrow prison. Let reason go. Dignity? Self-criticism? I am not here, my soul has taken flight some other where.

My little Madonna. My little hand. Who can console me? Me on me. Me with me.

Submerged, shipwrecked, I am controlling my own shipwreck.

I bathe my finger in my heaven.

I ought to have been keeping watch on the grass around me, on the beautiful weather, on a tall stalk nodding in the middle of the fields.

Sinking into a delicious chill, into the infernal heat of the allegro.

I am losing my strength, I am unfolding. Radiations from my sex, dusting of gold through my skeleton.

The horse looked at me, I looked at the horse. Electricity in the horse's coat, my contractions. His eyelashes, nostrils, silken shimmer, lack of interest, departure, and the stability of his whole world. I was abandoning nothing.

Three in the afternoon. Kneeling in front of the dead stove just before it snowed. The grey sky has taken over everything. It's going to snow. Strange, the cold air on the back of my hand.

The heart, the terrible heat. In my waking dream it was hot. A white sky, an absence. Cocks fighting. Above the poplar, above the cypress, the heat. A village asleep, a roof of geraniums keeping vigil, a blanket of fire over me. I closed my eyes to reach an ever more sharply etched inferno of heat, my heart was beating too fast. I failed. My head took refuge in the hollow of my shoulder. I offered my hands to the arrows of the heat. I am a null thing; is it a punishment?

Sordid hotel bedrooms tamed till they became as gentle as angora rabbits. Questionable sheets, an invitation. The table with its protective circle of plate glass. I set down my case. Hidden deep in the bed I caressed my solitude; it was a cradle for my poverty, since I had just arrived from my dishwater-coloured province. You'll never dare come out of yourself, the table and its glass circle told me. I did come out of myself; and I did victorious battle with the everyday.

My naked face in my darkness, my stretched neck. Someone has been unhappy but is now unhappy no longer. Unhappy no longer, and yet everything has gone out. I am facing myself and yet I am not giddy. I am going to scratch like an animal.

My coat opened. Rustle of falling soot, rustling inside a belly. I threw my panties as far from me as I could.

I shall succeed in grasping the agonies in my being, I shall succeed in taking them by the throat. That is what I believe. I am young every time.

My wide abundance, my panorama. My floral kingdom and my butcher's stall, I cannot see you. My skirt, my suspender belt, my shoes.

Freed of my panties, I am free of everything. I told myself that, and yet, oh mystery, my misery continued to unfold.

I shall sink to the bottom of the seas, I shall fall back on my straw.

My mechanism, my vertigo. My speed, my zenith. My legs, my pastels. It will all rot me away, it will all destroy me.

The avalanche of unreality. The vast sun of absence.

Hermine told me she'd learned from reading a book by Freud. Discovering she had made love to herself before she knew me somehow upset me. Later, when Hermine was already making preparations for her escape, I was forced to be absent one Thursday. That evening I asked her what she'd found to do with herself. 'I pulled the curtains and made love to myself,' she answered. I was shattered. What could I be jealous of in that? How could I not be enamoured of such frankness? It shocked me just how far apart we had moved. She vanished, and I tried to prove myself her equal, somewhat shyly, with a certain fictive element, a shred of morality, a tattered remnant of modesty. Later I made love to myself with daring, with perseverance, with immodesty, with studied postures. I closed the curtains one Thursday afternoon, I stretched out on the divan as she had stretched out on it. I wanted to imitate her in order to have my revenge upon her. I have never told that incident till now. I have taken off a gag. An absurd gag. If someone had caught me in the act, if he or she had told, then I should have fallen ill from the shame. At first I believed I was damning myself. I didn't say to myself: chastity and repression drive people mad. I said: these are nasty habits that you must rid yourself of or keep quiet about. You who are solitary, accursed, cut off from the world, the martyrs of loneliness, do not condemn yourselves for so small a thing. I shall soon be sixty. I am rather proud than otherwise to make it known that my vigour still returns to me several times a year. I yield to that dizzying monotony. But there is no shore of tenderness to rest on afterwards, as after an act of love between two. The fire burns everything.

One morning my concierge, a forthright, buxom woman, knocked on my door and handed me an envelope bearing the postmark of a town in Brittany. I knew no one in Brittany. I walked across the unfurnished room, I turned on the light. Some man or woman I did not know had written to me, care of Gallimard ... I had two addresses. I couldn't get over it. Perhaps, after all, I was a writer, then ... A writer who sold a copy of *L'Asphyxie* from time to time. I laid the envelope on my lap. Black ink, too black. No, I'm not a writer. Small, unexceptional writing. Black ink, that means a writer attached to what he writes. I close my notebook and forget it. My notebook doesn't exist when I go down into the cellar of the Vieux-Colombier to listen to Sidney Bechet and Claude Luter ...

I opened the envelope. The letter was signed Patrice. He liked *L'Asphyxie*, could he write me another letter? He lived locked up in modern literature; what solitude in his letter, from start to finish ... He wouldn't be an adolescent if he weren't alone, imprisoned inside himself. He had read my book. Was a reader a prey upon which I was now about to hurl myself? I reread his letter, I was tempted by the abyss that yawns between a woman of forty and a youth of seventeen. I couldn't escape the fact: my youth was that of others. I would be forced to chill, to refrigerate the girl I had once been if I wanted to reply to this stranger. A fevered boy in boarding school had read my book. I was flattered. I looked down into the street. There were women of my age coming out of the grocer's, out of the butcher's, out of the hardware store. They were snapping their purses shut, they were slipping their purchases into their bags, they were retying the scarves on their heads. They all looked alike, they were all, already, concentrating on the next meal to be cooked. I left the window. I rejected their prudence, yet not wanting to be imprudent either. At twenty-five I should have left this letter unanswered. At fifty I should have closed the correspondence with two definitive lines.

I wrote back to this fevered young man. I thanked him quite straightforwardly, but then, fearing to lose him before getting to know him, instead of writing: 'You aren't happy.' I wrote: 'I wonder whether you are happy.' That was the only point at which I became devious, at which I deliberately trained a bait. How hot my cheeks and forehead would have burned, what shame I would have felt if Simone de Beauvoir at that moment, or Jacques, had leaned over to read my letter. For I was being unfaithful to them both. I decided not to tell them about Patrice's letter. Something really new: a man, a youngster, was writing to me; a man, a youngster, couldn't see my face. My tone became stern again as I demanded to know once more, at the end of the letter, if he was really unhappy. It was my way of flirting, of introducing a note of flattering interest in an in-between zone where everything is possible, where everything is impossible. Then at the very end of my letter I gave him what I gave Simone de Beauvoir and Jacques, my enthusiasm for Van Gogh's letters to his brother Théo. I was planning a careful campaign. My formula for signing off was a snitch. I wrote: 'With sympathetic interest.' That 'sympathetic interest' had come to me originally from André Gide, to whom I had myself written a letter when I was sixteen ... I always use his phrase now. I took my letter to the post office on the rue des Boulets.

*

Paul Morihen, the bookseller-publisher, stopped his automobile in the centre of the little town and dropped me there with his errand boy. We skirted the pillars of the covered market. Order held sway in the little square of Milly. The place was like a Flemish interior; there were brass cauldrons glittering against tiles.

I fell immediately and passionately in love with the little cul-de-sac street where Cocteau lived. I have a passion for provincial streets that close up like buds, that become aloof as soon as a human step is heard. I staggered; every blade of grass, insolently green, was like a sword protruding between two cobbles. The door had an air of such simplicity ... My heart was beating too hard. I waited for Georges to ring the bell. I shouldn't have accepted the invitation. I turned my head; the grass was so energetic. In what world had Cocteau asked my advice before choosing this street that was now my street, my cobbles, my silence, my wall of silence? The door opened. Why run away, I had agreed to come. I walked in, less simple than the door.

'Cocteau isn't back from the studio yet,' Paul Morihen told us.

At that very instant, someone inside the house switched on the outside lights. A stage was flooded with light ten yards from us: a kitchen garden so well-kept it made you almost weep with love. Grey-green ribbons combed across the earth: the unruly leaves of leeks, a riot of verdigris shavings. I had only just arrived and already I was away.

'Georges! Come and help me pour the Pernods!' Paul Morihen called from inside the house.

Georges hurried inside.

Cocteau was shooting *Ruy Blas* in a Paris studio. Was that true? Was it really not him training a floodlight on the flowers? Snapdragons, lupins, stocks, flax, toadflax, mulleins, balsams, rosebushes, all accommodating themselves to the society of salads and cabbages, and all redoubling their preciosity thereby.

I went in; someone switched off the floodlights. Had Cocteau given orders? Had every detail of my arrival been planned? I liked the tiny hall. My path was blocked by closed doors on every side. My heart was beating still harder: the sixteen-year-old in Valenciennes who had admired Jean Cocteau's hands in *Comoedia*, in *Les Nouvelles Littéraries*, was standing in his home.

'Do you like ice in your Pernod?' Paul Morihen called to me.

'Even more ice in the evening!' I said.

Paul Morihen and Georges laughed. There were twenty years between me and Georges, fifteen between me and Morihen. Their laughter could not but be arrogant. I had never had a real youth and now, without a word, without a sigh, without handing over a cent, I had to pay for the youth of others. I was neither cruelly disappointed nor dismally afraid. That which had to come was coming. Though I was growing old, I still hoped to go to the land of the children who cling together in the métro, in the cinema, under the porches of houses ... To hope that, at the age of forty, was worse than growing old. It was trying to jump on a moving train with crutches. What was I to do with my raincoat? Cocteau's suitcase terrified me. My knitted top from Jacques Fath restored my confidence. Those two young brutes might tear me to pieces. Be careful, they're both sporty types. The dining room in Milly? A little circular casket, an austere candy box, a tower in a little round coffer. The pale walls, the round table, the unpretentious chairs warmed me the way my newly ironed nightdress warms me. I was where I belonged, even though I wasn't at home.

'Shall we see him this evening?' I asked Paul Morihen.

'No, he'll be back sometime during the night.'

In those days Paul Morihen looked like Errol Flynn. A neat little moustache, shined with shoe-blacking.

They began trying to knock one another over.

We carry within us, from the beginning to the end, all that we have received. Alone, and in the company of two young puppies engaged in mock battle, I sat in Jean Cocteau's dining room and drank the first Pernod mixed for me by Gabriel on the marble table-top of a café, in the Place Péreire. I wondered what I expected from this dining room in which two young men were letting off their excess energy, as I had wondered what was expected of me then by a man to whom there was nothing I wanted to give.

Paul Morihen vanished to see about dinner. We drank a second Pernod, they began rough-housing again. The second Pernod made me sad: we were three profiteers: Cocteau, at least sixty then, was slaving late into the night while we were drinking his drinks, wearing out his chairs, dirtying his glasses. On the Place Péreire I accepted what a poor man gave me without thought; now I was soul-searching on account of a writer who was certainly not a pauper. I was getting old: any posy thrown into my lap impressed me. Gabriel had made sacrifices for me: that was nothing to a cynical young man. Cocteau was being generous to me: that was something extraordinary to the worshipper of a famous name.

The housekeeper, a pleasant person with white satin hair, served us a simple and excellent meal.

'You're sleeping in Jean Marais's room,' Paul Morihen told me.

Plain Jane, you're going to snore in the bed of an idol.

The two young men made it clear that they did not desire to prolong the evening with me. Georges seized the handle of my old suitcase and we went upstairs. On the way I noticed Cocteau drawings, Bérard drawings on the walls, but I didn't dare stop to look.

The bedroom was beautiful. Too ceremonial. The mahogany Empire furniture inspired me with too much respect for comfort. And so, in a quarter of an hour's time, I would be stretched out in the bed of a hero, I would be laying my head on the pillow of Tristan, the Tristan of *L'Eternel Retour*. I abandoned the great mahogany bed, I made myself stop wandering around it like a stableboy around his horse. My suitcase. I had been parachuted into this miraculous room, yet I had eyes only for my case. I emptied its contents out onto the Empire table. The room was suddenly taken over by beloved smells stealing back at an inopportune moment. That too-languorous smell of fresh meat, the rustic smell of fresh butter. I closed my case up again. I wanted to hide it to protect it and keep it from all that ceremony. I explored the dressing room, looking for a closet, a cupboard. Yes, I permitted myself to pronounce the common word 'closet' in that place.

The sliding door slid open without sound, the interior lit up just as the kitchen garden had lit up at my arrival. Displayed were russet suède shorts, cinnamon suède shorts, beige suède shorts, with fringes, with flaps: Jean Marais's Tyrolean costumes for *L'Aigle à deux têtes*. Silence is sometimes a tempter. I stood for a long time, in the silence of his dressing room, fingering the flap covering the swelling of his sex; I felt the edge of the short suède leg where it was pressed by the hard muscles of his thigh, I touched the suspenders, the horizontal bands that pressed against his athletic torso. I could hear the slightly husky, almost common voice of Jean Marais, I was outlining the profile of a hero with my thumb and forefinger. A fagged-out face, a fagged-out voice, I said to myself as I stroked the suède, which is itself a soft, fagged-out sort of leather. I stroked the russet suède, the beige suède, the cinnamon suède with the steady rhythm of a pendulum; I felt nothing stir inside me, and yet, having Jean Marais's tired face in front of my eyes like that began to exhaust me.

My lovely curlers, my lovely lengths of dark and greasy string, shall I dare to use them? Would I dare to inflict them on Jean

Marais's hollow cheek on the pillow? If I sacrifice my little curls, tomorrow I shall have to appear before Cocteau with lank hair. I opted for my frizzers, and proffered the movie star my pity. He had no idea that a scarecrow was sliding down between his sheets while he faced the cameras. One question kept me awake in the darkness. Where was Cocteau's room? Would I go into it? Would he show it to me? It was kilometres away from me. A noise. I sat up. Was Cocteau back from Paris? Was he climbing the stairs? No sound. The house was sinking. I switched the light back on: not bad, my notebooks ... not bad at all on the Empire table; but the table in the middle of the room, that wasn't good at all. I wanted it in front of the window, in front of the sky, in front of the kitchen-garden. I got out of bed, I dragged it over, inch by inch, so that no one would know what I was doing, at midnight, in someone else's house. It was where I had imagined it; now I felt a little more at home. I switched off the light before getting back into bed: I wanted to spare that noble bed the spectacle of an ugly woman clambering into it wearing a flannelette nightdress. I could not spare it the contact of my long legs, my long arms. I sighed for a hot-water bottle. Now I had to sleep if I wanted to be in a good mood next day. I pushed my earplugs into my ears. One o'clock in the morning at Milly. I couldn't sleep. Was Cocteau back from the studio? Half past one. As I sink into sleep—is that the sound of his step in his house?

*

Seven in the morning. Too early to get up when you're a guest. The house was dead before; now it is resting. I have slept; I confuse my sleep with a brilliant feat of some kind. The daylight is singing, the daylight is chattering outside despite the thick, lined curtains. Arm lying outside the covers on the pillow, indolence after restoring sleep. What a marvellous invention, rest. A pastime: fingering the lace edging of the pillow ... It's really quite sympathetic after all, this big bed, as I wake up with one leg over to the left, one leg over to the right. The day has come back, what a godsend! Not a movement anywhere; however, I have my big bed to wallow in. I can do my waking up in comfort. They say the tree position is diffi-cult to begin with; my little bit of yoga isn't tiring me, one foot up against the other thigh, arm in the air, fingering the lace on the pillow, twisting the lace around my finger. Can I get up at eight?

That will depend on what sounds I hear.

What if I began thinking about Jacques? Who's to stop me? Certainly not the lined curtains: they're accomplices. It's Morse code outside, all those birds. What a frivolous message. I wonder whether I shall continue to go down into the toilet of that café in the rue de Courcelles before I visit Jacques ... I have every time till now ... It would be terrible if I couldn't control myself while eating at his table. Sheer nervousness. I know I'm going to see him, and the kidneys are sensitive too. The toilets in the cafés around his neighbourhood are gay; I powder my nose, I pencil my eyebrows, I daub my lips, I give the whole town a good kick where it hurts. If I urinate a drop or two, if I take my precautions, that's so that I can be sure of having a sex made of white tile while I'm with him. And him? He sometimes leaves his drawing room, but he never comes back buttoning his fly ... Does he have a fly? I've never seen it. He leaves the room: it is in order to bring you a lock of Rimbaud's hair, a Rousseau manuscript, a note from Proust ... My immoderate gratitude for his locked and bolted fly; but he must piss, must shit, and so on. I was trying to violate him with that 'piss,' that 'shit'; but nothing has changed. He doesn't piss, he doesn't shit: he is Jacques the melancholy, he is Jacques the intangible. He talks about Les Maîtres d'autrefois; I listen to him talk, I drink my own blood. He talks about Rembrandt; I am silent, I am in a kennel where thirty dogs are all baying at once: that is the chaos of my love.

Should I get up now? They're all asleep and I'm not at home. You were enjoying your lolling around; go on enjoying it. I'm unhappy because I've started thinking about Jacques. The birds in Milly are frenetic, they are making me sad. That's a lie. It's the rue de Courcelles, with the railings of the Parc Monceau along it, that is weighing me down, making me sad. Just now a kennel, now it's a greyhound sapping me. It is following the scent of its pain, the world isn't big enough, it is homeless, a wanderer. The greyhound, ah! it throws itself against the park railings ... If I were to get up, that would drive these thoughts away.

Cocteau is resting, let him rest quietly. It is bruising itself against the railings, it's fallen, it's beginning again. What does it want? It is hurling itself on to the gilded spikes to tell them ... I've had enough, I don't want to look at it any more. That's enough, enough! It's jumping higher and higher, it's falling back lower and lower. It ought to have smashed itself to pieces by now. Finish it off, that dog. Of course it's me. How could I love it otherwise?

*

I drew the thick curtains, I opened the window. A pretentious castle stood there with its back to Cocteau's house. Was it a dream, or was I seeing almond-green confetti scattered on bottle-green water? I had been curled up all night beside a moat and its duckweed, between tapestries of ivy ... A bridge. Yes, ivy streaming from its urns. A bridge at the end of the kitchen-garden path. You were sleeping in an actor's bed while a bridge, with the youth of a stag, was bounding upwards a hundred yards away from that bed. I ought to travel. You get up in the morning and the day is all discovery. How frail, how swift it is, that bridge; hazel branches, new leaves, dappled liquid sunlight, morning: only Cocteau could have given me all that; what if he came back to the house from that spinney, if he saw me in my curlers, in my flannelette nightdress ... I closed the window again. Where was the gardener? It was Sunday; everything had gone out of my head, I even looked for him in the sky, which had festooned itself with a single white cloud ...

Twenty past eight and not a sound anywhere in the house: this is becoming preposterous. I sat down by the window, I had the feeling that I was coming back to my birthplace, to my own kitchen-garden, after making my fortune. The power of stagnation in age-old bodies of water. The moat. 'It won't be a commercial book, Violette.' My first name, which she used very rarely, my first name slumbering on the stealthy water. Away with you, Narcissus, there's no room for you between the green roundels of the duckweed.

*

'Have you had breakfast?'
'No ... I didn't dare come down.'
'We'll have breakfast together then.'
It was brief and it was warm.
Ought I to say good morning to him and kiss him? He was already sitting. He laid his hands flat on the tablecloth. His dressing gown ... I would have liked it to be more sumptuous.
'Sit down, my darling ...'
By what right does he call me 'my darling'?
'You're not sad? It will be nice having breakfast together ...'
Why was he playing happy family?
How was I to manage it? Getting into a chair opposite him? His

thin wrists hypnotized me.

'Do you like your room?'

'Yes ... it's beautiful. Will Jean Marais be coming?'

I had managed to slide my knees under the table.

'I shall butter your bread for you,' he said.

The woman with the white satin hair smiled down at him fondly. I felt I was choking even before I had started to eat. He nibbled at a rusk. He was getting old, his emaciated face hurt my heart. Tendons stretched to breaking point all down his neck as he nibbled. I dipped my bread in my milky coffee.

'... No, Jean Marais won't be coming. He's shooting day and night.'

The shadow, the melancholy after he had said it.

He held his cup exactly as I was holding mine, and his hand was like a swift bird. His hands rustled with life even when they were doing nothing.

'Danielle Darrieux is wonderful,' he said. 'Do you like her?'

He meant it sincerely, so ... but why this sudden, impulsive question from the blue, killing all enthusiasm, all admiration?

'Danielle Darrieux? I didn't like her when she was a young girl. I like her better now.'

He surprised me when he lit a Gitane. This man so clever at everything, in every field, was clumsiness itself with a match ... Ill at ease, I felt I was dragging my breakfast out to eternity.

'Darrieux is a prodigious actress,' Cocteau told me. 'She has understood everything before you've even explained it. Such an intelligent actress ...'

He expected comments, approbations, but my mouth was full. I was growing steadily heavier and slower as his voice became warmer. I felt his presence was almost supernatural. I didn't respect him. I felt free to be myself, to let my cube of sugar melt in my mouth— a Northerner's habit—while blowing and blowing on my coffee to cool it. My lack of ceremony enchanted me.

I am sitting at your table, I am permitting myself to judge you. I wouldn't be Berthe's daughter if I didn't judge you. My mother is a judge who never leaves the bench. Why do you attract severity? Why do you confuse all the issues by talking so fast? You are generous with your talents, is it that you've never stopped still enough? You're not sure of yourself even at the age of sixty; you're not sure of anything or anybody, that's what moves me. There are resources in you to be mined since you can doubt, since you can lose your way.

You are loyal, the birds in your hands are always ready to spring into flight. You questioned me about Danielle Darrieux and I answered you. You weren't listening to what I said. What I said didn't count. That's not important. I am not here in your house to charm you. I am here to see you grow old, old angel Heurtebise. Cruel? Me? Demanding, certainly. You seem to feel the cold. I am ready to warm you ... But how would I do it: you never stay still anywhere.

I took a Gitane from his packet. 'Were you very late coming back?'

'About one o'clock. Did I waken you?'

'No, I wasn't asleep. I didn't hear you ...'

'I had been in the studio since seven in the morning,' he informed me.

A lesson in energy.

Pale-blue dragonflies fluttered over his wrists in their tight, pale-blue silk cuffs.

'Let's talk about Maurice Sachs!' he suddenly shot at me point-blank. There was no blood left in my veins. Cocteau had dropped the dead weight of a corpse, still warm, onto my lap.

'All right, let's talk about Maurice Sachs,' I said weakly.

I could feel it: that stone face, my face, was sculptured emotion and grief. What was the good of talking? But I was a guest, I must do as I was asked.

Cocteau stubbed out his cigarette. Who would begin?

'I read Le Sabbat,' he said.

He cleared his throat.

'Did you like it?'

'Yes, a great deal,' Cocteau answered. 'He has written a book at last.'

He was looking into my eyes. I lowered them.

Jean Cocteau rose from the table. He raised his voice. 'Can *you* tell me why he said things like that about me in Le Sabbat?'

I stood up, too. The corpse, deprived of its funeral rites, was insisting that we disturb ourselves for his sake.

I remained silent, I kept my eyes lowered.

'Why? Why?' Cocteau insisted.

I lifted my eyes at last. Cocteau was unhappy.

I told him the truth, as I told it later in La Bâtarde.

I put on gloves. '... We were in Normandy and he gave me the manuscript of Le Sabbat to read ... I gave it back, I asked him why he was so unforgiving ...'

Cocteau leaned over the corpse. 'You asked him that?' he said, moved.

'Yes, I asked him that,' I said in a quiet voice.

'What was his answer?' There was anxiety in Cocteau's voice.

'His answer was that he had suffered a great deal on your account.'

'That's all he said?'

'Yes.'

Cocteau reflected on this. He rested his eyes on some leaves. 'And yet I forgave him everything ... When he took all my letters ...'

'He didn't conceal that ... He told about that in *Le Sabbat*!'

'... and wheeled them away from my house in a barrow, I forgave him ... When I had to buy them back for their weight in gold, I forgave him ... I always forgave him ...'

Cocteau's voice became ever more distant as he recalled those past events.

'He's told all about those things in his book!' I cried.

It was a blunder, but Cocteau didn't pick me up on it.

He was weighing the pros and cons, not letting me see his thoughts. I wanted nothing to do with his forbearance; I felt it fitted in too well with Maurice's tragic end.

'Bah, what does it matter ...' he said finally.

He slipped his packet of Gitanes into his dressing gown pocket.

I remembered Maurice too well. Now his sufferings on Cocteau's account had become infinitely useless.

'Come along,' Cocteau said, 'we'll walk round the garden ...'

Why are there never miracles? Why couldn't Sachs come back, now he was becoming famous, why couldn't he and Cocteau have it out as equals, face to face? I would have tiptoed quietly away.

*

Cocteau walked out into his garden in fur-lined slippers. 'You see, my darling,' he said to me, 'the flowers and the seasons are like the bells ringing changes. One calls, another answers. A tulip falls, a pink opens ... Here the rosebush is in flower, there the pansy seed blows on the wind ...'

I'm the only one hearing this, I told myself, hypnotized, mute.

Cocteau in his silent slippers, Cocteau in his dressing gown, simple as the morning, was straightening the stake of another rosebush, lifting the leaves of one of those splendidly tousled leeks off a strawberry seedling. How had he sensed that he owed me a gardener's stroll through his garden on a Sunday morning?

We walked on along the path.

'The pollen, that's like the bells calling to one another too,' he said.

He threw his arms in front of him; his hands were holding his garden, he was already painting it on a wall.

I listened to him without listening. Maurice Sachs was beside me too, he was saying: 'No, Violette, I won't cut it, I suffered too much, too much ...'

Thought-transference: at that moment Jean Cocteau said: 'Do you know how he died?'

'I think I know. Maurice's closest friend made inquiries.'

I explained it to Cocteau: forced to leave a Hamburg prison at the moment of the Liberation, Maurice was also forced to leave the column of prisoners as they retreated with the army. He couldn't march quickly enough. The guard shot him point-blank, against a village wall. He was thrown into a mass grave. The mayor is thought to have his papers ...

Cocteau listened, examining his fruit trees. He was going grey, Cocteau; his electric hair was going white. It was receding too. I could see two rivulets running through his hair: his skin. It was the hair of an old actor retired from the boards. It was cloudier in texture, but it reminded me of the writer Colette's great mane.

To question Cocteau about Maurice Sachs would be to importune Maurice wherever he was.

We walked on between the rosebushes and the spinach leaves. I was silent.

Jean Cocteau leaned his elbows on the bridge. I did the same.

'Have you seen Genet again?' he asked.

'No ... I haven't seen him recently.'

I didn't want to tell him about Genet's temper, about the table, the tablecloth, the wine on the floor. Genet was over for me, leaving a wound that would never close.

'He's not easy. And it's just as well,' he said, as though he had read my thoughts.

Cocteau clasped his hands above the water. A plane leaf slid down the stream.

I nodded agreement.

Musing, ageing, he repeated one of his remarks so often quoted in print: 'You know, Genet is the greatest moralist of our time!'

'I find him harsh,' I said without rancour.

Cocteau looked at me. Was I forgetting myself, had I suffered on Genet's account? He leaned over the bridge; the pictures on the water were so clear, so delicate, the reflections of supplicating branches.

'He isn't harsh,' he said. 'He has true integrity. Do you think he spares me? He often accuses me of being stupid, but I don't hold it against him ...'

Cocteau was beginning to irritate me: he didn't hold anything against anyone.

He seemed sad, without being depressed.

'Let's walk on,' he said, 'and I'll tell you something about Genet.'

I followed him into a little spinney. It meant passing abruptly from the light and colours of the kitchen-garden into the half darkness beneath rather too neatly laid out trees; the transition sapped my spirits.

'And this isn't the end,' he said. 'You'll see, after this there's the wood ...'

I took his box of matches from his hands. I preferred him as the infallible conjurer.

He took a second puff at his cigarette. 'You know,' he said. 'It wasn't I who taught Radiguet to write, it was he who gave me lessons ...'

It was a great moment, after that confidence. But his eyes, unwavering, had nothing to confide.

The wood gave way abruptly to ploughed fields. Fields as far as the eye could see, horizons stretched to breaking point. You could suck in great lungfuls of freedom.

'Do you like it?' Cocteau asked.

'Let's say I'm mad about it.'

Of course I was mad about it; I had come back to my bushes of light flattened against the earth; to my larks and their piercing song.

'Genet was in prison,' Cocteau began. 'I wondered who, in Paris, should read the manuscript of his *Notre-Dame des Fleurs* first. I took it to Valéry. "Come back in a week's time, and I'll tell you what I think of it," Paul Valéry said.'

'Yes?'

'Wait. I went back after a week ...'

'Yes? Yes?'

'Guess what he said.'

'That it was a work of genius!'

'He said: "Jean, this must be burned. This would upset everything." I took the manuscript back and did what I could myself.'

'I can't believe it.'

'All the same, it's true,' Cocteau said.

He took another cigarette from his dressing gown pocket. 'We shall be playing croquet at midday. Do you like croquet?'

'I used to like it, I don't know if I still do ...'

I was thinking of Valéry's pyre for Genet.

*

I was writing in Jean Marais's sun-flooded room after my walk. Paul Morihen and Georges were playing football outside. They were shouting, they were yelling, they were shrieking their heads off. Poor Cocteau, I said quietly to myself. Writing the end of *L'Affamée* under the roof of a poet was tending to go to my head. It wasn't commercial, but perhaps I was going as far as the Surrealists ... A small edition for a great inspiration. I opened the window as wide as it would go ... My subtlety should outvie the subtleties of the pink and orange poppies. I put my elbows on the table ... Something wrong, Mallarmé? A bit discouraged, Lautréamont? Wouldn't it be better to draw crosses with a piece of charcoal on chalk cliffs?

They called me down to play croquet with them.

*

At one o'clock, Georges collected the mallets: we were going to eat lunch in a restaurant, in the forest. With Cocteau? Without Cocteau. He was expecting the Princess Paley, he was going to eat with her at home, but he was treating us to a meal in the restaurant. He was getting rid of us.

At three in the afternoon the princess hadn't arrived. We took up our mallets again. Cocteau would not allow himself to play with us before she arrived.

The bell rang at last. A little old lady dressed in navy blue, wearing a skullcap of the same colour, trotted up the gravel path. She saddened me. She had dwindled so, the insipid Garbo who had posed twenty years earlier for *Vogue*, for *Fémina* ... I held my mallet in one hand, I fingered my wrinkles with the other.

*

'How well you will be able to work here!' Cocteau had said during one of our croquet games.

How innocent. How ignorant. I write ... I write three notebook
pages a day. It's too much and it's not enough, that's the root of the
problem and there I am chained to my anxieties, there I am covet-
ing the sweeper's broom, the street cleaner's wheeled bin along the
rue Paul-Bert. I admire them: they have a job. I walk close to them
as I pass, paler than a turnip. They are whistling, they are content.
I stagnate in Paris, I am wasting my time in Cocteau's country house.
'How well you will be able to work here!' Yes, if work meant un-
loading sacks of flour from morning till night. I'm not ambitious,
and yet I have great expectations when I write: I live with the
hope of placing the mind-blowing word exactly in the place that
awaits it. I can't find it, I splatter about in my sweet whipped cream.
I say out loud that the primroses stream down the slope to the brook
... I am writing without a pen. I put it to myself that I should
write: the winter sky engulfs the tenements. I ring the word
'engulfs'; eyes closed, I exploit the grey sky of a Sunday afternoon. I say to myself: The winter sky is a belly, a great vault, a
fit of the sulks that could go on forever. And in the end I find myself all alone again with the verb 'to engulf.' Write? I haven't the
time. The setting sun races bleeding down the sky and carries me
with it. Why, why add my name to the list of authors who are not
read?

*

I walked alone through the kitchen-garden, onto the bridge; I
couldn't understand why I was sullying, soiling the flowers, the
plants, the trees, the leaves, the reflections gazed at by Jean Cocteau's
side. My aloneness was annulling the place and the dream. The
prayer was over, the candle was dribbling its wax. I fled out into
Milly's market square.
    Was it a citadel, Cocteau's room, that no one ever mentioned it?

*

An Oedipus, more Virgilian than Greek and sporting a throbbing
sex, is questioning a sphinx too graceful to stay dumb. The sphinx
has the wings of an Italian angel, the claws and tail of Puss-in-Boots.
Maybe it is Mme Seraphita, the hermaphrodite fortune-teller on the
Boulevard Magenta? She is holding three cards, you notice. Sig-
nificant. Oedipus, the student of fate, is laying three fingers on one
seraphic knee. All is mournful, all is twilight gloom. Two young

people finding one another attractive far from the curse of the Atridae. It was a Christian Bérard drawing behind the palm tree with the golden leaves in Cocteau's drawing room.

Christian Bérard. I was walking along with my suitcases full of sausages one day, after the Liberation; I recognized him walking along outside the windows of Hagnauer's antiquarian bookshop in the rue Bonaparte. The walls of bookshelves with their ladders some-how suited that dimpled giant better than the sports car or the taxi on the other side. Led by a Goya griffon, he was only just managing to keep hold of the lead, which was no more than a sort of bizarre length of string. In a dark-blue suit apparently bought from an old-clothes merchant, this character with the beaming face seemed to have stepped out of a Clouet canvas. But he was more moving, more beautiful than Francis I. More aesthetic; therefore, more complicated. His face: a countenance alive with grace and bordered with a gild-ing of beard. Christian Bérard looked at me without seeing me; but there was kindness in the look. These thunderclap apparitions hap-pen to us all. Christian Bérard was an apparition to my eyes at every step he took. I followed him. I crossed sidewalks if I overtook him; I dropped back, then closed in again. Drawn by his griffon, he simply progressed along the sidewalk without any apparent intention or effort. A cloud of nonchalance.

His great body was a languorous buoy bobbing between the passers-by. A wilting gait. Walking, for Christian Bérard, meant abolishing all straight lines. His docility as he followed his griffon ... The other people on the sidewalk were extinguished as his great bulk moved slowly on. Christian Bérard's sensuality, his ardent decad-ence. The butt-end in one corner of his mouth had an air of the eternal. I met him two weeks later at Madeleine and Marcellin Cas-taing's. He talked with great feeling about the village cafés he was collecting.

The bees of Milly are gathering their honey; I don't give a damn. The poppy that opened this morning still isn't tattered yet; I don't give a damn. The ten-week-stock is frothing against the wall; I don't give a damn. Moonlight there ... the heart of the cabbage lettuce; I don't give a damn. The bird ignores us, he knows where he's going: I don't give a double damn. This morning there is too much happiness and tranquillity here among the vegetables and fruits. I lean out of the window, I think of that Russian who under-stood and could feel the despair of the trees, the convulsions of their branches, the agonized pauses of the dead leaves. He was taken over, he was possessed by the tree's grief and torment, this Russian, when it was being tortured by the hurricane, when its topmost branches were bent down to sweep the earth in which its roots were riveted. The wind would cease, and the tree could not tell its sufferings. The Russian followed the path of the storms on the tree's behalf. And then he dived into his inner darkness, sitting on a chair, his head buried in his hands for hours, for days, at Lèves, when he was staying with Madeleine and Marcellin Castaing. The trees for which he was suffering grew. His stature is now the same as theirs. He sings the prophetic steel-blue light before the storm; he glorifies the stammering between the branches when the sky is a tiny fragment of stained glass, when it is sufficient for the immensity of a simple colour. Tree in all its glory on the Place Furstenberg; eloquent trees tensed and passionate in the teeth of storms across the meadows of Lèves, he understood you as we shall never understand you: your sap flowed in his veins. That Russian is the painter Soutine.

*

Second Sunday in Cocteau's house, second walk with him in his kitchen-garden. He had been away from morning till night every day for a week. Every night I asked myself: what time does he come home? Where is his room?

He repeated to me between the escaroles and the snapdragons: 'I didn't teach Raymond Radiguet to write ... It was he who gave me lessons!'

We ended up in the kitchen of the couple who looked after his house. Their Pomeranian stretched itself out on the table, paws in the air, offering itself and wriggling. Cocteau plunged his long hand into the white fur. It was playful, it was ambiguous. The narrow-minded nun in me took offence. I walked outside and waited for him there; I could hear his vibrant, metallic voice inside.

'Is that his little dickie, is that his little dickie?' Cocteau was singsonging.

I fled along the path, then retraced my steps. I was fighting with my father's Puritan family.

I went back into the kitchen. The couple were laughing heartily at 'monsieur's' attentions to their dog.

'Where were you?' Cocteau asked.

'Just outside,' I answered, embarrassed.

He left me to get dressed.

At noon the famous hands prepared our Pernods with water poured through sugar in an elegant perforated spoon. We all four touched glasses. Cocteau didn't sip and simper where alcohol was concerned. He mixed us a second Pernod. The sun flooded the drawing room, stripping the palm tree with its golden leaves quite naked.

'Ah, my children ...' Cocteau sighed.

I felt he was exhausted. Cocteau wasn't rich; his hospitality was beginning to present a problem.

'Pour the coffee for us,' he said to me after lunch, as though he felt I needed cranking up.

I poured the coffee.

Paul Morihen and Georges left the drawing room. Their haste was a pleasure to the eye.

Sitting on an uncomfortable gilded chair, he made small talk to me. Outside, the two young men were preparing for their game of volleyball. Cocteau began to doze off. His pointed chin sank down onto his long, supple necktie, then rose again; Cocteau fought against sleep, smiled. I was terrified, my sixteen-year-old self rejected an old man dropping off after a meal. Standing motionless beside him, I stared down at him, I shucked him, I peeled him as the *Boeuf sur le toit* bar sank slowly into the quicksands. Beautiful and prodigal young men, in love with adventures and dangers that went no further than opium, you made haste by night to approach him. He charmed you. Now you sit by your hearths and he falls asleep after his coffee. Other young men have come: they are shouting, they are yelling, they are drugging themselves with a ball. Meanwhile the beautiful, the indifferent lover is at his ease inside with us, he does not leave us, he does not speak to us, he is time, and he simply passes. The poet cannot resist the coils of sleep. Ah, how tyrannical age is! Why are these new young men yelling outside while you sleep?

You start, you struggle a moment, poor old bird. You emerge from your sleep, you try to take up everything where you left off. Your cigarette is about to fall from between your fingers.

'You know, Jean Marais, he's a hero. He must play heroic roles, he ought always to play heroes ...'

You had already told me that, you break my heart. Your cigarette between your limp and feeble fingers worries me.

He sank back again. The chin moved down once more towards the silk shirt, settled to rest on the long, supple necktie. Cocteau was sliding into old age like a simple peasant falling asleep in a farm cottage. Why must I witness the defeat of a being who was all dynamite and electricity? It was my duty to keep watch on that lighted cigarette between his fingers. The glowing point signified that we must die so that others may live. Cocteau was holding a future that was no longer his. The young men were growing and multiplying with their cries and their clamour. Cocteau was asleep. Sex, white sex, narrow sex, paper sex, tattooed sex, would I dare to remove you from between his fingers? I went closer; the palm tree with golden leaves was watching me. I went closer and closer; my boldness was offending the palm tree, the golden leaves were hardening; my confidence ebbed further. Old angel Heurtebise, I must; otherwise, you'll burn yourself. I took his Gitane from him. He started again; I stubbed out his cigarette. The two young men were yelling, shouting that's a point, no it wasn't, yes it was. Who will let him rest?

Cocteau was deeply asleep: he was sighing rather than breathing; his sabre-slash mouth was softening; his nose was diving downwards; his wrinkles were deepening, his frothing hair was growing even whiter in the beam of sunlight. He shook himself. Was he pretending to be asleep? Was it a game? No, the time for games is past when you are old. The poet who wrote in *Plain-Chant*:

> *Nothing inspires more fear in me*
> *Than the mock calm of a face asleep*

quivered in his sleep. I sat down on a gilded chair. I kept vigil, stood guard over him, observed him till my eyes hurt. Did he weep? When did he weep? The two young men were shouting more and more loudly. I didn't dare close the window; there were so many birds offering their concert to a man who wasn't there. I put my head in my hands: there are some sleeps as sad as foredoomed undertakings.

After I had sated myself on his features, I grew bored. Another game of volleyball had started, more yells, more shouts. He woke up.

'Have I been asleep?' he asked.

'Yes, for a while ... not for long.'

Already he was tightening the knot of his long, supple necktie.

*

March 15, 1966—Cocteau is dead. He had written me four notes. Last year I ran as fast as my legs would carry me to sell them to a bookseller on the Left Bank. I wasn't short of money, and four short letters take up very little space in a closet. Certain beings, dead or alive, will always force you into ingratitude and cruelty. Was I still repressing the letters from Maurice Sachs burnt out of bravado? Possibly. Jean Cocteau and Maurice Sachs are often linked in my memory. Cocteau had become as alone as Maurice. I am never apart from a pencil sketch of Genet by Cocteau. It is Genet to the life, the pride of a cock prepared for battle; he is stiffening his back, raising his head, making ready to attack first; even the lapels of his raglan are bristling—who is he about to leap on? The pencil sweeps down in an unbroken line for the profile. Affection: a little hook for the nostril. Emotion: the arc of the brow. The love of a writer for a writer greater than himself.

*

I receive a letter from Patrice every two days. The concierge is pleased with this transparent mystery: someone is writing to me, someone importunate. Who would be importunate except a man ... A woman without a man, oh horror, a kind of big kangaroo hopping about everywhere with its pouch always empty. A man is writing to me; the concierge is reassured. It was high time. There is praise in her eyes every two days. She will have some sharp things to say if she finds out that a provincial schoolboy is wasting his time writing to me about his passion for literature. To win the esteem of one's concierge. I would have smiled at such a preoccupation twenty years ago, ten years ago. Keeping up appearances. Yes, yes. Respect for principles. Yes, yes, oh, yes. As long as all that twaddle doesn't destroy me. It's already beginning to undermine me. My dignity? A rat gnawing at me, eating me alive. I am deceiving my dear concierge; she thinks I have a correspondent the same age as myself. She devotes herself to her family while I, bent over my microscope, study the bacterial flora of a lonely heart of seventeen. I walk up the six flights of stairs with Patrice's letter.

I turn the key, I let my shopping fall, I read, I reread; my own seventeen-year-old hopes and fears return, then leave again, between Patrice's words. My youth is over, and yet the brutal light of a neon sign going on and off outside a hotel bedroom window ... There they are, my feelings at seventeen, appearance, disappearance, on the ruled school paper of a provincial schoolboy. I thrilled to *Les Nourritures Terrestres*, he thrills to *L'Espace du dedans*. We wither, we die, everything goes on. I raise my head in the middle of one of his sentences; I hear a loud crack in a waiting room; it is the waiting room of a matrimonial agency, and it tempts me. Ah, wandering around outside a matrimonial agency; could that mean you want to remarry? No. It is my vague hope of a vague who knows what.

I answer his letter, and I am sullying him. What more sullying than superiority? I answer him with the superiority of an 'older person'; I play him maxims on a toy flute. A parrot puffing up its scarlet feathers. A parrot that talks to him about Van Gogh, about St. John of the Cross, about the Portuguese Nun, about Louise Labé, about Emily Brontë. I fornicate with the titles of books, I put on dog with the little I know, I serve up the talents of others in a fricassee, I juggle with geniuses. My mousetrap for Patrice is laid between the names Lorca, Pavese, Faulkner. I hide my traps beneath quotations from books. This young man, he's a real opportunity, a bargain, I am almost inclined to say, going cheap in the big store of adolescence. This young man, I mustn't let him get away. Oh, nothing dishonest; I'm not the madam of a cat-house. I feed his little flame for me by feeding his passion for literature. I answer his letters, this schoolboy who doesn't haggle over his enthusiasms, I weave my web: I advise him to read Saint-John Perse, Dos Passos, Steinbeck. And to what have I anchored my web? To a quotation from Nietzsche, taken from the most difficult of his books, from *The Will to Power*, of which I have as yet to grasp ten lines ...

But the day Antonin Artaud died ... that day my attempts at seduction were suspended. I cut the cackle. It was serious, Artaud's illness. A seared genius was leaving us. Later I told Patrice he ought to read *Héliogabale* and the lightning-lit text on Van Gogh. Sometimes the sun of the dead seems possessed of intelligence. That day it lit up my paper just as I was writing the capital A of Artaud.

When I confide my torments over my little, broken-winded sentences to Patrice, then I am sincere. When I tell him: 'Love, suffer, give yourself up to your inclinations, to your preferences,' then it's just padding. I don't give a damn about his morals or his absence of morals. When I write: 'Work, broaden your field of study with further reading. Tell yourself that your studies are merely a springboard,' then I feel too much the preacher, up in a pulpit. It's not up to me to talk about his studies; I never studied. I don't deny it, getting a letter from a well-brought-up young man every two days flatters me. I should no longer laugh as I did once, in an office of Plon the publishers, when my superior in that office came in at four o'clock and told me she had met 'a young chap,' that this 'young chap' read *Werther* in buses ... I hurry, I rush, I run to post my reply, I never hold his envelope on or under an envelope addressed to Simone de Beauvoir. No mixing up my compartments. If I talk about my correspondence with Patrice to the author of *The Second Sex*, she appears to be interested, with her usual, limitless good will.

'It's charming, your relationship with that schoolboy ... Does he still write to you?'

Sitting beside a woman so powerful in her work and striving, I no longer know what I think about, so insipid, so anodyne our little exchange of letters seems ... Simone de Beauvoir is a force, my schoolboy vanishes into thin air, and I am left there, no more, really, than a sort of vegetable.

The day after next I write another letter. The letter once slipped into the box, I return to my place among the old men and women buying their discount vegetables from Dominique's stall. I try to speak the way they speak, complain the way they complain, drivel on the way they drivel on. I take tracings of their hackneyed phrases, but I cannot obtain their sympathy. Men and women alike, the old people turn away. They can sense it: I belong to no society, not even to that of the discards.

*

Jacques, glacial as ever on the telephone, invited me to have lunch at his house one Thursday. Jean-Jacques Pauvert, recommended by Genet as a suitable publisher for the de luxe edition of *L'Affamée*, would be there as well. I would have preferred a piece of jewelry from the Place Vendôme, a fur from the Faubourg Saint-Honoré, a ticket from Cook's for a trip to Mexico, anything that would have signified a tribute to my femininity, to the woman of leisure as opposed to the writer. You're never satisfied, you never will be satisfied, a voice told me—Hermine's, I have no doubt. His publishing project disconcerted me. I listened to his voice in the earpiece, I hung up: a little white chalk crushed on my fingertips, that was me and my discouragement at his curtness every time. I walked out of the coalman's little bar ... the earth was turning, the sun was shining.

Jacques was in seventh heaven the following Thursday; his project was beginning to take shape. Jean-Jacques Pauvert was silent; for him it was a business deal; he wasn't going to interrupt his client. In those days he was a cold young man, very cold, distant, very distant, a sort of frozen work of art with a pleasant face that wore a contemptuous, Asiatic smile. He wore glasses and a skimpy suit. Shyness.

A retiring presence. He was just starting out, still finding his way. Emboldened by Denis's absence and Jacques's good humour, I began playing the luxuriously kept tart, the self-confident mistress of the house. Pauvert, sitting opposite me, avoided having anything to do with me as far as he could. Understandably. My suit, an old gift from Jacques Fath, altered, re-altered, dyed once, dyed twice, and a Russian-style rabbit hat encouraged me to eye the tyro publisher from something of a height, to take the furniture, the pictures, the collector's books for my own. Look at the poor idiot woman smelling a rose in the drawing room, trying to convince herself she is truly on home ground. Jacques was insistent on the rarity, the perfection, the quality; Pauvert, polite, attentive, didn't seem to give a damn about what I wrote. The price of each copy was to be so high I took fright; bibliophilia on such a scale filled me with dread. Pauvert took it all in and gave nothing away. Was it disdain he was feeling?

We went in to eat, and I effaced myself. Jacques's good humour must have all the room. They talked about rare books. Sometimes a being becomes two beings, can give you a child simply by being with you. They talked about the number of copies to be printed. On the Place de l'Opéra, hanging on my arm, I had a retarded child, a feeble-minded infant, an idiot, a halfwit. He wouldn't let go of my arm. Jacques glittered opposite me; Pauvert ate with gusto.

*

That Thursday lunch was an exception. Ordinarily I ate with them every Friday evening. Jacques began to yawn at about eleven o'clock if I was alone with just the two of them. He yawned. He was bored. His tomorrow-morning factory was telling him: To bed, to bed. I rose from the sofa, even though I would have liked to stay till dawn. To stay stretched out on the flagstones, near the door of his bedroom, near his bedside table, near his paper knife between the pages of a book. He walked across the drawing room, he opened the french windows. He was driving out my microbes, my miasmas, my adverbs, my clinging odours, my exaggerations. The weight below the small of his back. The curve and the weight that is needed to emphasize virility. He opened the thick curtains, I watched his every movement. Denis said it was freezing; he fled with the boxers over towards the bracken and the sofa. I waited, apprehensive, in the middle of the room. I convicted myself of uselessness while he was making everywhere sweet and clean again. The evening was floating to an end. The air wafted in. Was I an attack of flu? Was I a pollution? Some evenings I set off briskly towards the miniature cloakroom. The curve of Jacques's back, a memory, that of the bright-red flannel around the waists of Zouaves and old-style road-workers. I said good night. Denis looked at me, silently pitying me. He is jealous, Denis. He is spiteful, Denis. What thoughts! I was crazy: for him any battle was won in advance. Jacques stood silent, ready to open the door, ready to close it after me. His black, shiny slippers spattered me with their reflections. I had to go, I had to beg.

'When shall I see you again?'

He rushed to answer. 'Telephone! Telephone next week!'

I had begged, I went.

He closed the door after me, he shot the bolt. His life too was elsewhere.

The Friday before, the Friday after, I followed, I would follow the same route, back to the Courcelles métro station. It was always twenty to twelve, twenty-five to twelve. I listened for it, the sound of my heels through the deserted streets ... A companion was beating out the rhythm in common time. I slowed down past the Parc Monceau railings ... The sombre masses of the trees directed curses at me. A taxi passed in the direction of the Place Péreire, and I set off again. Charity, if you please, I said to the sound of my heels when I did not meet even the shadow of a passer-by ...

He succoured me, the painter Soutine's rabbit in Jacques's dining room. Always seated on my host's right hand, I never once found myself opposite the picture. I learned it by heart as I came in, as I left. Denis offered me a Royale between vegetables and dessert; what a dusting of delight as I looked up at the dead rabbit on the sly, while I was accepting Denis's cigarette. To die ... austere wonderland; providence had been kind to me if I managed to gaze at it a moment. Jacques asked me if I was working, if I was happy. I answered simply yes or no. Jacques and I, with out reticence, with our courtesies, were both being kept warm by a still-living coat of fur.

The métro plays a large role in my story. It was a refuge, a grotto, an asylum. I waited on the platform for the next train; the evening with Jacques was at an end; everything was coming to an end. A considerate man was knocking me to pieces, a courteous man was reducing me to zero. A noise: the train. Despite the two sacks of sand slung from my shoulders, I disengage myself from the bench, I watch for the train along the tunnel. The speed, the unstoppable weight: why go back next week, it would be over so quickly? The doors open, the doors close all on their own ... fidelity, fidelity. Why die, why not go back next week? The cattle have not abandoned me; other trains have thundered past while I was eating dinner with him. Yes, yes, I will go back. Avoid his street forever, send him an express letter to tell him so? Impossible. Why? Because if I run away from him, I shall be a deserter. The wreck of a *France-Soir* under a seat tells me about theatres, about cinemas where carefree people have been laughing with high hearts. I cannot find my own kind anywhere, I have been scorning them for four hours. I blow my nose. Now I can smell that shabby smell better: the smell of the thousands of people who have no life of their own, who make themselves into zeros just so they can eat when they're hungry. They are asleep; I roam the world sniffing their odour. I rub my cheek against the window; I say: Don't reject me *Dubo ... Dubon... Dubonnet*. Riding through the tunnel is a relief; but at each station I suffer everything that exists. A stunted little man cleans his nails with his nails. It is Jacques: he has failed in life. I look for him everywhere. I hide myself in order to weep, I control myself, I think of myself as living on the frontiers of grief.

*

Patrice writes to me every day. Big Nose receives mail six days a week, someone is thinking about Big Nose every day. It is unheard of, I am inspiring pages and pages of friendship from a young man.

*

I have another Genet story. The last?

There were about ten of us at dinner, Jacques's guests, and François Reichenbach was saying to me: 'You'd like New York ... Why not go?'

With what bread, my friend? But it was nice of him all the same.

'Genet's cold!' I cried.

'What? What's the matter?' Jacques asked, always too quick to become impatient.

'Genet is shivering!'

Everyone had fallen silent. Genet had lowered his eyes.

'Genet is wearing a summer jacket!'

Had I done the right thing? Had I done the wrong thing? It was winter. He was wearing a mere membrane. Genet was still silent. His summer jacket: a call to order.

I had heard that Genet was doing without for Lucien; that Genet was doing without for Lucien's wife; that Genet was doing without for the wife's child.

Jacques had left the dining room; François was telling me about his film *Les Marines*.

Two minutes later Jacques returned with a beige cashmere cardigan over his arm. He was upset.

'Keep it,' he said roughly to Genet.

Genet didn't want to. I did want him to: 'Go on, take it, since he's offered it to you!'

Genet hadn't deigned to look at me, hadn't deigned to answer me. Jacques helped him take off his summer jacket and put it back on. The others were all talking, the incident forgotten. Was Genet any warmer? I doubt it.

If I hadn't doubted it, would I have announced at the end of the meal: 'If I was asked to go to the scaffold to defend Genet's work, I'd go...'

'Ah! you and your literature!' Genet exclaimed indignantly.

He found it distasteful. I was exaggerating. I was unpardonable: I should have kept my mouth shut. I believed in Genet; he didn't believe in my belief. He loathed me; I venerated him. Why so much despair for someone I drove to exasperation ... He had warmed up by the end of the meal ... I have had that from him.

Next morning I wrote:

Dear Patrice,
         I won't harp on the fact that our letters crossed. Yours is dated the 1st. What a long time it took getting to me! I am sending you two numbers of *Les Temps Modernes*. You ask if one of your friends may write to me. Yes, let him write. You tell me that you are of no interest to me. If you were of no interest to me, would I clamour for more letters from you? No. Try to overcome your complexes. Why should I despise you? I was just like you when I was seventeen. It's so sad, so difficult, adolescence ... I am often an adolescent myself, despite all the advantages of being forty. You are a man, you have the possibility of making love with another human being (either sex). Do so. It's like gymnastics, it shakes out our black humours with its give-and-take, it adds to our vitality. So we have to retreat into our skins again afterwards, but never mind, we feel

less sorry for ourselves. Don't be in a hurry to write, don't force your-self to write if the desire to do so is not irresistible. To love, to die of love, to make love, all that it getting into training for writing. You will lack material if you don't go through the mill. Your quo-tation from Montesquieu is very fine. Don't despise others; that's just self-destruction. Don't avoid other people; you will end up a beggar even with your full hands. If you wish to create, then stockpile now; snatch up everything that comes to hand. As I see it, geniuses are wealthy adventurers who have made their pile and then go on to ruin themselves for us. They give us all they have amassed.

At thirty you will grumble, but you will find life incredibly diverse. It is a work of art if only you know how to open your eyes, how to stretch out your hand. I went out as evening fell. I had a date with the twilight. I was scarcely outside when I felt a slackening. That slackening, even in my own limbs, was a warning: the sky was just beginning to dust over. A touch of rouge on the cheek of a grey-blue apricot. I walked along from the Faidherbe-Chaligny inter-section as far as the Place de la Nation, and everything took my breath away. Even the long sausages of rags tied up with string by the street drains, on the grilles around the bases of the trees. What are they for? You never see anyone touching them. Always wet, always darkly stained, always repulsive. Caricatures of rolled-up carpets. Poor things—as we say 'poor chap.' What use do they serve? Mystery. It is almost a piece of life itself, one of those rag sausages in a street, of the life that is always stronger than ideas. Believe me, I don't want to preach to you. And how could I?

I understand you. You are all like Oedipus, you adolescents. You tear out your eyes, your eyes are worn out with their discoveries. You spit on the child you were, and the adult you are going to be seems merely a hideous grimace. Live in Paris. You want to. You will be put through that mill I spoke of; that will keep you on your toes. You won't starve. Unless you fast for no good reason. Why bury yourself in advance under this determination to find a job in a bookstore or a publishing house. You would have to take a course on how to run a bookstore ... The idea doesn't enchant me for you. I can see you better wielding a bush hook in a jungle. Bookstores in Paris ... bookstores in the provinces ... Yes, of course, if you owned it, or if you were a buyer selecting books from the *Booklist* ... Other-wise what will you be? A clerk, an errand boy ... You will arrange the books on the shelves, you will move books here, move books there; well in every field I suppose you have to begin somewhere.

Lend me your books, I will lend you mine. We shall have that excitement every time we open one of the packages. We are still children a lot of the time, and so much the better. I will reimburse you for the stamps you have to buy.

I haven't seen Pichette's *Les Epiphanies*. I don't go to the theatre. Yes, I've read some Kierkegaard. I am reading Benjamin Constant's *Journal*. He's like fizzy lime-tea, that Benjamin Constant. Do you love music? I hope so. Write to me. I shake your hand goodbye with all my heart.

*

What is written is written. Which doesn't alter the fact that my letter is a load of garbage. The hardware merchant's rose and lilac, lemon and jasmine Kleen-Air tablets, the circular bricks that melt away as they lend their perfume to our W.C.s are of more use. My letter is a malformation, a septic blister of pretentiousness. It is my decoy duck. Posturing hooker, I swing my little purse with my phony rocks inside: Benjamin Constant, Kierkegaard. A soliciting wink thrown in between my banal comments and all those authors' names. Cross your thighs, perch on your stool, fancy hostess, puff away at your phony idealist's smokeweed, take out your twelve-inch cigarette-holder stolen from the *Seducer's Journal*. Come on, doll, wow them as you peep around the bookshelves. Accost them with your half-read, half-digested books. O profoundly expendable vamp.

What was it I said to you in my last letter? I said ... Try to overcome your complexes, dear Patrice.

You have maundered on long enough, Vivi, now just run your tongue over that gum on the envelope...

I am on my way to meet Marie-Louise Villiers and Yves Lévy. A raised arm, the 86 draws to a halt. A ring of the bell and we're off again. Oh la la, what a conquest I am about to make of Paris over by Notre-Dame, over by the Hall aux Vins. The hour takes flight from a steeple. Seven o'clock? Seven o'clock in the evening is lightheartedness itself above the rooftops. We advance up the boulevard Henri-IV. Walls, buildings. Paris repairing her ravages on the banquettes of restaurants. Stones, rough stones, symmetrical stones, surly stones ... The bridge. Distant refinements in the sky, Oriental light glinting between the carved branches. Notre-Dame is wearing a grey veil, oh heady light. Whipstitch: my mouth sewn tight to admire you ... barges on a mirror. My swarm, my bees, my blond mist, all that coming out of my head. I admire, I hum. My distant beauty. In a veil. Texture and colour of wood-ash. Mouse-grey cocoon. This evening the sky around her has no colour. Notre-Dame. Notre-Dame ... your gentle tints, your towers. Towers of

Notre-Dame, without you I was deprived of infinity. My great
Dulcineas. Dusk . . . the city is in a suède glove. Human hands wielding trowels, and here is their prayer still with us. If it were just a wild
rose . . . the architecture, the bell-turrets. Women leaning over to
offer the builders a drink; their shawls: those swags of ivy. Rue
Cardinal-Lemoine. Ah, we are leaving her too soon.

Why am I going to have dinner with them? I don't read Taine, I
don't understand Husserl. They are friends, they like what I write.
I would walk along the rue Chanoinesse, along the rue du Cloître-
Notre-Dame; I would inspect the shutters of the Marché aux Fleurs,
a minced-pork sandwich between my teeth. Marie-Louise Villiers,
without stopping to think, gave me her best friend. I was forgetting,
I often do forget it: Yves Lévy psychoanalysed *L'Asphyxie* in a
remarkable article. I prefer the padlocks on the shutters of the
Marché aux Fleurs. They enchant me, they set me free. And Marie-
Louise Villiers is always there to read Taine for me.

End of line. Everyone off. I am in plenty of time to meet them at
the Restaurant des Catalans.

*

I wonder why it was that I was not one of them that evening, even
though I was physically there with them. They irritated me with
their education, with their witticisms. I had two glasses of claret
during dinner. They intimidated me, so I took my revenge by
picking them to pieces. I told myself: I am the poor relation they
felt they ought to invite. It didn't occur to me that I was being unjust
towards them. We finished the evening at the Tabou bar. Marie-
Louise wouldn't go down into the cellar: the noise of the jazz . . .
She was young, beautiful, witty, she couldn't stand the din . . . So
why not stay home? I consoled myself with two cocktails. They
all indulged in gymnastics with their brains. By midnight I had
become the maidservant of the poor relation they had invited. Yves
Lévy drinks a little wine with his meal, and that's all. As for Marie-
Louise Villiers, I am sorry to say that she is one of those people
always coddling and pampering their livers. I cursed them for
their sobriety, for their concern with their health. This Tabou, the
smoke here, it's absolutely unbreathable! Oh? So why not sit
quietly at home sniffing up essence of pine? I sulked: they were
drinking water.

I strained my ears: the jazz . . . the jazz came up to me in stri-
dent tatters. Young men and girls dressed in black jumpers, with

long black hair, came in like creatures possessed and hurled themselves down into the cellar. They were already in the grip of the
dance. I had been invited to this dinner because it was the evening
before the eve of my birthday, and now I was being punished.
Absolutely forbidden to crowd down among the crowd of beboppers.
Marie-Louise Villiers announced that she wanted to leave. All to the
good; I certainly wasn't having a ball. I must emphasize this: during the course of the evening I had two cocktails and two glasses of
wine, which was not very much, since I could take nine or ten
Scotches.

They drove me back in their automobile to the front of my building. I heard the door of the building close from the inside as if I had
no hand; that was it.

*

I woke up. I remembered nothing. What a weight the weight of
my bottom lip hanging under my chin the idiot thing is making an
idiot of me how strange I am a hanging lip I can't think how long
I can't think for a long time eyes or the shutters of the darkness or
the coal dust why is the coalman lying on my eyes he isn't cracked
he has a bed of his own why lie on my shutters he ca ... he ca ... he
ca ... what he can't join he wasn't asked to deliver I'm not a cellar
I am joining why a bag of coal slap on my eyes no my shutters no
my eyelids begin again a lip hanging further now who threw the
coal and the dust the grit on my shutters no no no again on my
eyelids the coalman has a telephone box some telephone directories
beautifully recited aren't reciting must call had to call can't remember must who said hurt hurts forget ah yes Berna Bernadette said
call so-tired so-tired the coalman his coalyard on my shutters so
tired exhausted always say tired always say exhausted doctor have a
balcony my mucous membrane my lip hanging

I am old my lip spreading all huddled up am I in a mould black-
currants blackcurrant bushes on lip after but head where is head
resting on a rim so tired I was tired is it rim must explain must find
out jam on lip hanging tired jam, mashed tired, sloshy tired, rabbit
coat soft smell sweet a bond what's this sitting in suit showing
beyond my hope broken worm-eaten breadcrumbs in ankles in wrist
you going to die you sitting in suit his blue suit suit him always pushing bridge of glasses later another time open mouth dead come in I
won't eat you come in make self at home hello my hand goodbye
hand goodbye forever hand I didn't remember you where you going

like that she's trying say goodbye in darkness poor mad little mouth open stupe ... stupefaction consol ... consolation don't come back hand don't come near my fingers my lip hanging mustn't find out any more pebble jam on lip hanging down our babies our dear babies give them my pebbles to suck like bottle they were sucking the statues bottle suck the bottle I suck you suck words to throw on dungheap too tiring must go too far or can't stand any more the cockroach fell back after I don't remember you've already seen it you a hand falling back onto knees of an asylum it's my hand my knees stone floor you cruel we were talking of one thing another now the stone floor butting in

I am defoliated like thirty-six autumns buttocks stuck to the cold sitting on a star I wonder mashed milled in mill of tiredness must find out the cold, oh oh oh who put me on top of steeple I so cold after love pull covers over curves over scratches would pray would betray anyone to be less tired sitting in suit a century will have gone by like a letter thrown into a letter box none can tell none can tell if a century has gone by like a letter thrown in the letter box you like saying none can tell yes I like saying it just a moment no strength none can tell old-fashioned words three words kindly the pain I have a pain is it my lip is it someone else's lip I don't dare go close to my pain ought to is it a wall in pain or is it me

I am sitting in my suit on the stone floor that's certain that's proved that's agreed there's no changing minds about that I am little I am pulled forward with the weight of my lip hanging I can't cry help it is still November it is horrid it is whistling my head falls back on the rim you yes you the little girl in me be brave you were before separate me from the cold I want to go I want to go back to our home I don't want to live on the stone floor at night there must be a remedy a solution yes of course children I have stood up it took me a long time it's the results that count chattering teeth yes those I've certainly got it's not pleasant at all perhaps its the end of the world I can't tell I'm getting mixed up in the darkness my teeth are chattering so much it's frightening if it was the chatter of a corpse courage now we shall win don't ask too much of me who's asking anything of you it was just a manner of speaking if I could find where my legs are I'd get out of here if I didn't talk so much it's true butcher I am asking you a question you'd be doing me a favour changing me into a nice pink escallop

I'm looking for the doorknob they were looking for their twin soul I don't think I'm in my normal state my lip is hanging my teeth are chattering my buttocks are orphans almost a comic song for an old time entertainer big success my feet keep going on and on frozen water lily leaves were you there precious were you there little love you were there my memory at last the promised land the doorknob we were waiting for you the table is set you will take a little vermouth won't you we've put it to cool take off your coat think of this as your own home I was near you doorknob I didn't know you were there you existed my hand is burning you are all frosted come in come in you are really welcome we were just going to eat you'll take a bite with us I'd die if you abandoned me doorknob come in don't stand on ceremony I was just carving it it will be tender it was larded I talk I talk a harvest doesn't talk I'm just restoring my spirits my sagging spirits I can see them in serried ranks little sisters of the poor I warm you up as I warm the doorknob why don't you come in there's a good fire rum pancakes

I'm opening the door you spend your life opening thirty-six doors onto the void this lip hanging down right down below my chin the earth is a magnet a burial a big eater she is everyone knows it we could all club together then we could have a stair light after all though there's intimacy in the darkness why get rid of it she shall have our last word I'm walking I'm going up the first step of the stairs will I raise myself above the history of civilizations what is my civilization the dirt the grease on the banister the dirt on the landings shall I get it this second story shall I deserve it this second story I'm only a little baby I'm dark blackness I'm soup for the people I'm billycan near Greek column and let's hear no more about it it's freezing in my bones four doors to one landing that's too many don't come in I don't know you don't force me to throw you out my children are doing their homework I shall call my husband if you don't go

I'm looking for a nose you haven't met a nose on the Rocky Mountains I'm looking for a few fingers you haven't met a few fingers on the fir trees in the Black Forest I'm looking for two ears you haven't met two ears in the African desert I'm reconstituting myself you've come too late revivifying scent of a sprig of thyme I am collapsing I have reached my door I am falling my body is saying a slow goodbye this is what steaming back into port means dozing off no impossible my lip's hanging sleepy-bye sleepy-bye little girl I won't rock you three months' overdue they are with nursie's pay I'll rock you if the money order comes sleepy-bye

sleepy-bye little girl I won't take you in my arms the money hasn't
come I am camping on my doormat the top spun on the merry-go-
round the merry-go-round spun too the top is stupid it's enough
to make you faint with happiness it's so idiotic on your knees I said
quicker than that who are you to say the clever little girl it's her turn
on your knees if you want to get onto your feet in front of the door
if you want to hold on to the doorknob I can't lift my head my lip
is hanging down I'm going to try but then little girl you'll leave me
in peace won't you leave me out on the landing to live oh to live
mouth open consolation of consolations I shall be in my own room
I shall see my lip I am afraid.

Report of anonymous observer. He saw her when she went out
at seven in the evening. She walked past the trash bins in the
passageway, she enveloped them in her gaze exactly the way she
does orphans out walking, on Sundays, in the afternoons. To be
noted: she said, Hello little sisters to them, I shall be back at eleven,
at midnight, at one o'clock...

Hello little sisters your ashes your dirt I recognize you in my
five-and-dime mirror a trash bin has come too close to me tonight
and I have fallen onto its rim and inside it well my chick that was
it, eh, a vision of horror, tell me little sister why have you wounded
me yes I enveloped you in a long gaze and you gave me the black
diamonds of your coffee grounds I collapsed on top of you I frighten
myself with your ashes and your dirt on my hanging lip.

Her hair, all sticky with caked blood, was falling into her eyes;
ashes, clinkers, peelings were stuck all over her head; her eyes were
ringed with broad smudges of coal dust. She pulled herself up from
the divan, she sat up on the divan without taking her eyes off herself. She couldn't manage to part herself from a poor woman who
daubed her lips with blood, with ashes, with filth. Her mushrooms
were growing before her eyes. One compensation: her rabbit coat
hadn't changed. Hodgepodge of refuse at twenty to five in the
morning. Nothing surprised her except the unharmed throat beneath her hanging lip. She began to tremble again. Her teeth were
once more chattering. Swollen lips came to meet her swollen lips
in the cheap mirror she held in both hands. Terror: she must clean
the lips with a piece of cotton. She miaowed, she hunted for it, for
the cotton. By miaowing, she lessens her distress a little. The five-and-
dime mirror fell from her hands without breaking. She picked it up
again carefully. It doesn't make life easy, a lip hanging down with
two mushrooms on it.

The piece of cotton terrified her. She removed the ashes, the coal dust, the trash with a handkerchief soaked in cold water. Her wound is deep, the roof over her head has been paid for for the next three months. Reassuring. It's comic, she's afraid of wetting her hair, of catching cold. She can't resist it, she must pick up the mirror again to make herself realize she is hurt. She looks at herself without wanting to look at herself. The mirror falls from her hands, she picks it up once again, she trembles, her teeth chatter, her two ulcers look like two lotto balls.

She got into bed. She hadn't the courage to ask herself at what time she had said good night to Yves Lévy and Marie-Louise Villiers, or why the fall had been so brutal. Her pain wasn't as great as it should have been. She accepted. Docile, she huddled down into her suffering. She talked out loud from time to time; she said: my bottom is still not warm yet. At last she went to sleep.

How did she manage to feed herself? By mashing everything into a thick soup. Then she tilted her head back and poured the liquid nourishment between her lips without touching the wound, the two mushrooms. She was a careful stranger to herself, an attentive stranger to whose ministrations she submitted. She dressed, did her hair, nothing was real, she was in pain. She walked round her room, round the unfurnished room beyond, as she might have walked round a hospital corridor in slippers and robe.

*

I was expecting Clara Malraux. She arrived at three in the afternoon.

She cried out: 'My poor child ... what has happened to you?'

Clara. That beautiful voice. Shadow, light, a soft, low note, a pool of peace, Clara's musical voice.

I told her.

'I shall kiss you all the same,' she said.

She was wearing a black leather jacket.

Had I seen a doctor? No, there was no point, I wanted to have dinner at Jacques's that evening...

I mustn't risk tetanus. She held my hand.

I began again: 'We had been to eat at a restaurant, I'd had two glasses of wine ... I wasn't drunk...'

Clara Malraux believed me. At what time did they drop me off? I had no idea.

Clara ran out to telephone Dr Carasso, Marie-Louise Villiers's husband.

I was alone again, and I began to worry.

Jacques. My God, Jacques. What will he say? Will he dare question me about it? He will think: She was dead drunk, she fell down dead drunk. And it's not true. I shan't be able to defend myself. I feel like howling. They will be sceptical, I shall be silent. How could I lie with two strawberries on my lip? If you fell, Jacques, I should fall.

Carasso came in.

'Good afternoon,' he said.

He drew the perfectly ordinary greeting out and gave it the sonority of a violin.

'You had a pleasant evening, I hear,' he said benevolently.

It was an insinuation: my two protuberances were illogical.

'Look at her lip, quickly,' Clara broke in.

Carasso came over. He opened his bag.

'Did you get back here late?' Clara asked.

'...It was twenty to five by Maurice Sachs's alarm clock,' I said without hesitation.

'No, my child, no! Marie-Louise was home at ten to one. I was working, I wasn't in bed. They must have dropped you here at twenty-five to one at the very latest!'

'That's impossible! I tell you it's impossible!'

'Boil this syringe,' he said to Clara.

He pulled over a chair and sat down. 'I'm listening,' he said.

I told my story again.

Two cocktails, two glasses of wine.

'I know,' he said. 'Marie-Louise told me the same thing.'

I wanted the key to the mystery.

'What happened to me?'

'You were in a coma. On a stone floor, for four hours.'

'Is that serious?'

'You could have died of pneumonia when you came to. But it's not serious any more. You've survived that danger.'

Death, with an iron fist, seizes you near a trash bin. Death, finding you distasteful, rejects you, lets you drop back among the refuse. And now, for good behaviour, an anti-tetanus injection.

He snapped his bag shut, he started to leave. 'How did you get up here?'

'I dragged myself up in the dark...'

'Is there no stair light?' Carasso asked, interested.

'No.'

'It must have taken you quite a while ...'

'I don't know, I don't remember ...'

My struggles the previous night: sawn-off stumps. The five-and-dime mirror reflecting ashes, refuse, and filth: a prism of hope.

'Can I go?' I begged as the doctor and friend was shaking my hand and refusing to be paid.

Carasso opened his eyes very wide.

'They're expecting me this evening.'

Carasso became an interrogator. 'Who are "they"? Who do you mean "they"?'

'Them,' I said stubbornly.

He didn't pursue it. He was perfectly willing that I should go and eat with 'them' that evening.

As soon as they were gone, I took up my mirror again as an addict takes up her syringe. I checked the gifts I would be offering then on the eve of my birthday: a papier-mâché face, two blue swags under my eyes, two revolting strawberries on my lower lip. A numbed soul's blossoming. Jacques ... he was asleep last night, he was as pure as the walls of a prison by moonlight. He weighs me down, oh, he weighs me down, I told the five-and-dime mirror.

And Simone de Beauvoir? Where has she vanished to? You fall into piles of garbage, you fall into a coma, you lie in death's antechamber, you crawl out of it, not a thought for her, not a single impulse towards her.

My answer.

Sitting at her table in the Flore, she writes. That is my miraculous picture, that is my miraculous memory in the present, in the future, and its colours do not fade. She must not be disturbed, even if I were dying on the side of the road. She is working, I am squandering; I waste my energies on my sentimental orgies and my debauches. Why should I importune her with my aberrations? She is not an intimate friend, I don't know her well enough to lead her down into my tragic circus rings, to offer her rides on my melodramatic merry-go-rounds. She would refuse. I would tell her everything if she were less admirable. What am I concealing from her? A dog. Here life is elsewhere, the dog can only sniff the scent along the bottoms of walls. Jacques reads *Cécile* in his bedroom, Simone de Beauvoir is preparing to write *The Second Sex*; where is there room for me to wriggle in?

Rejected without their having rejected me, idle, I wander off to kill time on suburban railway platforms. The irises are fading, I rest in the iris's wilting tissue-paper petals. Clock, my darling, you're wearing yourself out, but I have nothing to do but watch my ash falling, my sex is dead. I say Denis out loud, and I separate the syllables ... Denis will fade, he will no longer be a tissue-paper iris on which I can rest. Clock, my darling, nibble away his years. What shall I have more than I do when they have been nibbled? Melancholy on the newly painted bench, a long ribbon, is there any meaning there? Dead leaf, first sign of fall, take me with you. They have done a moonlight flit, they have left the carcass behind, should I wander over towards the market, it will be over at one? I won't go, they have forgotten their fox-terrier in the café, not a soul in sight as the dead leaves waltz. Charming little houses, but of course, nonchalant smoke plumes, scorched grass, blue-tinted funerals. I go back into Paris, but in good time. Denis ... if it were just the nutshell at the end of his meal with you ... give it to me, I will gulp it down. Quiet, foul toad, oh, quiet.

*

A letter from Patrice, received on my birthday, tells me that he is coming to see me. I shall open my door to him the day after tomorrow. Catastrophe. My lank hair, my greasy hair, my nose, my lip, my mushrooms, my blue swags, how am I to hide them? Buy a mask? My lip swings as it hangs; the mask will move. Refuse to answer when he rings? That would be despicable. I've never told him I'm beautiful. You've never told him you're ugly either, though ... Bah, my ugliness fits in with all that heavy parent stuff in the letters. We must just go on playing at pure spirits, only in the flesh. Impossible, my brain is empty. I want to be attractive to him, I want to be attractive to him. And then? And then nothing. He's just a kid. Too frail, at his age. And anyway the calendar is eyeing me from up there, reminding me of my last drops of blood ... Oh, how foul, such reasoning. Where will he sleep? In a hotel? In my bed. Mere youngsters don't have money. I shall switch out the light, we shall talk about Michaux, about Breton. You certainly think ahead, you've certainly got everything worked out, haven't you, madame hot-pants. Michaux, Breton in the darkness of your bedroom, and then? Then, curly head on my shoulder, away from my mushrooms, everyone will be happy, Michaux, Breton. And then, and then? A child, children are clumsy, they can't make up their minds. We'll force him. Young man, you were old in your letters. I am an adolescent with my enthusiams for Rousseau's *Confessions*, for Van Gogh's *Letters,* for Benjamin Constant's *Cécile* ...

Time passes. A permanent would work a transformation. With my hair in curls, I should look like an older version of him ... Who told me he has curly hair? Greece. Alcibiades. Plato. If I wash my hair, its silkiness will be a surprise for his fingers. But the letdown next morning ... It will be greasy again by then. Movements, that's what you need, mademoiselle. Just movements, as we call them. Waves. Like the summer breeze blowing through the wheat. Just the style for a sensible, serious-minded woman. No, it might make him serious-minded too. Short hair, in curls. Antinoüs disturbs everyone, with Antinoüs curls I shall disturb him. The rue de Charonne early in the afternoon, the first hairdresser's I come to will be the best. Not expensive, and ten years off.

*

Rollers, curlers, net, helmet, dryer, clips, pins, ringlets, less hot, too hot, hotter, ambition, pretentions, hope, heady desires, magazines, colours, photos, moonlight, Monte Carlo, Monaco, white shirt front, tails, evening dress, high life, gala, evening air, lighter, smoking room, seaside sound of the dryer, refrain of the fan, seduction factory, to seduce a sex you must be seductive. Rollers, curlers, net, helmet, comb-out, set, how much do I owe you, a tip for Patrice's sex. I shall be irresistible with my will power so tightly rolled and curled? They pick me, they pull off my petals. They blow me out, I am their candle. Who do? The queers, the others. I exist when I write. To be dependent on words, is that existing? To hunt for expressions, to find expressions ... Your home for the aged is assured. I emancipate myself: cock, cock, cock ... physical culture on a glacier. Modesty, a fortress. Let it be blown sky-high by the dynamite on my lips. Cock, ring on my front door tomorrow and I will let you in. Open your fly for the fireworks display, open up, open up ... I will curl it; rollers, curlers, clips, pins, a hairdresser on the rue de Charonne is what I must have. You'll find one a hundred yards along the street. Thank you. Don't mention it. What am I when I write? Quickly. Quickly, before you open the door of the hairdresser's. I am a forger making a bad copy of her neighbour's work. And who is my neighbour? The sky, the stars. Rollers, curlers, lacquer, comb. What am I when I write? A deliverance, but I am not there. Always me in what I write. Always. But I give without counting to this terrible paper. What-am-I-when-I-write? This time I've got you by the throat, my copyist. What am I when I write ... a peasant, a peasant giving away the Angelus; the page is so vast to be filled.

*

She consulted her big book. 'I can't take you now, madame. To-morrow at half past two. Would that suit you?'

Tomorrow? Patrice's sex will be too tightly curled, too formal.

'Tomorrow? Impossible. I shan't be in Paris by then. I'm flying out this evening. You can't fit me in now?'

To lose or not to lose a customer who flies in and out of Paris? The question is Shakespearean in stature. She hesitates, she throws her ballpoint pen down on the big book. 'Myriam ... take care of madame, will you?'

Myriam comes over, her hands in long orange gloves. She has been colouring someone's hair.

The owner's face is different now, she does not trifle with Viscounts and Constellations.

Is this a bad omen? She isn't helping me on with my robe. She has been colouring a pretty young thing's hair. Now she must turn her attention to an ageing noodle.

'It's too long,' she said, pain in her voice. 'Shall I cut it?'

One moment, graceful castratrix. What if I should want to let my hair pour down over his burning sex ...

'Couldn't you give me a pageboy?'

'It wouldn't suit you,' she said. 'It would age you.'

Why should she flatter me?

She is rivalling Solomon in all his glory with her long hair down over her shoulders.

'Why isn't it possible, the pageboy?'

'It just wouldn't stay in.'

She looked at my face in the glass, then at her own. Surely the comparison couldn't be necessary. To cut and set a hanging lip, two strawberries ... It was her job, why should I feel sorry for her?

'With a permanent, would it stay in then?'

'You wanted a permanent?'

I want everything.

She left me.

The salon was full. Full of women who got up at six and went to bed at eleven. Women for whom thinking about their own appearances was a theft between two loads of washing. Women who were knitting garments for their men even under the dryer, women who were afraid of missing their children out from school . . .

'Shall I cut it? It will be more practical . . .'

'Yes, cut it.'

My hair is falling on the hairdresser's floor, I am falling into ruins. All round, the gaiety of brightly clicking scissors as it happens. I love my hair, I yearn for it already as Myriam carries it away in her dustpan. Where will it end up, my hair? I loved it to the point of sobs, I would have stuck it back anyhow all over my head. Myriam has made a sacrifice of me.

*

Frizzed? Yes, I was frizzed as I had never been. A nylon scourer over a hanging lip.

I danced a wild savage's dance in the empty room, I hopped around it on one foot. I must terrify the wall, appal the wallpaper. I stamped on the floorboards. I jumped higher and higher, I lifted my arms to the ceiling, I ground my teeth, I adjured the ceiling, I accused the ceiling, I took the ceiling as my witness: I was a thicket, a frizz, a bramble bush. Panting for breath, I menaced the mirror. I pulled at my hair with both hands, I would have liked to pull the top off my skull. I was bellowing with fury. There was a ring at the door. Him already? I opened the door. No one there. The landing surprised me with its usual candour. I slammed the door it its face. I put my head under the tap. I was forgetting: rain makes hair curl. I sat and brushed my hair. Fifteen hundred strokes, two thousand strokes. The little curls uncoiled, then they coiled up again.

*

Next day. Port and bedside lamp. Classical preparations. But we must conceal the preparations. In an hour it will be dark. He's late. He's late, I said to myself. He is late, I say. I can speak properly when I want to. Correct and determined am I with my approach works. In brief . . . In brief, what? In brief, I am an old beau expecting a young lady. No, I haven't sprayed the pillow with scent. Port and bedside lamp. Bedside lamp and port. Atmosphere, that's your best mousetrap. A rosewater seducer. No hook, just a cottony atmosphere as I fish for a little damsel. Loathsome, that word 'damsel.' I am selling off disused stock. I loathe it and I employ it. Speaking and writing. Too late to begin an oration, it's getting dark. What if I were to rehearse?

'Good evening' (slower, slower). 'I hope you didn't have too much trouble finding it?' (Sing out more, envelop him in your voice.) 'Good evening . . .'

A ring. Patrice.

'Good evening . . . I hope you didn't have too much trouble finding it?'

'I read your name on the directory downstairs.'

'Come in.'

It is already in the past: he has seen the monster, he has stepped over it. No reflex, no start, no change of expression. He didn't show a thing; what style!

'It's through there. I've just moved, this room isn't furnished yet . . .'

He is dying of shyness. Stimulating. Don't lie, it's not stimulating. He's just the cautious type; he's taking you apart, my little one. Can't you see that head of yours, tiny curls, tiny ringlets, rolling on the cobbles?

Why is he waiting so patiently in the empty room? His suitcase can't be very heavy.

'Come in . . . come in . . . This is my room.'

His neck, a light-brown furrow around his neck . . . A warm Puritanism lurking there.

'We haven't shaken hands . . .'

'No,' I said, with the presentiment of friendship.

I had forgotten it, our handshake, I was examining him so intently. But he hadn't lost sight of friendship.

Sparing of words, so far: he has to emerge out of his secret shelter every time. He doesn't want to part from his case, it has the provinces written all over it it's enough to make you weep, the conscious way he's hanging on to that suitcase . . .

I say: 'Shall I turn on the light or leave it as it is?'

He stares at me, then answers: 'I prefer the half light.'

He weighs his words. A careful character who cares infinitely for literature, that I know already.

'Put down your suitcase . . .'

His lips part slightly; a young man vanishes, driven out by the man he will become; then the lips move together again. He has not spoken.

He brings himself to the point. 'I've brought you a present.'

'What is it? Tell me quickly!'

'A half pound of butter. You asked me for it.'

It is true, I did ask him to bring it.

Still, always, that need to keep my black market going, to extort, to push up the bidding.

He has taken it out of his case.

The butter is wrapped in a cabbage leaf still so fresh ... still with a bloom on it... I imagine a sculptor leading a double life: sculptor by night, grocer by day.

I take the butter into the kitchen, we are laughing, laughing... we don't know why.

'Take off your raincoat, then!'

I call the words through from the kitchen—and immediately regret them. That 'then' was too familiar.

I walk back into the bedroom and surprise him looking at the photos of Sartre and de Beauvoir above my table. He stares at me again; his gaze is warm. People will be attracted by him, this hermit; he has regular features.

'Why don't you take off your raincoat?'

'I prefer to keep it on.'

He is protecting himself, I understand that. Armour yourself, shield yourself, man-flower.

I lapse into idiocies. 'The journey wasn't too tiring, I hope?'

'No ... not too tiring.'

He bites his nails like a schoolboy.

'You don't look comfortable over by the door ...'

He bristles. 'I'm perfectly comfortable, thank you!'

An attack repulsed; he lowers his eyes.

Sometimes his regional accent comes through. It is bluff: a good drinking-man relaxing. Then it vanishes again; the serious and uneasy adolescent reappears.

He talks to me about *L'Asphyxie*, I tell him about my short sentences. He likes them. Let's change the subject.

There has been someone between us ever since he came in. *Nadja*. She lights up the room even before he lets André Breton's name fall.

'Why don't we have a glass of port?'

I have taken him by surprise. Artaud, Van Gogh, Van Gogh's

letters to his brother Théo, can all that be served in a glass of port?
Can it be nibbled in a biscuit?

I bring out the bottle and the glasses from under my table. A lot
of water has flowed under the bridge since my approach works were
dug ... My caressing hands are outmoded.

'I never drink,' he says. 'A little port, if you like ...'

And there he sits, losing himself in the Paris sky.

'A cigarette?' I offer the packet.

'Oh, yes, please!'

He smokes with avidity. The taste and smell of tobacco must be
new for him. I work it out: I have been smoking for twenty-three
years. It is something that never fails to surprise me: old age is
other people.

He smokes quickly; he is getting to know the Paris sky through
my windowpane.

My plane trip, my lie. My curlers, my rollers. My dance, my fury.
Yesterday crumbles away, yesterday would reduce me to hysterical
laughter if I didn't restrain myself. This evening is quiet and sensible. Yesterday was stupid.

He smokes, he smokes, he is awkward. He is sitting on the edge
of an upright chair, near the doorway. His uncomfortable position
... a supplement to his modesty, an extra precaution.

Is he wealthy? Is he poor? The provinces do not give up their
secrets just like that. Probably quite well off, though: he is modestly
but not shabbily dressed.

He likes my street, he likes my neighbourhood, he likes my room;
they are all part of the Paris he is exploring through a window.

'I can't stay long,' he warns me.

After he has spoken, a slight tremor of the lips. Is he ashamed
because of my loneliness?

Suddenly we have nothing to say. I pull myself together. 'Won't
you eat with me? Won't you sleep here?'

He stands up. I have frightened him.

'...I could have put the mattress down for you in the empty
room, we could have eaten there ... on the table where I write.'

I have reassured him; he sits down again. May he smoke a
Gauloise? He extracts it from his raincoat pocket, his battered,
beloved pack.

Where is he going to sleep? Where is he going to eat? At an
uncle's house. What if his uncle's name were Jacques ... My head
spins for a moment. An uncle who lives in the sixteenth arrondisse-

ment. I breathe again. But what if it is really a girl he's been writing to? I open my arms to them.

'I can stay another half hour,' he announces.

He is not trying to humiliate me; he is offering me hospitality.

Once more we are left with nothing to say. He stares down at his shoes; that's the best he can find. We wait patiently; the seconds stretch out.

It is really time I switched on the light; too much darkness might look suggestive. No, I won't switch on the light. I shall let myself steep in the gentle flow of my disillusions.

It is the dusk with its spellbinder's insinuating stealth? Is it a bat, this velvet against my forehead, against my cheek? It is my own sweet reason, my fortieth year. This young man has brought them to me. What is he for me? The acceptance of my age, my years. My fortieth year is a clear spring. I am pushing off, contentedly, down-stream towards my fiftieth year. He is wise, he sits in silence, I clutch a handful of grey hair in my hand: my sixtieth year, and I am at peace.

I draw the curtains; I go from acceptance to acceptance. He has brought me back to my realities without tears, without grimaces. I bring him back to his essential:

'How you love *L'Amour fou*! How well you write about it...'

His face lights up. It is the light of those who have given them-selves once and for all. He will admire Breton to the end of his existence.

Paris, despite its variety of greys, the quiet, meditative time of day, the insignificance of its noises, Paris, this evening, seems frivolous to me: I have beside me a true adept of the religion we call the love of books.

He has stood up again. The darkness is eating into him, the folds of his raincoat are catching night's first shadows.

'André Breton,' he begins.

His emotion paralyses him.

'André Breton ... is all I have ... I have nothing but him...'

'But he is enough.'

He gazes at me, speechless. Happy. Content. Mad with silence. Mad with being understood. Mad with sharing.

'I have Michaux too,' he says very quietly.

He moves over to the window. The shadows, the dusk, slowness of our inward collapses. Our defeats, all dreams; and our dreams fol-lowing the shadows, following the dusk.

He has left the window, he has cleared his throat. What are we waiting for?

Without warning, he recites several pages of *Nadja*.

It is our evening prayer. This young man's love for Breton's poetry works miracles. André Breton is there with us. In that room, above the roofs. I listen, I touch his prose with my fingertips. He purges us. The city darkens, we are deeply stirred, the poet brings us calm. It was the hour of defeats and collapses; it is the hour of salvation. Night, the beginning of the night. An adolescent boy has given me the most precious thing he has. If I did not write, then he would not have come to visit me. I feel gratitude towards my little book; it has raised me higher than itself.

I don't thank him, he is worth more than that. He goes back to gazing at his shoes. I, too, gaze at my shoes: this young man who hasn't yet lived has given me my today and my ancient future. I suggest a walk together along the Seine next day; I am freed from my approach works. He knows the way, he has closed the door gently behind him. It is night.

I undo my bed, I slide down into it, nothing must be disturbed. I stretch out on my back, my arms down by my sides. I am where I belong. Two tears and I am at peace. No more tears are needed this evening. A vista, a lark's cry opens in my head: it is hope stretching far ahead, it is lucidity.

An hour later I get up again and hug to my heart the notebook in which I have just finished writing *L'Affamée*. I pull on my nightdress, I get back into bed, I find myself back with my arms down by my sides, with that cry of light in my head; Patrice has given me a lesson, and tomorrow I am going for a walk with him.

*

The afternoon of the next day, a couple on the quai Malaquais.

'Hello,' the woman says to me.

She is inconspicuous, she is remarkable with her forget-me-not blue eyes, she is modest in her little fur coat. I am mad with happiness at having met her so unexpectedly.

'Good afternoon, madame,' the man says to me.

His great fur-lined lumber jacket spatters you with its strength and energy.

'Good afternoon, monsieur,' I answer, tongue-tied.

Handshakes all round.

'Your poor little face,' the woman says. She has noticed my swollen lip.

'See you soon. Telephone me,' she says finally.

'Oh, yes,' I say, overwhelmed by her gift.

They continue their walk.

'Aren't you going to ask me who that was?'

'I didn't dare,' he says.

'That was Sartre and Beauvoir.'

'Sartre and Beauvoir? Really them?'

We walked from the Boulevard Saint-Michel to the Place de la Concorde. He told me all about the evening he'd spent at *Les Lorientais*, with Claude Luter playing. Paris had won his heart, he was going to come back, he was going to study in Paris.

'I have a friend who'd like to write to you as well,' he said to me when our walk was over. 'His name is Flavien.'

'Then let him write.'

The ritual signings of one's press copies come around like the seasons of the year; they are always the same. I had reread and copied out the same names. Had I been away from Jacqueline Bour since the previous signing session? She was so very much the same as always. Amiable, eager to help. She is unbelievable; she defies wrinkles. I should like to say to her: Lend me your eraser ... But what would I do with it, her eraser? I was a shadow. I had come to sign copies of an uncommercial book in a windowless office, between glazed bookshelves all round the walls, surrounded by names as heavy as statues. I felt guilty: what I had written would serve no purpose. This book, its pages sewn together, was already tumbling down into the dungeons of the forgotten before it was even sent out to the booksellers. I would have liked to hide my face in my checked smock, to sob in it, to write without looking, at someone's dictation, the names of Messieurs X., Y., and Z. I would have liked not to have to think at all. I remembered only too well what

it was like when I worked for Plon. With what hauteur, with
what silent disdain we treated the authors when they re-emerged,
after they had done all their signing, when they asked for more
publicity, when they worried about their books. We rushed to read
the galleys of the most thrilling books, and after that the author was
merely a stray in the corridors. That was my state of mind as I
slid its card into each copy of *L'Affamée*. I would have liked to run
away, I would have liked to paint my skin and camouflage myself
with leaf mould from the forests, to give wild Indian cries rather
than to go on writing and coming to sign my name in a jungle where
no one attacked me.

*

Simone de Beauvoir told me over and over again: 'Just have confidence. It will all work out.' She said it to me firmly. How will it
all work out? Have I the right to live, have I the right to eat with
my two or three hours' writing a day?

*

L'Affamée has appeared. Not a single review except in *Les Lettres
Françaises* (if I remember rightly). Since then I throw grateful
glances at the windows of the humble newsagents I pass on the way
back from the Aligre market, from Dominique's, from the Reuilly-
Diderot métro station, from the Faidherbe-Chalingy métro station.
Simone de Beauvoir is patient ... She listens to my laments, to my
sobs, to my tirades; she is forced to sit through the same scene, to
watch the same bad actress giving the same old performance. I tell
her: 'I want to wash dishes in a café, I want to be your charwoman.'
She doesn't believe a word of it, and yet she replies with great
gentleness: 'No, Violette ... no. Don't lose confidence ... Go on
writing...' The dirty dishes, the brooms, the furniture to be
dusted in other people's houses ... I dig in my heels, I am determined to be ill-tempered with myself. I must go on writing because
she insists that I must. I am perplexed. Yesterday she explained to
me that I ought to try to remember Hermine and Gabriel, to tell that
story the way I tell it to her. She has almost convinced me. But to
remember Hermine, that means remembering Isabelle too, I told
myself in my beloved métro. To succeed. What does that mean, to
succeed? I pondered the question as I sucked aniseed candy from a
vending machine, as we went through station after station. To succeed means to go beyond oneself without showing it. I was suc-

ceeding when I strode through those meadows, alone in the world, bearing my burdens. I am not crushed with depression every day of the week, I am not demoralized every hour of the day. That is my undoing, and that is my salvation. My depression, my picking-up-of-pins profession. I was made for half measures the way the chameleon was made for varying colours. I have vitality, and I soak it soggy with tears. Much ado about nothing if I add the number of pages in *L'Affamée* to those in *L'Asphyxie*.

*

Patrice writes less. Flavien writes more and more. His letters are sad, passionate; I carry his photo in my wallet. Sometimes I make a mistake, sometimes I try to buy wilting lettuce with the image of that long, romantic face. Dominique smiles and hands me my image back. I hand over the right change. Flavien wants me to pay him a visit. I do not speak his name to anyone. He stirs something inside me, he is so sad. I struggle during my sleepless nights, I push this shadowy eighteen-year-old away from me ever more feebly. What if it were a conspiracy, a gang trying to make a fool of me: 'Go on, write to the loony old girl.' Impossible. Patrice was genuine. What if it were the idea of someone who wishes me well, who's giving me Patrice and Flavien as a compensation ... I don't know what to think. I can hear their hiccuping chuckles in the distance, I can see them swapping my letters during classes. I reread Flavien's at three in the morning, I tell myself I am despicable with my suspicions. He needs me. I shall go; tomorrow it will be too late, tomorrow I shall be fifty, sixty, seventy-five. Running after schoolboys ... My last flickers— let's hope so, anyway. And Patrice? He is madly in love with the modern poets, he sits reading them in his grandfather's house in Combourg. I'll go at the end of the week, there's not an instant to lose. Yes? No? Yes. He is a day boy, it will be easy. I shall leave on Saturday afternoon. I'm coming. Just a moment, I must file my nails.

*

My oilskin raincoat inspires no confidence in the receptionist of the town's best hotel. It is glittering, it is challenging their rainy town.

One grouch hands me a card to fill in, another demands to see my identity card.

We go upstairs. Three scornful fingers are curled through the handle of my case. People just don't travel with aluminium-rimmed plywood luggage. They have too much self-respect. Too flashy by half, too conspicuous. Oh, be quiet, old grog-blossom, trudging along the dark corridors.

'I am giving you our very best room, the hotel is empty. Whatever you do, don't polish your shoes on the bedspread. I would be held responsible ... One smudge of polish and I'm out on my neck. The telephone is over there by the bed. Shall I bring in the key for you?'

I have the tomato-juice-coloured moquette of the best hotel in town, which is more than I bargained for. What a bed! Big enough to tuck Flavien and his whole family into! Luxurious or shabby, hotel rooms are always adrift from life, they belong to no one. Who will shake it awake, this well-behaved room floating through time? Handed on from father to son. The hotelkeepers have procreated, the furniture has hardened arteries. The gallows-bird look of the chairs, the crushed velvet. Gallows-bird. I have to exhume it to use it.

I pick up the telephone, I put on my grandest air. 'I'm expecting a visitor at eight. Let me know when he arrives.'

'We would do that in any case.'

They know their job, bumpkin!

Seven twenty-five. What if he were coming to slit my throat at eight o'clock? What if he weren't a schoolboy at all ... The room is never let, the lift boy doesn't even take the trouble to open the shutters ... So much the better, I am not being cut off from Flavien. The darkness is Flavien. I don't know him. Unpleasing, that nose shining above the shiny oilskin. Shall I give it a tap with my puff? Gestures, always the same, made with the hope of not growing old, of not dying. Shall I tap it a little more? A third layer? A last cloud around my grouser's snout. God, what a drag, this room! It must be laughing its ceiling off at my clouds of face powder before my death, for I am dying, for we are all dying in the present, in the future. Lipstick, forbidden. I mustn't daub Flavien with it. Why Flavien? Patrice was enough with his three pages recited in the half darkness. No, no, no ... Flavien, just for the hell of it. Dress rehearsal at a quarter to eight.

Now let's imagine it. He knocks. Patrice knocked at my door, too. I open the door, not a soul. I ought to stop there. Pay for the room without having used it, and vanish. He knocks. In my imagination. Boldness and shyness, a delicious mixture. Come in! Too radiant. Do come in! Too hearty. You can come in ... Too syrupy. Come in,

I was expecting you ... Too lecherous. If I lie down on the bed I shall have to jump up, then the noise of the springs will be an embarrassment. What if I stay there as he comes in? He'll say to himself: That a woman? A bumpkin in black on white sheets. Why not? I can bite his lips for a little blood. I know! What if I stayed close to this Steinbeck book on the table, in front of the closed shutters. As soon as he knocks I can snatch it up, my fashionable American novel. Come in, do come in ... a far-away voice. I have difficulty freeing myself from Steinbeck's world, yes, I sink back into it. She was reading when I met her. That always places a woman. I can go on reading as he stands there. Flavien! So you came! Laughable, it's so old hat. What if I were to lean my elbows on the bedboard? I lower my eyelids, and now I look like an insipid Saint-Sulpice Madonna. He'll turn around and walk out with a stick of barley sugar between his legs. More imperious then? Come in! Do you smoke? I thrust the cigarette between his lips, I light it. Amazon-style. Dancing lesson on Thursday afternoons ... More of a curve to the arm (resting on the end of the bed), as if you were holding a basket of eggs in your arm, or better still a Greuze jug. Perhaps I've come a little too early, it's only ten to eight. Were you thinking? Yes, I was thinking. What about? About the falseness of this situation.

My elbow gets tired, I get bored. What if I were to call down for a Scotch? It would help fill the last few minutes. They don't have any Scotch.

Two minutes past eight by the station clock. There is a train due to leave at two minutes past eight, I am on it, the guard's whistle goes right through me, that's living, even if I do get out at the next village. But I'm not on a train, I'm in a bedroom waiting for a teenage boy. Three minutes past eight. No luck, I always pick men who play hard to get. Men? Two men: Jacques and Gabriel. Three minutes past eight: I am a woman abandoned, he doesn't give a damn about me. Suddenly the town is heavy to carry, despite the windowpanes, the curtains, the closed shutters. The room drifts on without me, the town ignores me, the hotel corridors are silent. Why am I here? Why did I come? Discouragement churns inside me, I am a battered barley-field; to live means to read, to write, to behave. I am not behaving. To live is to roll in the mud, poor stunted creature. I prefer scouring my saucepans. Tell me, lavender-blue ashtray, kindly witness ... but let me collapse a moment first

on the moquette ... Why wasn't Patrice's patience enough for me?
What am I about to play at with Flavien? Never mind. To arms,
the Band of No Hope!

I powder my nose again and quickly redo my hair. Four
minutes past eight. He will be an absent-minded professor, he has
no idea of time. If I take my arm off the end of the bed, he won't
come. Six minutes past eight. A bastard, a rotten swine. My mother's
all-purpose words of invective. Let me suck the words she used to
chew. The hatred in her mouth is no more than a faint sweetness in
mine; I lack her character. Windows? Those are windows? The
long downpour of depression starting. God, I must have been bored
in Paris to come all this way to stand sighing in a hotel room.

I pick up the telephone. 'Has no one asked for me?'

'We would have telephoned up to you ...'

So what do I do? Get into bed? Snore and pretend to be asleep in
order to humiliate him? At nine o'clock in the evening what can she
eat, this piece of surplus stock in a hotel bedroom?

'Can you serve me a meal in my room?'

'The kitchens are closed.'

'A sandwich?'

'The kitchens are closed.'

'A rusk? A biscuit?'

'The kitchens are closed.'

If she were to go out and look for some place ... She is too tired.
What has she come expecting to find? What has she come looking
for? Her failures with Jacques and Gabriel. A quarter past nine. He
has made a fool of her, her Flavien. Old? She, old? She may well
feel indignant.

A knock. At last.

Tears. What is one to do with tears? Quick, fingertips.

In her most natural voice: 'Come in ... Come in ...'

'May I turn down your bed now?'

Let us remember Paris this time last week. L'Artistic, my friendly
neighbourhood cinema. I am doing my two dishes after my meal,
the whim suddenly takes me, I rush out to the cinema. Very practical: the first show is over at half past ten. You see the film right
through, the next day you still look well-rested. I get there half an
hour early, but there is always someone waiting in the foyer when
I arrive. I wait panting among the posters and the portraits of stars
done in blackcurrant jelly. I have run and run along the rue Basfroi
with a pale-green heart between my teeth: a mint lollipop. I pay

for my seat, the usherette abandons me inside, I have the whole cinema to myself. That was the good life, that was the high life ... last Saturday. To come here and kick my heels in the very best room of the best hotel in town, when there are so many little neighbourhood cinemas ... What have I been dreaming of? I've got just what I deserve.

*

Next morning old grog-blossom brings me my croissants. Well, I have been well and truly taken in, and this evening I shall just go back home again. But on Sunday morning in the provinces there are those triumphant peals of bells. A little reading in bed till it's time to go, that would be a good idea.

A knock. If it's Flavien, he'll keep trying.

A second knock. That mixture of boldness and shyness: a reality.

'Don't come in!'

I pull on my oilskin raincoat over my nightdress.

'Come in,' I say.

He turns the doorknob with premeditated slowness.

The waiting is over. I repress a desire to laugh. No, it isn't James Dean. I wasn't expecting a James Dean. Well ...

There can be no doubt. It is Flavien's sombre face, his discouraged letters to the life. Huddled up inside his own sadness, lost inside his limp knickerbockers. I am ashamed of being ashamed of his knickerbockers.

He doesn't dare come any further, he doesn't dare shake my hand. He grieves me, he is behind a high wall.

'Why didn't you come yesterday evening?'

She listens to herself, she can hear herself.

'Yesterday evening? I couldn't. I live at home with my parents. I told you that in my letter.'

Flavien's complexion, that of a sacristan. Is it a perversion? Why do you always find those who always walk alone so disturbing? She is warm, ripe for picking.

'Don't your parents let you out on your own?'

He has just walked in, I am reducing him to his lowest common denominator.

'It wasn't possible yesterday. At the moment my mother's at mass, so I've taken the opportunity to come.'

A grimace intended for a smile. He is sickened by his own deceit.

'Is your mother aware of our correspondence?'

'She thinks you may be able to help me become a writer ...'

'Me?'

Is he telling the truth? This fearful, sad, apprehensive being wants to embark on such a precarious existence? I don't believe it.

In the end he has decided not to shake my hand. He has stowed his hands safely away inside the pockets of his threadbare jacket: another deception enabling him to keep his distance from an ageing woman. He smiles in embarrassment, not knowing what to say or do.

'I'm cold, I'm getting back into bed. Turn your back!'

'As you wish ... if you wish.'

Ultimately, I am his slave since yesterday evening.

He turns his back, and I do not waste the opportunity: no, he is not bundled up in those floppy knickerbockers; he is exposed to the most sarcastic of winds. His defects are not to be your private property, my little one; they belong to the whole wide world. It wasn't in search of a dandy that I took that train ...

'A Camel?'

'Why not?'

His fingers became entangled with my cigarettes and the pack falls to the floor. He sits down on the edge of the bed and the pack falls to the floor a second time. He begins to lose points as soon as he increases even slightly in boldness.

'I like being alone when I smoke, I like being alone with my headaches,' he informs me.

Not a particularly engaging confidence.

He consults his watch: he must go. He has been here a quarter of an hour. In that case I must return to Paris this evening. After all, he likes smoking alone, he likes being alone with his headaches. No, no ... don't go ... don't go yet ... The world becomes a gilded cage, a child is asking me to stay. He'll work something out, I must wait till he's got it worked out.

A priest, a doctor, an old friend; all three together took my hand. No impulsiveness. The hand is limp. Second confidence: he must continue his schooling, he must work for a law degree. His parents insist on it. What does he want? To write? Not to write? He raises his eyebrows. It's up to his mother to decide that. All he wants is to be left alone with his headaches. He will come back, he promises. He will escape during their evening walk. He has gone.

I pick up the telephone. 'A Cinzano with ice, a good lunch ...'

She will read her Steinbeck. The shutters can stay closed.

*

Sunday evening, eight o'clock. Unbelievable, he has come back just as he promised.
'Are Papa and Mama digesting their pudding in the park?'
Silence.
'Don't make fun of me, don't be cruel ...'
Another silence.
They look at one another. Season of cornflowers. Hundreds of years. Grey cornflowers. Faded. They look at one another. She draws him towards her. Advances. Delaying tactics. Unexpected success. Skilful manoeuvres. Barricades and further approaches. Season of grape harvest. Season of apricot harvest. Another grape harvest. Another apricot harvest. They kiss for a long while.
The End. He runs away again.
Tomorrow I am to leave the hotel with him, he will have somewhere to go to; tomorrow we shall live together day and night, he assures me of that. And Papa? And Mama? He has worked out a complicated plot. What is he going to give me, this still sad Flavien? The hotel will be modern, the hotel's owner will look the other way, he's in on the plot.

*

A knock. What time is it? A quarter to one in the morning.
'Don't be afraid, it's Flavien ...'
Thank heavens for my permanent at least; otherwise, I'd have to pull out my curlers and stuff them under the pillow ...
'Why are you here at this hour?'
'I felt like it.'
'And the night porter?'
'The night porter was dozing. He's in on things, anyway ...'
Flavien is in a bad way. His face, a metallic grey earlier, is now like wax. The mistiness has gone, he is bearing the weight of his pain, the burden of his sadness. I feel compassion but no pain for him.
He sits down on the edge of the bed. Not gone yet?
It begins, it begins all over again:
'Look at me ... look at me for a long time ... look at me for always ... always ... always ... always ... always ... My migraine, in your eyes ...'

I close my eyes before obeying him. Is this what it's like, the kind
of love that ends up in a psychiatric ward? I obey. I drown myself
in his eyes, he drowns himself in mine ... The room, our nonexistent hands resting on our knees, we are two good little people.

'Half past one. Time for sleep,' Grandmother said.

He closed the door, as he did every time, with the same premeditated slowness.

*

It had been raining for hours and hours. He carried my suitcase in
one hand, my bag in the other. We skated through mud, we drank
white wine in the decrepit hutments. A too-human town, a patched-
up town, a town that had suffered.

His little modern hotel glittered. He didn't want to fill in a
registration card. I insisted. I wasn't a child-stealer. The hotelkeeper was eyeing me. I could tell what he was thinking. She ought
to bring herself to her senses, she ought to send him back to his
family, to his homework.

'What shall we have to drink?' I said in deliberately coarse tones.

'You want to drink?' Flavien asked in fright.

I must shock him if I want to weaken his defences, I thought.

'What shall we drink?'

'I'm not thirsty,' Flavien said tearfully.

'A bottle of Mersault on ice!' I said with determination.

The hotelkeeper resented the order. I was putting on some sort
of an act, and he was beginning to find us tiresome.

The little maid was delighted with us, though. Off we go, all
three of us, with the suitcase.

Dismal unease as soon as the maid leaves us alone in our room.
The bed. What are we to do with it? It absorbs the whole room. Yet
it could be my battlefield if only Flavien would accept my exploits.

We turned and twisted round it as though it were a kennel har-
bouring a savage dog waiting to bite us. The hotel's silence became
oppressive.

He hid his face in his hands.

'Let's go to bed,' he said in a muffled voice.

He was nailed to the spot.

'Why so unhappy?' I asked from the other end of the room.

He can't come over to me. He is in his desert.

He has leaned his arm against the windowpane, he has buried his
forehead, his eyes in it. He is rejecting us: me, the bed, the room.

He offered his explanation.

I was to undress. Why? The bed filled him with horror. I mustn't show him my underclothes. That was not part of my plan. Women's underclothes are ugly, Flavien insisted.

Is he determined to make me suffer? Am I determined to make him suffer? I no longer know.

The lopsidedness of the bright-red oilskin curtain ... It hung between the room and the bathroom, and I took it for a friend. Just as I was hiding my underclothes in the wastepaper basket, a fall.

Fallen. Fallen full-length on the carpet. He was sobbing.

I die of pleasure, I go weak at the knees with happiness, I have had all my dreams answered when a man weeps. To drink their tears, to lick up their tears, that calming sperm, oh weep, I beg you, weep. I wet his face with lips wetted with his tears. Raw meat blossoming. Flowers bunched between my thighs.

Naked, I rubbed myself against his clothed body. I can give no explanation of the female who must beg. I clambered over the young man lying there in knickerbockers. Kissing, yes, that was allowed. Soon I had a pumice stone in place of a mouth. Bend your legs, I told him. I made use of his knees, I felt disgust at myself. If you wanted to, twisted body on the floor, it would be easy, I have an appetite to know you. Kiss, yes, we had to go on kissing. An inferno was distintegrating under my eyelids: I kissed, I kissed.

I lay down beside him. Hands behind his head, he was lost in contemplation of the wall.

Act now, but with care, with care.

I watched, between my eyelashes, the swelling, the cage, the liftings, the heart beating, the viscera, the thrust, the world wanting to be free. I let my hand fall on its prey. A wonder, my hand was full of wonder through the concealing cloth. The earth was breathing under my hand.

He seized my wrist and hurled my hand away.

'I forbid you,' he cried.

'Very well, then I shall leave immediately.'

'Don't go,' he begged. 'Get into bed, I'll undress ...'

'I'll get into bed if you come with me.'

I looked at it through the worn cloth, beneath the line of buttons. It wanted to measure itself against the sky, it wanted to swing free. Baroque, more baroque even than the summer weight of the hollyhock stem in bloom. Sheltering it, feting it with my hand, forbidden.

Why does he want me to stay?

*

I am in the bed, I am sipping the Meursault, I am smoking a Camel. The sheet pulled up under my chin is a sedative.

Kneeling in front of a hideous modern armchair, stripped to the waist, head in hands, back swept by intermittent tremors, he wrestles.

'Are you praying?'

'Don't be cruel ...'

'Come on, the Meursault is smashing!'

'I can't come ...'

'Who's stopping you?'

'My migraines ...'

'Are you beginning that again?'

'I can't fight them off ...'

'Bring them with you, we can share them.'

'You're mad!'

You have fire in your head when you abuse yourself too much, a maniac once told me in a café. I was remembering him now, twenty years later.

He took off his discouraged shoes, his sad socks, his limp knicker-bockers, his briefs. He contrived to conceal himself with agonies of modesty.

'What were you hoping for, when you brought me here?'

He jumped. He put his clothes away under the bed as though, even totally undressed, he was still trying to deprive me of his nudity.

'Hoping for?' he echoed, looking haggard.

He came over to the bed.

He was sheltering it, covering it, hiding it from me. I felt little and alone.

'... I was hoping,' he went on, 'I was hoping that I wouldn't love my migraines any more with you.'

'Do you love them as much as that?' I asked.

Where there's life there's hope. Who knows ... perhaps we are about to dissolve into an embrace.

'I love them more than anything in the world when I'm alone,' he said very quietly.

'Some Meursault?'

'No, after ...'

'After what?' I said brazenly.

'After nothing,' he said dishonestly.

'Let's not talk,' I said, weary of this five-and-dime sadism.

He is in the bed, he is lying beside me. He is on the alert. At the slightest gesture, if my hand were to move closer ... He has drunk some Meursault, I stub out his cigarette, I close my fists: my caresses would be insults.

'Let's dream ...'

'Yes, let's dream,' he says. 'Will you be good?'

'I'm always good.'

He doesn't understand the irony.

I drift away, he drifts away. We dream with our hands laid flat on the mattress. Every man for himself; sketching the outlines of love with gentle fingers, no, no, forbidden.

Silken brother, where are you? My sex is not a roll-on or a corset, I'm here to tell you. It was for you I took the train, my sex pleads. Let us couple together, it's so nice, a tablet dissolving in the water. Plough, you have fields lying here beside you. I promise you muslins and milky ways. Stir yourself, come couple with me. How can you keep apart from us old rovers of vaginas? All blind creators, all giants. Oh, prodigality. The act is over, streaming face, miles of beach in a room. O gift of self. Little brother, what do you say?

He said: I can't change, I am held fast in a vice, my head is inside a fire.

*

And then? A lamentable padding-out of the time left. I begged him for the weight of his body on mine; he refused it. He refused himself with the obstinacy of a dumb animal. He scissored his legs, he locked them together. I got him drunk on champagne, on Camels, on Meursault, all to no avail. His gentle, cruel eyes when he seized my wrists ... I had to kiss him for quarters of an hour together, we had to look into one another's eyes for half hours together, our erosion drove him mad with pleasure. A pleasure that he concealed from me. Embraces sufficient to break every bone in our bodies. Then we had to begin all over again, without ever going any farther. If I lifted the sheet unexpectedly, then he brutalized me. I couldn't escape, he pinned me to the mattress. We were well on the way to losing our reason, what with the drink, the lack of air, the moistness of our naked bodies, my prayers, my kneeling supplications in the bed. He refused. If I had been repulsive, he would not be there, he said. I believed him without believing him.

As a result of too many contractions I had a bad hemorrhage. He was terrified. Would he now? No, he wouldn't. I sponged the sheet, I asked myself what it was I had come to that room to expiate? What was it they wanted me to make amends for, these schoolboys? He confided in me, he told me about his terrible moments of loneliness. I told him about mine, I began to take heart again; I was forgetting that he was just a child, that he despised me.

Next day:

'The police are downstairs. They want to speak with you,' the little maid told Flavien.

He was already dressed.

'I'll go and see about this!' he told us.

He vanished with the assurance of a little pimp. The little maid couldn't bring herself to leave. Stop drinking, stop smoking, stop holding him in your arms, her gaze signified.

'I'll let you know what's happening,' she said.

She closed the door quietly, she was presumably hoping I would go to sleep.

She came back. '... His mother didn't want to make a charge. He'll be back in an hour.'

'Good, good,' I said with detachment ...

He did come back in an hour. A pity. I was resting, though not dozing. His hour in the bosom of his family had refreshed him; he was breathing more freely. He apologized for what had happened. What had happened? His mother ... she had asked the police to look for him ... but she had insisted ... he hasn't run away ... I was here to help her son break into the literary world. Break into! Ha. The whole thing was too grotesque.

Why had he come back? To conduct me forthwith to the railway station, to put me on the train. There was a train this evening I could take, his family had made inquiries. They were seeing me off. I retrieved my underclothes from the wastepaper basket.

'I'm a brute,' he said at the station.

'A brute? You?'

'Yes, a brute.'

Ambition had gone to his head as the moment came for parting.

There was a train due to leave in ten minutes. He insisted on coming with me onto the platform. Why not just say goodbye and turn our backs on one another?

The train gathered speed. A long face, a young man's face set in sadness, receded, receded ... Then nothing. Despite myself, I staggered out into the corridor and found my way along to the dining car. Such a failure required something substantial in the way of nourishment.

*

L'Affamée isn't selling, I don't see my book in any bookshop. Thanks to *L'Affamée*, I can now consider myself unsuccessful on a grand scale. I don't think of myself as not understood. I think of myself as nonexistent. Jacques is delighted, Jacques loathes vulgarization. He prefers to hide the things he likes. Jacques can eat. Soon I shan't have enough left even to eat. He ought to make it his concern; has he forgotten that he is encouraging me as a writer? He ought to give me work, whether it made him any profit or not; he could if he wanted to. Copy out 500,000 addresses, he would say in a dictatorial voice. What luck, I would copy out his address 500,000 times with all the others. He would tear up my 500,000 envelopes in secret, but I would receive a remuneration. In the name of what? In the name of my literature, which disturbs his soul. I am shocked: he doesn't even ask me how my finances are going. The more rebellious I feel, the more I make myself suffer. Why doesn't he stop to consider my situation? I see the truth only too clearly, and it is hard to bear: I keep his evenings from being completely empty, even if I don't amuse him, even if I bore him to death. I leave, he forgets me, me and my anxieties. The luxury he lives in, that's the problem. It makes me forget my true condition, my everyday existence, when I am there. He goes to bed, he goes to sleep, I go round the bend in the métro. I can always stop seeing him. I love him, why shouldn't I visit him? I feel remorse when I remember Simone de Beauvoir: I am being unfaithful to her. Idiot. Genet told you, it's possible to love two people at once. Is Genet in the right?

*

Jacques has written to me. Jacques has invited me to visit the house and land he has bought outside Paris. We shall eat lunch out in the open air; he will inspect the work he's having done. The next day will be Sunday, where will I be? Swimming in my tears. I ought to say no. I shall write and say yes. What more wearisome than ⸗

struggle with yourself that you know your worser half is going to win. I shall go.

*

A memorable incident: one of the other tenants has spoken to me out on the landing. She barred my route, she moved in to the attack. Do I live the way I live because I like it? How do I live? Like a savage. I come in, I go out, no one ever hears me. Yes, a real savage. I mustn't be annoyed: she is sorry for me. Living the way I live, it's not normal ...

All the time she talked to me, she was also on the lookout for something or someone, leaning over the rail of the sixth-floor landing. My quarters, did I like it in my present quarters? No, I didn't.

She was in a peignoir, a flimsy flapping garment, always falling open, covered in a pattern of extravagant poppies.

The milkmen at five in the morning, didn't they wake me up? Yes, the milkmen did wake me up. And the deliverymen, too? And the deliverymen, too.

'Let's swap quarters!' she said.

'...'

Her decisions, her resolves flashed ahead of her like a drum-majorette's baton. The word 'quarters' had all the warmth of an isba.

Now, on the courtyard side, you could hear a pin drop ... But she, she preferred the bustle of the street ... It couldn't have worked out better. When should we move? Right away?

'...'

A glance at her big, man's watch. A sigh. What could her Ferdinand be up to? Shall we move now? Have I made up my mind? No, we weren't going to move now. We must notify the owner ...

She moved away from the stair rail. Her face was overcast.

I would never get anywhere, I was too slow, according to her.

She pulled her peignoir together and retreated into her flat.

Who was Ferdinand?

They are swarming all over the grass, round the piles of paving stones, along the narrow-gauge railway tracks, dozens of shovels working away, diggers vomiting up fresh earth, men loading the little railway cars, the little train setting off, foremen walking past one another, men running across the lawn, a workman laying down a paving stone by a tree, rolling a cigarette, picking the stone up again, the little train passing on the other side of the lake, the driver disappearing beneath an arch of leaves. They opened the gates, the trucks filed in. They tipped out all sorts of manure, they unloaded building materials, three foremen supervised the operation, the trucks drove out again, the workmen closed the gates, the foremen dispersed. A gang was re-formed, they were laying paving stones along a walk between two lines of Italian poplars. The little train came back, the driver climbed down, a foreman stood talking to him. The house stood with its back to the road, almost chilled, one felt, by all those trees shading it. Is it too close to the road? Oh no, the lawn, the park, the lake, the trees wouldn't be a theatre if the house with its white walls, its white columns had been built close to them. I wouldn't be imagining concerts, plays, masques as I sit under the portico, as the birds fall silent in the sombre masses of the trees. Wicker armchairs and chaise-longues add to the drama of the five or six steps. The evening would recite, the glow of the sunset would declaim.

We were lunching in the open air, near the main gates, near the caretakers' lodge, the legs of the table wobbly on the gravel. A sunbeam lit up our juicy joint of meat. Jacques was bustling around the mound of paving stones, along the miniature railway tracks, between the poplars, among the foremen. He vanished, like the train, through the leafy arch; he reappeared, I forgot my fork. A foreman crossed the lawn and went up to Jacques; workmen were bowed over the stones they were levelling between their feet.

Denis served me another slice of meat. Jacques. Why wasn't Jacques with us? I ate with one elbow on the table, I listened to Denis with a distracted ear.

He stood up. 'Would you like to come? We can walk round and I'll explain to you what Jacques is trying to do.'

'I'd rather stay here.'

'Very well, my girl, stay, stay! I'm going for a walk.'

The caretakers' dog followed Denis as he walked away.

What are the caretakers going to say? Blanche wants to clear the table, Joseph will want to take it back inside . . . They are peering from behind the curtains. I look everywhere for Jacques, I must wait for him here, sitting on my chair. I must make a gesture, a movement; otherwise I'll never see him again. How common if I were to applaud a presence, his presence. I must improve my manners. I must watch myself, I must behave better. Ah, the saltcellar! Dare I scatter salt on the gravel? No, I daren't. Jacques and Denis deplore impulsive people, people who act on whim. You must corset your personality if you don't want them to criticize you, drive you away. I talk, I talk . . . can I struggle with the word-mill inside me? It won't be the little death if I managed to halt it.

The train hasn't reappeared, the leafy arch is quite still, the shovels have ceased to ferret, the foremen are having an argument in a silent film. My lip is swelling, that's my emotion; my lip is quivering, that's with shock. The workmen and the poplars are depriving me of Jacques. I pull myself together. A leaf, long dead, swings at the top of a beech tree; shall I be less tenacious than a dead leaf?

One workman has called to another workman, I heard him. Everything lives, everything breathes, Jacques is in everything, Jacques is everywhere. The trees draw nearer to one another, there is a brotherly feeling between them, the leafy arch sinks lower, there is a bustle of friendship for the earth. My eyes are misting, I am becoming confused; it is as though I were singing so as not to weep, Jacques is everywhere, Jacques is in everything. Jacques was talking behind a bush.

Will I always be lucky enough to hear his voice raised in discussion? Sitting beside a table long since cleared, my fingers interlaced, it is suddenly soft and sweet to wait in patience. Fragile instant, let yourself be photographed. I am listening to Jacques, he is looking after his young poplars in advance. Saucepans, strainer, dishcloth, I shall be back with you this evening, I know that. That instant was enough for me, now the instant is not enough for me. A rending desire to look back. It will rain before the day is out; it will have rained, it will stop raining, the smells will all be new, the cascades of pearls so generous; the blue light will creep away, every grass blade will suggest a walk, a yellowing leaf will cling to the west shoulder of the statue at the far end of the walk; we shan't be here. The future, the future ... I speed up its coming, I dramatize it. I thrust my bunches of white hair into my eyes, the statue refines its smile into infinity; ah, what amazement, what nuances between human beings and stones.

Jacques was exaggerating with his alterations, his complications, his plans; the dogs would be bored having to stay in the drawing room all this time. Denis wanted to get back to Paris before dark. And I, what did I want? My dear girl, one doesn't come out to the country just to sit and never stir a foot ... Look at that animal over there, how he gives himself up to the joy of movement ... The caretakers' dog was jumping higher and higher, asking Denis to play with him some more. Denis hurtled with him out across the lawn; he shouted: I'm leaving in a quarter of an hour. He picked up a stick, he ran into the long grass, liberated like a child. Liberated from Jacques? I thought tenderly of Denis. The park became more human. Denis, I don't think about him enough, I thought. They disappeared behind a thicket, I stopped thinking about him. Tomorrow, the day after tomorrow, ducks and swans will glide at eleven in the morning on the lake; this evening it is spattered with flakes of cruel light. Jacques will throw bread; the other will push the boat out from among the reeds. Their new life thirty kilometres

outside Paris oppresses me. I lean down from the height of my hell:
the wake of a swan or a duck across the lake, Jacques claps his hands
against the small of his back, he is happy and terribly alone; sometimes the vast park is nothing but shadow and silence, but they
call to one another and meet at the turn in a walk. I'm not jealous,
I am just gnawing away at an old bone, the same old bone.

They will think I'm paralysed, spastic, if I don't get up from this
chair, if I don't move away from this table. His park is my dungeon.
Jacques is going into an ecstasy over a statue, over a tree. If I leave
the table, I won't see him coming.

Two workmen made a detour round me. They exchanged mock-
ing glances. I was a penniless idler, I was a guest who didn't count.

Now Jacques was giving orders, explaining everything more fully,
in more detail, with greater emphasis. Why had I come? What use
was I? Was I happy there? No. Was I unhappy? No, oh, no. What
did I feel? Nothing, a sugary aimlessness.

If I fold my arms, I shall snap out of this caterpillar state. If I cross
my legs, I shall cease to be a bug stuck to a chair. Not bad, my
grey slacks. Something Anglo-Saxon in the greenery. Grey worsted
trousers worn by Denis. I asked him for them, he gave them to me.
I like my royal-blue pullover. I'm as flat as an ironing board, impeccably decent. Strict, severe, and not expensive either with its
long sleeves and its long cuffs. My hair was so manageable this
morning. Poor child, you are consoling yourself with what you have,
and you don't have much. He's going to come soon. I shall say to
myself: You must leave, barnacle, you must run away forever. I will
leave him in a little while. I am despairing to the point of hope.
Hoping to the point of despair. I am sick with him. Where is Denis?
Gone back to Paris.

'Will monsieur want some tea?' Blanche asks me.

It occurred to her; it certainly didn't to me.

'Tea?' I repeated stupidy. 'I don't know ... I think it's too late.'

Monsieur. Monsieur is Jacques. Monsieur, the moisture between
your toes, your dirty socks, your body smells, my love. Run away
forever without looking back, I said a moment ago. I turned my
head, I followed him with my eyes. Love is beyond us. Railings of
Jacques's park, imprison me, imprison each of my hairs, I will not
go.

*

He came towards me. Love leads us astray and gives to us in such

profusion. I was detached from everything, and yet I possessed what
he possessed: he was coming. He pushed at the bridge of his glasses,
he had made himself at home inside me. I set out to meet him, I
brushed a plant with my fingertips, I said goodbye in my joy to a
blade of grass. Shall we be blind? Would you like that? Let us hurl
ourselves on one another. Let us roll together on the lawn, and
autumn will bury us there.

'Have you been for a walk round?'

'No, I haven't been for a walk round. I waited for you . . .'

I am irritating him. I have gone too far.

'Why didn't you go with Denis?'

'I don't know.'

Lying like that makes you want to die.

He has taken out his cigarette case. I shall busy myself with a
cigarette.

'What do you think of the house?'

'I don't know.'

'Would you like to come and see it?'

'If you like.'

He has taken my arm. I am stepping on the match he has thrown
away.

Here we are in front of the steps, the columns, the chaise-longues,
the wicker armchairs. A whole future of warm evenings, of visionary
nightingales.

I am shivering. I searched for him too long through the arch of
leaves.

'You're shivering. Would you like a wood fire lit?'

If a wood fire were enough, I would soon have the forests de-
pleted . . .

'Tell me about your improvements.'

He tapped a cigarette on his case. A man's cigarette for him all
alone.

'I should only bore you.'

There are twelve cigarettes lined up in your case; I've just counted
them. Twelve. Plus the one you're smoking. Plus the one you're
about to smoke and the one you gave me. Twelve and three make
fifteen.

Two foremen emerged from a clump of trees; they discussed
springs, streams, brooks, humpback bridges; they discussed them
with Jacques.

His Gitanes, lined up in their tight row in his black leather case,

fascinated me the very first time he came to see me in my black den.
Now they obsess me. I go to Neuilly-sur-Marne, to Gif, to Evry-Petit-
Bourg, and I covet their little gardens there. The flowers they call
snowballs are collapsing on their stems, they go to my head, they
calm me down: the sleep of Jacques's cigarettes in their case. I
haunt the Gibert Bookshop one October 1, the notebooks lie open
in the stationery department: Jacques's cigarettes, Jacques's candour,
Jacques's virginity at ten years old. I dream that he is offering me a
Gitane, and I roll it between my fingertips before I light it.

They were talking about sick trees, trees to be felled, trees that
must be saved, measures, ramps, planks, calipers. I drew half circles
with the toe of my shoe. The poor must hack out their own dignity.
Shall I meet it this evening on a sidewalk, his empty packet of
Gitanes? I hope that will happen, I yearn for it to happen. I close my
eyes, and it makes me tremble.

He will pay for the humpback bridges, for the trees to be saved,
for the trees to be felled, for the narrow-gauge railway, for the
foremen, for the workmen, for the leaf mould, for the fertilizers.
He is paying for me in an agency. What? Private detectives. Are
you sure? I'd take a bet on it. The detectives go round distributing
empty Gitanes packets to men out of work, to professional loafers,
and they pay them. Then the out-of-work men, the loafers go round
during the night putting them in certain places, here and there,
along the rue Paul-Bert, the Faubourg Saint-Antoine, the Place du
Marché d'Aligre, the Boulevard Voltaire, the avenue Ledru-Rollin,
the rue de Montreuil, the rue Saint-Bernard, the rue de la Forge-
Royal, the rue Titon, the rue Chanzy, the rue Jules-Vallès, the rue
Jean-Macé, the rue Basfroi. I come out at ten in the morning, the oilskin shopping bag banging against my calf, I lower my eyes, I think
of Jacques at the bottom of the walls, along the edge of the pavements.
He wants me to think of him, so he takes the necessary steps. A
stab in the heart; there's one under the letter box between the florist
and the hairdresser's. I push it with my foot because it's too near the
wall. Lightly: I mustn't hurt Jacques.

I go on further, I take up my position outside the furniture store,
I look back at it from a distance. No signs, but our adorable secret
code inside the flap. We communicate in the heart of sounds: the
bell on the police car unites us. I don't dare pick it up and take it
with me. I push it again with my foot. Jacques mustn't be crushed.
Some mornings I feel very, very shy. I recognize it just as I am saying
good morning to the fishmonger, and I push and pull at the flesh on

my forehead. Already there, at nine in the morning, there in the
middle of the sidewalk ... look at it in the mirror on the front of the
Nicolas Wine Store. It has spent the night waiting for me, half open,
gaping, patient, no longer of any use. Jacques was asleep, Jacques is
reliable and logical and sensible. I love it in the mirror, then I move
away as though it doesn't exist. The stall covered with oranges and
grapefruit fills me with remorse. They are caressing the skins of the
fruit for their sick lying in hospital. And I, I have just pretended
to scorn his Gitane packet, I have rejected what he is offering me to
start the day with.

I retrace my steps. Too late. A sole has dirtied it, a heel has
squashed it. Ought I to look at what I ought never to see? Jacques
trampled on. I pick up the bream by its tail, I check a sole's gills to
see if it's fresh, I throw an imploring glance back towards the packet.
Everyone is walking on it. All the better. Jacques's anonymous gift
takes on an even greater value, our secret bond becomes tighter
still. At noon the apprentices, the workmen, the clerks insult me,
hustle me, make me stumble. I am just idling; they have their
lunches to heat up, they have no time to spare, I feel excluded from
the twentieth century. But I'm not just idling: I am observing it, I
am staring it out. I go into the dead-end street, I shall be able to
stand undisturbed there and cherish it. You load of idiots, look at
your feet, can't you see how it intensifies the summer sky? What if
I were to pick it up, to take it away with me ... I must covet, I
must not possess. It is a present from Jacques, but it is nevertheless
a mystery. A passer-by has smashed into it with his foot. It has
fallen in the gutter. It is floating along on the water. Tomorrow
I shall come upon another. Do they really come to me from him,
these empty Gitanes packets? What if it were a trap, an evil omen
at the bottom of the walls, along the edge of the pavements ...

*

I was shivering but I didn't want to admit it. I am cold, and I
shall be cold again if I come back here. It is too grandiose, his park.
I am shivering, shivering. Yes, let's leave as soon as possible, the
night is coming down with its great cat's silences. I am cold, I am
always cold with Jacques. I have no voice, I keep trying to clear my
throat. Tell me, Violette, tell me, my darling, what is the use of living and loving? Appalling woe. A belated insect in a hurry; it will
soon reach the shelter of the lawn. A prayer: to be changed into an
insect. Be patient, my poor little girl, the grass will cover you when

you are dead. He's bringing the automobile round; I am dumb in advance. My feelings for him are too religious; he has so few really for me. The night is pitiful with its insinuating softness. Now I'm warm, I'm too warm; the clamminess of my hands when I was twelve, when I was thirteen; child, you are doing me no service, he is going to close the car door soon; I want him gloved, hands just touching the wheel, a speeding conqueror. And I wait, in anguish, for the moment when I must be parted from him. The lake is fading into darkness . . .

'Are you coming? We must go!'

Yes, commander; just one second's breathing space.

The lake is fading into darkness; other trees, other theatres become sombre masses, the little railway train is a bas-relief, the night superimposes its drama on the thickets; already a timid dawn at the far end of the walk? The statue lying on its side.

'Denis must be there by now.'

Oh, how totally I don't give a damn! You wouldn't believe your eyes: I open my skull, I imprison you inside it, you and your navy-blue suit, then I lower the lid.

The key turns in the ignition, the car moves across the flags of what was once the stable yard; we are on our way back to Paris.

*

I move my flat. It is all over in a flash. A snap of the fingers, olé, and there I am in my new surroundings. Mme Gavotte, nurse in a home for incurables, directs the operation. She knows how to keep people on their toes. Live people, dead people, she sees them all; well, you can imagine. No time now, but she'll tell me all about it later. She goes on duty at three, she comes off at eleven; there are three eight-hour shifts in every twenty-four hours apparently. Old men, old women, so many of them, an endless procession through her beds, through the wards. The things she's seen, oh, and is still seeing when it comes to old men and old women sick in hospital. They lie there dying, they give her their ration of wine. They are just fading away, pegging out, and all their goodies they offer to her. La Puce is allowed to choose from their little bags. Six last month, La Puce was, her little horror, her little girl. Where is she now? At Les Lordes in the country, with her grandmother. The coachdriver hands him down to her without even stopping now, he's so used to it.

Well, must get down to it, tomorrow everything must be scrubbed, where would she have been if she'd dawdled through life? Tomorrow's her day off, everything must be ready, Ferdinand will be coming. I don't know him? The other day, when the idea came to her about moving into the front, that's who she was on the lookout for. I must know him, the postman who brings the money orders. I never receive money orders. But it's not just the money orders, there are the streets with Ferdinand there to be seen. Can't I think who she means, can I really not call him to mind? Tall. Hair combed flat on his head. A mat complexion. People always notice him. Always well turned out. A deep voice. Not like any of the other postmen at all. She'll call me, she'll point him out from the window.

We really must get down to it. It won't take me long, I've no furniture. Can I live like that, without furniture? Yes, I can. The poor things, she can't give them back their bedroom, their dining room, they died in the ovens, they were Jews, she hid their son. He was a child then, now he's a young man. She was polishing the linoleum, Ferdinand came in with the allowances. Good morning, postman. Good morning, little customer. Use the pads. The pads? You'll dirty my floor. She remembers so well, it seems only yesterday, and it wasn't so very long ago. A nice place you've got here, little customer. I'm dead-beat, can I sit down a sec? He is so well-mannered, Ferdinand. He hung his bag over the doorknob, he checked his accounts, he organized his rounds. Twelve old-age pensions to pay, seventy-three steps to climb. He hunches himself over when he's counting. He hadn't noticed the bottle of grenache by his bundles ... He counted, the old people were waiting for him. Are you offering me a drink then, little customer? He pays them, then he meets them down in the bar a half hour later. They are celebrating their money, they prance like gazelles; a banknote, it makes you young again. Are you offering me another drink, little customer? You're sweet, you know, I shall come again. Her peignoir was coming open; anyone else would have thrown himself on her. He came back the following week, he took the trouble to come up all this way just to see her. Now he waits for her in the evening outside the hospital. He hides, he watches her, she looks for him along the wall of Père-Lachaise, he's jealous.

Yes, it's ten o'clock exactly, she'll be finished by twelve. The owner? It's just an exchange, they're the same rent. If you stop to think about every step you take, you'll never get anywhere. Why don't we begin by drinking a glass of Granvillons together? It's so smooth, so sweet. Her water heater, her refrigerator, she'd gladly let me have them, she'd like to go out and buy the latest models ... but she can't. The soapholder affixed to the wall, that she will let me have. And those three planks, the ones hiding the electric meter, I can have those. What is it, actually, my occupation? I don't work? What do I do with my days? I write books. Well, as long as I can manage, that's the main thing. One day she'll tell me her life story. Poor Dad, he drank, it killed him. Why do I go out with my curlers on? Everyone wonders. I go out with my curlers on because I'm depressed. You mustn't be depressed. You mustn't go out with those things on. Here's the sun, I shall have sun in every room, I shall have flowers, I shall have plants. She will give me some begonias, she has too many. Living without furniture like that, living without curtains, she just couldn't do it. Why do I wear trousers? They have some very pretty material on the Place d'Aligre. A peignoir, it's more feminine. She will give me some netting; nothing at the windows, it's just not right. Why don't we call M. Chantelauze? Who is that? A neighbour. He yells sometimes, but he's not violent, it's just a habit he has. His dining-room wall is also mine. He yells but he's always willing to help. He's at home now, he works in the evenings. What at? In a theatre. Is he an actor? He works the lights. I mustn't be frightened if I hear him shouting through the wall. She'll just go and fetch him, I can look round her flat while she's gone.

I look round. How spick and span! Her windows are gardens ... And her green plants ... as though a President were expected. How gay the begonias with their hilarious swags of bloom ... No canary, I notice to my surprise. She has chosen a goldfish instead. Her bad taste enchants me, I begin to expand. It is homely her little home, but it's champagne too, bubbling and generous. Bad taste served warm.

They appear.

'M. Chantelauze,' she says.

M. Chantelauze. Briefs below his navel. Dying of heat. Briefs of yellowish cotton, skin too white. Soft, black felt hat. Maroon socks. Cracked, oxblood shoes. Brush-cut under the hat, straight nose.

He walked into Mme Gavotte's flat, slid the case back inside his briefs. He offered me a cigarette. He didn't lift his head, he didn't address a single word to me.

I looked at the cigarette in the palm of my hand. It was so slim ... it was like a chocolate cigarette.

'I was forgetting myself,' he said.

He didn't take the trouble to lift his eyes.

He retrieved the case from his briefs, he picked out a cigarette almost as thick as a small cigar. He wasn't forgetting himself.

So I was changing my digs without a moment's notice ... Well, I was right to get out if I felt like it ... The street is going to the dogs anyhow ... What about his cat, Cantor, a real Don Juan, always kicking up that terrible noise on the stairs, did I ever meet him? I'm a funny little beggar, you know, he said. He didn't mean it.

'They're nudists,' Mme Gavotte yelled from her bedroom.

'Nudists and campers,' he corrected her. 'My wife as well.'

Mme Gavotte was dragging her double bed.

'They go to a camp that's too posh for them!' she added.

With a flick of one nail, M. Chantelauze tipped his hat onto the back of his head. Obviously a fan of all those Prohibition era Chicago gangster films. He showed me his eyes. They were depths; they were sad, unhappy creatures.

'It's true, we've got to find another camp. It's a pity, we had a terrific time at this one,' he said lugubriously.

He poured himself some Granvillons in Mme Gavotte's glass. Whereupon Mme Gavotte bounded out of her bedroom. She just couldn't resist white wine. We clinked glasses. The thick rims of the mustard-container glasses seemed to me an added attraction.

He talked about La Puce. I would see what a little madam she was. I liked his nerve. They are rare birds, those who will dare wound a mother's heart without circumlocution.

Swathed in her extravagantly bepoppied peignoir, Mme Gavotte defended her child: a heart of gold, such intelligence, a love.

She was talking, wearing herself out quite pointlessly. M. Chantelauze knew La Puce too well, I didn't know her well enough.

She drank, then she folded her arms below the deep cleavage of her peignoir. A vague look in his eyes, head thrown back, the nudist expressionlessly eyed the long, firm, full shape of her breasts. Two shells, or two watermelons.

'I'm a funny little beggar, you know,' was his refrain.

Mme Gavotte was complaining: her Ferdinand sometimes appeared like a whirlwind. She hoped he wouldn't come now, he would run away again, he hated visitors.

M. Chantelauze began to talk, went on talking, his empty glass in his hand.

In the end our move did begin.

*

Zézette would have helped us; she was out at the Co-op. Mme Gavotte was carrying the doors of her wardrobe; I didn't dare ask who Zézette was. I followed her with her brooms, her dish-cloths, her basins.

I dropped the entire load on the landing, I seized her wrist: why was he roaring like that? I would have to get used to it. M. Chantel-auze always roared like that when he banged his fingers.

She crossed my unfurnished room. Almost noon, almost a victory. She eyed the pink bird, the dark-brown branch with sullen gaze, she eyed them as though they were her enemies. I lacked furniture, I was a source of depression to her.

'Later on I'll change the wallpaper,' she said.

We returned to my new flat. M. Chantelauze was unhooking Mme Gavotte's rustic light fitting. He was roaring underneath his hat.

Our move was completed at two in the afternoon.

*

Mme Gavotte would give two rings on the bell when she was dressed. And there she is ringing already: what if I were to become a doorman?

Yes, I must eat it; otherwise, it would only be thrown away. And she was gone. She always took a shower directly after lunch, you see; she always lived with her doors wide open, you see. But I closed mine as cautiously as a thief. How was I to get rid of her piece of calf's heart? How could I make it vanish? By throwing it down the lavatory, idiot woman. I hadn't met my new lavatory. I opened the door and was filled with wonder. A throne. A throne from a wooden hut at the bottom of a country garden ... Brimming with gratitude, I no longer had the courage to throw the piece of braised calf's heart into the pan. I sat down fully dressed on the hole, I chewed the rubbery slice of muscle. Alone at last, home at last, I said to myself. Two short, sharp rings. I laid my plate down on the back of the seat. She appeared: showered, combed, made-up, neatly shod. A suburban beauty. Eight minutes to three. She leaps on her bicycle, at three she is in the hospital, the matron is pleased with her. She earns her living, I don't earn mine.

I have opened the window, I have checked the intensity of the

silence. Precious silence, precarious silence enclosed inside the buildings of Paris. How I like qualifying it, that narrow, bad, alien
silence like a cold current of air. That leaden silence. And those
distances: pearly grey, are they? ash grey, mouse grey, pastels,
jewels? A whole city of delicate shadings out there. Shall I not
need to snatch up my oilskin shopping bag any more, not need to
go out on my errands in order to caress you with my gaze, grey
distances? Lumpy chimney with your coolie hat, I shall be able to
see you from my table, from my bed. I was sending down my
friendship to the window of my black den, to my sisters the trash
bins. At the risk of tumbling out on top of them. I lean my elbows
on the sill, the clouds are mine, the sky comes right into my room.
Silence, but a whole swarm of windows opposite. I know that thirty-
year-old matron at the window just facing mine ... the snags are
beginning, I know her, I loathe her, what bad luck, her dining room
is exactly, yes, exactly opposite the bedroom where I shall be writing.

Whiplashes. No, strap lashes. Why has she opened the window
while she beats him? Cruel, and subtle in her cruelty. I must hear, I
must suffer with her son as she straps him. She beats him, and on
top of that she calls him 'Spud.' Why 'Spud'? He's got a nice little
nose. I ought to close my window, but I can't: I fear and I long
for the hiss of the split strap. How quickly we become accomplices
of vileness. He makes noises of pain but will not weep. A mother
must correct her child. Poor little boy already undergoing his apprenticeship ... his apprenticeship to humiliation. No, we mustn't interfere with things that aren't our business. I closed my window. Weep
as I wept after losing an umbrella when I was seven ... I can't any
more. I open my window a crack. Is it over? A mother and son are
singing *Star of Wonder* in unison.

*

'You do understand...' I said to the young salesman.

He was dying of boredom among his Godin stoves.

'You do understand,' I said yet again. 'I have to heat two rooms,
a hall, and a kitchen, but since I work in my bedroom I need the
stove itself in there with me. Will it also heat the rest?'

'It will heat it if you buy one big enough!'

I had become dumb.

'The area your floor covers, do you know that?'

He left me to think it over. He began a debate with the girl at
the cash desk.

The young salesman wandered reluctantly back. 'How many square yards?'

'... Two rooms, a kitchen, a hall.'

My repetitions were more than he could stand. So were all the forever unlit stoves around us.

He fingered the enamel, the iron. I touched it after him; he was an expert.

'Take this one.'

'It's so big!'

'You say you want to be warm.'

'Does it burn much?'

'Three hundredweight a month.'

He wandered away. Why bother to sell, his pay packet will still be the same.

Three hundredweight a month ... I have enough money left to live for three months provided I go on using my little round stove ...

'Let the girl at the desk have your address,' he said to me from a distance, his elbows resting on a maroon Godin. He seemed to have vanished into a dream.

'It will eat me out of house and home,' I exclaimed, almost without meaning to.

He shrugged his shoulders. He preferred the rumba to such problems.

'Choose the smallest.'

'I should just shiver with cold.'

He took pity. 'It's what we sell for offices, for hospitals ...'

'I'll take it!'

A mastadon for a cubbyhole.

*

Fury, whirlwind, passion in my bedroom, but for an instant only. It's drawing on a sixth floor, I'm lucky, all sixth floors don't draw like that. The deliveryman was paving the way for his tip. I paid the bill, I handed him a tip. Two short, sharp rings on the bell.

'I've brought La Puce to see you with some carnations ... we're just on our way back from the market ...'

'Already!'

It was ten past nine.

The stove man vanished.

La Puce. On her knees in front of the Godin. She was playing at slamming my airflow regulator to and fro. It was hurting me.

La Puce. Six or twenty-six with those big inquisitorial eyes? A Paris doll. Bare thighs, dress with hooped skirt ending level with the sex, panties showing, the titillating panties of little girls on the ball. Non-stop stream of questions, non-stop showing off. A knowing smile. She threw me completely with her silent quizzing stare. I bit my lips. That way I wouldn't commit the blunder of asking why her lips were blue, why her bitten nails were lacquered blue as well ...

'Offer her the flowers,' her mother told her.

She picked the bunch of carnations up off the divan and proffered it to me. She was making fools of both me and herself. She was aping a little ape.

'That, madame, is my little chip-off-the-block,' Mme Gavotte informed me.

She lifted her little chip off the floor and the little chip wound its legs round its big mumsy.

I was gooseberry. Where could I vanish to?

The demonstrations of love and affection having been completed, the chip leaped down from the saddle and made a beeline for my worktable.

'How jealous Ferdinand would be if he could see me,' Mme Gavotte sighed.

'Jealous of what?' I asked rebelliously.

Mother and daughter had been making love in the presence of an impartial witness, where was the harm in that?

'Jealous of you, jealous of my being here, jealous of everything.'

'Leave, then.'

'Ah, no, I enjoy being here with you.'

Her lack of logic, her muddleheadedness annoyed me.

I had suffered for the regulator on my stove, now I had to suffer for my bronze bird. La Puce was using it to rub and scrape my table with. She let it fall on the floor. On purpose. Then she stood on it. Then she picked it up again, held it as high as her arm would stretch, and let it go once more. It bounced off the table and fell on La Puce's foot. Not a whimper, not a cry, even though she had her shoes off.

'Come here, ducks, come and show what you can do.'

La Puce ran to her. She pulled off her white socks too.

'You have to teach them to stand anything,' Mme Gavotte explained to me.

La Puce fell on her mother's lap and sent her legs flying in the air. I moved away. I would have been forced to hide my eyes: the sex of a child of six is obscene, despite panties and elastic. She had her eyes closed. I could see only her blue lips.

'Where are you going?' Mme Gavotte asked reproachfully. 'Watch ... it's for you we're doing it.'

I moved back towards them.

'Shall I begin?' the mother asked.

'Yes, begin.'

Mme Gavotte, like her daughter, had closed her eyes. She leaned forward, and at last she began. She tickled the heels, the insteps of her little girl's feet with both hands. La Puce went pale, but her blue lips became darker and darker until they were navy blue.

After having endured being tickled like that for several minutes, she opened her eyes. Her immense pupils were questioning me: wasn't that extraordinary, wasn't that remarkable? I found it very distasteful.

'More,' La Puce insisted, staring at me.

She was challenging me because I hadn't complimented her.

Mme Gavotte complied.

'A simple matter of willpower,' she observed.

She tickled at varying tempos. She soaped, then she titillated.

Finally she put her phoenix's shoes back on.

La Puce informed me that she would have liked to take off my big nose, that it was too big...

Little Miss Stoic had a fit of hysteria shortly after her demonstration. She rolled on the floor, she jumped up and down, she shed copious tears of rage. Galvanized with fury, she shook one of the table legs: the bronze bird quivered, the water slopped out of the vase. The Bible and other books began to slide on my polished table. La Puce shook another table leg: the books tumbled in a heap on the floor. The lifeless bird, shaken by her fury, quivered with life. Little Miss Stoic didn't want to go home.

'You've got a big nose, you've got a big nose!' she yelled as her mother dragged her by her feet from my room out onto the landing.

My forgiveness was for her blue lips, her blue-lacquered, chewed nails. I would be brought tripe at noon and netting later on. So Mme Gavotte informed me on the landing.

*

I closed my door as cautiously as a thief. Eleven o'clock. A morning wasted. If only it were the first, if only it were the last ... My bedroom, I bleed for it. They have taken it away from me. I've known them two days. They've taken everything away from me. I had a black den, a flower to hide in. My den closed up by day as well as night. Yes, you lived inside a pretty-by-night, and you scorned it. My Godin. They touched it before I did. But they haven't robbed me of its enamel, its mica, the weight of its lid. Calf's heart yesterday, tripe at noon—why should I try to restrain her impulses? They will come, they will execute me, they will discuss my big nose. I shall smile, they will have finished executing me. My lips glued against a pair of blue lips.

I am your kind nurse, table mine, my paperweight will purify you, my walnut shuck will give you back your colour. Bible, close again; bronze bird, sink back into the sleep of death. Open your exercise book and begin. Those last words were spoken to me by Simone de Beauvoir photographed by Cartier-Bresson. Melancholy, reticent, a little wan on her balcony, she was ready to help me as soon as I began telling my story. What story? Hermine, our love affair, our life, our hell in that little house just outside Paris. I shall call her Cécile. Poor Cécile, she has failed to win her first prize at the Conservatoire ... What else can I tell about? Gabriel in love with Thérèse and Thérèse in love with Cécile. I shall call him Marc. Poor Thérèse. Tomorrow she won't have a cent to her name to buy greens at Dominique's ... Am I beginning all that again? Ah, how sudden, how piercing, money worries are. Yes, I shall call him Marc. It's sober, it's austere. Simone de Beauvoir wants me to tell about how Marc came between Cécile and Thérèse. How disturbing he was, how equivocal, and always master of himself. Poor mixed-up creature, he paid dear for what he did. It will be somehow shady. Shady? You'll be telling the story of your own life. Cynical, that Thérèse. Cynical? A good pupil: men are rotten pigs, all men, her mother told her. The readers will be disgusted. I don't have any readers. Close your inkwell if you can't write. Terror.

Isabelle. Was I forgetting her? Was I trying to jettison her? Impossible, I carry her embedded inside me. It would be a travesty on my youth if I changed her name. I met her before I knew her. Basket, distribution of rolls in the recreation yard, bell going mad, end of school, tinkling bells for classes, rings sliding along their rod, my cubicle curtain opening, animal warmth for scales of diminished sevenths in the music room ... Isabelle and my divine ignorance of her. Isabelle spits on her slipper, the stakes are down. She has entered, my dishevelled queen, she has forced me to yield. Did someone ring my bell? No. I thought I heard my doorbell. I shall sit on the floor, I shall push my fist into my cheek. No one has rung; I need not leave my winding path back to her. Her nomad lips, the long journey of her hands. She initiated me, I could tell her to stop, twist her wrists, escape the strange, lost feeling round the lobe of my ear. Later she became cruel, barbaric. Why a woman with a woman? Why Thérèse with Isabelle? Why did I accept? Why did I love her, adore her? Until then I had been aggressively solitary, I stayed away from boys, from familiarities.

My virginity ... my wealth, my relic, my incomparable treasure. I wanted always to be a virgin, iron-fisted, a woman gangster who would never stoop to sully herself. I didn't flirt: that was an iron rule. Reading *Les Nourritures Terrestres*, a drunken ecstasy; yet I didn't even know such a thing as homosexuality existed. And then I was invited to Estelle's wedding, and there I was with a handsome, a daring young man for my escort. I was behaving like a young girl with a young man. He was not conventional. Drunk, and knowing how to drink, he vanished into Estelle's parents' garden. I ran after him. He must have been throwing up. He was lying in the grass. As though in submission to the moonlight, as though he had been brought peace by the quivering of the leaves. He turned his head, held out his hand, pulled me down to him. A dog barked. He kissed me, a barley-sugar kiss on inexperienced lips. We went back in to the party. I wasn't disappointed.

Isabelle came into my life three months later. I shall have to tell everything if I write about her. Our bed. Our avalanches, our paroxysms. I don't dare try. I am afraid in advance. It will be disgusting without my wanting it to be. The body is secret ... it takes, it gives nothing back. Up to you to make it transparent then. Wasted effort. The body doesn't remember. It will be pinchbeck stuff, thin fancies ... Slacker, come on, no excuses ... pleasure comes from the brain. In that case I can't imagine those pleasures twice. That's it, back down before you've even tried to do battle with your mock modesty. Mock modesty? My chivalrous exhibitionism. Shall I show less strength of will than a tickled child? She controlled herself. I shall open Isabelle's sex, I shall write inside it with my blue ink. Our butcher's slab, it has aged. It was fresh then, we lay dying of exhaustion on it. I shall buy roses the colour of scallops, I shall plunge into them as she plunged then.

Why upset people? Why shock people? Presumptuous, open your exercise book first. Mme Gavotte will point the finger at me. You were writing for Simone de Beauvoir before, are you writing for Mme Gavotte now? Simone de Beauvoir will read that? I will dare to give her that to read? Do you take her for a silly goose? Write, remember and write; that's what she wants. A writer without a name embarking on such an adventure? What adventure? The daybreak in our folds, the dusting of dawn light in our hole. Isabelle has vanished, Isabelle must not perish. How am I to describe her? Three fingers, three bandits every night. Shall I write about our fingers then? The spasm of sex is not a catechism class. The unsayable melting away, the unsayable melting together. I shall never be able to do it. Come to me then, smoothness of the lilac leaf, unfolding of the clouds ... In other words you're going to deluge us with a lot of sugary drivel about your sensations ... Don't ask me to carry the breeze in a basket ... It is a fugitive, that sensation, I can't just stop it as it passes. A load of sticky jam with two adolescent girls embalmed in it ... But we were warrior maidens, we were fighting so as to fall on the field.

Sex isn't charming, sex isn't exquisite. Sex. The terrible tom-tom in our heads when the rules kept us apart. Always, always ... we fought our way through the bush, one in her chemistry class, one in her art class, at the urging of that inexorable drum. Sex. How I would like to have our yearning meat naked on the page of my exercise book. Naked as the side of beef delivered to the butcher, and words as sober as cypress trees. Two women find their way to one another: what follows is not compensations, not consolations, not erotic engravings. I want funeral ceremonies mingled with carnivals of legs, of lips, of hair to write about you, to write about us, Isabelle. Our pastels were blood-red.

Shall I dare write it, the beginning of my next book? What shall I live on? You forget: Simone de Beauvoir is looking after you. They will say: it's filth. Who will? They don't read you. I pity you, slave of your fear of what other people will say. It is so easy to slip into mere repulsive description ... Sensationalism. It's a crazy idea the whole thing, I can't remember a thing about it all. I married, I disowned them, those two adolescents ... I am faithful to them, though, I obey them: I make love to myself. My sex? So as not to betray Thérèse and Isabelle. It is disgusting exploitation. Will you sell your sex for the sake of your pen? I would sell everything for greater exactness. Can you see yourself while you write it? I can see the result: an exact word, just one, and I will say go to hell to all the opprobrium and all the sin. What shall I make of my three

months with Isabelle? Three days and three nights? Quickly, my
shopping. Dominique will be closed.

*

I opened my door with my thief's caution; her door flew open at
the same moment. They leaped upon their prey.

I dared to go out with my curlers still on at a quarter past twelve?
I dared? The scarf? It hid nothing, the scarf ... She pitied me,
I was to be pitied, I just didn't realize. I bore with their sarcasms.
La Puce was walking round and round me. I fought back: if I
took them out too soon, then it didn't curl.

M. Chantelauze opened his door slightly, then closed it again
quickly. We were disturbing him.

I wasn't supposed to go out, she was giving me some tripe. Had
I forgotten? An escarole from Dominique's? Here was La Puce,
my little errand girl. Had I forgotten that, too? Did I forget everything?

I stuttered out excuses. Neighbours under my feet, fed on tripe and
calf's heart, drunk on Granvillons, I felt guilty, in the wrong ... She
was too generous, I mustn't take advantage ... I had hurt her.
Wrinkles appeared, the poppies were withering, the peignoir closed.
I can always feed her when she has nothing left. I trembled. Feed
her with what? With the fruits of my labour perhaps? Innocent
creature.

I needed bread. Oughtn't I to go out for bread?

Bread she had plenty of. The patients turn out their lockers:
bread they don't need any more. She could give me bread.

Newspapers. I must buy the newspapers.

She raised her arms to heaven. I wanted the last word? Very
well, I should have it. La Puce could accompany me. She, meanwhile, she would make herself beautiful for Ferdinand ... Wouldn't
I like to see how she had transformed my old flat?

I made to enter, but she pushed me back. Without pads, I would
dirty the floor.

I looked in from the doorway. My old flat was unrecognizable.
The colour prints were like carnivals flattened against the pink birds,
against the brown branches of my wallpaper. The ruched curtains
at the windows made you think of the inside of padded caskets. The
divan is its 'cozy corner' looked like a million others in furnished
bed-sitting rooms. The table: too small. The chairs: better concealed by people. The long, modern sideboard: a combuggerance.

But the gleaming linoleum, rivalling taffeta with its texture, warmed the ceilings with its glow. At last, I said to myself, at last a personal note. She wanted to be complimented. I gave her as many compliments as she could carry.

La Puce and I walked down the stairs slowly. Her nails clutched in my hand terrified me. I asked her all the time if she was tired.

'Do you want to listen to my heart?' she asked.

'Later.'

'No, now.'

I mustn't thwart her.

I knelt down on one of the stairs. I listened.

'What can you hear?' she asked, as though it were a game.

'... I can hear your heart beating. That's all.'

I listened to the gush, the pressures, the hissing valves of a steam engine.

'Everyone who comes to see us listens to it,' she confided in me.

M. Chantelauze passed us. Dressed, he went unnoticed on account of a certain distinction.

'That little horror,' he said as he passed.

La Puce was meant to hear.

He went on down the stairs, hat over his eyes, wearing the surly air of a conspirator. He wanted to be alone with his own tranquillity, with the bottles in his string bag.

I bought the newspapers.

*

This project of telling about my nights in boarding school with Isabelle is an error. The sixth floor, the top landing is against it. I shall be abusing them if I write it. Do I write for them? Do I live for them? I live near them. How can this ugly creature, how can this old trollop who goes out into the streets with her nightdress on under her skirt ever get back to that adolescent girl straight out of a bandbox?

*

Heavens, so that's Zézette. I used to pass her. I used to meet her in Florale the grocer's six or seven years ago. She hasn't grown any older. She was aloof. I always found her very impressive with her navy-blue tailored suits and her white blouses. She had a flat facing the street even then. They're all much the same in that respect: they don't have much to do with the tenants living in the back. Never a greeting, just a vague sign, a communication ... We live in the same building, we come to the same grocer's. Not arrogant, not haughty exactly. She avoided me, and I understood it. I was the tenant of the dark den that used to be let at one time to a butcher's boy ... And what emerged from the den? A Jacques Fath hat, a Jacques Fath outfit. They talked. She's a tart, she's a kept woman. Does she recognize me now? I've aged, and yet nothing has changed: I have no job, and everyone knows it.

'You see,' Mme Gavotte said to her, 'you see whose place I was invited into. Our neighbour is a little more civilized nowadays. I am taming her ...'

I sat down beside Zézette. She fascinated me: she seemed about to give birth at any moment. Her belly: a fabulous display counter.

'Basile is being friendly to Liliane this evening,' Mme Gavotte explained to me, from where she was wallowing on her daughter's bed, the divan in the 'cozy corner.'

Zézette made the introductions. Basile is her husband. Liliane is M. Chantelauze's wife. My eyes opened very wide. Why was Mme Chantelauze sitting so close to Basile? Almost, though I wouldn't have dared swear to it, on his lap. Did her husband leave her on her own too much? Why was she stroking Basile's hollow cheeks and lean neck with her hand? Did her husband reject her caresses? Zézette's fingers weren't paralysed. Why was he pecking at Mme Chantelauze in front of Zézette, a Zézette about to become a mother? A pregnant woman isn't a cripple. I was outraged. Was I seeing evil where none existed? Basile had been well brought up. Now he was letting himself slide. But his laugh was the laugh of an embarrassed man. Don't think about it any more, don't try to understand. Take your cue from Zézette, she's the one most concerned. Why was she so much more indifferent to what was going on than I was? It shocked me. Zézette was a full womb, nothing shocks a full womb. She continued to chatter on in a world far removed from their nibblings and teasings. A mare was gasping for it, so what? So a mare is gasping for it. A husband was unable to resist a mare in heat ... So what? So nothing. Zézette didn't get worked up about such petty things.

Mme Chantelauze was cooing, the dining room was packed with purring onomatopeias ... Was I the eyes and ears of the Ten Commandments? No, no. I concentrated on Mme Chantelauze's unbelievable thighs. I quenched my thirst with her peachlike skin, I dreamed in her rose complexion, I was ready to fly away with those rolled-back eyes of hers, like a Madonna being carried up to heaven, her mouth squeezed into a heart-shaped adoration of a prepuce. I shook myself. Was it her fault if she was in season? Zézette showed no reaction at all, she was amazing. She went on discussing rum, vanilla sugar, orange-blossom essence with a Mme Gavotte left smooth and shiny by Ferdinand's caresses. I had been invited in for crepes. Mme Gavotte and Zézette disappeared into the kitchen.

Why had I been left alone with Basile and Mme Chantelauze? To be punished? For what? For thinking of bringing Isabelle back out into the light? I twiddled my thumbs, I went round the bottom of my pullover making sure the hem was turned out properly; I ran one nail to and fro along the hem at the front.

Mme Gavotte called to me: 'Zézette would like to speak to you...'

Zézette emerged from the kitchen, her face ablaze, her hair embattled. 'I'd like to show you my layette,' she said.

I felt myself melting with happiness.

We crossed a no-man's-land of silence between Mme Gavotte's door and hers. M. Chantelauze was roaring in his flat. He kept yelling: 'The whoring tart, the whoring tart.'

'His theatre's closed this evening, so he doesn't have any lights to see to,' Zézette explained to me.

We were in her flat.

Love at first sight. Where had she bought it? How much did she have to pay for it? It's 1900, isn't it? It's Henri II. Where could I find one like it? She has no idea. Her grandmother gave her the furniture when she gave her the lease. I have fallen in love at first sight with her Henri II dining set. I shall ask Jacques to give me one. He owes it me. Why does he owe it me? I don't know. He owes it me, he owes it me. Their flat has cast a spell over me; I could sit there patiently for years and years. Everything in the flat seems to suit Zézette's blond lashes, her sparse and unruly hair, her straight nose, her kind and energetic eyes, her rather piercing good-wife-and-mother's voice. I am crazy about their flat.

Now she has produced her dreams, her hopes, her ambitions from the Henri II sideboard. The pile is impressive.

She announces each item: 'The little jacket. In moss stitch!'

She listens. Basile and Mme Chantelauze are laughing on the other side of the wall. She folds the little jacket, unfolds it again, moves over to the wall. Mme Chantelauze has the pearly laugh of a woman of the world.

'When you've seen one garment, you've seen the lot,' she decides, in a hurry to settle her layette back in its cardboard box.

I help her. We go back over to Mme Gavotte's. At the double, because crepes must be eaten hot.

*

I spent a sleepless night. I had fallen into an ambush. They were being kind to me so that I would go over to my table, so that I would open my inkwell, so that they could guide my hand across the paper, so that they could help me draw and illustrate, with words, with sentences, what repelled and will always repel them: homosexuality. They were dictating to me to proscribe me, to convict me. I wasn't one of them, because I must hide everything from them. I must conceal from their eyes what Jacques prefers, what he has chosen; and my feeling for Simone de Beauvoir, my offerings and my designs on her. They would laugh at the posies, at the handkerchiefs, at the scarfs I take her. They were calling to me, yet they wanted nothing to do with me. Where was I expected? That was no way to behave, the mare in heat before the young bride's very eyes. It was an enigma, it was undermining me.

I shall go away, I shall live on an island. I shall walk and walk till I am with Simone de Beauvoir again. And that La Puce ... she is destroying my worktable. And that Mme Gavotte ... she's teaching me to drink as though I'd never heard of drink before I met her. I am unjust, I am wallowing in the pettiest of pettinesses. I am wholly in the wrong. What is it I want? To be praised to the skies by them? I should only yawn, only drop off to sleep. Hug La Puce in my arms until she suffocates, until I can't hear her heart any more, that, yes, that I do want. Poor, poor little steam engine. I want to smooth everything over. I am timorous, why are they infiltrating my life? Won't I get bored with them? That's not a question, it's a piece of treachery. I shall grow to resemble them. I resemble them already with my hair-splitting. They don't split hairs. I mistrust them because I mistrust myself. Tomorrow I shall feel better. I shan't get tired of them. They are my childhood and my book of songs. They despise me, they haven't asked me what I do, what I live on. Do they think of me as a shady character then? Perhaps. There's no reason why they shouldn't hide it from me if they do.

*

Next day. Must have mustard with pot-au-feu. I shall have to dash out to the grocer's for a pot of mustard.

Seventy-five. Why 75? Why that number of all numbers, I asked myself aloud in the street. I had never noticed it before, yet suddenly I was looking out for it. I was being drawn towards it, and towards the registration plate it was on. I was being driven towards it. I bought my Dijon mustard, I hunted for the number, I hunted and hunted for it. I was afraid of it. A special number, a fearful number. I shall see it, I know. It's on my track, it's bound to catch me. The death ray is driving me towards it, driving me closer and closer to it. I strode along like one possessed, my fingers playing scales on my bottom lip. Ten past twelve; the city was closing up, contracting. I was furious with impatience.

End of the rue Chanzy. I put my finger on the wound. Why that number? Why, precisely, the number 75? They are invisible, they are invincible, they won't reveal it to me. They send me the number that will disturb me most. It was such a nice idea, my little walk to get some mustard. But they had their tortures waiting for me outside. I had never thought about that number in my life, yet now I was condemned to see it everywhere.

I crossed anywhere, where the rue Faidherbe runs into the rue Chanzy. I was aimless, and sought to use my aimlessness as a disguise. I dragged my feet. Ah, here it is, the holy of holies. I have slid so many letters into its mouth, letters for her, letters for Jacques. I stationed myself outside the baker's and watched indifferent strangers from time to time mail their letters. The metal lip fell back, hiding the slot again, and that signified: Write, write to them, but you will receive no reply. Why didn't they reply? Because it would encourage me. They are busy. They read me, but that is all. Why persist? They are not interested in my everlasting refrains.

The number 75 had forced its brutal way into my life a little while before. Now I was at bay as it hunted me.

An old woman came out of the baker's carrying a loaf bigger than herself. She asked me what I was doing there, why I was moaning. I wasn't doing anything, I wasn't moaning. She walked away without even glancing back at me. So sprightly, so spick and span.

The number 75. I want it and I don't want it. They have put it away in its garage, it is sitting there ready. It is waiting for me, keeping watch for me. I want to look and I want to hide.

All I had was that old woman with her big loaf, and now she's been gobbled up by a tenement block ... Still the bakery window, the cakes on display ... Gabriel didn't want to pay for my dreary cake ... Let me just wander through my past woes, let me stand coaxing and stroking my miseries ... I can see the mailbox reflected in the window. Time to move on.

A black automobile, solemn as a great hearse, drew up alongside a wood-veneer warehouse. The figure 7. What is the figure 7? A matter of life or death. Oh, what a relief, to have found the answer at last. I was born on a seventh, in 1907. Am I going to live or am I going to die with that 7 painted in white on a black ground? Some children stood staring at me open-mouthed, then fled. What if it were Jacques ... what if it were Jacques who was giving me the number 75, just so as to be giving me something, anything, despite his indifference, his aloofness ... I was talking to myself some of the time now; my voice was plaintive, a lamentable echo along my shabby passageways.

'You're getting in everyone's way,' a cruel man said to me.

Another automobile. Speeding past, bearing the mysterious numerals. The drivers have received their orders. They are to drive past, they are to show them to me without forcing them on my attention. They are to check that I am where I ought to be: out of doors, nowhere in particular. The numerals are spying on me, nibbling at me. They will gnaw me away, destroy me. What is to become of me if I don't drive that number out of my mind? But I can't. Seventy-five, an old man's age. My life will come to an end at seventy-five; it's a warning.

I was sitting on a seat in the rue Faidherbe, I had my eyes closed, I didn't want to see 75. I imagined it was there, white on black, in front of my closed eyes. The number wouldn't go away.

Sometimes it's Jacques. He is trying to make me lose my way, he wants to inhabit me, he wants to possess my soul, my thoughts. He sends me a present from one end of Paris to the other: 75. At other times the numerals on the registration plates are enough in themselves: 75 can torture me without my needing to link it with Jacques.

The jar of mustard fell to the sidewalk. I fled.

I ran in the direction of the Square Saint-Bernard with its little garden in the middle. Would I be able to shake 75 off?

The numerals were burning into my retinas. How tenacious that 7 was, how cruel that 5! If only I could take a sponge and wipe them off all the registration plates ... What is a garden in a square? An abortion. Protect me, abortion of a countryside, apology for woods; there is a pack hunting me, the number 75. Why are there swarms in front of my eyes, why is there a crowd in a single number? I want to rest ... Branches, leaves, do you hear me? My reprieve: ugly gardens in squares. The weather is fine, but I take shelter in the shelter, nevertheless. I close my eyes, I struggle, I recite: they have gone to Les Lordes, she has gone to visit her mother.

I left the little park, the furniture van crushed me without moving, just with its number 75. Why hadn't I noticed it before? It must be a very large organization. They are still there even when I forget them.

I shrank back into the park, I took shelter again in the concrete shelter. A young workman was feeding the birds with the remains of his lunch. Why was he in the park? Young workmen don't feed birds. Retired people do that. He has his back to me. I've guessed it. He is trying to excite me, he wants me to lose my reason, Jacques sent him. He is trying to disturb me with his indifference. Jacques, the workman. The workman, Jacques. Whose orders are you obeying? Why are you pretending to feed the birds? Your back is spying on me, your back can see me better than a mirror.

I fled again from the gardens; the driver of the furniture van was having lunch, but the number 75 was still on duty. I was caught in a vice.

I went to earth in my kitchen. What is this charcoal-like beef, what are these blackened vegetables stuck to the casserole? Enemies. I know how to regulate a flame, how to simmer things. Someone must have turned up the gas; someone came in while I was out. They have ruined my meal; as punishment they have set me a chore. I used a knife to scrape out all that could still be scraped out. I scratched, I scoured. Funereal scales fell into the sink. In order to eat like other people, I must rub and rub with a scourer, scrape with my nails, with scouring powder. It took two hours to clean my casserole. My hands sloshing about in greasy water, the casserole, like a big dead fish, wallowing in dirty suds.

I lunched on bread and Gruyère, flopped across the kitchen table. The casserole shone beside me; I had been granted a moment's reprieve.

Aie! Oh, how that hurt. Oh, what a pain! A stabbing, a jabbing, a scalpel thrust. I have sniffed you out, yes, you, the enemy I shall never meet. I recognize you even though I can't see you. You scratched the label on my bottle of mineral water with your nail. My bottle, not someone else's. A simple sign, a little sign of your rage and your spite. You mean to wear me down. An invisible being is giving me visible proof of his savagery, of his underhand methods. The tiny, scratching claw of a murderer. Oh, quiet, all this meaningless exaggeration of yours ... No, wait it's true: they are murdering my peace of mind. I'm listening to you, I can hear you. I've got it now: you bribe the deliveryman, you bribe the grocer; a bottle of Vittel, or Evian, is waiting down there every day for me with your signature on it, that little nail mark. A little pinch in the pink paper. He doesn't want me to love him but he wants me to think about him, to think about him all the time. What have I done, in what way have I displeased him? He is showing me his anger: the little pucker on the label there. No, it isn't Jacques ... It's a gang. The most mysterious sort of gang. I am at their mercy. It's a sign, it's a message, it's the trademark of their cruelty. Tomorrow I shall buy my mineral water in some other neighbourhood. That puckering, that pursing of the paper: a concentrate of cruelty.

*

They returned from Les Lordes at six in the evening. I was waiting for them, listening behind my door. I followed it all: Mme Gavotte's heavy tread ... Had she overdone the white wine at her mother's? I heard it all, her voice full of door knockers and warning rattles as she commanded: 'No, don't ring her bell now, I tell you she's writing books.' I am writing books? Where? When? 'Open the door for me, you're old enough to turn a key, you can see I've got my hands full ...' I know it so well, that odorous return from the country, warm as a pie fresh from the oven, arms full of good things brought back from country villages, your companion putting the key into the lock for you. What have I done with my day? Which of them banged the door like that? How many minutes must I wait before presenting myself in their flat? I won't wait. I'll go down to the grocer's this moment, then I'll come up and knock at their door with a bottle of Granvillons ... What have I done since this morning? Isabelle ... Thérèse ... Tomorrow, later; it is possible, it is impossible?

That poor Mme Leduc, she knows nothing, she's always the last to know ... Zézette left us last night ... Left us? She'll be back at the end of the week. My darlings, my sisters, my engendering sweethearts, be delivered quickly, recompense me a little; I suffered so much to have my abortion. They will soil the misty veils over my meadows, your newborn babies. The day is breaking and the dawn is a love story. The dew, the hymen of our shooting wheat, of our chilly spring acres; but the beams, the great golden sexes of the sun will sweep across you, the great sun will strip the village cross naked.

Mme Gavotte, well-organized countrywoman that she was, made me gifts of frilled parsley, of the chervil's fairy lightness, of infallible tarragon, of her shallots from Les Lordes. She loved her mother and her mother's garden. She also said, without any false shame, that she loved wine the way her father had loved it. Why not? And yet I was concerned: there were those purple patches on her cheeks. One day she would tell me her life story so that I could make it into a book: that was her leitmotiv. Her ward sister was an ally. But the matron loathed her. A life of perpetual subservience, of pettiness imposed by a duty roster. I felt privileged with my unencumbered billfold, with my duty roster as light as thistledown. Hospital, incurables, operating rooms, laboratories, anesthetics, diagnoses, repotted begonias, tripe and calf's heart, chicken in white sauce, I must have it all, all, in just a moment. The shades on the ceiling light were quivering, celebrating the triumph of Mme Gavotte's red corpuscles. She strode hither and thither in her old flat as at home as Mme Sans-Gêne in her laundry. Nothing stopped her. She walked through furniture, through closed doors, the poppies of her peignoir already scarlet with vitality at eight in the morning, one lumpy foot retrieving an escaping mule with an acrobat's skill. The clotted fat on her thighs merely expressed the vast reserves of courage and obstinacy lying untapped inside her. She pulled her peignoir together, but it flew open again: Isabelle forced herself into my memory. Mme Gavotte stood stripping a shallot with the point of her knife.

Such a pity I'm not successful. But what does being successful mean? Mme Gavotte shrugs her shoulders. Drink, she orders me, drink. Would I like her to tell me what being successful is? For example, she wanted to become a nurse, and that's what she's become. Right? Granted, of course, that she will never be a sister, a matron. Not enough education. So? Oh, a whole ragbag of circumstances ... Success, I just haven't got there yet. Although she has to admit it: the building, this one, the tenants, Marie-Lou's mother, they feel sorry for me. The other day, Marie-Lou was explaining it down in the lodge: It will come later, when I'm dead. It is my turn to shrug my shoulders: fame when you've stopped breathing, well, it's at once too much and too little. I pour out more wine, we clink glasses. Let's drink, let's drink. La Puce could sew like a little fairy, she could sing like a little angel. She went out to the grocer's swearing like a navvy...

*

We are living in joy, in euphoria, in happiness. We are moved, we are grateful and reasonably Christian: a child was to be born, it has been born. We glorify it as we drink our sparkling wine. We are all fathers. Basile is proud after having been afraid, Mme Chantelauze speaks on his behalf and she is right to do so, she can talk like a book. We listen to her. Basile asks me if I remember the crepes, and I wonder what he's getting at. His elegance surprises me. He is careful with his clothes; he doesn't wear them outside working hours as a rule. He learned how to dress at La Canebière, and how to hold himself at athletic meetings. He looks at you, he is looking down at you from his tower. He isn't haughty, he is deferential. He avoids raising his eyelids when he is near you. No, I don't remember, I tell him. In fact I ate two; but I prefer to lie.

M. Chantelauze, in whose apartment Basile is giving his party, roars that all we any of us remember is that! Still sporting his black felt hat, wearing a short-sleeved shirt in a violent check, he is pointing at the area of his wife's sex. I am the only one who takes him seriously.

'Papa, calm down, and don't yell,' Mme Chantelauze told him.

M. Chantelauze is a do-it-yourselfer. I am shown a set of chimes of his invention with tubes, chains, and a brass doe's head.

Zézette gave birth to a little girl twenty-six hours after our rum crepes. That is what Basile was getting at.

Mme Chantelauze is Basile's publicity agent. He is radiant now that he is a father. Look at him, she says in admiration, gazing and gazing at him herself.

It's true, there are green flames dancing in his eyes. He takes great care not to get dirty even when he's not doing anything. He smooths down his smooth hair. He knows he's got what it takes now, but he wants to be modest, and he is. We congratulate him, we plonk kisses on his hollow cheeks, he is moved by our attentions. Mme Gavotte is mute, she is standing on her dignity. She is not playing the leading role. She uncorks another bottle of sparkling wine; she swears, she talks to herself, and the cork hits the ceiling. Bustle and noise, oh, it's a grand life.

A young girl walks in. The straightforwardness of a shower of rain, her entry. One more female, M. Chantelauze grumbles. He hooks the chains along his tubes.

'Now, Papa, Papa! Your own daughter, Papa...' Mme Chantelauze miaows tenderly.

She rolls her eyes, it is her way of rubbing up against her husband without going over to him.

The young girl, about fifteen, informs us that she wishes to drink what we are drinking, smoke what we are smoking. M. Chantelauze has crept over with catlike tread. He looks like an extravagant clockmaker with his amazed eyes, his elliptical spectacle lenses. She is his daughter, she is nevertheless a female ... a slut ... What have we got to say to that?

'Papa, you're scrumptious!' the girl cries.

She leaps on his neck.

Everyone goes quiet, the girl starts to laugh. Her horse laugh is contagious. We laugh, we laugh; the sparkling wine shivers in our glasses, slops over. Needless to say, I am forcing it. And I go on forcing it, and my efforts to be one of them are like a long pilgrimage on foot.

Clans form. Mme Chantelauze knows how to give a party. The young girl brings round olives, canapés. I was sitting blissfully on the split sofa. I stood up, I allowed a compliment to escape me, I dared to say: 'What a body she has!' in a stifled voice. Mme Gavotte cannot forgive me. The sparkling wine has corrupted me, I have betrayed her Granvillons and her cooking. Of course she has a pretty body; anyone would have, if they spent their lives on rivers with boys ... She stalks out.

The baby is to be called Béatrice. Before long, Baba, I imagine. And the christening? Basile is the centre of attention. In two months, in three months, got to save a few pennies first. M. Chantelauze is tying his tubes together again, you can't hear yourself speak through his bell-ringing practice. A preoccupied Spanish grandee with his white cigarette-holder, a big Camargue landowner with his loud check shirt, he can sell me a set if I'd like one. I say yes without asking the price.

'Good night, madame, I must get back off to my friend...'

No goodbye for the others; she knows them too well. The girl has left us, she has flown away in her pleated skirt.

Weighted down by the white wine and the sparkling wine, numbed by all the conversation, I had reached the stage of wondering whether I myself was ever going to get out of the Chantelauzes' dining room. Liliane's friendliness, the arabesques of her voice, her disturbing, sensual, schoolteacher's face, her lordly air of indifference, her floppy blouse, her lace were all holding me there the way a shady corner holds one on a hot summer's day. Sudden uproar. What's happening? Objects bouncing down the stairs, an avalanche of shoes from step to step . . .

M. Chantelauze seized my wrists. 'Interference forbidden,' he told me.

Basile and Liliane were laughing.

Yes, Ferdinand and his things; yes, she throws him out, then takes him back a moment later. M. Chantelauze seemed very happy about their disharmony.

I sneaked away five minutes later.

His postman's shoe broke one's heart under the fire escape. Was I going to see him one day, her Ferdinand? Their quarrel depressed me, their reconciliation stimulated me.

*

It is unbelievable and it is true: she came in a taxi, she climbed the six flights of stairs. Now she is sitting in the armchair, under the wall shelves bought for a thousand francs in the market in the Place d'Aligre. She is smoking, she accepts a glass of champagne. She says: You will be warm with a Godin. I am hot, I am too hot, she has come to visit me. She wanted to see my room, she has seen her photos on the wall, above my worktable. I am ashamed, she has caught me out. I am an immodest adolescent; she is seeing what I do: I hang photographs of her on my wall. She has caught me in the act. Where shall I sit? On my divan? Too intimate, too unbuttoned. Where, then? On the chair facing the armchair. The chair near the door, that will be less positive. The chair on which I fold my little girl's clothes every evening. She has come here. What wisdom, what reticence over by the window where I hear the nickname 'Spud' yelled through the windowpane. She gave me notice of her visit, but I tremble all the same at the idea that she might have caught me in Denis's grey trousers. I am sitting opposite her, I am hiding my feet under the chair, hiding my hands in the sleeves of my pullover. I am ashamed of my feet, of my hands. Why? Are my hands too naked when she comes to see me; are my feet too arrogant resting on the floor? Now shall we talk about this project, this book ... Thérèse, Isabelle. I resist the idea, I don't want to discuss it. We can talk about it somewhere else, in the evening, over dinner, in Harry's Bar ... Not here. Why write? I must go on writing. I mustn't cry, I shall soon receive a letter from Gaston Gallimard. From Gaston Gallimard? Yes, she has talked to him about me, she has been to see him on my behalf. Is it true, all that? Is it certain? I am too weak to thank her. I am limp because of my gratitude. If I dared, I would ask: 'Are you working? What are you writing?'

But she talks to me about me, she crushes me with her concern. I have a nice place to write in, it's nice and quiet, she has never seen that photo of Genet before ... She must go now. I understand, yes, I shall always understand. I efface myself, I shall always efface myself, even though I am also talking about myself in a drunken fury of egocentricity, even if I am weeping over my lot in life with maniacal despair. I can eliminate myself for her sake without a revolver, without any idea of suicide. A shower is falling on a village in the distance; what rectitude in the slanting lines of the rain! That rectitude is her; now she must go and discuss things with others, serious topics I can never grasp. She is about to leave, she leaves my flat.

Ring, my Angelus bells, to receive her going. I submit myself to her absences; the wheat ripens. Yes, I need furniture in the empty room. She wants all the things for me that I want myself. It is excessive. Why not thwart me, contradict me? Is it indifference? No, it is considerateness. She wants to make me stronger, she doesn't want to weaken me by thwarting me. Mme Gavotte ... A good thing, I am so alone. The Granvillons, I drink too much ... No, one needs a pick-up occasionally. Is she smoothing away all the difficulties in my daily life as a way of smoothing away all the difficulties in my relations with her? The thought buzzes round me, poisoning me a little as I see her out. Are you reading, she asks me. I must read. Am I reading? Recently I pressed Beckett's *Molloy* against one cheek, then against the other ... A great writer is a great brother, he just falls into your life, it is a bond stronger than any bond of blood. He arrives quite unexpectedly. He has cleared the ground, you are ploughed. Molloy throws a last glance at his little suburban garden, he closes the gate forever. Beckett with his speleology, his simple words ... and my prison and my condition are turned to crystal. Nothing has changed, but all is transparent inside me; I have read *Molloy*. I don't dare tell Simone de Beauvoir about it like that. I will tell her about it differently at our next dinner together.

La Puce is curious. She has run out on the landing as I say goodbye to Simone de Beauvoir. She wants to see everything, hear everything, learn everything, understand everything ... She's at that age. And besides, I intrigue her. I leaned over the stair rail and watched Simone de Beauvoir quietly walking down the stairs. I was set free, I am set free every time she leaves me, as if meeting me were for her the most onerous duty in the world.

'Is that her?' La Puce asked.

She was sniffling. She had just been smacked.

'Yes, that's her,' I answered sadly.

I could no longer hear her step on the landings below. She was on her way to find a taxi at the Faidherbe-Chaligny station.

La Puce was leaning over too far. I pulled her back, and she sobbed. She wanted to see her, she was so lovely in the photo ... I, too, would like to see her again, now she was gone.

I thought I was free; I said to myself: I shall be silent, I shall console myself by sitting in silence in the room where I entertained her. But I was chained to a child that needed minding.

I took her hand. I would gladly have knocked her down. Trampled her underfoot. They were leaving me with nothing, nothing.

'If you're quiet, you shall have some champagne...'

She stopped crying. 'What is she like?'

'You know. You see her every day on the wall!'

La Puce let go of my hand. 'Auntie Leduc, I wish I could take off your big nose!' she cried.

A stab and an endearment in the same breath.

How could I hold it against her? She wanted to relieve me of a burden.

'Why do you call me auntie? You've never called me that before?'

La Puce didn't answer. Her eyes were wide as she lifted them towards me. Eyes full of love.

We went into my room on tiptoe.

'Did she sit there?' La Puce asked.

'Yes,' I said, 'she sat there.'

*

Jacques is going to give me a dining-room set. His general manager is looking for one for me.

*

Gaston Gallimard has written to me. I can't believe my eyes. Why shouldn't Gaston Gallimard dictate letters to his writers? I am not a writer, I am a guilty ghost in his corridors. A letter from him, typed, signed with his first name, with his family name. Fascination. I concentrate on the first name. This 'Gaston' is the Gaston of Maurice Sachs. This 'Gaston' recurs frequently in Maurice's letters from Hamburg. This 'Gaston' was Maurice's guest on ... on Maurice's last evening in Paris. And in his letter Gaston tells me that I have none but friends in 'the house.' I believe Gaston. Who are they, though? Apart from Jacques Lemarchand, apart from Jacqueline Bour ... mostly I meet totally indifferent people on Gaston's stairs. They don't see me, and I don't try to make them see me. A moment's pause, all the same, for the 'house' of Breton, of Céline, of Dostoevsky, where I have none but friends ... That's not all, though. I shall receive, from now on, a monthly allowance of 20,000 francs; I shall be able to write in peace. A curler has fallen on his letter. Is it a sign? It is a warning. If I don't write every day, I shall be stealing what is given to me. I am being paid, I have a job. If writing is no longer a choice, so much the better. I want to work and be handed my pay packet. Writing is a chore, a punishment, an iron ball chained to one's foot. Then stop writing. That would be a punishment worse than the first, a curse, an affliction you could die of. Now I really think I'm something: I shall be paid for what I do. My thin first drafts, my flabby adjectives, my asthmatic sentences, my cheap mannerisms are going to provide me with good lean meat, with croissants. I shall strut into the best grocers. Asparagus, please, your best. Farewell, Dominique.

When Gaston Gallimard's letter had been replaced in its envelope, I imprinted a long kiss on Simone de Beauvoir's wide brow in the Cartier-Bresson photograph. I owed her my monthly payments, I owed her everything. An hour later I was playing the successful writer with my radio, letting it blare its head off. Two hours later, carefree and sure of myself, almost disdainful, I took in a bottle of Granvillons to Mme Gavotte. Did I confide in her? Did I tell her what had happened to me, how much I was to receive every month? No, I am too much of a peasant to confide such things. We clinked glasses to toast some good news. What good news? I'll tell you later. Mme Gavotte listened to me with a preoccupied ear; she was looking for bruises on her legs, on her arms: Ferdinand's love bites. He loves her, he bites her. Don't I want to look? Come on, now, I must look. No, no, a really good look. Do I find it distasteful? I can't understand, a man has never been mad for me ... I must hold the purple stamped arm, I must bend over her tattooed thighs, I must stick my nose into her love bites. Am I still disgusted? I am growing accustomed ... They're the colour of pansies in country gardens. Pansies in gardens? Mme Gavotte has to hold her belly with both hands, she laughs so much.

*

I knocked at their door one Saturday afternoon. 'Come and see ... I have a dining-room set!'

'I'm shaving, I'll be with you in a moment,' M. Chantelauze called out.

'Jacques has given me a Henri II dining-room set. It's arrived! Are you going to come and see?'

'I'm washing my hair, I'll be there in a minute,' Zézette called.

As for Mme Gavotte, she was always ready to bestir herself in her gaping peignoir.

They all arrived at the same time. Basile, with Zézette with Baba in her arms, Mme Gavotte, M. and Mme Chantelauze. La Puce was sleeping.

They looked at one another, they couldn't make up their minds.

Zézette transferred Baba to Mme Chantelauze's arms. 'In your place, I'd have chosen something else! It's too heavy. It makes the room heavy.'

Basile crossed his arms. He was exasperated. 'Be quiet, you idiot!'

His garb: striped pyjamas. He was saving his suit.

'I would have liked it so much to be like yours,' I said to Zézette.

'Oh, really?' Basile said. Gentle and dreamy.

By way of consolation, he offered me a denicotined Gauloise.

'I had a choice of three. I chose the one with the most work in it ...'

'The most elaborate,' Basile said. 'What carvings ...'

He caressed the hollows, the bosses on the sideboard doors.

I went over. 'That's Saint George. He's slaying the dragon.'

'Oh, yes?' Basile said.

He looked at it for a long time.

'Here, take your child back!' Mme Chantelauze said to Zézette.

Arms free once more, she turned to me. 'Madame Leduc, I just don't understand you...'

She held her audience with her eyes.

'There's nothing to understand. I like it. But go on, all the same...'

Zézette was walking up and down with her baby between the six chairs.

Mme Chantelauze did go on all the same. 'What do you want all this crimson on the seats of your chairs for? Why crimson curtains? It's too glaring, too hard on the eyes.'

'The chairs and curtains were a gift,' I said with a hangdog expression. 'Don't you think the studs around the seats...'

'There's nothing very special about that kind of thing,' M. Chantelauze mumbled grudgingly. He was chewing his long white cigarette-holder.

'I prefer a pure modern style,' Zézette said.

'Idiot, be quiet!' Basile told her again.

Mme Gavotte recovered from her consternation. 'But that's just a dust trap, an old piece of furniture like that...'

Suddenly a change of mood. They all went over. Some intrigued. Some blasé.

'This is a Louis XI chair,' I announced, very simply, like an actress formally announcing the author's name at the end of a preview.

'If I'd been there when they were making it, I'd have told them not to bother,' M. Chantelauze muttered. He was still chewing at his long white bone.

'Now you, Papa, you were brought up with Henri II stuff... What do you think of her dining set?' Mme Chantelauze asked her husband.

Mme Gavotte had lowered herself into the Louis XI chair. It was a rocking chair, and she was rocking back and forth. Basile was passionately engrossed in the hills and dales of the sideboard doors. Zézette told me she'd show me how to make curtains ... Portières in the Italian style? No, sorry, she didn't know a thing about those.

What did he think of it? Well, St George was a funny fellow all right, in his way. The dragon was a fiasco. Carving? Don't try to give him that. He preferred ebony heads in medallions. He'd had his bellyful of Henri II, he'd been brought up with it ... I would roast in summer with all that red felt ... But Cantor at least would have a high old time with it, sharpening his claws...

Then suddenly Basile, Zézette and Baba, Mme Gavotte and M. Chantelauze all flew off together, like a flock of sparrows, all at precisely the same moment.

*

Swathed in her long lilac quilted wrap, Mme Chantelauze was examining her face in the bevel-edged mirror bought for a thousand francs on the Place d'Aligre. They were having people in that evening, would she look her best? Papa has his head full of these wild ideas; you know what he's like. The latest is they've got to put all their things in cardboard boxes, redecorate the flat ... Finished satin ... She raised her arms and began to hum a soothing love song. Plum curtains with a light grey lining ... She was distressing me. Luxury can become an obsession.

'I have a cigarette with a gold tip,' I told her. 'I've been saving it for you. I'll get it.'

Her eyes shone.

She stood smoking a jewel of a cigarette, her elbow resting on my mantel. Why was this languorous creature with her peach skin, her temptress's shoulders, still in my room? Did she know I was writing about Thérèse, about Isabelle? Did she want to test me, to provoke me? She was wasting her time.

'You must feel sorry for me, I know,' she said.

Now she was looking at herself in the mirror because she was smoking a cigarette the colour of a fading rose.

'The hardest part,' she confided, 'is the nights. Can you imagine his breath? He sleeps with his mouth open ... The whole room reeks of it,' she added.

She came towards me. What was about to happen?

'I have understood you, you must understand me,' she began. 'Someone you love has given you these crimson curtains, this dragon, this Henri II table ... Mme Gavotte and Zézette have told me about it. You are going to be living in a nest he has made for you. Oh, I'm not saying a thing against it. Oh, no! All those studs on the chairs will be so many thorns, so many caresses. As for him over there, sometimes he will be St George, sometimes the absent beloved ... We are women, we understand these things ... Do you like pale-pink carnations? Yes, I've understood you. Now please try to understand my situation. We have bought the latest-model camp bed. On credit. And now they are at our throats. Lend me five thousand francs. Could you lend it to us immediately?'

She had caught me off-guard. Five thousand francs. What aim the woman had. Bull's-eye, first shot. Five thousand francs. The industrious ant must pay the grasshopper. But what a sum. Why didn't she ask Mme Gavotte for it? Why come to me? I earn less than she does! But then, I work so much less than she does! In a factory all day, and two bouts of pneumonia. How can I bear to humiliate her? Yet Mme Gavotte has warned me: money just runs through her fingers, she has ideas way beyond her means ... A quarter of my monthly allowance. How does she even dare to ask? I would never have the nerve. Oh, how cunning she is when it comes to wangling money out of you.

I held out my five-thousand-franc note.

'Now listen,' I said, 'listen carefully ... Yes, I will lend you the five thousand francs, here they are ... But you know my position ... A woman on her own, without a job ...'

'You write books,' she said with scorn.

I had disappointed her. I wasn't Pearl Buck.

'I write, yes. But I can't live on what I earn from my writing.'

I began the lecture again. I would lend her the money, yes, I agreed to lend it her. But I didn't want to have to beg for my money back. I didn't want to have to demean myself by having to ask her for it.

Mme Chantelauze yawned. That went without saying. Of course I wouldn't have to beg, of course I wouldn't have to demean myself. She would bring me a dozen pale-pink carnations and my five thousand francs next Saturday, without fail. And without a thank you, she was gone.

I envied her nerve, her lack of concern.

Limbs shattered, sapped by the virus of discouragement, I went to buy my wilting, rotting vegetables from Dominique. I was punishing myself for my generosity. She had sapped my very foundations, that siren. I have done her a good turn ... and here I am, crawling on the floor. Will they let me be one of them if I become their flunky and their basset hound? Bang to the left, bang to the right, that's the heavy machine she works at in the factory. She told me how her back hurts ... I who write for three short hours a day ... Always accusing myself, always the same. I shall wear my knees out if I go on abasing myself like this. But if they knew what I'm writing ... That again? They won't know. How could they know? Spies wriggling their way in. Private investigators. They are invisible. How am I to describe the sensation? How am I to pin

it down, that sensation? I shall never manage it. I must make love to
myself, I shall make love to myself for the sake of the truth. I will
be Isabelle. There's no other course. I am committed to my exercise
book.

*

I got up at one in the morning. I went into the kitchen in my bare
feet, without turning on the light. I was angry with myself; I had
bought the bottle without thinking of the danger. I hoped, I feared
I would see the enemy's mark. A being to be feared. Impregnable.
I was chilled, I was too hot. Who wants me to suffer from the
scratch of a nail? What is it he suspects me of, this pitiless being? I
sit on my stool in the darkness. The coldness of the white oilcloth on
the table. The oilcloth coming to my rescue. At last I had found
absolute indifference! I withdrew my hand. The night was letting
me know the extent of my torment. The great cats lay asleep, their
circus act over, their claws in wait for me. The silence? The clenched
teeth of those who had it in for me. I will lay my hand flat against
the label. If it is unharmed, then it will be smooth, it will give me
fresh life. I dream of a sky-blue skin on a bottle of eau de Cologne,
my head falls on my knees. Why has what had to happen happened,
why am I the bull in the ring with my hand flat against the bottle
label? I don't move, and yet, ah! and yet I stagger with the band-
erillos in my neck. The pucker left by the scratching nail is there.
Serve me up in slices, I am their bull spouting blood. Primordial, it
is primordial: was the nail mark there when I carried it out of the
grocer's? Perhaps they come into my flat when I'm not here. A
slash of the paw and they are away again. Even if I fled to the end
of the earth, the nail would be ready, the claw sharpened and waiting.

I switched on the light. Violated in one corner, the label. Withered,
puckered. He has also vented his rage on the letter *a* in *Eau natur-
elle*, the letter *a* mangled unrecognizably. Regretfully, he has left
me an *n*, then *tu* and *elle* without an *r*. *Tu elle*. That could easily
be *tue elle*. *Kill her?* Who is it I must kill? What woman must I
eliminate? Is it telling me in advance about a killing on the Stock
Exchange? Or can that mangled *a* be my father, André, who died at
the age of thirty-six? Is it telling me I shall die of tuberculosis as
well? Tomorrow I shall throw them off the scent, tomorrow I
shall buy Contrexéville water in Damoy's, or in Nicolas's. I shall
lose myself in the crowd, I shall shake them off. Who am I trying
to fool? They are waiting everywhere, at every hour of the day and

night. Ready to leap to the attack, determined to possess me. Ready with their justice, which is futile because I haven't done anything wrong.

I told Simone de Beauvoir about it and upset her. She looked at me at first as though she wanted to speak very sharply to me. I mustn't frighten her with my silly notions. They aren't silly notions. They are slaughterhouses that kill you with scratching pins. If only it were an axe, or a mallet ... I could see who was killing me. Violette, now think ... 75 ... that's the registration number for Paris, didn't you know that? The torn labels ... They aren't torn, Simone de Beauvoir. A paw has slashed them, a claw has puckered them. I don't dare say the claw of an inquisitor. The torn labels, Violette, are just where the bottles have scraped against the crate slats—what possible meaning could they have! I ought to believe her, I don't believe her. She ought to believe me, she doesn't believe me. Simone de Beauvoir can't go into a pin factory where all the points are intended for me. There isn't someone tracking her down, there isn't someone suffocating her, there isn't someone poisoning her existence with the scratches left by a nail. I shall not be able to convince her, she will not be able to convince me. She will not give way to my hallucinations—she calls the mark of a tiger's claw a hallucination—and it seems to me she is deserting me. My dishcloth wasn't born yesterday ... It wasn't a real tear even this morning; but a savage finger has ripped through my piece of linen in its rage. Who has torn my dishcloth, who has loathed and hated me through my dishcloth? Things wear out, Violette, we forget that ...

'Have you been working?' she asks with her usual kindly look.

That is what counts for her. That is the bond between us. I shall leave her, I shall throw myself on my torn dishcloth, I shall be alone with my pain. I shan't get better, despite her kindness. My heart contracts. I wanted an accomplice, I have a lucid friend. I shiver as I sit beside a warm fire. Yes, I have worked. Isabelle spat on her shoe. I have begun like that. Can I begin like that?

'Show me.'

I open my notebook.

Shall I tell her? Shall I hide it from her? I can't stop myself. Someone looks into my room through a little hole in the ceiling, someone reads it before she does, someone reads it as I write.

'What is there above you?' she asks sceptically.

'... A loft, it's the loft.'

Her face lights up. I had distressed her; now I have reassured her.

'It's the rats you hear.'

'It's not rats! There's a trap door on the landing that's always open ... Someone goes up into the loft, someone goes up the fire escape ...'

Her face darkens. Why are you deliberately making things worse for yourself, her eyes ask me. I give up the idea of trying to explain that the scratching I hear up above me is the nail of someone watching, implacably watching.

'You're not well, you're really not well,' she says sadly.

'Is that true? Am I not well?'

I hear noises that she will never hear. She wants to dispel my misfortunes; they are inside me, inside my womb, they belong to me.

She reads, she turns the pages of my notebook. But the gang is ready, preparing fresh torments, fresh thorns for me.

*

Mme Chantelauze hasn't returned my money. The days go by, I listen to her step outside, I hear her voice. She ought to be coming in to see me, but she doesn't. I suffer, I fume, I foam with rage. I avoid her when I ought to confront her, force open her purse without a word, take out what is mine. Shall I go this morning? I count up to eight hundred. Still, I don't dare go. I count up to three hundred ... I stop counting. I go. And I lie: give me back my money because I need it. Yet I am not lying. I do need it, because I love it, my money, I want to put it safely away in my canvas sack. My darling money ... If you give me back my five thousand, you will be enriching me with what I already possessed before, and all in you will be perfection. Money, my lovely little baby, come back and let me throw the bolts behind you. I am to have pale-pink carnations tomorrow morning ... Oh, yes? But I am fingering you, that's what matters, my reconquered five-thousand-franc note. Do I prefer the flapping of my notes to the frothing of the chestnut trees? No, I prefer the chestnut trees. Suddenly I let the five-thousand-franc note in my pocket lie there deserted and neglected: the return of the prodigal had begun to bore me. Money can do anything; it signifies nothing.

No, Liliane Chantelauze doesn't mind. She lets me sit down on her split sofa, between the window and the fireplace. She lets me have what I wanted: to sit in their flat. The tiniest, the tightest packed. A palace. That of my yearning for coziness. Peddlers had unpacked their bundles in the Chantelauzes' home. Their table, divinely close to the sofa, as in a nursery school. The sofa has hair like an old woman's bursting out of it, and I am blissful sitting there beside it. I put my small five-year-old's hands on their table. The flowers are about to be born, their window is a cradle covered in greenery. Paris, when you begin remembering the countryside ... Cantor struts from one bundle to another, he is looking for somewhere to sit befitting his dignity, he strikes a pose in the greenery frame. Liliane is wearing a mauve linen housecoat; it is as new as a brand-new mauve sky in February; the cat has gone to sleep on a pile of napkins waiting to be ironed. I must get some table linen. That's what Zézette tells me.

Liliane offers me a liqueur. 'Verbena? Tarragon? Chervil?'

She opens her sideboard. What stores she has, what snooks cocked at the winter, those regiments of jars!

'May I look?'

'Of course. Don't stand on ceremony.'

Gherkins with tiny black stars of cloves and peppercorns; onions as perfect as partridge eggs. Asparagus so obscenely big it looked like sheaves of sexes. As for the tomatoes, they were balls of raw meat. The macédoine of vegetables chirruped away in its jars, and un-identified plants stood soaking in greenish alcohol.

'It's an orchard, it's a whole kitchen-garden, your sideboard ...'

'We like orchards and kitchen-gardens,' Mme Chantelauze said.

She poured us glasses of tarragon liqueur. That evening they would camp by the water's edge, they would sleep under the latest-model tent, on a camp bed that's the latest thing. Pity your poor old friend always shut up in her flat, I said to the five-thousand-franc note folded in four in my pocket.

*

I wrote, I wrote at their dictation. I wrote with one hand, and with the other ... I loved myself to love them, to find them again, to translate them, to make sure I did not betray them. I told them about that. Always the same circle, always that monotony. I threw my pen-holder down on the exercise book. It is a perpetual motion, and it insists on having all of you. An arm stayed free on the table, my head fell on the arm. I talked to them. My hell is thinning out, Isabelle, my sky is widening. I want to be an explosion of pebbles hurled at the stars. Thérèse, my prison is dizzy with the movement. How shall I ever manage to transcribe it, the wave carries me off on its back, pleasure is on the prowl. Come back, Isabelle. Ah, you have come back. Your hair in my arms, in my lap, between my legs, I have found you again, and so goodbye, captivity. High tension, I am overcharged. Speed and communion. Am I dreaming or did someone knock? I am being wedded to myself where nothing exists. A knock on the door. Impossible, my finger is being betrothed. The great betrothal for the great absence. The terrible divagation without words. Knock, knock. Impossible, I am on my way to see Pasiphae. Someone shouting outside my door. The catastrophe is there, in my body; my sky has shivered. Don't call me, I am diving. Someone in danger outside my door. Calling me again now. I would kill if I were forced to stop. I was the summer, I am a few drops of rain, I am dying of gratitude. An open flower, a trembling flower, smoke drifting all through me. A body throwing itself at my door. Someone shouted my name. I tell you it's impossible. My feet? Water-lilies opening. Decay, spreading your filaments. The great advance. Don't interrupt me, don't knock like that, don't shout like that. My left hand, my brand-new darling on the table, my fragile one, you have dragged me back out of my underworld. It is serious, someone outside my door, someone who won't go away, cries for help on the landing. You are burning me, snowdrop, a sigh, one must help one's neighbour.

'Who is it?'

'Zézette. Open up ...'

I open the door. I don't recognize her.

'Why didn't you answer?'

My disorder is in her hair. My fever is on her cheeks.

'My little girl is dying.'

I followed Zézette into her flat.

The baby is on the table, the oilcloth has alopecia. Zézette has the light on, though it's bright daylight. The baby is barely breathing.

'She's not asleep,' Zézette said. 'She's ill.'

That was quite apparent. Not enough life left to open its eyes. Where did I live through that beginning of death under my lowered eyelids? In a clinic. After an abortion.

'Sit down,' Zézette told me. 'You must hold her while I fetch the doctor ...'

Zézette was going out of her mind, I could see it in the wide eyes. This crazed, dishevelled creature was her.

I stretched out my arms and she laid Baba on them. The baby was heavy, despite the life leaking out of it.

'Her eczema is going,' I said quietly.

Zézette was counting her money before setting out.

'Take good care of her,' she said.

Then she was gone.

'Take good care of her.' As if it was in my power to escort the lady with the scythe back over the border.

I am so afraid of death ... I would not help a wounded or dying person if I chanced on one. I would find excuses: one dies alone. What am I holding in my arms? A box with 'Fragile' stamped on it. Ah, a godsend: the fly on the ceiling. I see the fly, I need not look at the baby. Yes, sniffle, little cocoon. I shall stand by my cowardice. The baby was silent, the street went quietly on existing. The alarm clock, with its dry noise of flaring twigs, was getting on my nerves. So was the sullen grey of the sky pressing down on Paris. I can't let it die. I must fight for it. I looked down: I was less frightened when I saw how shapeless it was in its covers. I could feel the back of its neck wetting my arm. A deathbed sweat? I must look at its face. Dummy, the world is bursting at the seams with children. This is Zézette's, though, the baby on our floor. I couldn't make myself look at it. Is it breathing?

You are all set, and death sweeps aside your fun and games. Remorse. Go on then, wallow in it. After all, it's not my child. I'll help it to live. The pure-wool blanket is hiding its mouth. A baby, is it, or a shrivelled-up mummy? Both. I'm getting used to its gasping for breath. Baby, I don't dare look at you ... I'm wrong, death won't find your feet in that overheated bundle. You're dead, you're too white. Eyelids the colour of honey. Lift your eyelids? Never. The child's struggle continues, ticktock, ticktock, we are dead, my child, the ticktock goes on too. What would I see if I pulled up its eyelids? It's just vegetating, it's not dying. Its hands. I was forgetting its hands. Check its hands, examine its hands. A baby has cool hands when it's in good health. I can't check them, I can't examine them.

Where is Zézette? Has she lost her way? Where is it breathing? When is it breathing? Take heart, babies have always been mysterious creatures. It's stiffening. Is this the end? I bent down close to its sick little lips. Where was it living, if it was living? Where was it dying, if it was dying? I felt a breath, oh, hope! Will it live till she comes back? How can I get up from my chair with this sacrosanct package, how can I switch off that pointless light? It will live, I shall have the strength and the regularity of that hated ticktock to make it live. It must live, I will lend a five-thousand-franc note to every tenant. You're committing yourself without thinking, my little one. It will live, I am breathing myself on behalf of its goddamned little life. I kissed its hand, finger by finger. Revulsion. I shall never win if I can't forget myself.

Key in lock, here is Zézette.

How is she? Is she just the same? How would I know, Zézette? Death hasn't let me in on any secrets.

Zézette came over. She smiled at the waxen eyelids. She had hope. She was back with her child and it was as though nothing had happened.

'We shall save her, you'll see,' she said.

A knock on the door.

I opened it and admitted an oily-looking man. My trousers and my turtle-neck sweater surprised him.

We undressed the baby on the table, away from the mother collapsed in a corner. Once naked, Baba began kicking and whimpering. My calm manner surprised the doctor too. Was I a nurse? No, I was a volunteer.

He would be back that evening, he would save her, he would give her another injection. He certainly had the best part. Zézette complicated his rescue work with talk of forms and money. Later. Let's save her first. I liked that Zézette: she had her feet on the ground. It was necessary; she must do her counting. I forget now what Baba had wrong with her.

*

Jacques has given me a Tuscan lamb jacket. I would have preferred young fox, blue fox, mink. We must be happy with what we are given. Jacques couldn't stand me any more in my old, mangy coat, Denis told me. Denis restrained me, kept me calm while we were buying it, while I was trying on coat after coat. Thirty thousand francs, that's quite a sum. We mustn't spend more than that. Champagne, the colour. It makes me invisible. My old rabbit has got its own back. I suspect I have red albino's eyes when I go out with this champagne-coloured froth all over my back. It will never wear out, the saleswoman told me. How could I ever complain of its weight? It is the weight of Jacques's money. I put it on, I go out. Ten degrees below, outside; but my mattress laughs at the cold. A woman in trousers walks alone through the streets; she need not even think about the cold spell we're having. She looks at herself in the store windows, she sings to herself. No. She sings a song of love for Jacques. He has given her a warmth worth having, a wall of comfort between her and the cold.

My evenings have changed. I possess the spirit of decision on Sunday evenings since he gave me my Tuscan lamb. The last mouthful swallowed, plate and knife wiped, I consult the what's-on columns. Five minutes later I am on my way, debonair and carefree. I lock my door with a double turn of the key, and I listen. Everything is all right, everything is normal: Zézette and Basile having a row, M. Chantelauze roaring, his wife calling him 'Papa.' I jump. Unexpectedly, Zézette has opened her door. She is taking La Puce back to put her to bed, she is looking after her while Mme Gavotte looks after her patients.

'If you're going out, put something on your head,' she says.

This happiness at rushing out into the deserted streets on the way to a good film would be perfect without the turds; but, alas, there are the turds. Before, I used to look at them without seeing them, without paying attention. Then I saw them. It hurt. I averted my eyes; but that made the pain worse. So I looked at them. Openly, stoically. Seeing those segments hurt very much indeed. When they were fresh, I reasoned thus: if you have a dog in a flat, then you must take that dog out at night; it can't be avoided. But that argument did not stand up for long. Someone has deliberately trained a dog, you see, in order to make an impression on me. Someone knows when I am getting ready to go out, where I shall be going. Someone walks his dog just ahead of me. Someone hypnotizes it. Someone makes sure his dog relieves itself precisely where I shall walk, under my very feet if I'm not careful. It isn't just excrement, real, ordinary excrement. I can't bear that as it is, mine or other people's. But this is worse: a calamity. My disgust is exaggerated, but I can't change myself. How many times have I wished I could extrude the pellets of rabbits or hares ... They're dry, they're neat and clean. The softer the excrement, the greater my horror. I live in terror now the minute I put my nose out of doors: I shall see dog droppings on the pavements. I do see them, and I am in shreds. The enemy clenches his teeth, the spy keeps his watch, the organization tightens the net. I leave the turd, I move away, I force myself to walk with the unconcerned tread of someone with a limp, trying to disguise it; I too am disguising an infirmity, that of having to escape from turds.

I thought I was free, but they were all round me. They've got what they wanted: I am in a state of utter misery now that I've seen that excrement. Those turds against the walls, or else in the gutters, they signify failure, mockery, derision. I emerge from my flat: derision. I wrote this afternoon: derision. I'm going to a film: derision. I am walking fast: derision. I shall go into a cinema: derision. They are strong. I was forgetting the pointlessness of all I do, but the turd has forced it back into my memory. My invisible enemy never lets me out of his sight. I wouldn't wish anyone the vastness of my resignation when I walk through the streets in the evening and they are walking their dogs and I say to myself: my enemies are made of steel, the turds are eternal and innumerable. Those who have humiliated me in the course of my existence so far were simple indeed alongside these anonymous torturers, these secret beings hunting me with dogs. I run to L'Artistic; a turd, another, yet another ... They are steaming, they are evenly pieced, they are repulsive, I am dying of disgust and curiosity, I want to see who it is that hates me, that wants to kill me. Who will take turns with me in the streets? I could rest then. But who would do it ... ?

The more neatly formed they are, the more precise the sarcasm. If you knew with what purity I remember the cow pats and the piles of horse dung in the country. The cow and the horse are separate from what they produce. It is manure, it is butter for the buttercup. But dogs' turds: a hell peopled with dwarfs who write anonymous letters. I would believe in them less if I could weep. But I can't manage tears. I sight them ahead of me, I cross the road, I examine them from closer-to, I am less and less able to ward off the dagger blows of the being who sends them to me. I hurry along the pavements. I am always seeing them, always studying the very objects that horrify me; who can imagine what I have to bear? My suffering doubles if I pretend I haven't seen them, because they know I've seen them from near and from far, from too near and too far ... It triples if I attempt to mock them with my glances ... I would like to grip the head of a bed, I would like to be a stump of dead tree on the edge of a field, I would like to lie down in a church. They aren't in my exercise book, or on my chair, or in front of my table, or in my inkwell, or under my nails, or in my hair, or in my billfold, or on my seat in the cinema. It's worse. They eye me. The little girls and the old women hate me when the lights have gone down in the auditorium of L'Artistic. They tell me so with the noise of their shiny candy wrappers. They want to cancel out my evening, turn the silence into gangrene, make my hair stand on end. No, I won't tap them with my foot, I won't squash them. That's what they would like. They are sucking and fiddling with their paper. I will bear their coils. But how long can I bear them? Show me my enemies. Shall I see them some day? What have I done, what have I done? I am destroying myself in my search for an answer.

*

The daughter of the grocer's wife has affinities with the angels: round face, soft features, curly hair, a halo of question marks round her brow, a small mouth, clear complexion, limpid gaze. Her pen friend is fighting far away. He writes to her and will soon be engaged to her. Their cat, so spiteful tongues relate, pisses on the spinach. Too bad. I like people who like cats. We talk about Fort-Mahon. Why? It's the beach where Marie-Christine goes for her holidays and also the beach where Jacques and his nanny used to go for theirs. His Mémée. As who should say his adored grandmother. The customers come in one after another; I stand aside to let them be served. I cherish the thought of Jacques and his Mémée, Jacques's rake, his butterfly net, their boat at the photographer's ... Loving Jacques, a melancholy secret. I hid it from Simone de Beauvoir, am still hiding it. But loving Jacques is no secret on the sixth floor. I am letting myself slide, I am degrading myself, I have parted with the secrets of my heart. Marie-Christine hasn't lived. Yet all the same she possesses the subtle generosity of the mature woman. She has experience, and she is my consoling angel. I confide in her.

She weighed my spinach and I embarked on further details. A little boy came in and smiled. Jacques. He waited patiently. Jacques at Fort-Mahon. Jacques, ironic, obedient. His spade, his rake, his butterfly net ... I fell silent, dazed and dumb.

She served him. He wanted a bar of Suchard chocolate. He paid, then stayed to watch us. He was his own master. Then Red Indians summoned him from outside. He vanished.

Marie-Christine's curiosity had to be sated. I continued my story. I was still concealing the essential: Denis.

'But there is some hope all the same,' she said.

'Not the slightest.'

I was proud: I was imposing my misfortune on another.

'Not the slightest little hope?' the angel persisted.

'Not the slightest. I can assure you of that.'

She selected a Petit Pâtre cheese, not too firm, not too soft. Whatever happens, one must eat properly. Her eyes filled with tears.

'I'll give you an address. You can go and see her, I'm sure she'll help you ...'

Two customers came in. Marie-Christine weighed out blood oranges for them.

I must go there at half past one, she has all her wits about her at that hour ... I must go along the side of Le Palais de la Femme, take this street ... She wrote down the address.

I walked along the side of Le Palais de la Femme, the private apartments ... The starched curtains of the Salvation Army officers' quarters called me to order. 'Read the Bible, sister. It will help you to believe in another life.' Another life? I was in a hurry.

Is that it, the house of hope? It's tumbling down. That wretched, two-story hovel? They'll be demolishing it tomorrow by the look of it, so there's no time to waste. I walked into a passage where darkness held perpetual sway; I started up the stairs. Doll's house banisters and landing. Greasy walls that will be mere child's play for the demolition men ... A door at the end. Hers. Like a wish come true.

The door opened only the slightest crack. Then there appeared arthritic swellings, brown liver marks, veins puffed out with violet blood. Should I bow my head for it to bless me, this ancient hand? I hadn't come for a blessing. I handed over my paper. Rapaciously the hand clutched it, then withdrew.

'Did anyone see you come in? Did you meet anyone?' I was asked from the other side of the door.

'No ... No ...'

Her rooms smells of scented soap and stew. She moves to and fro. She has the stiffness, the false confidence of those no longer able to see their way. Will this blind woman penetrate my future?

She seats herself at her fortune-telling table. I sit opposite her. Ah, how perfect her hands are on the mauve table-cover. The whole city sighs in my throat. Her eyes open. She can see, she can see me. I must remove my Tuscan lamb, make myself comfortable. Get ready, future, get set, 'cause here we come. No, she is collecting her thoughts. She is looking at her hands as they lie on the table. What has she done with her life, with her days? I can read nothing in her.

'About what exactly did you wish to consult me about?'

Inquisitive old woman, exercise your trade. You should be inundating me with words, not asking questions.

She seems bored; her hands are helping her pass the time.

'If I am to help me, you must talk to me . . .'

Each word she utters falls and is lost among the ancient objects cluttering her room. They lie in piles. The flame in her eyes had become disconcerting.

I recovered the use of my tongue. 'I am in love. My feelings are not reciprocated. Marie-Christine said you could help me . . .'

Have I shocked her? She has withdrawn her hands. A swift gesture. What if the old age were just a disguise . . .

'Can you help me? You haven't answered.'

'It's not easy,' she says.

Now she is holding a conversation with her table-cover. 'I would have preferred a bond of love to strengthen, an erring heart to guide back home!'

My case is a poor case, without interest. I folded my arms. Straightening my back as I sat—that meant I was keeping my shadow out of her light.

Her hand was tapping out a rhythm on the table. Was she trying to conjure spirits? Without looking, she pulled a silk cord: the mauve percale curtain swished, the rings squeaked along their rod.

'Hand me my tins,' she said curtly.

I picked up the two cookie tins.

She introduced me. 'The thirty-two-card deck. The fifty-two-card deck.'

Her eyes ferreted inside me. She drew out a thick deck of tall, grubby cards.

'The tarot pack,' she announced.

She opened a fan of grease and grime. She was getting her hand in. Dog-eared apparently, the future. The narrowness of the tarot cards bewildered me. She lowered the fan and showed me the pictures: a naked woman dancing inside a crown; an angel-king getting drunk; a hanged man attempting a Charleston up in the air; a bright blue crab keeping company with German-shepherd dogs baying at the moon; a sun weeping big tears onto twins; death scything off hands. Bizarre medieval pictures, childishness, dark sorcery. I could see the future: it was skipping rope on a belly.

She raised the fan again. I missed the pictures. I felt respect, veneration for the tarot cards. I felt a yearning for the jolly world of the Middle Ages. Jesters embodying what we call hidden meanings. She was slowly shuffling the thirty-two-card deck.

'The big deal or the little deal?'

'The big deal.'

I cut with concern for equality. Half good fortune, half bad fortune. We would see later.

A black dog tried to turn round in its basket under the sewing machine. Crippled by rheumatism, it fell back. Its blue-ribbon bow didn't make it look any younger.

'That's Kiki,' she said.

'. . .'

'Think! Think hard. Think for a long time.'

I closed my eyes. I wanted to concentrate on something. On what? On Jacques? On my mother? On Thérèse and Isabelle? On my monthly stipend? On everything? On nothing? Kiki was breathing heavily in his basket, so I concentrated on him.

'Have you thought hard?' she asked.

'Yes ... Yes ...'

'Now cut!'

Again ... What am I separating? Sun from rain? Stars from bawdy-houses? It was done long ago.

'Not with that hand! That's bad luck!'

I cut more indecisively.

She scrutinized. 'Sensitive nature,' she said in a far-away voice.

A feast for the ego. A sphinx, albeit a sphinx in a small-business way, was talking to me about myself.

'. . . You are a worrier.'

Bliss on bliss, she seemed to care one way or the other.

'Yes, I would say I'm a worrier,' I said.

'Concentrate, concentrate as hard as you can ...'

I concentrated on her hair. Before receiving her clients, she evidently ran a wet comb through it. I envied Kiki's detachment. Why not sit him up on my chair. He can have his fortune told, and I will sigh comfortably there in his basket, in his misty oblivion.

She dealt out cards apparently at random on the mauve table-cover. Her yellowed index finger tapped each card as she laid it down. She turned one over. Her worn eyes questioned me.

'You are in trouble. Nothing is going the way you'd like ...'

I shifted on my chair. 'It's true,' I bleated. 'Nothing I do seems to make it any better.'

At that instant the enemy whispered in my ear: have you ever heard of things getting better for anyone when those things have been worked out and planned for him?

She was showing me my troubles, my heartaches: the dimpled seven of spades. She pointed out a little source of anger: the merry-cheeked seven of diamonds.

'You have suffered a great deal. Nothing has turned out as you would have wished ...'

As I listen to her, my past and its terrifying currents become tiny wavelets. My suffering is the merest banality floating up to the surface.

She scrutinizes me. 'Am I wrong?'

'No, you're not wrong.'

What she has revealed to me is meagre, unfrightening.

'I'm going to cover you now.'

She covered me with one mysterious card: the very nub of my misfortunes.

An old woman, someone who didn't know me five minutes ago, was rummaging round for my disappointments, my blighted hopes, in her storeroom. I felt I would like to kiss the top of her head.

'You need peace and quiet. You're always being disturbed,' she said.

'I live alone, I am always alone! No, I'm not always being disturbed ...'

A shadow passed over her face. You don't interrupt a wise old woman when she is reading the secrets of your failure in life.

I wanted to see exceptional qualities in her. She at least expressed herself without vulgarity.

'Are we in agreement if I tell you that you have not obtained what you wished to obtain?'

'Absolutely.'

Kiki opened one eye. We were still talking. He went back to sleep.

'Think,' she said. 'Think for a long while ...'

I cut.

'Think, go on thinking ...'

I had been empty before I arrived. Now she sought to make me even emptier with her 'thinks' and her 'go-on-thinkings.'

She opened her mouth. 'A man, are you listening?'

'I'm listening, a man ...'

A stranger. Featureless. Important. It can only be the darkness at the bottom of a mine.

'A man will set out.'

'Yes, a man will set out ...'

I was the darkness, I was the mine, I was the lump of coal they were pulling from the wall. I shuddered.

'... He will be with you before three weeks are out. Remember: before three weeks are out. You will meet him at a party.'

I had already met him. He had come to my den with Genet. Was she making fun of me?

'Another man? This one will ring your bell within the next three days ...'

I racked my brains. Who was it? The jack with two heads and the leg-of-mutton sleeves?

'Within the next three days?'

'They will both play a great part in your life.'

They are the policemen coming at dusk in Lorca's poem.

'Two men ... I used to know Maurice Sachs,' I said tentatively.

'Maurice Sachs? I'll find him for you ...'

Lugubrious, her willingness to help, her failure to grasp.

'Don't look for him! He's dead.'

'I would have known that!' she said sharply.

Kiki got up and turned round several times in his basket.

She laid out a cross with long, long arms, the cards all face-down on the mauve cover.

'Mlle Lenormand's cross,' she announced.

'Mlle Lenormand's cross!'

'Pick a card.'

I picked up a card.

'That's him!' she said. 'The card you chose is him. Give it to me!'

I handed Maurice over without hesitation. Then I steeled myself. 'May I see the card?'

She handed me the king of hearts. Maurice. His fecundity. His corpulence. His smiling erudition. A piece of Maurice's heart was missing at the top on the left, and again at the bottom on the right. That's how cards are designed.

She turned over another card. 'Yes,' she said with supreme indifference, 'he is dead.'

She shuffled her tarot cards. 'Would you like us to find out more about him?'

'I didn't come about him. I came because of someone who's very much alive!'

She laid her tarot pack down again. Her spirit is working on my behalf, I told myself. I was content to rely on her powers. But the old like to be methodical about the future. She still hadn't quite finished with Maurice.

'He was an able man,' she said, ignoring her cards on the table.

'He was a writer.'

She did not pause. She would have preferred an engineer or the head of a legal department.

I became specific in my demands: I wanted to see the man on whose account I was suffering, I wanted her to tell me about him.

She counted out a score or so of cards: then she showed him to me. He was the king of clubs. He looked very much like the king of hearts, and the resemblance disappointed me. Could the cards just iron out the differences between people? The fortune-teller became loquacious. The king of clubs is alone despite his friends, his money; he is solitary and he is powerful. He is sad, but he does not confide his sadness.

I must concentrate. The same thing all over again. I must think about him, there was plenty of time. I wanted to concentrate, but I couldn't do it. I had forgotten everything. She looked to see how Kiki was resting. I lowered my head over my homework. I summoned up all my strength, I could just manage to say to myself: I love him, I have never been so near to him and so far.

'His name is Jacques,' she said.

'His name is Jacques?' I answered, terrified by her gifts of divination.

'He is very much alone. He is unhappy.'

'Don't talk about him any more!' I cried.

I asked her to predict a happy outcome to my afflictions.

'No, the card doesn't answer,' she said, offended.

I had asked if Jacques would love me by the time I was eighty.

'Try again ...'

She tried again. 'The card doesn't want to answer your question.'

'Shall I come back tomorrow?'

'Tomorrow? That's too soon.'

Perhaps it will become a terrible addiction? I was to come back in three or four days. I handed over my three hundred francs.

*

Not the slightest hope? Who knows, I have a new address.

Mme Lamballe? On the top floor. Can Mme Lamballe see me? Mme Lamballe is out. The maid squeezed me into a corner near the rosewood piano. Will she be back one day? What use would a waiting room be otherwise? Why don't I caress my adolescence on that rosewood? I have plenty of time, so stroke away. She seems to have grown up a bit twisted, that adolescent I once was. You starved yourself to pay for my piano lessons, dear, dear Mama. Starved herself? What an exaggeration. You sat turning the pages of expensive wallpaper collections. While mademoiselle took her private lessons. Chopin Polonaises in the Peter edition—the most expensive. Result: dear mother, your down-and-out daughter, your good-fornothing daughter is holding out her hand to fortune-tellers.

Here is Mme Lamballe, content with her few little purchases. She is a confectioner's construction, I've seen set pieces like her before. She is immured in a corset. Another inch or so and her breasts will be tickling her chin. She leads me across the waiting room. Hair piled high, geometric in its perfection. A woman with a shiny black basin on her head walking inside a steel sheath.

Here we are in her bedroom. A card table, a table for two. What are we going to play?

'Would you mind splashing some ink on this sheet of paper?'

Such imperiousness! I will do as you say, anything you say.

I splashed her ink for her with athletic vigour. At last, good honest blots instead of my misbegotten words, instead of all my deserts of sterile adjectives. The pen spits. And so do I, cruel paper, I spit and rage with it. Mme Lamballe shall have no grounds for complaint, she shall have Roman fountains of ink. White page, yesterday afternoon I gave you my ink, do you remember? But you, miserly sheet, you gave me nothing in return.

'That's enough! Now fold it in four!'

I folded the paper in four.

'Very interesting,' she informs me.

She is interpreting my handiwork. Am I the new Oedipus? I am burning with curiosity.

'I can see you. Tormented, struggling ... Look for yourself ... Here you are, over in this corner on the left ...'

'Yes, I see,' I told her, without conviction.

She tilted the paper to the light. 'You see this spider? That is you. Caught in this web. In the web of your difficulties. So you are struggling. Do you see it? Look closer.'

'Yes, I see it.'

This woman was depressing me. Her bedroom was the spider: black, hairy, dangerous.

I ought to have thought how we are all spiders, how we all weave webs for ourselves. But she was crushing me with these struggles, these difficulties of mine that were nothing to do with her. She was gobbling up things that didn't belong to her and leaving me starving. And yet I wanted to believe in her. Being told by somebody else what we already know can be a help.

'... There are unimaginable complications. Here, you see. Here and here. There and there.'

The word 'unimaginable' was flattering. It somehow endowed me with a little of the imagination that I am doomed always to lack.

'Look round the edge here,' she said. 'That's where it's particularly noticeable.'

The coastline was a broken one. I toiled up the cape of my griefs, I skidded down the slope of my desolations, I halted in the creek of my torments. I stared, stunned, at my crises, I forgot that they had all come out of an ink bottle.

She twitched the paper away from me again. They were not my property, the despair and the melancholy on this map I had made with my splashes of ink.

She tilted the sheet, she tilted it this way and that. I had been unfortunate, she told me. I didn't reply.

I wanted to fight my way out of the darkness, but I couldn't fight my way out of it. I was having to battle on every front ...

Yes, I had been very unfortunate, she repeated.

In the end she was rocking me to sleep with this evocation of my past days, with this vague bla-bla-bla of sad and bygone years.

In her poverty she had no stories, no inventions to offer me. But the chestnut tree, outside her open window, the chestnut tree was lavishing them on me in profusion. The breeze was a Scheherazade charming its leaves. They quivered with parsimony and generosity; the slightest breath touched them into life. Only trees, only leafy branches can offer themselves in just that way to the gentle evening air.

What was she saying, the tachist? She was pouring oil on my past, she was smoothing out old events. No, I wasn't fighting my way out of the darkness. Why should I fight my way out of it? I was living in a chestnut tree, I was in the hollowed lap of time, warmly sheltered from turds and empty cigarette packets. Why desire to know the future?

Did I live alone? Where did I live? Had I been married? Her questions shocked me. One doesn't break and enter people's lives instantaneously like that. Did I work? Yes ... in a way ... Sssh, sssh.

She was collecting her thoughts.

'You write,' she informed me after a brief pause.

She had found the answer. It rejuvenated her.

I didn't dare to say outright: yes, I write.

'You have published two books.'

She wasn't telling me anything I didn't know. So what? Who hasn't published two books these days? She put away her ink and her paper. She handed me the ownerless sheet on the card table. It was included in the price. Did that mean it was all over?

I mentioned Simone de Beauvoir. Her eyes opened. I knew her? She went pale with emotion. Not only did I know her, but I had dinner with her every two weeks. I took her breath away. Dimwit, couldn't you have told me all this earlier, her eyes reproached me. She was someone, Simone de Beauvoir. What a woman, what a writer! She had read all her books. I sat silent. I scowled. I wasn't jealous of Simone de Beauvoir's fame, I never have been. I just felt that her admirer was not of sufficient stature. Did I want to try the ink blots again? No, I didn't.

Hands behind her back, heels firm on the floor, globulous eyes unwavering, Mme Lamballe paced to and fro across her room. Simone de Beauvoir was inspiring her with a different attitude, with further considerations.

'You must persevere if she says so! And now ask me anything you like,' she said, eyelids lowered.

I asked her. She stopped talking. She reflected on what she should say in reply, she stared at a chest of drawers with wrought-iron fittings. Where to put myself while she sorted out her yes and her no? I contemplated the chestnut tree again. Not a leaf stirring.

Mme Lamballe caught me at it. I was escaping when I should have been preparing to receive her oracle.

'Your work,' she began.

What is that to do with her? My work belongs to someone else. She tugged at her bodice. She concentrated all her attention on it.

'Your present work, I see it drawn in a chariot of roses, a triumph.'

She's dotty.

She wound up her watch. I loathed her. Her and her affectations of activity.

'Alas,' she went on, 'it won't all go smoothly. You'll have spokes in your wheels; you're not out of the woods yet...'

'And Jacques?' I said without transition.

'Jacques?' she continued, as though he were someone she had

known for years.

Ah, it is for Jacques she has gone over to her table in the middle of the room, it is for Jacques she has sat down.

Mme Lamballe was holding her head in her hands. Where was I to wander off to? Jacques? No reverberation from the big chestnut tree. A perfect masterpiece. At that moment I heard a weak moan. She wanted Jacques to be inside her.

She straightened up but kept her eyes closed. I didn't dare look at her. I, too, closed my eyes.

Our Father which art in heaven, make it so that Jacques loves me one day, I asked between a chest of drawers and an oak bedboard.

My prayer finished, I waited.

'Good,' she said. 'Good, good, good,' she added.

I opened my eyes, I tilted my head over to the right to conjure my fate over on the left, I clasped my hands together. I was worshipping in advance what she was about to tell me. I shivered. A miracle?

'It won't go much further than friendship,' she told me, 'and if I have any advice to give you, it is that you keep away from those regions, they are dangerous...'

I burst into sobs.

'Oh, madame,' I cried, 'what a thing to tell me, what a thing to tell me!'

I fell forward on the table. Against my tear-stained cheek I could feel the cold flatness of the paper spattered with my misfortunes. My cottages, my palaces, my disappointments, my hopes, farewell. Farewell.

'I didn't realize it went so deep,' she said.

A little balm in the depths of my wound. And yet she wasn't saying anything, she was gauging something.

'... Next time you must bring me a specimen of his handwriting and we'll talk about this again.'

I calmed down. I handed her a thousand francs.

'Remember the chariot of roses, remember the triumph,' she said as she showed me out.

The Gare du Nord. Billowing memories. I walk in on a Sunday
morning, I pin my black crepe bows on the soot from the engines,
I am commemorating all Gabriel's tricks and deceptions. He used to
wait till the whistle blew; then he would get on the train without a
ticket and join me in my journey. I walk into the station, I pin a
butterfly to the glass roof. What colour? Navy blue. A bow from my
mother's dress after I had been expelled from boarding school.
There is the barrier where she was waiting for me. And the other
day ... I picked up a pink-wrapped candy under a baggage trolly.
What was it? It was us: Musaraigne, Julienne, Violette. Those three
sausage-bearing Graces meeting to take the train to Evry-Petit-
Bourg. We shared an orchard in a tiny patch of raspberry canes.
My past: a game of hide-and-seek in every corner of the Gare du
Nord.

I walk into it on a Sunday morning at half past nine, I harry all
the clerks and porters with my unnecessary questions. Is it still the

same track for Flurares? Is it still the same platform? Has the time been changed? A farce. I know the time of the train better than they do, I go to Flurares twice a month. I am just play-acting. I am the first into the train; I inspect my quarters, I dust the seats. Shall I be alone? I am fifty minutes early; I brush my coat off with my hand; I decipher the empty train on the track next to mine. Then one by one, two by two, three by three they settle themselves noiselessly down on the other seats in the compartment. I display my ticket to them: I am going to Flurares, and I want you all to know it. My ticket tells them: Flurares is not a dead fish floating on a pond, not a piece of melon rind drifting in the current, not a layer of flies buzzing on carrion.

The train pulls out. I know what is to come. Flurares will be exactly what it is. An innocuous avenue. A quiet café back from the road. A disenchanted square outside the station. Lead colour everywhere. I shall adore it. It will be the place of my dreams, I shall never have enough of it, I shall have returned to it at last. I shall see shadows and notebooks. I make a mental note: 'We wanted to go even further with the next embrace, but we fell back exhausted.' Jacques will come to meet me. I shall recognize him in the distance through the train window; the cottage will be buried in long grass, painted with moss, its walls cracked beneath the Virginia creeper. Jacques will be alone on the platform. It will be autumn as it was last time, as it always is when he is wearing his Sulka silk scarf. He will hug me. What should I think of his brotherly kisses? Of my sisterly kisses? The season is a brazen hussy: garlands of scents strung gaudily along the platform. I shall follow him into the station. I shall hold myself too straight, I shall walk quickly to keep up with him, I shall tell the rosary of my regrets; what if I were to get straight back on a train for Paris?

'Did you have a good journey?' he will ask me.

We shall walk through the deserted station entrance. As always, there will be two packages on the scales ready for forwarding. I shall hand in my ticket, the station will take pity on me. I shall stop my mouth with two fingers; he won't see what he doesn't want to see: my phrases meant for him. My phrases? Reverberations of sun on snow; reflections; the blue windowpane of the sky. My confessions, oh, they would be so precise. Like the outline of an ivy leaf. But it must all remain blocked in my intestines. What shall I kill myself with? The nests I make for you. I will destroy myself by keeping all that is meant for you inside me till it poisons me.

How can I not hate you tomorrow, up on my sixth floor, thief forever refusing to take anything from me? We shall walk out of the station, I shall stumble. Careful, he would be disgusted with me if I fell. A sly invitation to suicide as we emerge from the Flurares station: the elusive landscape sketched in grey pastel. Why kill ourselves, we are sliding downhill so fast anyway. I must keep a strict watch on myself: he is the sort of man you mustn't cross. The place will be slow and sinister, there won't be any sun to be seen. We shall walk along the road towards Flurares. I with my nausea, he with his silence. I shall say: Just a moment, please, I have a pebble in my shoe. I shall stop, I shall linger, I shall imagine the smell of the tweed covering his elbow. But my forehead and my temples as I halt will stay calm, so calm: everything would be lost if my love were to flutter free. A model pupil, I shall regulate my steps so as to keep exact pace with him.

He will ask his usual question. 'Have you been working?'

Yes, at loving you and hiding it from you.

I shall reply: 'I have been working ... not as much as I would like.'

I shall remain silent about Mme Gavotte and her Granvillons, about my hours spent talking to Zézette. Recent memories, embarrassing memories. Shall I drive them away? How could I. I would no longer be myself. I shall ask myself where I am, where I was, where I shall be. To love is to be sure of nothing.

He will ask his second question. 'Is Simone de Beauvoir pleased with what you have shown her?'

Simone de Beauvoir. My cheeks will flame, and the flames will be my bad faith: I never tell Simone de Beauvoir how much I love Jacques. Confusion. I could sacrifice everything for Simone de Beauvoir's sake.

I shall say: '... Without her, I wouldn't be able to find my way. Without her, I would never find my stride. She has the sense of form I lack.'

I shall have a vague feeling of intimacy between us ... his question asked, my reply given. But then Denis will make his presence felt, even though he's half a mile away with Blitz and Bahia. We shall cross the main road, between the insane automobiles that won't slow down, and the little boy will come towards us as he always does. He will lower his head as he lowers it every Sunday. He will have badly polished black boots; a black, threadbare pinafore; black socks sagging. We turn to look at him; he is our light, he is our childhood. He will lose himself in contemplation of a drain, just as he did last time. We shall each take him by one hand without a hello, without a goodbye. We shall stop at the cake shop on the crossroads. Flurares will be dusty; the little boy will run away; a quiet road will close up behind him. The other Sunday a sparrow had been run over where the four roads meet. It is possible that my sadness leaves such flattened traces as I pass by in my loneliness with Jacques? We shall be within two hundred yards of his house. I shall stumble again, jibbing at the sacrifice ahead. I shall hide my lips, he won't see my muzzle. I shall see the pink wall of his workshop again. The hour will have chimed. Loving and disgraced, I shall be wholly insignificant. I shall be afraid of Jacques when he says to me, as he did the other day at Compiègne: Come on, be honest, you do want another Pernod . . . If I were honest . . . I would devour him.

'Let me look at it again . . .'

He won't answer. The house, just along the road from his, draws me to it.

'You don't think I could rent it?'

'It's not possible,' he will answer.

I would be importuning him if I were to live near him while he sleeps. The house will never be for sale, it will never be to let. I should be a weight round his neck, an encumbrance. Why accept his invitation? I am afraid of him, I fear Denis. I shan't dare to drink if I'm thirsty. Crossing my legs will be a big production. Yes, Jacques. No, Jacques. I don't know, Jacques. Just as you like, Jacques. Barnacle, make an effort, get back on your rock. But how to react, to resist? I shall be bedridden, I shall be near him. Shall I die? No, I shall just bear it.

His park will intimidate me. I shall pick a daisy, I shall think of myself as a vandal. I shan't dare walk across his lawns, I shall feel too much respect for the mown grass. His laws, his turf make me into a timid little girl in a public park. The shade of Rousseau is at home in Jacques's park. Why am I so jittery if I stop to refresh myself with a holly leaf? I shan't dare pull it off the tree: the gardeners would notice. I shan't dare live, I shan't dare laugh despite the bold scent I'm wearing. If someone were to proffer me a bunch of lilacs at a bend in the path, I should sob into it. And here I am again pulling myself together, drawing myself up so that I shall look sufficiently distinguished walking along between the Italian poplars . . . Why so frozen, you're his guest, aren't you? His park is a proof of love, a gratitude for the solitary stroller, an offering to the trees of the forests, the grass of the fields. Sing the praises of his thickets, for Jacques is a romantic; he is revealing his passion for wide walks, his devotion to winding paths. Why am I not his little path? If wishing were enough ... The pomp of the tall poplars, the symmetry of the flagstones frighten me. Take heart. It is pure modesty, his kind of modesty. He sees big like that in order to hide himself. That's as may be, but my teeth will still chatter.

*

Drama. A tree's life is threatened. Gardeners rush to and fro across the lawns, frantic, directionless. And Jacques is running faster than anyone. It was a titan of a tree; must it be felled? Jacques's face is dark with concern. Not yet. Three doctors meet in consultation: Jacques and the Messrs Dutaillis, father and son. I await their diagnosis. Will they be able to save it? Two of the doctors depart in search of a cure. Jacques remains beside his sick tree. He touches its scorched leaves. He runs his hand over its bark. Tree, don't torment him. Jacques, don't suffer.

I can feel his anxiety. I need to hear his voice.

'Can it be saved?'

'We shall do everything possible,' he answers curtly.

He seems to be holding something against me. He was almost savage then. Why did he invite me? Should I leave? Let him give me a kick and I will roll under my table. Let him insult me outright just once, let him spit on my skirt. Then I shall run away, I shall refuse to be his dog. I could leave his park, yes, let's think about that, leaving his park ... But I am nailed to this tree he is so concerned about, I must wail, I must lament for his sick tree. You speak to me harshly, yet I still speak to you sweetly.

You need have no fear, silent man, my sobs are forced down into mute gulfs. I imprison myself to leave you free. Denis insists it's a fact: you are brutal with those you love. But that doesn't include me. So why should I worry, why should I be interested in your emotional hang-ups. I give myself up to hate as one gives oneself up to a drug. You owe me everything and you have asked nothing of me. I am often a stupid mongrel determined to tear you to shreds. Forgive where there is nothing to forgive! I come to heel every time.

'Would you like to go on with our walk? Would you like to go along this path?'

Ah, now then you were really trying to be kind. The tree is dying. Your eyes are blank, you are sad. A forbidden no-man's-land. And so back to this plan for breaking my chains when I am beside you. But after all, why not go on with our walk together, it's not far, it's a path that wanders off into the long grass. In order to live, I must walk for a moment behind you. In order to live, I must moan against the back of your neck without you hearing me.

*

Winding paths, leaves, shade, humpback bridges, swans, ducks, a mule, a donkey, hidden statues, springs, a washhouse, shelters. Jacques will open his cigarette case. Gitanes ... I won't remember the empty packets on the edge of the pavements. What were they? Jacques in his absence. Jacques will be with me. I shall choose the one that has no number on it, I shall remove it from between its white-clad sisters. Jacques, in order to name you I am going to burn you, I am going to smoke you, your sex didn't count, I loved you too much, your sex is vanishing in smoke.

'A row in the boat?'

'No, Jacques.'

I shall refuse to be a woman sitting opposite a man rowing.

We shall meet his mother and his brother. Denis will ask how our walk was. I don't know; I spent all my time holding back my tears.

'Shall I fix you a Scotch?'

'If you like...'

Everyone will try to ignore the fact that I am stupid, stubborn. Everyone will try to make me forget that I'm going to drive myself into an early grave if I keep it up. I shall be a dead weight on a beautiful day. Unshakable, Jacques will read his papers. You can eat dinner with us, but then for heaven's sake go, go quickly ... You make us sad. Jacques will open a book. You are so dismal, can't you keep a check on yourself? Just look at yourself looking at him, that should be enough to make you mend your ways. And Jacques will read his art magazines.

*

Denis dressed me up the other day. He wanted a 1925 look. He got it with an ostrich feather stuck in my hair and a beaded dress way above my knees. Jean Genet was there; he said we were going to shoot a film in one of the broad walks. He was to be the baby, I was to be the mother. Genet swathed himself in a bedsheet. Denis gave him a bonnet, a real baby's bonnet. Genet wanted to be baptized. Jacques's brother was watching our preparations from a window ... he was to be the priest, Genet decided. I would like to laugh, but I can't: Genet is rehearsing, he is working out his part. That, a baby? A caterpillar, an incredible earthworm in a bundle of linen. He crawls, he drags himself along, his feet are swaddled in the sheet, he advances along the gravel walk in a series of contortions. He seems delighted. It's my turn. I give a start, I had forgotten: I am acting in his film as well. Genet's pink face under the white bonnet had driven everything else out of my mind. The camera turns. I emerge from a thicket, I rush towards my child. I think I am acting well because I am remembering the jerky movements Charlie Chaplin always made in his films.

I run, I run, I feel liberated, I am grotesque; under Genet's influence I am desanctifying the park. At breakneck speed I rush up to my baby. My baby whips me with a branch and a length of cord. Then he crawls: he has just been born, he drags himself over the ground. We do it again. The slower Genet is, the more I force the pace. I have the vitality of a circus horse with my plume. And the baptism? When do we do that? Later, Genet says. I must take my baby in my arms. I will whip you, I will beat you, Genet says. I obey my big earthworm, my big, my stupendously big baby. Genet whips me with his branch and his cord, he beats me, and Denis laughs as he shoots the scene. Jacques pretends not to see us, he is having a discussion with a contractor. Now a close-up for Jacques's brother. The felt flowerpot he has put on his head is a stroke of genius. It is a baptism reduced to its simplest elements: Jacques's brother reads from a book, then he blesses us. Genet whips me with his branch and his cord all through the ceremony. End of day's shooting.

That evening Denis puts up his screen. The film begins. I see a madwoman obviously just escaped from an asylum, a nut, a hag with St Vitus's dance, left over from the era of the foxtrot and the shimmy. Why didn't they stop me plunging headlong into such idiocy, such absurdity? But after all, as a daft old crone, well, it's really not at all bad! I laugh. Jacques laughs louder than anyone. As for Genet, he is extraordinary, a genius. He crawls across the bosom of the earth. Three of the actors in the film were bastards.

*

My adviser Simone de Beauvoir advises me to take a few weeks' holiday. I ought to get some fresh air into my lungs, I ought to get away from this room, this building, this street, this neighbourhood. But why take a rest, since I don't do any work. Writing for two or three hours after a day of gossip and too much Granvillons—you can't call that doing a full day's work. You can scarcely even call it skimping one's homework. Maybe I exaggerate, though. The fact is that writing for one hour or writing for twelve hours comes to much the same thing. What counts is getting off the ground. I wrote *Thérèse and Isabelle* at a steady three hours a day, with Isabelle's river tresses in my mouth, in my throat. What Isabelle brought me, what I gave her, all of it was rendered in my exercise book. I sacrificed my reticence and my principles; it was love itself I wanted to describe. I meant to tell everything. And I did tell everything. That is the only thing I did not fail in. My text is full of images, and that's a pity. My roses, my clouds, my sea monster, my lilac leaves, my spices and birdsong, my paradise of deliquescence, I don't disown them, no, but I was aiming for a greater precision: I was hoping my words would be evocative yet accurate, not just approximations, comparisons. There was more to be said, and I was unable to say it. I failed; there is no doubt in my mind about that. I don't regret my labours. It was an attempt. Other women will go on from there, others will succeed where I failed.

*

'Yes, I will go. Yes, I will go and get some fresh air in my lungs,' I said, but without really believing all that Simone de Beauvoir had said.

'You can still work,' she said.

She had confidence in me. She always has confidence in me. That is why she is the dawn of a beautiful day when I am sitting beside her.

I lit her Chesterfield. Yes, she believed in me.

'You're working so well, you must go on . . .'

'You think so? Really?'

I didn't doubt her word. The question was merely a way of doubling my happiness.

She said that Sartre would give me a cheque.

Colette Audry suggested Camaret. She was going there herself, I wouldn't be all alone, we would see each other every day as it were . . .

Mme Gavote thought her Les Lordes a much better bet. There's only one countryside, only one kind of holiday, she told me, and that's a garden with vegetables and flowers to tend. That shook my resolve. I woke up in the night, I suffered agonies of indecision. If I go, my plants will die of thirst. I got up and drowned my begonias and petunias at two in the morning.

Zézette has divined my problem. She has promised to be foster mother to my 'darlings' in my absence. I am not wholly reassured. It means entrusting her with my keys. As long as no one scratches my table, picks up all my things, moves them about, puts them back a centimetre to this side, a centimetre to that side ... Provided everyone isn't allowed to wander into my room ... Everyone? Who is everyone? I don't know. There are two chips in the marble of the dining-room fireplace. They were there when I moved in. Things wear out, you forget that, Simone de Beauvoir had told me. Marble doesn't wear out. Cracks have appeared, slivers have come off since my arrival. Who is it? Though I know it would hurt me if I were to find out. Why has someone struck this blow at me by striking blows at the marble of my fireplace? He must have gone at it with a hammer. Who heard him? What have I done? Genet liked the bevelled mirror over the fireplace, was that the reason? You are jealous of Genet then, but who are you?

My petals and leaves pinched between two fingers, that's La Puce's work. I catch her at it, I scold her; then she does it again. That situation is perfectly clear. Yes, but what about the marble cracking like that? Who is it who has left me these clues to say he is displeased with me? That dark-blue inkstain on the sheet, just where my feet go in the bed, where did it come from? And my salt shaker can't have slid back against the wall by itself. It is a deliberate signal, the work of a mysterious hand.

Leave for Camaret? What for? To encounter yet another set of signals? Oh, my back and my bowed head, they weep with the discouragement of it all. I am hunted in the marrow of my bones. How is it done? Oh, head, head, how you weary me. Those pin-holes in the wall around my divan ... I've seen them before, I can see them now, yes, there they are. Is it woodworm? Wormholes? The worms that will eat me when I'm dead? Do they mean the insignificance of my days? Their holes are so neat. If I stick a pin in anything, the whole is never clear-cut as those are. The news-paper the day before yesterday, and my *France-Soir* yesterday, its print is so much thicker, blacker than the others ... One of the printers is on my track and wants me to know it. As your eye reaches a certain news item, I shall pounce, the print told me. And he did pounce. He is letting me know that if he makes printing mistakes he does it on purpose to make my torture even greater. I pierce you with the letter V of your first name, he says, and with the letter L of your family name. I made them stick up above the line on purpose. Two explosions sent them up into the air. You perished twice over. And there's more to come. The word 'gold' has turned head over heels (you love gold, you loved the story of Goldilocks when you were little). Gold will never be right side up again. It's on page 8. What if I were to go for a holiday on an island? Boats would come to taunt me. What if I lost myself in a desert? An oasis would still stalk me. What if I rented an attic in Pigalle? What if I lived disguised as an old woman escaped from a home, huddled in an all-night café? What if I went into a convent? The doors would shut me in. Leave me alone, head up there, leave me be. Stop spinning, carousel. They still let me listen to cantatas and toccatas. But for how long now? Why shouldn't I admit it to myself?

The radio is becoming an infernal instrument of torture. Jean Witold. What about Jean Witold? He rises to such heights when he talks about J. S. Bach's Passions. 'Music and Musicians' is a staggering programme. But Jean Witold ... Go on, say it; it will be a relief. I shall say it; but it won't be a relief. Jean Witold is being sarcastic at my expense when he talks about duchesses and countesses. My name ends with *duc*. It does sometimes happen that I behave affectedly towards poor people ... Jean Witold won't let me forget. What if he were alluding to my dinners at Jacques's house, to the luxury of Jacques's way of life, to my feelings for him? Jacques isn't a count, Jacques isn't a duke. Jacques is a businessman. I shall do without Jean Witold's programmes, that's all. I shall turn the knob. He was poking fun at me, he shall be silenced. What liberation, what a feeling of superiority: to switch off a radio, to wring its neck, to eliminate a voice, the sound of a voice. And the laughter, the hysterical laughter of the girl announcer on Europe I ...

The concierge's big stick, I'll bet it's disappeared. They will have taken it away in broad daylight; there is nothing they can't do and nothing they won't do. I shall see some things if I switch the light on. I shall see others if I don't. I switch it on. Putting my trust in Providence. A piece of black thread? It didn't find its way to my bedside rug by itself. I haven't been sewing and I shook that bedside rug this very morning. I would have seen it last evening because I notice everything. Could those be thumbtack holes in the beige wall? I have no photos around the divan ... Shall I count them again? Three more holes than yesterday. They are piercing holes in my wall while I am asleep. They are destroying me, yet they leave no fingerprints. Never, never. I shall say: I have observed these facts; the answer will be: you are mistaken. Yet I am not inventing that piece of black thread on its grey background. If I removed it, I would be working for them. I wager it won't be there at eight tomorrow morning ... Suddenly I see: the thread is a message. An omen. They mean that my life is suspended by a thread. That thread is the fragility of my existence. But why is it black? Is it an allusion to the black soldiers when I bought the chewing gum and the chocolate in the café? What have they got against me?

Ah. At last. The big stick is there in its place. Nothing untoward? The wood hasn't been scraped anywhere? They haven't bent the scraper? My big stick makes me want to laugh and laugh every time. None of the other tenants has one anything like it. A wonderful invention of the concierge's. I am safe from flood. And turds as long as my big stick, those they'll never find.

I scraped the dead leaves, the leaf mold, the mud out from the drainpipe under my window. I threw ten or so bowls of water down it. Half past two in the morning. I was leading my life, my double life: the other innocents on my floor were asleep, all unawares. Suddenly, my exercise book. Threads hanging. They are deliberately damaging its binding. Go, get out, the white wood of the big stick was saying. I shall go.

Three boisterous children. They were waiting for me in the train
compartment. They stared me down. They sized me up. We left
Paris and they organized games. They wouldn't take their eyes off
me. They played checkers, they ate sandwiches, they fought over
who was to sit by the window. They folded their arms, they swung
their legs ... I held up my open newspaper as a shield, I fought back
with the cover of *Les Temps Modernes* and its contents listing, I
asserted myself with the flame of my lighter. Their father was reading a book by Cesbron; to make me think he hadn't noticed me,
he turned every page with the anxiety of a man on a quest. Their
mother was taking a respite from her children by resting long, con-
tented looks on the French countryside. I observed everything carefully. Their checkers game was in a leather case. Their sandwiches
were soft bread with lettuce. The Cesbron book was in a white-
leather cover with embossed fleur-de-lis. Her ring was a solitaire.
That checkers, now ... An allusion to my black-marketeering? The
checkers checking our bags? And what about the young maid? Was

she really an employee of theirs? Not for a moment. Could she perhaps be a police spy travelling incognito? She was reading Dostoevsky at the far end of the compartment. Baffling and exciting. Did she mean to make me go mad with *The Possessed*? She kept sliding her foot out of her shoe, then back in. Heartrending, her old old shoe. She read, she was passionately involved in what she read. First prize for good acting? She, too, turned the pages with the avidity of one on an important search. The eighth seat? Not occupied. A trick. The travellers standing out in the corridor would have occupied it if it were truly empty. It is Jacques, the unoccupied place. We escaped from the train at the last moment. We didn't leave, we didn't say goodbye to one another, I am not here. We are drinking a Scotch in Dupont's, just outside the Montparnasse station. What time is the first film at the Gaumont?

Time to change our tune. Here's the ticket inspector. Your tickets, if you please. I begin with the young maid.

'I don't have a ticket,' she says serenely.

'No ticket?'

He folds his arms, he leans against the doorway. She has taken ten thousand francs from the toe of her shoe.

And then . . .

*

And then . . . A coach full of Breton coiffes. And me? Squashed in on the back seat. I laugh behind my hand. I am not laughing at their lace towers of Pisa. They are pinned into sparse heads of hair; they have been lovingly starched, lovingly ironed, lovingly fastened in place. These ladies are decked out in finery fit for a ball. The precision of their black velvet bodices, the comical look of their chin straps, the toughness of their tanned skins. The city has bleached me, the city streets have faded me, and they make me know it. I sit in the coach with its load of old Breton women; the raw, bright light in village after village scrapes the grime off my Parisian's eyes. Healthy gusts of wind sweep in from the ocean, they rebound from walls eternally freshened by brisk sea breezes. The air is scoured clean. And the wind from the ocean widens the coach window. I glimpse village crosses. More and more I believe in freedom; it is freedom lighting these luminous vistas all round me, freedom and not the capricious wind. Then my eyes return to the blue in the coach, the blue that can never wear out, the eternal blue of the old women's eyes.

I arrived in Camaret at seven in the evening. I picked up my case and walked. The windows and bow fronts of the Grand Hôtel. Table napkins folded into mitres, wild flowers on every table. The enchantment of their decoration was a spell that imprisoned me. Would there be a bed for me? Colette Audry was supposed to be there; but she wasn't. I am a child, I go mad with excitement when I reach the seaside. Oh, let me go on with my ride on the coach... I was a sword pierced with light, and I pierced the villages all along the edge of the sea. The driver handed out the packages to the post-office clerks, the wind lifted the oilskins hanging out for sale. I looked down the narrow alleys to catch a glimpse of the waves. I want to set out again, I want to ride on like that day and night for weeks on end.

I dragged myself as far as the restaurant Colette had given me the name of.

'That is correct,' the man said after he had read my piece of paper. 'You are eating here, and Mme Audry will be in when you've finished your meal...'

'Is Mme Audry staying here? Has she booked a room here for me?'

He did not deign to reply. He brought me my steaming soup.

'Unfold your napkin,' he told me.

No question of washing my hands or taking off my raincoat. I unfolded my napkin.

'Mme Audry...' he began.

He looked down at me with pity, he served me a brimming plate of soup.

'...Mme Colette Audry? She is spending her holiday at a hotel outside the town. This is only a restaurant, madame.'

Eat your soup and be quiet, poor creature, or else watch out.

Where was it hiding, the vast, liberating wind of the Breton villages?

I have a particular weakness: I always think I can make an impression by spending large sums of money. I asked for the menu. A half lobster meant a three-quarters-of-an-hour wait. I ordered a half lobster. I kept my eyes glued with exaggerated anxiety on the door through which Colette Audry would enter. Why so many lorries? Where would I lay my head that night if she didn't come? And what about tomorrow? Tomorrow the sun will rise, my mother always used to say. And she's right. The sun does always rise. What will Colette Audry think if she finds me eating grilled lobster?

Hundreds of kilometres on a railway train, and for what? To dazzle a Breton restaurant-keeper with my extravagance. How expensive, the lobster? More expensive than it would be in Paris. And why so many lorries in Camaret?

He serves it. It is dry, it is tough. For the same money I could have had a good bed in the Grand Hôtel. I couldn't see the sea, or the people passing, or the lorries; I chewed at my toughened cardboard. I sat stagnating in my cellar, I listened to the motors overhead.

Colette Audry arrived, bubbling with excuses, just as I had finished my banana and two wafers. I would have liked to say to her: Your excuses come a half century too late. But I didn't dare. I felt I had already had my holiday. In that coach, gulping down the sea wind in deserted villages.

She wasn't pleased with me, Colette. The restaurant-keeper had helped her find me a room on condition that I take all my meals with him. But I refuse. His half lobster just won't do.

We followed a path through the dark of Camaret's hinterland. I was going in the opposite direction from the sea, the sand, the rocks. Colette Audry overawed me: she was professorial. I didn't dare ask her where are the waves and the sand and the rocks. She talked to me about *Les Temps Modernes*, about Sartre, about de Beauvoir. How was she going to get back to her hotel? On foot? A companion was going to meet her in a little while with his car. A companion? Hers, not mine. I am excluded. Excluded from Sartre and de Beauvoir's holiday, from Nathalie Sarraute's holiday, from Jacques's, from Colette Audry's. Zézette, why did I come? Zézette, why did I come? Zézette, lend me your housecoat of Pyrenean wool, warm me up in your dining room, Zézette.

Colette Audry recognized the little houses. One street lamp for a whole neighbourhood; rather stingy. The gravel paths between the seemingly identical houses demoralized me.

'It's over there ... It's that one.'

Grandma was knitting black wool with four needles, maman was reading the local paper, two little girls were sharing a picture book. The *tableau* put me into a sweat. And to think that, close by, the sea was unfurling its waves, the ocean hollowing out caverns, the breakers hurling themselves, doomed and untamed, at the shore.

They had been expecting me at four. They were lying. There is only one train all day. My arrival, with all the fuss they made, became twice as embarrassing. Nine o'clock, such a late hour. Colette Audry excused herself, she was expected elsewhere. I would gladly have begun a night of cigarettes and whisky with her and her companion . . .

They followed her up the stairs, this ugly woman who was there to make free with their furniture. Please think about my feet, about my shoes, because I was going to be living over their kitchen. Water? From the well. The little girls will be very glad to show me the way. And the lavatory? At the bottom of the garden, and here's your bucket for the night. I must be tired. Good night, see you tomorrow. Quietly now, children, it's late. Was her husband asleep? No, madame, my husband isn't asleep, he's been called out on a job; he's a long way away, he's a policeman. Sleep well. The stairs creaked, the wood of every step groaned. What a pretty pickle I was in. What a way to come just to sit in a prison cell. The room was in mourning for want of light. What alternatives did I have? Either not to read or else to read and wear my eyes out in the faint glimmer of their twenty-five-watt bulb. Oh, the warm water for washing back in my own kitchen, in my own sink! A dream in another life. I am in a trap here. Oh, those footbaths in my dining room, oh, my creature comforts . . . To blazes with you, I shall say to the aborigines first thing in the morning, I'm off back to Paris. Listen! I listen. They are talking down in their kitchen. The floorboards are just so much tissue paper. She, she, she . . . Who is she? Me, sitting on this bed. And the bed groans, too. They were talking about me, and now they have suddenly stopped: they heard my bed lodge its complaint. The mistrust is reciprocal. My raincoat is too bright a blue for my age . . . My shoes are in really bad taste . . . My hair . . . who ever heard of letting one's hair just hang down like that. My big nose? Spared. I am in a death trap here, I shall never have a moment to myself. I shall go back to Paris first thing tomorrow morning.

I slid my case under the bed. At least my darling little case should keep her illusions. They went to bed at last. I swallowed two sleeping pills and plunged into the pit of sleep.

    *

Something stinging me. What is it? Something biting me. Something jumping on me. On my shoulder. Now on my instep. What is it teeming in my bed.

I threw back the bedclothes. A flea. I knew it. But such a tiny flea, and such a resourceful little flea, what's more. More malignant, more acrobatic than any mere creation of my obsessions could be.

Do such tiny fleas really exist, though? I am frightened. And there's no armchair to spend the rest of the night in. Another. On the pillow. Is it my own eyes that are giving birth to these tiny creatures? Idiocy. I am damned, accursed. We had fleas when I lived with Hermine ... Hermine, the incomparable Hermine, she killed them and consoled me. It's Mme Gavotte's La Puce, she's followed me here, dear child. Oh, what a bedtime story for poor Violette! I wasn't going to leave Paris, so of course I leave it. Why? To come here and shack up with a load of vermin. A fourth, a fifth. On the eiderdown. A sixth. On the bolster. The bed is a nest of fleas. They will attack me. That's just not true. But I'm frightened, I'm frightened. Colette Audry will say: oh, she's a neurotic, she's just imagining the whole thing. But how can I put up with this plague, this scourge, for three weeks? Why don't I have a suit of armour I can climb into? I would be saved if only I were a knight, a Duguesclin.

One in the morning and the room in ever-deeper mourning. Yes, I must just go back to Paris, there's nothing else for it. Wait. A choice: the Grand Hôtel with Sartre's cheque, or the fleas? I chose the fleas. You must have something left for a rainy day, otherwise ... Otherwise, you will just have to scratch yourself till you bleed for another twenty-one days. No bites. Worse: tickles. Poor little sea fleas, poor little sand fleas. I must go back to bed, I must throw myself back into it like a brute beast hurling itself into icy water. I'll warn them I'm there by banging my feet on the mattress, I'll frighten them off. Oh, heavens, my simple-mindedness is beyond belief! Of course! The organization got here before me. It was waiting for me in this mourning room. And what organization the organization has! How did they get their fleas up here into my room? That's their affair. And their aim? My destruction. My sentences will become ever more anaemic, my words will languish on hospital beds. I mustn't blacken my pages with my insect's scrawl. Blacken? No, drain the vitality. Decalcify. Drain the blood from the whiteness, the calm white surface, the inner peace of each page in my exercise book.

My pen spreads leukaemia. What can you expect? They've poisoned my ink bottle with a special virus.

*

The mother of the two little girls didn't like living in Camaret. She preferred Touraine, the bracing air of Touraine. I won't com-

plain about her café au lait. A pure miracle, Maurice Sachs would
have called it. The taste of an iron bar. Mme Audry has told them
all about me. The children will play outside so it will be quiet for
me to write. All we ask is to survive in a blind and deaf world. I
shall survive. And there's a restaurant next to the tuna-canning
factory that has a set menu, so I shall be spared agonies of worry
every time lunchtime comes round.

I sat and searched for a word, I was setting out on my hunt for
adjectives, I was concentrating so hard I forgot what I was looking
for. I threw back the bedclothes and they fled. My narrative was
absorbing my whole being. Strange, how the organization with
its meticulous plans sometimes displayed this incomprehensible indulgence towards me. There were periods when the coincidences
just faded away of their own accord, like the last dying sparks of a
fire.

I screwed on the top of my ink bottle; an emaciated twelve o'clock
chimed from their kitchen. No water in my room. How was I to
go down? How was I to get out of their house? I shortened my robe
by hitching it up on my leather belt. I apologized to myself in the
mirror: the brutal blue of the enamel jug fought with the lavender
blue of my new dress. They were having their midday meal already.
I disturbed them at table. The elder of the two little girls was told
to show me the way.

One has to talk to children. But what to say?

I asked: 'Do you go to school?'

No reply.

'There's the spring,' she said.

Then she turned on her heels and was gone.

A crowd. A crowd of housewives clustered round the spring.
Those rinsing their washing in buckets were bowed over the task.
They showed me their behinds. Those shaking their salad shakers
sprinkled my face. Those waiting their turn with pitchers or wet
washing nudged one another as they stood in line. They were seized
by sudden laughter. At first I had shocked them, now I amused
them. Why such ill will and hostility? I would amaze you if I bared
my misfortunes before you. How gladly I would throw myself into
your arms! You are wrong about me. I am not proud, I am not
aloof. I am baroque to look at, but don't hold it against me, I
didn't will it to be so. I am your friend, your sister, your colleague.
You wash, I wash. You count, I count. I write? Yes, but what of
it? I am one of you, and yet I must pretend to be an outsider. What

do I have that you haven't? The terrible privilege of living alone? Is that what frightens you?

I move towards you with my imbecile stammering: 'Do you mind? So sorry to disturb you ... Only a moment...'

They wouldn't let me make a fool of myself. They fled at my approach.

I returned with my water. The icy water must punish my belly and my back, my shoulders, my buttocks, my feet. The little house is solid, my room is only temporary. My loofah glove ... Yes, I've brought it, it's in my case ... Rub yourself hard all over and pretend it is the warmth of human touch you are feeling.

Having got myself ready to go out, I sat down on the bed. The fleas were jumping on it. They're fairy fleas, I told myself. Must I go through their kitchen a second time? I was not free to go where I chose; the organization's plan was becoming clearer. I moaned very quietly; I tried to put a name to a face, to a party. Impossible. The nearer it was, the farther away it became. It was hidden, yet staring me in the face. Could it be Jacques? He is often there, being warmed in my heart. He wants me to concentrate my thoughts on him.

They had come back to the spring, and they watched me as I walked away. Laughter, chuckles. No, I wasn't in fancy dress. If you knew, little sisters who find everything so funny, if only you knew how ashamed I am of my white arms, of my pale skin. Be patient, tomorrow your Flemish visitor will be red and blistered.

'You'll see how good the food is,' the one-legged man all alone in the harbour said to me.

I walked into the new restaurant.

Full to bursting. The one-legged man must have negotiated on my behalf: I have a table well away from curious eyes. A woman alone, what a music-hall turn. Move over, I can't see her. Oh, what a chuckle! Oh, what a laugh!

I am hungry.

I must be cunning, I must throw out bait to catch the restaurant-keeper. I haven't come to eat à la carte, monsieur, I have come to eat my midday meal with you for eighteen days. I shan't eat here in the evenings, I'm not living in Camaret ... So here I am with a little home of my own: a glass, a plate, a saltcellar, a check tablecloth. I stuff myself with bread and mustard.

'Just taste this, then!' the restaurant-keeper says.

A crab. A snowy crab. No. A crab becalmed in whiteness. Its

flesh lay sleeping in its shell. I ate it religiously. I sucked up confidence again as I emptied each claw.

'Will there be any tomorrow?' I inquired anxiously.

'There will be crab every day. It's on the set menu.'

I sighed with contentment. It isn't everyone that can count on crab every day when on holiday, even at the seaside ... I sucked and whistled every day of my eighteen days in every claw, and I never got tired of it. At least, almost never.

'Well?' the one-legged man inquired. 'Was that what you were looking for?'

He was sitting on a bollard, waiting for me.

'Yes, that was it,' I said enthusiastically. 'That was it exactly...'

Where did he eat at noon? Did he sit guarding the port while the others replenished their energies? I was never to know. The poor have their no-trespassing signs too. His blood-shot eyes probed me. Was I telling the truth? He refused a cigarette. Happiness doesn't come singly: I was offered a seat beside him on the bollard. His wooden leg was swung to one side on a slant, the rubber disc on its end just touching the harbour wall.

'This evening you will see the tuna boats, you will see the lobster boats brought in ... They always come in before it gets dark.'

He was proud of his port.

He explained how to reach the beach: two kilometres, on foot.

*

What a chore, that walk. I was in a bad mood to begin with. What I really wanted was to walk across wide plains when the young wheat is like turf. But I had to follow treacherous winding paths, tangle myself up in traps set for me by the weeds. I made my way round holes and fell into other holes. I had to walk down a slippery slope, I slipped on it, I found myself on my behind. I was furious. Oh, what rage I felt! And that wind! My scarf blown down about my throat, my hair smacking against my eyelids. I was eating a meal of sand; the wind was forcing me backwards, tearing me to shreds.

I halted in the midst of expanses of yellowish, sterile terrain. I checked to see that I still had my Chateaubriand, my ball of yarn, my needles, and my notebook inside the beach bag bought so hopefully a week before. I set off again. I looked down balefully at my espadrilles: they were too new, the thongs were too white, my skin was too white.

Two Englishwomen reassured me. I was on the right path for

the beach. Soon I would be in sight of the sea.

The beach was a disappointment. Too tiny to be called wild. I looked down on it from among my hummocks of stunted grass, I followed the hairpin bends of the path down to it. Brightly coloured towels made ugly splashes on the sand. Everyone was silent, the sun-bathing service had begun. The sea is dangerous, you must swim somewhere else, a fully dressed man told me. He was warning me, he was hoping to lessen his own disappointment by sharing it. Swim with their arrows in my back? Never. They would see my feet; they stick out of the water as I float. They shall not see them. Where am I to undress? And how? In *Marie-Claire* last week there was an article that said the skin needs to breathe. Mine will just fry. I am bored. Already I am bored. Today the waves are as gay as coxcombs. I undressed as surreptitiously as I could and sat watching the waves for an hour. They were only half alive. Shall I go now?

First I must remember who the actress is with the little dog... Then I'll go. The dog is like Christian Bérard's. Her turban makes her look different, it undresses her face. What a back, what carriage. I would like to write pages and pages on the power in that back. She stands like a poplar. But of course, it's Maria Casarès ... yes, it's her. I am content, I have put a name to a face. She is an athlete. She throws out her chest. She is as solitary as a cross-country runner. She fills her lungs. She walks barefoot. She is leaving; ah, what a pity. Do they know who she is? Athletic today, so fragile on the stage tomorrow. Her little dog: a tousled white rose. I am beginning to fry. I shall stay, therefore, because it's going to be pain-ful. She is leaving us now, Maria Casarès. With her straw mat rolled up under her arm she looks like someone who doesn't give a damn, like someone who knows just where she's going.

*

'Hurry up, they're loading...' the one-legged man said from his bollard.

Yesterday evening's lorries. Or different ones. Two robust men were putting up the tailboard of a five-tonner and sliding the fasteners into place. They were blocking my path, so I was forced to halt. Their lorry was bursting with tuna and lobsters. I could see red men, russet-coloured men, seaweed-coloured men, putty-coloured boots, orange boots, hardened and cracked oilskins, petrified rain-coats. They were handing up full baskets, handing down empty baskets, thudding down from the lorries, slapping their boots against the ground, leaping down into a lobster boat's hold, then leaping up out again.

'They will be in Paris tomorrow morning with the fresh lobsters,' the one-legged man informed me.

The lorry would drive through the night with a cargo worth millions of francs ... Overcome by the sheer scale of such commerce, the one-legged man sat shaking his head for a long while.

*

I am organized now. I write with my right hand from nine till noon; and with the other hand, every half hour, or every quarter of an hour, I press the lid of my tin of powder. I press, and the lid yields to the pressure. I throw back the bedclothes. No victims to be seen. A tickle, I press the lid again. Where are they hiding? Doesn't my powder smell nasty enough? I sneeze. The smell? That of old, peppery files. The colour? Dirty white mixed with very pale beige. My legs are covered in wholemeal flour. Every evening I lay a sheet of powder for them on the bottom sheet. Result? The tickles grow no less. I have vaguely mentioned the matter to the wife who is in love with her lovely Touraine. They are tiny fleas that do no harm, they are the local fleas ... Yes, well, I wouldn't mind if the local fleas would only let me sleep.

Why has Colette Audry dropped me? I rack my brains. I met her only rarely in Paris, why should she come running to visit me every day here? So I reason, but the doubt persists. Every day? She hasn't been once. It has become a dismal refrain; twice a day I repeat: 'Has Mme Audry asked for me?'

They haven't seen anyone, they are terribly sorry. She was so nice when she booked the room ...

Why doesn't she come? She's the only person I know here. Is it my poverty, is it my failure as a writer that keeps her away? I ponder the matter, I accuse myself. She is ignoring me. Why? Why not just admit the obvious truth: Colette Audry has better things to do than visit me. But I refuse to admit it. I am perpetually on the lookout for her: as I fetch my water from the spring, as I discuss the rain and the shine with my one-legged man, as I suck my crab legs, as I bake on the beach, as I use my insecticide powder. Could she have gone back to Paris without letting me know? I am proud of knowing her and make no attempt to hide it; she has a degree, she has published two books, I let everyone know what a remark-

able person she is, and all in the hope of drawing her to me. I must
be lost indeed to need her so much. I wait for a letter from her
bringing me good news, an invitation. No mail. If I write to her,
then she will have to write to me. But I don't write. I simply writhe
on the horns of my dilemma : I want her to come, and she doesn't
come. I am beating my head against a brick wall. Tomorrow. Tomorrow there won't be any news of her either.

Eight days ... Ten days ... No news of Colette Audry. Her
silence is crushing me, her absence is freezing me. I shall go to her
hotel on Sunday afternoon.

*

The harbour is dozing, Maria Casarès is leaving the Grand Hôtel
and returning to Paris, a lobster boat covered with tarpaulin sways
on the slapping swell. I walk along taking great strides, head bare,
in the rain that has been falling since morning. I go through a forest;
the rain and the trees were what I needed. They are my youth re-
discovered. I say my prayers : don't let her have left like Maria
Casarès, arrange it so that I see her from time to time. A bird. Dead.
I pick it up, I steal it from the night, from the showers, from those
that would devour it. It is warm, untouched, only that moment
dead. I shall give it to them when I arrive. It is there at the bottom of
my pocket. I run, I slow down, I run again; the rain falls on the
leaves and beats against my face. My hair is wet and keeps straggling
over my eyes.

The modern hotel among the pine trees frightened me. The
swimming suits hanging out on the upper-story windows reminded
me of the very posh hotels in La Baule. I paused in the teeming
rain. I didn't dare go in. Then I decided I had to risk it.

A porter showed me into the dining-room-cum-lounge. He felt a
certain sympathy because I had been rained on so copiously. He
didn't know that I had received the lonely rain with open arms. I
was no longer looking for Colette Audry; I stood gazing round at
her world. They were playing cards, they were smoking cigars, they
were drinking Scotch, they were like extras in a film. The rain
slithered down the big windows.

Colette Audry, at a table by the door, made a great fuss over me.
She dried my hair with her handkerchief while her companion
helped me off with my coat. Eventually, after a great to-do, the
porter took it. How quickly disappointment can set in! I had come
in quest of a liberator; now I shut up tight. I knew I wasn't going

to talk to her about what I was enduring. The dead bird lay on the table. I had given it to her for her little boy, but the gift had not been to her liking and I had taken it back.

No, I shan't tell her about the old, dry grasses that scratch me when I am out walking. What is the good of telling such things? Yes, I am enjoying myself at Camaret, and that's that, the rain went on slithering down the windows. No, I am not delighted at this renewal of friendship. I shall leave as I came. They put away their playing cards, their Scotch warmed me up, the children brought life to their lounge-cum-dining-room. She swam, the air was relaxing. And Sartre and de Beauvoir, where were they? She had dinner with Jean-Paul Sartre before she left for Brittany. I am going back to be with my insecticide powder, I am going back to my little house ... No, I am not to go back on foot. They will take me in the car. It's raining. I was free on the path through the pines, before their hotel came into sight ... Yes, it is raining; all right, I won't walk back through the bountiful curtain of rain. No, I don't go swimming. It's dangerous. Yes, that's true, what a pity. Yes, there are other beaches. A gong sounds, right in the water. Shall we start? It is I who ask. It will soon be dark. It is I who point this out. To live waiting to leave is not living at all. Let's go, let's go ... Oh, why doesn't she go, this sad woman, this boring woman with nothing new to say. What if I were to invite them to dinner? The Grand Hôtel? Why not? Just once. They refused. Their hotel doesn't like them eating out. After all, I have my fleas and my insecticide. Are we ever going to leave?

My high hopes as I rushed to be with them, I now see them carved in the pink bark of the pines, the pines in the rain. The monotony of the pine forest in the rain is startling. We drive over the pink carpet of pine leaves. They can't come up to my room, they must get back to their hotel. I understand. See you again, have a good drive back, thank you for bringing me home.

I consoled myself with a snack eaten in bed at six o'clock. I slapped a layer of mustard on my slice of ham, I pressed the lid of my tin in and out between the sheets.

I telephoned Colette Audry the day after next. She was back in Paris already ...

*

'Why don't you go up in the airplane?' the one-legged man said to me Monday morning. 'There's an air show. It will cost you eight hundred francs ...'

Why not?

I didn't take the bus. Avarice? Fear of being laughed at. I was red as a tomato. My silk scarf, worn pirate-fashion, did nothing for me at all. It didn't hide my greasy hair. I walked alone with wings on my heels for two hours: I would soon be flying in an airplane. To rise up into the air, when you think about it ... Goodbye, ugly conks. Farewell, ugly laughter. Hail, consoling clouds, now we are neighbours.

I soon recovered from my disappointment at the improvised air-field. I became accustomed to the barbed wire stretched round a simple meadow, to the sentry box selling bus tickets. Maiden flight, eight hundred francs. It was painted in big letters on a placard. What a mine of information he was, that one-legged man! Was I going to go up in a plane? That's what I'd come for. Was I going up? Just a moment, I've just got here. Am I going up? Where are they? It's no good expecting a squadron. Here it is. It will be your turn and you will taxi round the field and your handkerchief and your hand will have nothing to wave at. I have plenty of time, I have all the time in the world. Why should I go up right away? An influx of peasants. I'll go up later. That an airplane? It looks like a dummy one to me. What an adventure, my friends. Who are my friends? The strands of barbed wire I am leaning against. I seriously won-der whether I am going to go up in the cockpit of that cockchafer. Two passengers are going to take off. Two. The plane is a small one. It will be cozy. The flight lasts ten minutes. We shall fly, I shall see the ground as patchwork, as I have in films. I ought to present my-self at the sentry box; I am holding my eight hundred francs in my hand ... I would rather wait. I'll go up towards the end of the day. Is it hot? My money is getting damp. No, it isn't hot. I would like to go up and I would rather not go up. All the others are deciding to go up. I can't decide. Old men, old women, parents, young people ... all up in the air. They will talk about it during the winter. Has it been thoroughly serviced, that plane? Here it is again. They look delighted as they get out. I'll just let this couple go ahead of me, then I'll be one of the next two ... Liar, liar: I'm afraid. Look, they're taking a baby with them. I'll make up my mind to it in half an hour's time ... If I prefer a hot-water bottle in my bed, that's my right. You're chicken. Agreed. A chicken with its feet firmly on the ground. Will the one-legged man ask questions? How long before I am due to go back to Paris?

I am at home with my treasured habits once again. I consult Mme
Kikimauve twice a week. On Mondays and on Fridays, at half
past one in the afternoon, my tattered old sphinx reveals to me what
I already know. We begin by talking about the cost of living, about
how meat is not what it was, about the wonderful Indian summer
that is in fact turning my stomach—day after day with the sun
merely growing slowly paler and paler. Mme Kikimauve's husband,
an insignificant little man her own age, comes in or goes out, taking
Kiki with him or not taking Kiki with him. But Kiki is a well-
behaved dog: he stretches, he goes back to sleep. I sit gossiping with
her in the hope that eventually she will rend the veil of the future for
me. Occasionally she offers me a mint.

'Let's begin,' she says then.

I cut. Today's vein is mined out, but tomorrow shall be mine.
I cut a second time. She ought to have been struck dumb long ago
by the inaccuracy of her prophecies. I turn up a card: it's me. But

I have come out too quickly, it seems. Whereas last time I wouldn't come out at all. I left Paris, I was disappointed. Is she mistaken? No, she isn't. She is telling me nothing; but without her my saliva wouldn't have that minty taste of days to come. My past, my last month's past blooms again. She talks to me about it without hurting it; she rocks it to sleep. Her old face has a power. The laughter, the mockeries, the unkind remarks in Camaret sink to burial beneath each of her old wrinkles. I sigh with contentment and Kiki sighs with happiness in his sleep. Talk on, talk on, Madame Kikimauve.

'This gentleman's mother lives by the sea ...'

She makes the assertion without assertion, she lingers for a word from me to make it a certainty.

'Yes, she lives by the sea ...'

I don't accuse her of incompetence. The words she utters are newly minted. A solitary woman living by the sea ... She is visiting us without having come in person. I had forgotten all about his mother. She is the woman who lives by the sea.

'She will fall ill ...'

'She will fall ill?'

'He will be left all alone.'

'...'

'We shall see what will happen then,' she said.

My head whirls. Desire for rejuvenation for him, desire for motherhood for me. He is a fifty-year-old baby, he will be an orphan. He stretches out his arms to me. His face is a grimace of grief. She turns over several more cards. I thrill at the sight of the king of clubs and the jack of hearts. They will tell me whether this baby left all alone in the world will nest his head on my neck.

She looks at me, she prepares me. Her yellowed nail holds the interrogated card prisoner beneath it. 'He will need you. You will live with him.'

'Soon?'

'No! But it is certain. He will send for you.'

Certain. I don't hear any of her other predictions.

She has increased her prices during the holiday. It is five hundred francs now. I hand her a thousand-franc note, she gives me back five hundred francs in tattered small notes. I have a nasty thought ... Our money: a chicken, chopped steak for Kiki, champagne to drink our health with ... He will need me, he will ask me to come and live with him. A prediction like that is worth gallons of champagne, unlimited chickens. Not a word if I meet anyone ... I would get her into trouble. I creep out on tiptoe.

*

The workman spat. I was coming out of her house, I passed him, he spat. He was carrying his toolbox slung over one shoulder. The carefree air of a Bohemian painter, of a young newspaper photographer. He was spitting in my face when he spat on the ground. What have I done? Half past two. I am cold, the streets are slow. Quickly, quickly, back on your chores. Is it my fault if I am free? About-turn. I will follow the workman. If he spits again, I am saved; it means his spittle wasn't intended for me. Place Voltaire: he hasn't spit. again. He was telling me he despised me. But what have I done to earn your disgust? I can hear your answer: slut, you are taking our money from us; slut, you are living off us, sitting twiddling your thumbs; slut, you are robbing us of our bread and our toil, you are giving our pay to an evil old woman who is growing rich on your credulity! It wasn't your thousand-franc note, it was mine. It was ours. That man an old workman? How simpleminded can you get? They are disguising derelicts as plumbers, they are transforming their turds into toolboxes.

I was seeking consolation at the fortune-teller's, and they were throwing a cordon around the door of her building. The happiness I have been promised: a lump of spittle on the pavement. How can I be ashamed? I have not been marked for felling, yet you are felling me. Why do I look down at the ground so often, why? I am looking at a chalk circle in front of every door. A circle that always has the same letter inside it. It isn't the *V* of Violette. It's worse than if it were me. It's the *B* of Berthe; it's my mother. Why does she live inside a circle like that? Does it mean she has unconquerable enemies? The same circle again, the same letter again in front of the next door. What is it she's trying to say to me? That I mustn't go home and scribble on my paper? Is that what you're saying to me, Berthe? I mustn't go on writing about Thérèse, about Isabelle, about Marc, about Cécile? Is that what you're telling me, Mother? Are you ashamed of me? Someone answers my question with 'shit to you' written on the wall. My work is worthless, I know that, there's no point in insulting me. Scarcely visible waves, waves sketched in pink chalk ... they are my verbs and my stringy adjectives. A broken line. I am broken on a wall, I am a zigzagging chalk line of pain. Paris, you are too big. I have to escape up your walls, I am a pink spider swinging on a pink thread. Say hello to me, shake my hand, please.

Who is it I want to say hello to me? To shake my hand? The baby carriage, the tarpaulin over the piles of food in Les Halles, the baker's door, the forgotten bunch of parsley. Uniprix and Monoprix, my beloved windows, my adored displays, my cherished cradles, a sign, I beg you, give me a sign. I shall be safe among your bright materials, it will be a gala day surrounded by your lengths of colour, we will laugh, there will be such a crowd of us. It's Friday, Jacques is lunching with his lady friend. I can't escape from my top-security prison. Even if I did get out, I still couldn't intrude on them. I was better off in Camaret. What lies! It was there that I listened to the sound of the spade, it was there that I couldn't see the gardener and ran away. Living means digging one's own grave. Was it a warning, the clinking of that spade turning the earth? Possibly, quite possibly. Someone close to you, someone who will die soon. They are digging a hole for that person. We are informing you and we are tearing you apart with vague suggestions. The pretty blue silk with the white dots ... that's Jacques. It was Jacques who had it put in the display ... He is telling me to wear navy blue if I go to dinner with him ... Impossible, my treasure. I would have to learn how to cut, how to sew, how to notch armholes ... It would take me months.

I shall feel better as soon as I see a spade, a spade for turning the good earth. Shall I go and see one? Hesitation. I hugged the wall that was telling me: 'Anyone who reads this is a bloody fool.' Still the same pink chalk. I read it, I reread it; someone was preceding me, pursuing me with his waves, his dotted lines, his circles, his letter Bs. And now they were sending me filthy telegrams.

I hesitated, I wanted to walk it, I wanted to save on the two bus tickets after having thrown five hundred francs down the drain.

You're making a mistake, my chick. Go back to your room; there the multitude will become a solitude. But I shall hear their cracks. Oh, if only they were proper loud cracks ... But no, it is the subtlest of noises. A hair. A hair moving. A hair brushing against the ceiling. I hear it where I want, when I want, their tickling hair. It is in my mind. You would forget yourself if you went back to your room, if you wrote. Forget myself? I am incapable of such a thing. That piece of string there, crawling along ... They knew a long time ago, then ... She will be walking towards the Bazar de l'Hôtel de Ville. Scatter them where her feet will tread. Scatter them along the pavements, along the bottoms of the walls. A piece of dirty string.

Can it be my next book, already printed, sent off to the critics, already reduced to this piece of refuse on the pavement?

*

'The spades, please.'

I had sidled in among the afternoon crowd, the half-past-four-rush. Schoolgirls dawdling along, asking to smell the scents at the perfume counter.

'Spades?' a little shop boy called back as he passed me pushing a wicker hamper on little wheels. 'Try tools!'

The inside of a big store: a punch in the stomach. Salesgirls at the end of their tethers; teeming customers. My derelict's existence shall cease, I will write till midnight.

'Tools?' the girl said from beyond her rows of toothbrushes. 'Ask the section head!'

The section head was an old saleswoman. 'Spades? They're in the basement.'

The basement of a big store is restful.

'The spades, please.'

'At the far end,' the salesman said.

I chose the last, I gripped the handle in both hands. I lifted it, I touched the cutting edge, my four fingers slid across the flat blade. Its handle, a dimpled sex. I kneaded it with my cat's paws.

'Which one would you like?' the frivolous salesman asked.

'None of them. I was just looking ...'

*

'Look,' Mme Gavotte said to her daughter, 'just look at the state our neighbour has come home in. Just look at her!'

Mme Gavotte stamped her foot on the landing. Mme Gavotte stared me up and down.

'La Puce has knocked on your door more than twenty times ... Where were you? What have you been doing? One just doesn't stay out for six hours straight like that. You should let people know, damn it all!'

I confessed that I hadn't worked that whole afternoon.

'And just look at the mess her hair's in,' Mme Gavotte said.

I explained that it was raining.

She rushed back to her mother's flat.

'It isn't true,' La Puce cried. 'It isn't raining!'

Mme Gavotte lost her temper. 'She is behaving like a devil! She can't stand Ferdinand ...'

She led me through into her kitchen.

La Puce was daubing her blue lips with an old raspberry-coloured lipstick. She threw the lipstick down on the table: she wanted her suck-suck.

She will be good, we shall be left in peace if she has her suck-suck. Mme Gavotte poured us both a glass of wine.

Shapeless as a lump of mashed potato on their Formica-topped stool, I racked my brains. Her suck-suck? Why not? I was Jacques's bow-wow.

'Here, have your suck-suck.'

Of course ... Mme Gavotte had pulled out one breast.

La Puce sucks away, I sip my wine, I listen to the saliva-lubricated shlu-shlu-shlu of the sucker-lips. La Puce is fastened to her mother's thighs like a mountain climber to his pitons. Blooming, ecstatic, Mme Gavotte presses kisses on her big baby's hair.

Epilogue: La Puce fell in an inert lump on the granite-chip pattern of their composition floor. Her gums snickered up at us. Then she closed her mouth.

'Off with you! And close the door!'

She did as she was told after she had begun to daub her lips with the old lipstick again.

*

Then she insisted that we go into her mother's bedroom too. We went in. Mme Gavotte seemed to think I was a backward child as she explained to me that the disorder left in a bedroom is another sort of love, another pleasure to be enjoyed after the lover has departed.

She plunged her face into Ferdinand's pyjamas while I brushed the back of my hand against the flounce on their pillowslip and La Puce jumped wildly up and down on the big rumpled bed.

We all had to sit down on the bed. We had the right to share the fruits on her arms, on her thighs. She was loved, he loved her, he had given her a harvest of damson plums. It was his teeth, he bites her.

I made my escape.

*

Half an hour past midnight. Must look, posthaste, to see what is going on in the coal bin. If I lift the lid, what shall I find? It's not possible: the anthracite level has gone down again. Gone down by how much? You are taking my fuel. I must check. We must organize, we must pit organization with organization. They can't carry my fuel away along the street shovelful by shovelful ... Can't they? Anything's possible in this world. We must start our check.

First I spread the old newspapers out on the floor. Around the Henri II table, in the kitchen, in the hall. I worked it out: I need four shovelfuls of coal in the morning, four in the evening. I removed the fuel from the bin. By hand, with two fingers. Finally the level began perceptibly sinking before my eyes: there was an avalanche as the mound collapsed. I ran off into the kitchen, then came back again. Another avalanche. I escaped into my bedroom and looked at my black nails. I slid eight shovelfuls of fuel onto each newspaper. I still hadn't emptied the bin. I spread out more newspapers on the divan, by the window. I counted my piles of coal. I had enough to keep warm for eighteen days. I marked the date with a cross on my post-office calendar. If I run out of fuel before that date, it means someone is stealing my coal. Who is stealing it? I went from the bedroom to the bin, from the dining room to the bin, from the kitchen to the bin, from the hall to the bin, every time with a newspaper and the eight shovelfuls of coal allotted to it. Fifty percent of the time, the newspaper burst and the coal fell and rolled under the chairs. I lay down on the floor and retrieved the coal piece by piece. I hid behind the bed ruffles. The din I was making terrified me. I set off again on tiptoe, I hunted out the dust the anthracite had left, I salvaged it with my dustpan and brush.

Ten past one in the morning. I'm hungry. Why aren't the Chantelauzes knocking on the wall? They ought to be. I've woken them up. It's very suspicious.

Still in my oilskin raincoat, I swallow down a fried egg, a piece of Petit Pâtre cheese, standing up. I made up my mind: I must clear out the stove, I must cram it with newspapers and wood, I must light it, I must keep myself warm. I must live the way they do, I must have the same orange rectangle at the bottom of my stove as they do. Terrible, that stove. I had filled it at half past one that afternoon, but it hadn't started up again.

I went to bed at half past two in the morning. The orange mouth was saying: I am eating your substance, I am heating your room.

*

Sitting on my Formica-topped stool, my bare feet on the kitchen's composition floor, I picked up my bowl in both hands. I drank my Legal coffee, the sugar melting under my tongue. Five past ten. My bedroom window was open. I had leaped out of bed, I had pulled back the curtains. Precision as far as the eye could see. Light like a knife sharpener.

A ring at the door. Is it her?

I open the door. What a presence, what bearing! Black worsted skirt, white blouse, her formal wear. No makeup, no nail polish. And what an inviting smile!

'You were having breakfast?' she said.

I was indeed having breakfast. She apologized.

She has put on her corset and her brassière. She has removed her lover's signet ring from her finger. Her hands have become simple again. She inspects my kitchen table.

'Eat, it will make you less sad ...'

She took me by the shoulders; there was something confidential in the gesture. 'Will you do me a favour? Will you keep an eye on the saucepan?'

'The saucepan?'

She was gone, already waiting for me outside my door.

'What saucepan?' I asked, more and more bewildered.

'Ssh! ... Don't shout so loud!'

She has become ceremonial, she is still standing patiently on my doormat. 'Come ... Now, at once,' she says in a low voice.

'I'm coming.'

Her flat was clean yesterday; this morning it is spotless. At what hour must she have got up? She walks ahead of me in her low-heeled shoes, I would swear she has never had a drop of Granvillons since the moment she was born. Not the minutest thing out of place in her kitchen.

'I will light the gas. You must watch it!' she said in a low voice.

It was the cutting voice of a superior.

'What must I watch? Your saucepan? Why?'

I went over. I leaned over to look into the saucepan.

She went on: 'You see this syringe? You see this needle?'

'Yes.'

A patient? That's what she is going to tell me.

She unstrapped her wristwatch.

'Take this,' she said. 'Use it to check with ... The water must boil for a few minutes. When it has, turn off the gas, and don't touch anything ...'

I understood less and less. 'And you, where will you be?'

She smiled.

'In there ... I am not to be disturbed for any reason whatever. Close the door quietly behind you as you leave, but just loudly enough so that I will hear you. I must go now ...'

She walked away towards the dining room. I don't know what to think. Waiting for the water to boil is tedious. I flop against the white wall, I lean my rickety elbow on the white enamel of the stove's rim, I watch a needle, a syringe. Is she playing a joke on me? I am performing a task. But what task? She has scoured the whole place since she got up. Her little girl would be a danger if she didn't have that toohf-toohf in her heart: no running at play-time in school. The water begins to sing. A little stainless-steel sauce-pan. It's expensive, stainless-steel, but it never wears out, so they say. You're a real little darling, little saucepan. It is singing, it is a lament, it is a yearning for what was. The water is foaming away at its purifying task. What the hell am I doing here? I am awed by the needle and the syringe. They have boiled for four minutes. I turn off the gas. I leave without making a noise. I'm not curious: I have other failings.

*

An hour later.

'Open up, open up ... It's me with the Granvillons!'

She has recovered her voice. She is shouting out on the landing.

I was polishing my floor. I am dripping with sweat: her Gran-villons is a splendid idea.

She has undressed. The ceremony in the depths of her flat is over. She has undressed and got back into her nail polish, her lipstick, her mules, her poppies.

She leaps on the old skirt I use as a polisher and, hey presto, I have a floor like satin. This morning is a festival of mutual aid.

'Sit yourself down in my armchair ...'

'Let's have a drink,' she says. 'You've had breakfast, haven't you? I haven't! Give me some bread, some sausage.'

'Haven't you eaten anything at all since yesterday?'

She has closed herself away inside her peignoir.

'... I prefer an empty stomach. My hand is steadier. You under-stand?'

'I begin to understand.'

I go and fetch her some nourishment. Work well done leaves you feeling hollow. I have no doubt that her work is well, nay, impeccably, done.

And I serve her, and I watch her as she eats with such hearty appetite. Why didn't I know her before? Why didn't I know her then? The idea makes me forget the difference in our ages.

'I always give them the injection,' she tells me with her mouth full. 'It's better to be safe than sorry.'

I am sitting opposite her, on the corner of the divan. I cut her another slice of bread, another slice of sausage.

She refuses them. But she would love a cigarette.

I hurry to get her one; no trouble is too much.

'Was it for a girl? Was it for a woman, the injection?' I ask as I shake out the match.

'A girl. Twenty-two. She was three months' gone. Her boss. She's a secretary . . .'

She takes the cigarette from between her lips, she massacres it against the side of the ashtray.

'Couldn't you keep an eye on it yourself, your saucepan?'

'They come in, they're frightened. I put myself in their place. Oh, madame, what are you going to do to me? They are quite beside themselves . . . Will it hurt? Are you going to hurt me? Me hurt you? Come now, my dear, just think. Do I look like a monster? I shall be gentle, you'll see. They are panicky, they are distraught. Take off your gloves, put your purse down on the bed. I have to build up their confidence. They would upset themselves again if I left them alone while the water boils. I keep them company, I never question them except about the number of months. After three I am adamant. More than three months? Keep it, I should be robbing you of your health. You must live, my dear, you mustn't die. So young, so inexperienced, I have to be careful how I handle them. Sometimes they're trembling all over, so I bring them some coffee. Sometimes they're shivering with cold. Never without the injection. It keeps them going. They are running no risks, and you can imagine I certainly don't want to run any . . . Oh, madame, I'm in a terrible spot, are you going to get me out of it? Of course I'm going to get you out of it. You mustn't contract, that's all. I never fail. They trust me. If they get married later, they send me an announcement . . . They have lovely children, they send me photos, they send me sugar almonds from the christening . . . Discreetly. Others just vanish, but I never worry about them. Some get very emotional; they swear they owe me their happiness, their home. Very few forget me, they're all so nice ... I'm strict with them: you must keep coming back until ... but they never have to come back more than twice at the most.

'But I'm sitting here talking about it as though it's my profession ... I help them out, I'm broad-minded. I can hear children, is school out already? La Puce will be coming home ... She'll be looking for me ... Would you mind leaning over the banister and shouting down to her? Tell her I'm here, say I'm waiting for her here. The last one came in sobbing, a blonde, curly hair, a pretty dress with a white collar ... Oh, madame, madame ... if you can't get rid of it for me, I shall be in terrible trouble! I shall lose my job ... But she didn't get into terrible trouble, she didn't lose her job. Are you unhappy? Has it depressed you, what I've been telling you?'

I went over to her. I took her hand. Me, unhappy? If I had only known her ten years before ... I was still forgetting the difference in our ages ... Fifteen times. I had gone back fifteen times.

'At five and a half months?' I said. 'At five and a half months, was it possible?'

She freed her hand from mine. She was aghast. 'At five and a half months, one would be killing two instead of one.'

At that moment her little girl appeared and leaped up into her mother's ample, wholesome embrace.

My heart was clenched day and night in an iron hand during my ten-day family visit in the Charente. My stepfather moved so slowly, so tentatively as he picked the beans out in their field. He did it sitting on a little stool between the rows. My mother was too fastidious: she cleaned out the cowshed and the hen coop several times a day. I could have sobbed. Why? For her galoshes, for her beautiful townswoman's legs. A sober house besieged by anxiety. They are all busy hatching out a great disaster, I thought. Stop, fold your arms, the disaster will beat a retreat. As for Michel, he was out ploughing their little plot of land, plodding listlessly behind their elephantine ox. My mother would have gone mad if the ox had collapsed, if the cow had fallen ill. They sold its milk, they carried the churn out to the roadside in time for the delivery man to collect it. They will never get anywhere. They are wearing themselves out for nothing, nothing. Every morning is a drama: my mother is always afraid of being late. She shakes them out of their beds, frantic with anxiety.

She is hypnotized by the quality of her eggs; in the evening she watches her red chicken till it goes to roost, always last. I call it Madeleine because of the Boulevard de la Madeleine and the fancy women there, she tells me. Such are her consolations. They have a walnut tree. It is their only tree. No other habitations anywhere near theirs, which is a dismal and self-contained little farmhouse. Wasteland, vines in the distance, ineffable threats in the sunset. The sunsets behind their house are not reassuring: vaster than in other places, more stained with blood.

'Come and look at the cowshed,' my mother says.

We go into the cowshed.

'Sit down.'

I am five, I am wearing my white gloves, she is putting on a dress, she is taking it off, she is putting on another instead, we are going out somewhere, I shall have the best-dressed woman in town for my mother. Her galoshes brought me back to earth.

'You see how I look after them?'

'It's unique, the way you look after them.'

The fork in one corner of the cowshed bears witness to her ritual changing of the straw an hour before: her countrywoman's smock is less elegant than the straw she gives her animals. Is it a mistake? Can my mother have somehow been changed for another, the way children sometimes are as little babies? My eyes fill with tears, but the sight of the ox's blond lashes, the candour of those pale jute fringes console me.

'And your work?' she asks.

I watch my mother walk around Blanchette. Already soiled, her straw.

'My work? The same as before. I've begun a new book, but I don't want to talk about it. I'd be ashamed if you read it...'

'Ah,' my mother says simply.

She seems to be afraid for me.

The cow dung has fallen, it has spattered the straw ... The cow pat is as big as a puddle.

'And Mme de Beauvoir,' my mother asks. 'Is she still as kind to you?'

She is trying to be pleasant, but her cross-examination irritates me.

'More than kind. She will never change, she is my friend.'

My mother talks to me about my old age. She is worried for me.

I listen with one ear.

'And Michel? Isn't he going to get married?' I asked in turn.

My mother didn't lift her head. Leaning against Blanchette's flank with one hand, she was examining her cow's teats one by one.

'He is going out with a girl,' she said sadly and irritably.

She raised her head. 'Didn't you know she was expecting?'

'Who? The girl, or Blanchette?'

'Blanchette!'

We didn't laugh.

Michel appeared with two milk pails. That renews an atmosphere somehow, a man appearing. The ox and the cow both turned their heads towards him.

'Later I'll show you how to really paso-doble,' he said as he took the milking stool from me.

They sit milking, face to face. It isn't a noise, it is a beam of light in the glittering pail, it is a white plume emerging from the teat.

'She learned how right away,' Michel said, referring to our mother.

We drank dark-red wine before dinner, Michel danced paso-dobles with me in the kitchen while my mother fussed over her best chicken for us, while my stepfather finished nailing a new stair-tread. I danced, and listened to an owl hoot between two bars. Outside, misfortune had not lifted its siege. The owl fell silent; Michel waltzed with me in his socks, a Gauloise stuck to his lower lip.

I walked and read while they had their siesta. I raised my head: I saw wasps plundering a bunch of grapes, swarming over the black, broken skin. Disheartenment: the crushed ear of corn on the edge of a field. I advanced across perpetually trampled grass, I read without grasping what I read. The blackish, russetish wreck of a man's shoe awakened me; an empty Gauloise pack disturbed me with its newness. Never any indulgence for yourself, the abandoned shoe hummed. I walked on past bushes, and a gnawed leaf signified: an invisible power wishes you to remember it kindly, wants you to take me as a sign that it has forgotten nothing. If I had been asked to draw my suffering at that moment, my drawing would have been like a jetty leading out to a lighthouse, the open sea on either side. The infinity of my silent grief.

*

I returned to Paris with a coated mouth. A layer of sadness on my tongue. What was to become of them on their smallholding? How were they ever to make it work?

And the or-ga-ni-za-tion? And Jacques?

The or-ga-ni-za-tion has not been wasting its time in my absence. It has a vampire on its payroll now, and a very special kind of vampire, too. It doesn't drink blood, it doesn't suck blood. It claws things and feeds on my nerves. It uses its claws to rip the covers of the two Proust volumes on the mantel in my bedroom. *Du côté de chez Swann* is becoming just so much dried glue, so old and brown, a mere caked concretion of printed pages. It is obscene. I get up at dawn, at midnight, just to check on how much the vampire has scratched away. Yes, he's been there, destroying, gnawing. He has scalped the back of my book. I look, I gaze, I am empty, I am desolate, I am a school visitors'-room during summer vacation. It is Jacques, not the or-ga-ni-za-tion. But Jacques is a bibliophile. Why should he damage my books? Jacques is elsewhere, yet he is making his presence felt in my flat with his nails. He lives far away, yet he leaves his marks here. What powers of dissimulation, what determination to find a way in. Show yourself, rip my bedclothes, then I shall be able to catch you at your work. I hurl the two books on the floor, but he remains silent.

Jacques, have I hurt you? Vampire, horrible vampire, you shan't have my blood. Jacques, is that you up on the ceiling? I can't see you. But I can hear you. Why do you answer me with those cracklings and rustlings? You are too delicate. I am your jailer, I never leave your side. Quiet, filth! All I have is tears. And I melt, I melt into sadness and tenderness. Jacques has short nails, so it can't be him. Why isn't he here with me, my Jacques? I rub the tears from my nose across my cheeks: consolation. Is it true, Jacques? You aren't hurt? Vampire, foul vampire, do you think I'm deaf or something? ... Afternoon. I am writing at my table. The noise of a little chain. Indescribably delicate the noise is. It doesn't like the adverb I've just used. It's warning me, telling me that my short-winded sentence has offended it. You are too inquisitive. Just who do you think you are? I lie down on my bed so that it shan't see my paper. The cracklings and nibblings follow me there. If only they were regular... They are fantastic surprises. One of Jacques's black eyelashes on the sheet, another yesterday on my exercise book. I raise my head, I wait for it as it is waiting for me. It can see me; that is the advantage it has.

You are draining away my strength, I shall defend myself with my only weapon. I climb on the bed, I stand on the eiderdown and bang at the ceiling with the handle of my broom till a rain of plaster begins to fall gently on my hair. I yell and yell. Will you be quiet, will you please be quiet? My mother's voice. I am bullying the child I used to be, just as she was bullied in reality. I let myself fall on the bed still holding my broom. Can you tell me to whom I was speaking? I am full of grief and full of rage. I shake with emotion, I tear my handkerchief with my teeth, I pull out fistfuls of hair if I can't find a needle or a duster. It means hidden forces have won a victory; they are using an invisible door. They are snatching away my tiniest possessions minute by minute, second by second. I wander wildly from one room to the other. What flock, what herd would want anything to do with such an animal? Yet I am disappointed when I find what I was looking for. It makes the mystery less compact. It makes holes in it. Does it mean that there isn't someone living with me after all? Someone closer to me than my own skin over my bones? What is the meaning of the pin in the crack between the floorboards? Of the grease spot on the linoleum? Of the way the framed

photograph of the Gare St Lazare is aslant? That they are always
there above me, there below me. They are sapping me all the time,
and they will never give up. I wear my spies on my shoulders the
way a soldier wears his epaulettes. I shall die without having found
out who they are. They are watchers, they are enemies.

I tormented myself for a whole morning over the browned corner
of a dishcloth. I knew I hadn't scorched it myself. Yet, despite
everything, I have not lost my appetite. I eat my stew from the saucepan, my elbows on the aluminium rim round my table. I am feeding an animal, I lap up the gravy. Despair is an animal. I am a dog.
A dog belonging to Jacques; belonging to Simone de Beauvoir; belonging to *Les Temps Modernes*; belonging to Gallimard; belonging to Sartre, whom I don't even know; belonging to the editorial
board of his magazine. I have so many masters, why don't they
beat me? Why don't they keep me on a shorter leash?

Yes, I am a dog. Like Frisette. Poor Frisette, poor little bitch
being used out there in space ... You're not the only one, my poor
Frisette. They're using me too. We are two unfortunate, defence-
less creatures. You'll see, Frisette, you'll see what I'm going to do ...

I open my exercise book and tear out two pages. One I throw
away; the other I keep. Will it be big enough? Will people notice it?
Yes, it will do. My name is the same as yours, Frisette, I am just
like you now: I unscrew my fountain pen, I begin. I write FRISETTE
in capital letters, in blue ink, in the middle of the page. Let's take a
look from a distance. Yes, that's visible enough, it stands out nice
and clear. Now I take my sheepskin jacket down off its hanger, I
spread it out on the eiderdown, I look for two safety pins in my sewing box. This one and this one. There, my little dog, you are nicely
attached to the middle of my back. I take out my old umbrella ... en
avant, label and all!

Bizarre, very bizarre, more than bizarre: they are all playing
possum in their holes. So they won't see me on the stairs with my
sign between my shoulders. What if I made huge gestures as I
come out of the building? What if I bent over and limped?

The street wasn't about to help me. The street was deserted. The
few passers-by I saw were blind and indifferent. I shall edge my
way round the other passengers in the métro, then they'll have to see
it because my back will be in front of their noses. A dog wearing a
Tuscan lamb jacket, standing on her hind legs, paying for her
métro ticket, that's something you're bound to notice.

I walked backwards. I walked from one end of the coach to the other, then back again. They didn't notice me. Not a whisper, not a comment.

I got off the train at Chaussée d'Antin, and someone pulled at the sleeve of my jacket.

'Madame...' a voice addressed me gently.

'What?' I asked curtly.

She was old, well dressed.

'Madame ... Someone has played a joke on you ... Someone has pinned a piece of paper on your back ... Would you like me to take it off?'

She was peeling off her gloves.

'Can't you just mind your own business?' I snarled at her, making my voice deliberately coarse.

I stared at her aggressively, I swung my umbrella in menacing circles. Round and round you go, sharp black ribs, round and round.

She pulled her gloves back on. She vanished down a tunnel.

I sat down beside my refuge: the candy-vending machine on the platform. My head sank down on one shoulder.

I walked back into my bedroom. I threw my umbrella down on the table. I unpinned the label. Frisette had ceased to exist. But Frisette still existed.

Frisette still exists. I also throw my jacket down on the marble hearth, under where the two Proust books stand on the mantel. I jump up and down on my jacket. For ten minutes, watch in hand. Icy silence as I tear up the label. My pieces of paper ... Frisette and *L'Asphyxie*, Frisette and *L'Affamée*, Frisette and her two or three pieces printed in *Les Temps Modernes*, Frisette before long in the trash bin. I jump on her again, higher and higher. My things on the table and the wall shelves fall off and break. I console the glass and the porcelain, I hurl them into the hearth. Vampire, disgusting vampire, if you can see me, so much the better. I am angry now and I am Frisette. Who is there I can show my anger to if not my own four walls? Frisette can walk on all fours if you want. Do you want that?

*

And Jacques? And Jacques?

He appeared in my dark den, I created him. I fashioned him as I opened my door to him. He is a nest, Jacques. The nest of all my woes. He wanted me to like him. He succeeded only too well. Who is to blame? The fool, lady. That's me. I let myself be caught. We are quits now. No, that's too simple. I shall always be there at square one because I am always waiting. Waiting for what? For La Mer de Glace, for a glacier that will suddenly open and close again with me inside. Ultimately, yes, that is what I am waiting for. I don't tell myself so, though. I tell myself that what I am waiting for is something quite different. A field of forget-me-nots for a smile from him. A block of ivy-covered stone for a visit from him. He liked *L'Asphyxie*. Now I live in expiation. I am hatching him. He is my child. It is when I am coiled hatching him that I am most viperlike. My venom will spurt out onto the back of his hand as I bend to kiss it. I am afraid of him, I mustn't let him see anything. I say good-bye to him, and it is playtime for the Furies.

He is rich. He is rich and is not helping me. A frightful obstacle. I fling mud at him, and I am more spattered than he is. I ought to scrape my tongue before beginning to love him again. He is my loathed father, he is the man whose feet I would warm between my breasts, at noon, on the Place de l'Opéra. He is my torturer, he is my little boy for whom I would steal bread. I vomit him up, and then I swaddle him in finest tulle. He is also my wasps' nest of impossibilities, a nest in which I am queen. He is the greatest error of my existence, he is proof of a constancy, a tenacity of which I would not have believed myself capable. So much faithfulness for nothing. The energy I put into demolishing him carries all before it in his absence.

I see him again: I am his slave, I am his poplar leaf. I wouldn't rend and tear him if he hadn't subjugated me. His affection? A trap. A saint in a picture is kissing me, putting his arm round my waist. That's what his gestures are like. I am his bewildered Cinderella. At his fireside, in his gardens, as I arrive, as I leave. I talk to myself, I say that I detest him, that I hate him, I fall on my knees, I pray to have his hand in mine, his socks to wash, his back to rub. Does he feel any pity? He is incapable of pity; he is too strong. His arm around my waist will make me lose my reason. The shadow of a lady's man is darkening my mind. I dream, then I think it has really happened. Was it some gust of sudden nostalgia that inspired him to that gesture? Too bold, yet not bold enough. He ought to think what he's doing. He ought to think of the implications. A homely woman is a fragile thing: one oughtn't to squeeze her. A lonely woman is a touchy thing: one oughtn't to stand too close to her. He says it just came over him. But doesn't he know it completely crushed me? I am destroying myself by loving him, I am destroying myself by demolishing him. I adore him. That's easily said. What does adoring mean? It means praying for the soul of the ball and chain round one's ankle.

The other day ... Five past twelve in the afternoon, I was wandering round ... I was looking for him. Everywhere, everywhere. On the plate glass of a big store's windows, on the bedcovers displayed behind it. What was that I just saw! A Renault Dauphine, covered in dust, parked in the parking area on the rue Saint-Bernard. Is it his? Is he somewhere in my neighbourhood, then? Is he keeping watch on me? Shivers and cold sweat. My cheek pressed hard, very hard against the window. No, it isn't his automobile. I want him. I want Jacques here with me. I shall invent him, I shall invent him so that I can have him here and look at him. Who is to stop me writing his name on the hood? What childishness! All right, then; I'll be childish. I took my time and wrote his name. What foul air we're forced to breathe. Who is that whispering? An old man walking with the aid of two sticks. Idiot, if the air weren't so polluted, I wouldn't be able to write his name in the dust ... The old man with his sticks is the last straw. I open my arms, I hurl myself forward ...

I ran, I beat my wings, I was a crazed airplane, I was a bird out of its tiny mind, it was noon, it was hot, I was determined to escape, but where was there a way out? I was at the very end of my tether. They refused to shoot me down. Please shoot me down, please destroy me, then I can fall. You won't? Then I will do it for you.

I fell full-length on the pavement, just outside the little gate into the square gardens. I closed my eyes. What good fortune: utter capitulation. Goodbye, sky; farewell, sky; for all you gave me, for all you are giving me ... Why was I looking for him? He is here, he will always be here. You can never take Jacques away from me. He is a black dot under my eyelid. Here they are. Here they come. What will they say? Keep well away, don't meddle with such things, don't have anything to do with such things, it's an epileptic, it's someone who's mentally ill, a policeman will take care of it ... No more sick than you and I, was the comment of other passers-by. Finally they left me alone, and I got to my feet again.

'Why did you do that? Why did you do that?'

The question came from an old woman, a drab old woman idling there, loitering there, watching me and keeping her distance.

Yet her question was like a prayer too. Perhaps she was my mother.

'Surely at your age you can tell when someone is desperately un-happy?' I said.

'Filthy slut!' she shouted at me.

I fled into the gardens.

Tears, tears, tears, ejaculation, woman's sperm. So many tears cascading into my grief-butt. The more I sob, the more refreshed I feel. To weep harder, that is my one goal. Who would there be to help me if I didn't have my sobs? Too many tears, and too much talk about tears. I am only talking about what exists. My despair, my symphony. Pain, and the giving of myself to it. Suffering, my suffering, come deeper inside me, fill me, expand me. Even six nurses could never tear Jacques out of my mind. He is my cross, my tailor-made cross. You can't see it. It is behind my forehead, it is very tiny. Time to leave the square. The gate of the gardens closing, banging so brutally. Jacques is beating me, he never stops beating me. I say so. Where is he now? He was there a moment ago ... Up on the geranium on the top floor; on the rag round the tree trunk; on the next mail-collection time; on the baker's almond tarts. Soon he'll be up on my ceiling. So quick, quick, back home again. Go away, horrible creature, I haven't any blood left for you to suck. And I fall to my knees again beside my divan. Praying for a miracle, for fulfilment. He would come every day. Room, things, don't lean towards me like that. I know that you suffer with me, but perhaps you are disturbing God in his heaven ... Imagine that he can hear me, that he is listening to me ... He would come every day. Sometimes repetition is the best thing. The silence refuses to slink away, and I am nothing now, after my prayer. I shall trample on all that Jacques has given me.

*

I take the case stamped with the name of the store La Gerbe d'Or from my Louis XI drawer, I open it, I gaze down at the satiny secrecy all round the chain bracelet that Jacques gave me. I clutch it in my fist, I walk out on the landing with another of Jacques's gifts: the sheepskin jacket. I listen at their doors. They are all out. I spread the jacket out underneath the bell just as I spread it out under the two Proust books. I drop the bracelet from as high as I can onto the fur. A dramatic gesture, then I begin. I stamp on the sleeves, on the collar, on the pockets. Now the bracelet. I begin to dance on it. First on one foot, then on the other. Zézette has opened her door. So they weren't all out.

'I thought I heard something out here,' she said, still hesitating to emerge altogether from her reasonable world.

I dance and dance. I trample and stamp. And I stare Zézette full in the eyes.

She comes towards me. 'You're ruining it! Tomorrow you'll be sorry . . .'

I grind my teeth.

She has pushed me aside. She has snatched up the bracelet, she has rescued it.

'I'm going to keep this for a while, I'll give it back to you this evening,' she tells me in a sad, sad voice. Then she leads me back into my bedroom. 'You mustn't think about him any more . . . He is not for you.'

Does that mean she has the gift of divination?

She has gone back into her own flat. I collapse.

Kisses one after another on the inside of my wrist. That's where he looks to see the time. To punish me for having trampled on his bracelet. I go to bed at half past two in the afternoon, I look for my future in the cards until half past four. I must have Jacques on the king of clubs, I must have happiness on the ten of hearts. I give the cards no quarter until they have given me a man and my happiness. I throw my deck of cards at St George. St George is Jacques, he is valiant, he is laying low the dragon on my sideboard. Not enough. I run round and round the flat, I want nothing left standing. I howl that Paris is bringing me misfortune, that Paris will be the death of me in the end. They are coming back from their offices. I can hear Mme Chantelauze's heavy tread; she is bowed down with her weariness. I must put all my unfair leisure to the fire and the sword: I snatch up my cleaver, I smite my chopping block thirty times, forty times. The block rolls on the floorboards, I push it back on the marble, I smite it fifty times, sixty times. What is possessing me? Absolute fury. What am I? A tart without customers. I open the window, I shout: I am a tart without customers, you have your washing to wash, your lunch tins to fill, your dinner to make.

I shall never be one of them. I roar like M. Chantelauze, and I waltz. I walk all over my nightdress with my shoes on; I rush out, white as a ghost, and find my way to the Parc Monceau. After an hour of struggle I finally force my way into the closed park. The shutters shower me with their alms, with the light from Jacques's house. I pant and lament my lot. The trees appear divinely tranquil in my eyes. I mustn't see them, my own world is calling me; I must wring my hands, make tragic faces, stand before his windows, and gaze at what is carved in my memory. Oh, imperturbable privet thickets. I am grief itself, I am possessed. Free me from him. Lead me back into the ways of lightheartedness. Oh, gravel trickling through tiny fingers. I am a ghost, I have been stranded in a cinema and the film has already begun. The actor is Jacques. The actress is Jacques, too. I am alone, I have indigestion : Jacques has taken over the whole screen. I moan. I was hungry, now I have eaten too much. I am driven out of the auditorium. He exists, I invent him. Who will set me free?

*

And Nathalie? I have lost her. I was rotten to her. I told her she was a miser.

*

And Genet?

Finished, all over. I avoid him, I am in awe of him, I am afraid of him. I gave him my adulation. It wasn't enough. I prostrated myself before his misfortunes and his prisons. I debased myself. Now I flee his presence, and I respect my flight. I irritated him, so I have relieved him of that irritation. Someone once said that I was afraid of falling in love with him. It is possible. I venerated him. I was just taking a different path. Every one of the looks he gave me—none of them kind—found its mark and is embedded in me. If I keep away from him, it is because he has kept me away. He refused to compromise. He could not pretend. He rejected me. He was good for me.

And yet ... What if I were to transform myself for him, to make a final attempt, a last effort ... Very well, let us dream that dream ... Quickly there, dresser, bring me my costume and my props.

A pageboy bob in shrieking green nylon. A flame-coloured eagle on my head. The mask of James Dean. A raspberry body stocking. A dancer's body. My breasts crushed flat. A false penis. The penis of a leading male dancer beneath the body stocking. Pigalle. Three in the morning. Genet is alone at his table. I come in, I wave hello to everyone there. The softness of softest pigeon's down, a wave of the hand in greeting to Genet. No insistence. I go from table to table, I have a word for everyone, I am funny. I am a cheeky kid and a camp lady, I have a tongue like lightning, I have animation; anything to please him. The eagle falls over my eyes, but that's nothing, it's only me titfer, darlings, and with an exaggerated, old queen's gesture I push it to the back of my head, I debase myself utterly to please Jean Genet. I go from table to table making them laugh, I smoke a Baccarat rose. Genet's table. He yawns, he leaves, it's all over.

*

And Simone de Beauvoir?

Secretly, surreptitiously, she is becoming my remorse. I have cheated her, I am still cheating her in every way. I arrive, I complain about my lack of money. Yet only the day before, I opened a national savings account. Would she be annoyed if she found out? She is never annoyed. 'A national savings account?' She would laugh. 'It's not a capital crime. Have you been working?' But it is a capital crime. I am lying. I am concealing things. Sometimes Simone de Beauvoir reduces me to a heap of rubble with her indulgence. She pays no attention to my petty little tricks. Remorse is like an attack of flu. You would like to retrace your steps, but the pain is doubling you up. The past is a germ. 'I'll ask them to increase your allowance,' she goes on, with her usual kindliness, always as fresh as the very first day ... I wish I could explode like a great sheaf of sparks in response to her candour.

Too little money did I say? Last week I bought myself table napkins, dishcloths. I am cheating her for the sake of a few scraps of linen, a few rectangles of woven cotton. I would rather vanish from the face of the earth than tell her about my little stockpile of linen. If she were to speak sharply to me sometimes, I'd stop harping on my poverty. But national savings, pillow slips, to her they're just laughable. They aren't ideas. I was strong when I met her first, I walked with pride in my step. Now I am a sticky smear, a leukemic squid. I crawl before her and expect to be attractive. I repel her and I whine. What if the handkerchiefs selected for her with such feverish anxiety, what if the posies composed with a purist's application were merely hypocritical props ... Why such a destructive thought? Why do I slash at the hand choosing fine linen patterned with clematis, why do I hack at the fingers mixing balsams with scented roses? I want to let in the light. Forget it, just go on choosing your posies; love is a dark night. Love as you can, just drag your cart along. What if they were just tricks, my handkerchiefs and my flowers? Well? What if they were? She will still always be your sun when you see her again. Yes, she is the new day dawning in my today.

But what is my purpose in taking her all these handkerchiefs and flowers? (Can't we just drop the subject?) To give something to someone greater than myself. Is that all? I don't know? Not to achieve success? Not to become someone? What sort of success? I've no idea. Climbing on Simone de Beauvoir's shoulders. Is it possible you're jealous of her? That I shall never be. I am pure in that respect. I shall go on buying her handkerchiefs and flowers. Oh, I shall go on and on buying them for her ... It means a presence. Her presence. I was ungrateful towards Simone de Beauvoir the day I went to dine at Jacques's house, the day I went crackers over him. I ought to have told her everything. Why? She isn't interested in my love-at-first-sight rubbish. I am free just as she is free. She doesn't confide in me, so why should I make her my confidante? She is my friend. It isn't my fault: she walks into the café and everything else ceases to exist. Next day, the artichoke sits down and writes passionate letters to him and to her ... I can hear her: 'It's nothing ... If it's of any use to you ...' It's nothing, because her life is elsewhere. A revolver shot: it hits me but I get up all the same; her life is elsewhere but, all the same, life must go on. I hide Jacques from her, I want the image of her reigning over my heart. When will I admit to myself that such things just aren't of any interest to her? Yet she is asking a great deal of me precisely by asking nothing of me.

She is my conscience, she is so conscientious. I have an appointment with a past master of torture when I leave her: my bad faith. I walk round and round the Place Maubert, I run under the bridges, I walk across the Place de la Concorde without looking. I have concealed a man from her, a man who is not my lover, I have repressed him, I have been dishonest. No, I haven't been an opportunist. Because she does still count more than everything when I am sitting beside her. Am I her prisoner? She hasn't shut me up. She is radiant when my work pleases her. Have I flattered her? No, I haven't flattered her. She is beautiful and I have embellished that beauty. I may conceal Jacques from her, but I also know how to make myself invisible when I go to a preview of one of Sartre's plays or to the advance showing of one of Hélène de Beauvoir's exhibitions. My handkerchiefs, my flowers ... They aren't an indulgence. They are an antisepsis. What? Am I like a shameful disease, growing invisibly underground? Tell me what I am doing that's wrong, master of tortures. You are always sniffing round her fame. You go to meet her without a glance for the poor, for the failures of life, because that would make you late. Fame, glory, that's her, not them. But I shall come back to you, my flocks, my friends. Remember the hands of France's workmen, Madame Leduc, they are the feather in the cap of your writing.

If I loved her, I wouldn't be unhappy. The certainty of seeing her again in two weeks would be a festival lasting the whole of those two weeks. I don't tell her that he's the first man I have ever loved, that I shall love him to the end. She is Simone de Beauvoir, not Miss Lonelyhearts.

She doesn't know how much I suffer because I don't attend the meetings of the *Temps Modernes* editorial board. How perverse. I wouldn't open my mouth if I did. I don't know how to argue. I should be a gaping carp. Their magazine isn't a pond. She would be ashamed of my stupidity. I should suffer more on account of her shame than on account of my own idiocy. I am beginning to be wary of *Les Temps Modernes*. The typographers who set it up are beginning to have it in for me. They use misprints to let me know they've got their eyes on me. They juggle the type about on purpose. They want to upset me, to intrigue. A definite article is misplaced onto the following line ... That signifies: get off Simone de Beauvoir's back, you are an encumbrance to her. If someone writes in the magazine about a traitor, that traitor is me. They are using a political allusion to tell me they are on to me. I keep myself in check. If I have been a traitor, it has been only on the most penny-pinching, errand-boy level. But the editorial board is warning me: I am rotten to the core, and what's more they know it. I open my Larousse, I scribble on the word 'traitor' until it is obliterated. Their reproach, coming to me by such a devious path, crushes me more than any public condemnation. I hurl the magazine up at the ceiling; I would like to see it fall apart, the pieces held together by a single thread.

What have I done? I tittle-tattled when we were talking about my stepfather to my mother. The merest trifle. I have been indiscreet, I have been thoughtless. I pick the magazine up from the top of the stove where it has fallen; I search through it, looking for allusions to my inadequacies on every page. I end up thinking that Sartre himself has something against me. But then he wouldn't publish you,

you goose. It's much simpler: I am dying of envy. They haven't announced the extracts from *L'Affamée* they're going to publish, there's nothing about it on the back cover. They're ashamed of me. I'm not well known. My name is worthless. It's been buried away somewhere. After my dizzying climb to first place on the List of Contents, I have now tumbled into the bargain basement of Other New Books. I shall never clamber back up into their List of Contents again. I have withered like the grass of the field after having blazed in the firmament of a magazine. Yes, Sartre has something against me; he is pushing me to one side with his foot, and yet I am never in his way. I slide the magazine under my divan, I smear lipstick on my mouth from ear to ear, I walk round the apartment whimpering and shouting like a Mongoloid child. I am a clown, why should anyone take me seriously?

I suffered when I heard about Simone de Beauvoir's relationship with Claude Lanzmann. I was astounded. Didn't I know about it? No, I didn't know about it. They thought I was putting on an act. But I have never known anything about her private life. They are sceptical when I say that. I heard about it from others, and I could not forgive them. I hated Simone de Beauvoir that day. Vampire, please, please, I beg of you. I don't want to threaten her, I don't want to shake my fist at her as I shake it at the ceiling. All of them up there in the loft would see that she doesn't deserve my spite and my fury. She doesn't look after me enough ... She doesn't know that I am under a spell. It is a great misfortune in my life. My cigarettes and my coffee are tampered with; they have an unknown drug at their disposal, they pour it into my mineral water, I am possessed. Protect me, pull me out of my shrunken little world. Nothing happens by chance, everything is directed against me. If the birds sing in a tree when I go into the Luxembourg gardens, that is because they have been told to sing. I must beware of the song of the birds, of the cheekiness of the sparrows. Is even the great wind in the trees still its own master, I wonder. Why, oh God, why do you allow me to destroy everything? Will the day come when I insult Simone de Beauvoir in her absence as I insult the passers-by in the street? She works beside Sartre in all her innocence, and I who do nothing but contemplate my own navel am on the verge of dancing with fury on her name simply because she won't stop to wipe away my tears ... Oh God, don't let that happen.

I walked into a grocery. A poor woman smiled at me. A sketch of the kindness and tenderness in her heart. I immediately gave that frail smile to Simone de Beauvoir. It was more than flowers, more than a handkerchief.

*

And my writing?

It saps me. What does it inspire in me? Laziness, hollow hours, excuses for lazying my life away. I am literature's parasite. I must write. Then I change my mind. I spend my time at the cinema, in empty churches, in grimy little parks. I run away from my exercise book. It is my refuge. Yet I search for places where I can take refuge from it. I neglect it without abandoning it entirely. I am sickened by it all. I ought to be making a new life; all I do is write about my past life. I sink further and further into the silt of my past. I sew fresh frills on dramas that have become mere trifling incidents with the passing years. My abortion a trifling incident? Now I'm exaggerating. The past in the present, magnetizing one another. Last week I spent several days in succession hanging around baby carriages, gazing at little eiderdowns sewn with ribbons and frills. I reread the account of my abortion in my next book; I stood by the old woman who looks after the push-chairs outside the Prisunic store, I stood guard with her. The babies emerged from the store in their mothers' arms, and the sight gave me perfect satisfaction. I was as round as a great plump apple with a stalk and one leaf still attached. I asked myself, so many years after all my abortion attempts, what it means to bring up a child. I searched for the answer as they buckled the straps of the push-chairs around the children. It meant cossetting life.

I followed the mothers as they pushed their babies in front of them along the avenue Ledru-Rollin. I looked at the hardened fat on their thighs. At their weak ankles. At their dragging feet. At their neglected appearance. A letting go, and yet a blooming. Our daily lives were too different. I could never enter theirs. I am a little more than they are and yet much, much less: a writer steering her way, a woman crazy with love, a crackpot refusing to follow her madness to its conclusion. Their pink tongues. They licked at their two balls of ice cream; they lapped up the delicious flavours of their double cones. They were living, they weren't writing. Their walk, their outing was enough for them. Whereas I was exploiting them, since I had gone looking for them, since I am now describing them. To write is to inform against others. Most of the time I am an informer in my own pay as I walk through the streets of Paris. The people I pass are precious exhibits, even when I insult them. I accuse myself if I let a face or the back of a head slip by me. I retrace my steps: I needed that haircut for my collection, the collection I am trying to complete before I die.

To write means to give out warmth. I gave my warm hands to a hacksaw in the display window of a hardware store. I hypnotized myself following the even zigzag of its teeth. I climbed up its mountains, I slid down into the abysses of its seas. An ant making a journey round the earth. I slid down the stream of the world's slowest river on the other side of the blade. Flawless, the deep grey of the steel. I bought up the world's forests, I gave them as a present to that deep grey. The handle, with its painted bay twig, was a welcome in itself. To grasp it and saw would be to feel one's hand grasped in return. A tool is a chanted response in church. How much was it? I will be back, I will think it over. The salesman took it out of the window to show me. I held it as though it were on a cushion, a crown in a procession. It was pure, I had no idea I would ever write about it. Now it is rusting in the slush of my sentences. I used to go and visit it when it was freezing, my blessed damozel. The little teeth always smiling, always in a good humour as I passed by on my way to pay for my seat in the Saint-Antoine cinema. Now it hangs out on the other side of the store, the cheap side. We have prostituted ourselves together, I have put it out on the streets.

To write is to prostitute oneself. It is to give the come-on, to sell oneself. Worse perhaps, because whores don't feel anything. Every word is a new customer. Want to come with me, adjective? Come on, darling. I can show you a thing or two, adjective, you'll get to heaven if you come with me. How much? The price of the book when it's published. No exaggerating where writing is concerned, if you don't mind; no throwing out the baby with the bath water just because we don't have a writer's vocation. I eat my sauerkraut and sausages in a brasserie just closing for the night, and that's living just as much as writing is. To write means to dip one's pen in sea water on the first day of one's holiday. The rest is tricks and permutations. The rough diamond belongs to everyone: the sun when we open the window. Everyone can see the sky, so everyone is a writer. Anything after that is done with mirrors. Everyone is a poet when dusk is falling and the lamp is lit. To run in a certain way trying to catch a butterfly, that's having a style.

A child's logic. It makes it all too easy. Then come the days of desolation. I stagnate, I drag about the streets without writing, and yet I am writing too. Mutely, I wail at four in the afternoon on a bench on the Boulevard Voltaire. The dead leaves rustle. The wind carries away the ashes, the wind gathers the leaves round my bench. Death has made its harvest, and the wind drives the leaves across in front of a bank. They crackle and rustle. No, I shan't be Verlaine. No, I shan't be Rimbaud. No, I shan't fire a revolver shot in London. No, I shan't be Genet; no, I shan't go to prison in Mettray, in Fontrevault. The stakes are down, too late to change. My pen and my clothbound exercise book. Let's eat a palmier together.

To write or to remain silent?

To write the impossible word on the rainbow's arc. Then everything would have been said.